LITHUANIA

COUNTRY STUDY GUIDE

VOLUME 1

STRATEGIC INFORMATION AND DEVELOPMENTS

International Business Publications, USA
Washington DC, USA - Lithuania

LITHUANIA

COUNTRY STUDY GUIDE

VOLUME 1 STRATEGIC INFORMATION AND DEVELOPMENTS

UPDATED ANNUALLY

We express our sincere appreciation to all government agencies and international organizations, which provided information and other materials for this guide

Cover Design: **International Business Publications, USA**

2015 Edition Updated Reprint International Business Publications, USA
ISBN 0-7397-7910-9

For customer service and information, please contact:

in the USA: **International Business Publications, USA**
P.O.Box 15343, Washington, DC 20003
Phone: (202) 546-2103, Fax: (202) 546-3275.
E-mail: rusric@erols.com

Printed in the USA

LITHUIANIA

COUNTRY STUDY GUIDE

VOLUME 1

STRATEGIC INFORMATION AND DEVELOPMENTS

TABLE OF CONTENTS

STRATEGIC AND BUSINESS PROFILE

COUNTRY OVERVIEW

Capital and largest city	Vilnius 54°41′N 25°19′E54.683°N 25.317°E
Official languages	Lithuanian
Ethnic groups (2011)	84.1% Lithuanians 6.6% Poles 5.8% Russians 1.2% Belarusians 0.5% Ukrainians 0.1% Jews 0.1% Tatars 0.1% Germans 0.1% Romani 0.1% Latvians 1.3% others / unspecified
Demonym	Lithuanian
Government	Unitary parliamentary republic
- President	Dalia Grybauskaitė
- Seimas Speaker	Loreta Graužinienė
- Prime Minister	Algirdas Butkevičius
Legislature	Seimas
Independence from Russia / Germany (1918)	
- First mention of Lithuania	9 March 1009
- Coronation of Mindaugas	6 July 1253
- Union with Poland	2 February 1386
- Polish–Lithuanian Commonwealth created	1 July 1569
- Partitions of the Commonwealth	24 October 1795
- Independence declared	16 February 1918
- 1st Soviet occupation	15 June 1940
- Nazi German occupation	22 June 1941
- 2nd Soviet occupation	July 1944
- Independence restored	11 March 1990
- Joined the European Union	1 May 2004
Area	
- Total	65,300 km^2 (123rd) 25,212 sq mi
- Water (%)	1.35
Population	
- 2015 estimate	2,921,920 (139th)
- 2011 census	3,043,429
- Density	45/km^2 (120th) 116/sq mi
GDP (PPP)	2015 estimate
- Total	$83.105 billion

- Per capita	$28,245
GDP (nominal)	2015 estimate
- Total	$51.002 billion
- Per capita	$17,334
Gini (2013)	▲34.6 medium
HDI (2014)	▬0.834 very high · 35th
Currency	Euro (€) (EUR)
Time zone	EET (UTC+2)
- Summer (DST)	EEST (UTC+3)
Date format	yyyy-mm-dd (CE)
Drives on the	right
Calling code	+370
ISO 3166 code	LT
Internet TLD	.lt

Lithuania officially the **Republic of Lithuania** (Lithuanian: *Lietuvos Respublika*) is a country in Northern Europe, the largest of the three Baltic states. It is situated along the southeastern shore of the Baltic Sea, to the east of Sweden and Denmark. It borders Latvia to the north, Belarus to the east and south, Poland to the south, and a Russian exclave (Kaliningrad Oblast) to the southwest. Lithuania has an estimated population of 3 million as of 2012, and its capital and largest city is Vilnius. The Lithuanians are a Baltic people, and the official language, Lithuanian, is one of only two living languages (together with Latvian) in the Baltic branch of the Indo-European language family.

For centuries, the southeastern shore of the Baltic Sea was inhabited by various Baltic tribes. In the 1230s the Lithuanian lands were united by Mindaugas, who was crowned as King of the Grand Duchy of Lithuania, the first Lithuanian state, on 6 July 1253. During the 14th century, the Grand Duchy of Lithuania was the largest country in Europe: present-day Belarus, Ukraine, and parts of Poland and Russia were territories of the Grand Duchy of Lithuania. With the Lublin Union of 1569, Lithuania and Poland formed a voluntary two-state union, the Polish–Lithuanian Commonwealth. The Commonwealth lasted more than two centuries, until neighboring countries systematically dismantled it from 1772 to 1795, with the Russian Empire annexing most of Lithuania's territory.

In the aftermath of World War I, Lithuania's Act of Independence was signed on 16 February 1918, declaring the re-establishment of a sovereign state. Starting in 1940, Lithuania was occupied first by the Soviet Union and then by Nazi Germany. As World War II neared its end in 1944 and the Germans retreated, the Soviet Union reoccupied Lithuania.

On 11 March 1990, the year before the break-up of the Soviet Union, Lithuania became the first Soviet republic to declare independence. Prior to the global financial crisis of 2007–2010, Lithuania had one of the fastest growing economies in the European Union. Lithuania is a member of NATO, the Council of Europe, and the European Union. Lithuania is also a full member of the Schengen Agreement. The United Nations Human Development Index lists Lithuania as a "Very High Human Development" country. Lithuania will hold the Presidency of the Council of the European Union in the second half of 2013

ECONOMIC OVERVIEW

Currency: Lithuanian Litas
Market Exchange Rate : US$1 = 4.00 Litas
Nominal Gross Domestic Product (GDP) : $11.1 billion; **:** $12.1 billion
Real GDP Growth Rate : 2.5%; **:** 4.0%
Inflation Rate: 1.7%; **:** 2.3%
Unemployment Rate : 11.4%; **:** 11.0%
Current Account Balance : -$668 million; **:** -$698 million
Major Trading Partners: Russia, Germany, Denmark, Latvia, Belarus
Merchandise Exports : $4.14 billion; **:** $4.47 billion
Merchandise Imports : $5.17 billion; **:** $5.53 billion
Merchandise Trade Balance : -$1.03 billion; **:** -$1.06 billion
Major Export Products: Machinery and equipment 19%, mineral products 16%, textiles 15%, chemicals 8%, foodstuffs 8%
Major Import Products: Machinery and equipment 30%, mineral products 18%, chemicals 9%, textiles 8%, foodstuffs
External Debt : $2.6 billion

ENERGY OVERVIEW

Proven Oil Reserves : 12 million barrels
Crude Oil Production : 4,180 barrels per day (bbl/d)
Oil Consumption : 67,000 bbl/d; **:** 68,000 bbl/d
Crude Refining Capacity : 263,000 bbl/d
Natural Gas Reserves : minimal
Natural Gas Production : none
Natural Gas Consumption : 113 billion cubic feet
Proven Coal Reserves : none
Coal Production : none
Coal Consumption : 0.27 million short tons
Electricity Generation Capacity : 6.3 gigawatts
Electricity Generation : 15.6 billion kilowatthours (Bkwh)
Electricity Consumption : 7.8 Bkwh
Net Electricity Exports : 7.8 Bkwh

ENVIRONMENTAL OVERVIEW

Total Energy Consumption : 0.3 quadrillion Btu* (0.1% of world total energy consumption)
Energy-Related Carbon Emissions : 4.5 million metric tons of carbon (0.07% of world carbon emissions)
Per Capita Energy Consumption : 90.6 million Btu (vs U.S. value of 350.7 million Btu)
Per Capita Carbon Emissions : 1.2 metric tons of carbon (vs U.S. value of 5.5 metric tons of carbon)
Energy Intensity : 54,900 Btu/ $1990 (vs U.S. value of 13,400 Btu/ $1990)**
Carbon Intensity : 0.74 metric tons of carbon/thousand $1990 (vs U.S. value of 0.21 metric tons/thousand $1990)**
Sectoral Share of Energy Consumption: Industrial (58.9%), Residential (16.0%), Transportation (15.2%), Commercial (9.9%)
Sectoral Share of Carbon Emissions: Industrial (59.3%), Transportation (26.4%), Residential (8.2%), Commercial (6.0%)
Fuel Share of Energy Consumption : Oil (41.6%), Natural Gas (34.1%), Coal (1.4%)
Fuel Share of Carbon Emissions : Oil (60.8%), Natural Gas (36.6%), Coal (2.7%)
Renewable Energy Consumption: 26.2 trillion Btu* (61% increase from 2001)
Number of People per Motor Vehicle: 3.8 (vs U.S. value of 1.3)

Status in Climate Change Negotiations: Non-Annex I country under the United Nations Framework Convention on Climate Change (ratified March 24th, 1995). Signatory to the Kyoto Protocol (signed September 21st, 1998- not yet ratified).
Major Environmental Issues: Contamination of soil and groundwater with petroleum products and chemicals at military bases
Major International Environmental Agreements: A party to Conventions on Biodiversity, Climate Change, Hazardous Wastes, Ozone Layer Protection, Ship Pollution and Wetlands. Has signed, but not ratified: Air Pollution-Persistent Organic Pollutants.

Background: Independent between the two World Wars, Lithuania was annexed by the USSR in 1940. In March of 1990, Lithuania became the first of the Soviet republics to declare its independence, but this proclamation was not generally recognized until September of 1991 (following the abortive coup in Moscow). The last Russian troops withdrew in 1993. Lithuania subsequently has restructured its economy for eventual integration into Western European institutions.

GEOGRAPHY

Location: Eastern Europe, bordering the Baltic Sea, between Latvia and Russia
Geographic coordinates: 56 00 N, 24 00 E
Map references: Europe

Area:
total: 65,200 sq km *land:* 65,200 sq km *water:* 0 sq km

Area - comparative: slightly larger than West Virginia

Land boundaries:
total: 1,273 km
border countries: Belarus 502 km, Latvia 453 km, Poland 91 km, Russia (Kaliningrad) 227 km

Coastline: 99 km

Maritime claims: *territorial sea:* 12 nm

Climate: transitional, between maritime and continental; wet, moderate winters and summers

Terrain: lowland, many scattered small lakes, fertile soil

Elevation extremes:
lowest point: Baltic Sea 0 m
highest point: Juozapines/Kalnas 292 m

Natural resources: peat, arable land

Land use:
arable land: 35%
permanent crops: 12% *permanent pastures:* 7% *forests and woodland:* 31%
other: 15%

Irrigated land: 430 sq km

Natural hazards: NA

Environment - current issues: contamination of soil and groundwater with petroleum products and chemicals at military bases

Environment - international agreements:
party to: Biodiversity, Climate Change, Hazardous Wastes, Ozone Layer Protection, Ship Pollution, Wetlands

signed, but not ratified: Air Pollution-Persistent Organic Pollutants, Climate Change-Kyoto Protocol

PEOPLE

Population: 3,620,756

Age structure:
0-14 years: 19% (male 357,712; female 342,796)
15-64 years: 67% (male 1,177,732; female 1,259,682)
65 years and over: 14% (male 163,470; female 319,364)

Population growth rate: -0.29%
Birth rate: 9.77 births/1,000 population
Death rate: 12.87 deaths/1,000 population

Net migration rate: 0.16 migrant(s)/1,000 population

Sex ratio:
at birth: 1.05 male(s)/female
under 15 years: 1.04 male(s)/female
15-64 years: 0.93 male(s)/female
65 years and over: 0.51 male(s)/female
total population: 0.88 male(s)/female

Infant mortality rate: 14.67 deaths/1,000 live births

Life expectancy at birth:
total population: 69.09 years
male: 63.07 years
female: 75.41 years

Total fertility rate: 1.34 children born/woman

Nationality:
noun: Lithuanian(s)
adjective: Lithuanian

Ethnic groups: Lithuanian 80.6%, Russian 8.7%, Polish 7%, Byelorussian 1.6%, other 2.1%
Religions: Roman Catholic (primarily), Lutheran, Russian Orthodox, Protestant, evangelical Christian Baptist, Muslim, Jewish
Languages: Lithuanian (official), Polish, Russian

Literacy:
definition: age 15 and over can read and write
total population: 98%
male: 99%
female: 98%

LARGEST CITIES

Rank	City name	County	Pop.	Rank	City name	County	Pop.
1	Vilnius	Vilnius	542,932	11	Kėdainiai	Kaunas	29,824
2	Kaunas	Kaunas	336,912	12	Telšiai	Telšiai	29,107
3	Klaipėda	Klaipėda	177,812	13	Visaginas	Utena	26,804
4	Šiauliai	Šiauliai	120,969	14	Tauragė	Tauragė	26,429
5	Panevėžys	Panevėžys	109,028	15	Ukmergė	Vilnius	25,866
6	Alytus	Alytus	63,642	16	Plungė	Telšiai	22,287
7	Marijampolė	Marijampolė	44,885	17	Kretinga	Klaipėda	20,748
8	Mažeikiai	Telšiai	38,819	18	Šilutė	Klaipėda	19,720
9	Jonava	Kaunas	33,172	19	Radviliškis	Šiauliai	18,436
10	Utena	Utena	31,139	20	Palanga	Klaipėda	17,234

GOVERNMENT

Country name:

conventional long form: Republic of Lithuania
conventional short form: Lithuania
local long form: Lietuvos Respublika
local short form: Lietuva
former: Lithuanian Soviet Socialist Republic

Government type:

parliamentary democracy

Capital:

name: Vilnius
geographic coordinates: 54 41 N, 25 19 E
time difference: UTC+2 (7 hours ahead of Washington, DC, during Standard Time)
daylight saving time: +1hr, begins last Sunday in March; ends last Sunday in October

Administrative divisions:

60 municipalities (savivaldybe, singular - savivaldybe); Akmene, Alytaus Miestas, Alytus, Ankšciai, Birštono, Biržai, Druskininkai, Elektrénai, Ignalina, Jonava, Joniškis, Jurbarkas, Kaišiadorys, Kalvarijos, Kauno Miestas, Kaunas, Kazlu Rudos, Kedainiai, Kelme, Klaipedos Miestas, Klaipeda, Kretinga, Kupiškis, Lazdijai, Marijampole, Mažeikiai, Moletai, Neringa, Pagégiai, Pakruojis, Palangos Miestas, Panevežys, Pasvalys, Plunge, Prienai, Radviliškis, Raseiniai, Rietavo, Rokiškis, Šakiai, Šalcininkai, Šiauliu Miestas, Šiauliai, Šilale, Šilute, Širvintos, Skuodas, Švencionys, Taurage, Telšiai, Trakai, Ukmerge, Utena, Varena, Vilkaviškis, Vilniaus, Vilnius, Visaginas, Zarasai

Independence:

11 March 1990 (declared); 6 September 1991 (recognized by the Soviet Union); notable earlier dates: 6 July 1253 (coronation of MINDAUGAS, traditional founding date), 1 July 1569 (Polish-Lithuanian Commonwealth created)

National holiday:

Independence Day, 16 February (1918); note - 16 February 1918 was the date Lithuania declared its independence from Soviet Russia and established its statehood; 11 March 1990 was the date it declared its independence from the Soviet Union

Constitution:

several previous; latest adopted by referendum 25 October 1992, entered into force 2 November 1992; amended 2003 (2012)

Legal system:

civil law system; legislative acts can be appealed to the constitutional court

International law organization participation:

has not submitted an ICJ jurisdiction declaration; accepts ICCt jurisdiction

Suffrage:

18 years of age; universal

Executive branch:

chief of state: President Dalia GRYBAUSKAITE (since 12 July 2009)
head of government: Prime Minister Algirdas BUTKEVICIUS (since 22 November 2012)
cabinet: Council of Ministers appointed by the president on the nomination of the prime minister and approval of the Parliament
elections: president elected by popular vote for a five-year term (eligible for a second term); elections last held on 11 and 25 May 2014 (next to be held in May 2019); prime minister appointed by the president on the approval of the Parliament
election results: Dalia GRYBAUSKAITE reelected president; percent of vote - Dalia GRYBAUSKAITE 59%, Zigmantas BALCYTIS 41%; Algirdas BUTKEVICIUS approved by Parliament 90-40

Legislative branch:

unicameral Parliament or Seimas (141 seats; 71 members elected in single-member districts, 70 elected by proportional representation; members to serve four-year terms)
elections: last held on 14 and 28 October 2012 (next to be held in October 2016)
election results: percent of vote by party (proportional vote) - DP 19.8%, LSDP 18.4%, TS-LKD 15.1%, LS 8.6%, DK 8%, TT 7.3%, LLRA 5.8%, LVZS 3.9%, other parties 13.1%; seats by party - LSDP 38, TS-LKD 33, DP 29, TT 11, LS 10, LLRA 8, DK 7, unaffiliated 4, vacant 1

Judicial branch:

highest court(s): Supreme Court (consists of 37 judges); Constitutional Court (consists of 9 judges)

judge selection and term of office: Supreme Court judges nominated by the president and appointed by the Seimas; judges serve 5-year renewable terms; Constitutional Court judges selected by Seimas from among nominations by the president, by the Seimas chairperson, and Supreme Court chairperson; judges serve 9-year, nonrenewable terms; note - one-third of court judges reconstituted every 3 years
subordinate courts: Court of Appeals; district and local courts

Political parties and leaders:

Christian Party or KP [Gediminas VAGNORIUS]
Civil Democracy Party or PDP [Algimantas MATULEVICIUS]
Democratic Labor and Unity Party or DDVP [Kristina BRAZAUSKIENE]
Electoral Action of Lithuanian Poles or LLRA [Valdemar TOMASEVSKI]
Emigrants Party or EP [Juozas MURAUSKAS]
Homeland Union-Lithuanian Christian Democrats or TS-LKD [Andrius KUBILIUS]
Labor Party or DP [Loreta GRAUZINIENE]
Liberal and Center Union or LCS [Arturas MELIANAS]
Liberal Movement or LS or LRLS [Eligijus MASIULIS]
Lithuanian People's Party or LLP [Kazimiera PRUNSKIENE]
Lithuanian People's Party or LZP [Joana SIMANAUSKIENE]
Lithuanian Russian Union or LRS [Sergejus DMITRIJEVAS]
Lithuanian Social Democratic Party or LSDP [Algirdas BUTKEVICIUS]
Nationalist Union or TS [Gintaras SONGAILA]
Order and Justice Party or TT [Rolandas PAKSAS]
Peasant and Greens Union or LVZS [Ramunas KARBAUSKIS]
Republican Party or RP [Valdemaras VALKIUNAS]
Russian Alliance or RA [Tamara LOCHANKINA]
Socialist People's Front or SLF [Algirdas PALECKIS]
Way of Courage or DK [Jonas VARKALA]
YES-Homeland Revival and Perspective or YES Union or TAIP Union or TAIP [Arturas ZUOKAS]
Young Lithuania Party or PJL [Stanislovas BUSKEVICIUS]

International organization participation:

Australia Group, BA, BIS, CBSS, CD, CE, EAPC, EBRD, EIB, EU, FAO, IAEA, IBRD, ICAO, ICC (national committees), ICRM, IDA, IFC, IFRCS, ILO, IMF, IMO, Interpol, IOC, IOM, IPU, ISO, ITU, ITUC (NGOs), MIGA, NATO, NIB, NSG, OAS (observer), OIF (observer), OPCW, OSCE, PCA, Schengen Convention, UN, UN Security Council (temporary), UNCTAD, UNESCO, UNIDO, UNWTO, UPU, WCO, WHO, WIPO, WMO, WTO

Diplomatic representation in the US:

chief of mission: Ambassador Zygimantas PAVILIONIS (since 5 August 2010)
chancery: 2622 16th Street NW, Washington, DC 20009
telephone: (202) 234-5860
FAX: (202) 328-0466
consulate(s) general: Chicago, New York

Diplomatic representation from the US:

chief of mission: Ambassador Deborah A. MCCARTHY (since 5 February 2013)

embassy: Akmenu gatve 6, Vilnius, LT-03106
mailing address: American Embassy, Akmenu Gatve 6, Vilnius LT-03106
telephone: [370] (5) 266-5500
FAX: [370] (5) 266-5510

Flag description:

three equal horizontal bands of yellow (top), green, and red; yellow symbolizes golden fields, as well as the sun, light, and goodness; green represents the forests of the countryside, in addition to nature, freedom, and hope; red stands for courage and the blood spilled in defense of the homeland

National symbol(s):

mounted knight known as Vytis (the Chaser)

National anthem:

name: "Tautiska giesme" (The National Song)

ECONOMY

Lithuania gained membership in the World Trade Organization and joined the EU in May 2004. Despite its EU accession, Lithuania's trade with its Central and Eastern European neighbors, and Russia in particular, accounts for a significant share of total trade. Foreign investment and business support have helped in the transition from the old command economy to a market economy. The three former Soviet Baltic republics were among the hardest hit by the 2008-09 financial crisis. The government's efforts to attract foreign investment, to develop export markets, and to pursue broad economic reforms has been key to Lithuania's quick recovery from a deep recession, making Lithuania one of the fastest growing economies in the EU. Lithuania is committed to meeting the Maastricht criteria to join the euro zone, which the government expects to achieve by 2015. Under the Conservative Party's leadership, Lithuania raised the monthly minimum wage in January 2012 nearly 25% over 2011. In January 2013, the new Social Democrat-led government increased the minimum wage another 25% over January 2012. Despite government efforts, unemployment remains high.

GDP (purchasing power parity):

$67.43 billion
country comparison to the world: 86
$65.19 billion (2012 est.)
$62.92 billion (2011 est.)
note: data are in 2013 US dollars

GDP (official exchange rate):

$46.71 billion

GDP - real growth rate:

3.4%
country comparison to the world: 100
3.6% (2012 est.)
5.9% (2011 est.)

GDP - per capita (PPP):

$22,600
country comparison to the world: 65
$21,700 (2012 est.)
$20,800 (2011 est.)
note: data are in 2013 US dollars

Gross national saving:

16.5% of GDP
country comparison to the world: 100
17.2% of GDP (2012 est.)
18.9% of GDP (2011 est.)

GDP - composition, by end use:

household consumption: 64.4%
government consumption: 17.2%
investment in fixed capital: 16.8%
investment in inventories: 0.9%
exports of goods and services: 85.4%
imports of goods and services: -84.7%

GDP - composition, by sector of origin:

agriculture: 3.7%
industry: 28.3%
services: 68%

Agriculture - products:

grain, potatoes, sugar beets, flax, vegetables; beef, milk, eggs; fish

Industries:

metal-cutting machine tools, electric motors, television sets, refrigerators and freezers, petroleum refining, shipbuilding (small ships), furniture, textiles, food processing, fertilizers, agricultural machinery, optical equipment, electronic components, computers, amber jewelry

Industrial production growth rate:

2%
country comparison to the world: 126

Labor force:

1.452 million
country comparison to the world: 131

Labor force - by occupation:

agriculture: 7.9%
industry: 19.6%
services: 72.5% (2012 est.)

Unemployment rate:

12.4%
country comparison to the world: 126
13.2% (2012 est.)

Population below poverty line:

4% (2008)

Household income or consumption by percentage share:

lowest 10%: 2.6%
highest 10%: 29.1% (2008)

Distribution of family income - Gini index:

35.5 (2009)
country comparison to the world: 88
34 (1999)

Budget:

revenues: $14.5 billion
expenditures: $15.43 billion

Taxes and other revenues:

31% of GDP
country comparison to the world: 88

Budget surplus (+) or deficit (-):

-2% of GDP
country comparison to the world: 87

Public debt:

40.2% of GDP
country comparison to the world: 89
41% of GDP (2012 est.)
note: official data; data cover general government debt, and includes debt instruments issued (or owned) by government entities other than the treasury; the data include treasury debt held by foreign entities, debt issued by subnational entities, as well as intra-governmental debt; intra-governmental debt consists of treasury borrowings from surpluses in the social funds, such as for retirement, medical care, and unemployment; debt instruments for the social funds are sold at public auctions

Fiscal year:

calendar year

Inflation rate (consumer prices):

1.2%
country comparison to the world: 32
3.1% (2012 est.)

Central bank discount rate:

3% (31 December 2010 est.)
country comparison to the world: 112
2.06% (31 December 2009 est.)

Commercial bank prime lending rate:

4.5% (31 December 2013 est.)
country comparison to the world: 148
5.28% (31 December 2012 est.)

Stock of narrow money:

$13.83 billion (31 December 2013 est.)
country comparison to the world: 70
$13.77 billion (31 December 2012 est.)

Stock of broad money:

$20.59 billion (31 December 2013 est.)
country comparison to the world: 84
$20.58 billion (31 December 2012 est.)

Stock of domestic credit:

$22.02 billion (31 December 2013 est.)
country comparison to the world: 79

$22.69 billion (31 December 2012 est.)

Market value of publicly traded shares:

$3.964 billion (31 December 2012 est.)
country comparison to the world: 80
$4.075 billion (31 December 2011)
$5.661 billion (31 December 2010 est.)

Current account balance:

-$567 million
country comparison to the world: 104
-$231 million (2012 est.)

Exports:

$30.4 billion
country comparison to the world: 64
$28.76 billion (2012 est.)

Exports - commodities:

mineral products, machinery and equipment, chemicals, textiles , foodstuffs, plastics

Exports - partners:

Russia 19.8%, Latvia 9.9%, Estonia 7.5%, Poland 7.3%, Germany 7.1%, Belarus 5.1%, United Kingdom 4.9%, Netherlands 4.3%

Imports:

$32.52 billion
country comparison to the world: 66
$30.44 billion (2012 est.)

Imports - commodities:

mineral products, machinery and equipment, transport equipment, chemicals, textiles and clothing, metals

Imports - partners:

Russia 29.3%, Germany 10.3%, Poland 9.3%, Latvia 6.1%

Reserves of foreign exchange and gold:

$10.37 billion (31 December 2013 est.)
country comparison to the world: 75
$8.529 billion (31 December 2012 est.)

Debt - external:

$29.55 billion (31 December 2013 est.)
country comparison to the world: 73
$32.84 billion (31 December 2012 est.)

Stock of direct foreign investment - at home:

$16.57 billion (31 December 2013 est.)
country comparison to the world: 78
$15.56 billion (31 December 2012 est.)

Stock of direct foreign investment - abroad:

$3.029 billion (31 December 2013 est.)
country comparison to the world: 68
$2.729 billion (31 December 2012 est.)

Exchange rates:

litai (LTL) per US dollar -
2.658
2.685 (2012 est.)
2.6063 (2010 est.)
2.4787 (2009)
2.3251 (2008)

ENERGY

Electricity - production:

12.27 billion kWh
country comparison to the world: 90

Electricity - consumption:

10.3 billion kWh
country comparison to the world: 88

Electricity - exports:

186 million kWh
country comparison to the world: 71

Electricity - imports:

1.17 billion kWh
country comparison to the world: 64

Electricity - installed generating capacity:

3.82 million kW
country comparison to the world: 82

Electricity - from fossil fuels:

70.6% of total installed capacity
country comparison to the world: 106

Electricity - from nuclear fuels:

0% of total installed capacity
country comparison to the world: 125

Electricity - from hydroelectric plants:

3.2% of total installed capacity
country comparison to the world: 129

Electricity - from other renewable sources:

5% of total installed capacity
country comparison to the world: 47

Crude oil - production:

9,111 bbl/day
country comparison to the world: 93

Crude oil - exports:

2,181 bbl/day
country comparison to the world: 67

Crude oil - imports:

190,100 bbl/day
country comparison to the world: 33

Crude oil - proved reserves:

12 million bbl
country comparison to the world: 89

Refined petroleum products - production:

197,400 bbl/day
country comparison to the world: 54

Refined petroleum products - consumption:

70,390 bbl/day
country comparison to the world: 91

Refined petroleum products - exports:

155,000 bbl/day
country comparison to the world: 36

Refined petroleum products - imports:

16,110 bbl/day
country comparison to the world: 117

Natural gas - production:

0 cu m
country comparison to the world: 154

Natural gas - consumption:

3.3 billion cu m
country comparison to the world: 68

Natural gas - exports:

0 cu m
country comparison to the world: 135

Natural gas - imports:

3.4 billion cu m
country comparison to the world: 40

Natural gas - proved reserves:

0 cu m
country comparison to the world: 159

Carbon dioxide emissions from consumption of energy:

16.05 million Mt

COMMUNICATIONS

Telephones - main lines in use:

667,300

country comparison to the world: 89

Telephones - mobile cellular:

5 million
country comparison to the world: 110

Telephone system:

general assessment: adequate; being modernized to provide improved international capability and better residential access
domestic: rapid expansion of mobile-cellular services has resulted in a steady decline in the number of fixed-line connections; mobile-cellular teledensity stands at about 140 per 100 persons
international: country code - 370; major international connections to Denmark, Sweden, and Norway by submarine cable for further transmission by satellite; landline connections to Latvia and Poland

Broadcast media:

public broadcaster operates 3 channels with the third channel - a satellite channel - introduced in 2007; various privately owned commercial TV broadcasters operate national and multiple regional channels; many privately owned local TV stations; multi-channel cable and satellite TV services available; publicly owned broadcaster operates 3 radio networks; many privately owned commercial broadcasters, many with repeater stations in various regions throughout the country

Internet country code:

.lt

Internet hosts:

1.205 million
country comparison to the world: 43

Internet users:

1.964 million
country comparison to the world: 75

TRANSPORTATION

Airports:

61
country comparison to the world: 81

Airports - with paved runways:

total: 22

over 3,047 m: 3
2,438 to 3,047 m: 1
1,524 to 2,437 m: 7
914 to 1,523 m: 2
under 914 m: 9

Airports - with unpaved runways:

total: 39
over 3,047 m: 1
914 to 1,523 m: 2
under 914 m:
36

Pipelines:

gas 1,921 km; refined products 121 km

Railways:

total: 1,767 km
country comparison to the world: 76
broad gauge: 1,745 km 1.524-m gauge (122 km electrified)
standard gauge: 22 km 1.435-m gauge (2011)

Roadways:

total: 84,166 km
country comparison to the world: 56
paved: 72,297 km (includes 312 km of expressways)
unpaved: 11,869 km (2012)

Waterways:

441 km (navigable year round) (2007)
country comparison to the world: 87

Merchant marine:

total: 38
country comparison to the world: 76
by type: cargo 20, container 1, passenger/cargo 6, refrigerated cargo 9, roll on/roll off 2
foreign-owned: 8 (Denmark 8)
registered in other countries: 22 (Antigua and Barbuda 3, Belize 1, Comoros 1, Cook Islands 1, Norway 1, Panama 3, Saint Vincent and the Grenadines 9, unknown 3)

Ports and terminals:

major seaport(s): Klaipeda
oil terminals: Butinge oil terminal

MILITARY

Military branches:

Lithuanian Armed Forces (Lietuvos Ginkluotosios Pajegos): Land Forces (Sausumos Pajegos), Naval Forces (Karines Juru Pajegos), Air Forces (Karines Oro Pajegos)

Military service age and obligation:

18 years of age for voluntary military service; service obligation 1 year; Lithuania converted to a professional military in the fall of 2008, although the decision continues under judicial review

Manpower available for military service:

males age 16-49: 890,074
females age 16-49: 875,780

Manpower fit for military service:

males age 16-49: 669,111
females age 16-49: 724,803

Manpower reaching militarily significant age annually:

male: 20,425
female: 19,527

Military expenditures:

0.97% of GDP
country comparison to the world: 104
1.04% of GDP (2011)
0.97% of GDP (2010)

TRANSNATIONAL ISSUES

Disputes - international:

Lithuania and Russia committed to demarcating their boundary in 2006 in accordance with the land and maritime treaty ratified by Russia in May 2003 and by Lithuania in 1999; Lithuania operates a simplified transit regime for Russian nationals traveling from the Kaliningrad coastal exclave into Russia, while still conforming, as a EU member state having an external border with a non-EU member, to strict Schengen border rules; boundary demarcated with Latvia and Lithuania; as of January 2007, ground demarcation of the boundary with Belarus was complete and mapped with final ratification documents in preparation

Refugees and internally displaced persons:

stateless persons: 4,130

Illicit drugs:

transshipment and destination point for cannabis, cocaine, ecstasy, and opiates from Southwest Asia, Latin America, Western Europe, and neighboring Baltic countries; growing production of high-quality amphetamines, but limited production of cannabis, methamphetamines; susceptible to money laundering despite changes to banking legislation

IMPORTANT INFORMATION FOR UNDERSTANDING LITHUANIA

Official Name: Republic of Lithuania

PROFILE

Area: 65,200 sq. km. (26,080 sq. miles); about the size of West Virginia. Cities: *Capital*--Vilnius (pop. 592,500); Kaunas (430,000); Klaipeda (206,000); Siauliai (148,000); Panevezys (129,000).

Terrain: Lithuania's fertile, central lowland plains are separated by hilly uplands created by glacial drift. 758 rivers (many are navigable) and 2,833 lakes cover the landscape. The coastline is 99 km (62 miles) long. *Land use*--49.1% arable land, 22.2% meadows and pastures, 16.3% forest and woodland, 12.4% other. With four distinct seasons, the climate is humid continental, with a moderating maritime influence from the Baltic Sea. January temperatures average -5°C (23°F); July, 17°C (63°F). Annual precipitation averages 54-93 centimeters (21-37 in.).

People

Nationality: *Noun and adjective*--Lithuanian(s). Population: 3.75 million, 146 people/sq. mile.
Growth rate: -0.4%. *Birth rate*--13/1,000. *Death rate*--11/1,000. Migration rate--4 migrants/1,000. *Urban dwellers*--68%. *Density*--56 people/sq km (1989). *Divorce rate*--33% (1989).
Ethnic groups: Lithuanian 80.6%, Russians 8.7%, Poles 7%, Belarusians 1.6%, Ukrainians 1.1%.
Religions: Catholic (80%), Lutheran/Calvinist (10%), Jewish (7%), Orthodox (3%).
State language: Lithuanian. A minority speak Russian and Polish.
Education: *Years compulsory*--9. 60% of the adult population has completed secondary education, and 11% have completed higher education. *Attendance*--640,000 students at 2,326 schools, plus 55,300 university students at 15 universities and institutes of higher education. *Literacy*--99%.
Health: *Infant mortality rate*--18/1,000. *Life expectancy*--66 years male, 76 female. Work force: 1.6 million: *Industry*--33%, *Science, education, culture*--14%. *Construction*--13%. *Agriculture, forestry*--8%. *Health care*--7%. *Transportation/communications*--7%. *Trade and government*--10%. Other--8%.

Government

Type: parliamentary democracy.
Constitution: On October 25, 1992 Lithuanians ratified a new constitution, which officially was signed on November 6 that year.
Branches: *Executive*--popularly elected President (Chief of State); Prime Minister (Head of Government). *Legislative*--seimas (Parliament--141 members, 4-year term). *Judicial*--Supreme Court.
Administrative regions: 11 cities, 44 rural districts.

Principal political parties/coalitions: Homeland Union/Conservatives (70 seats); Christian Democrats (16 seats); Center Union (13 seats); Democratic Labor Party (12 seats); Social Democrats (12 seats); Democratic Party (2 seats); Independent candidates (12 seats); (4 seats are vacant)
Suffrage: 18 years, universal
Central government budget: $1.1 billion (education 20%, public order/safety 9%, social services 8%, defense 3%)
Flag: horizontal tricolor: yellow, green, red.

BASIC FACTS ABOUT LITHUANIA

THE REPUBLIC OF LITHUANIA lies in the center of Europe (the geometrical center of the continent is in eastern Lithuania, near the village of Bernotai, 25 km north of Vilnius). Lithuania is on the eastern coast of the Baltic Sea (the length of the Lithuanian coastline is 99 km). The northernmost point of Lithuania is 56 27 degrees latitude, while the southernmost point is 53 54 degrees latitude.
In the North, Lithuania borders on Latvia (610 km of common border), in the East and South, on Belarus (724 km), in the Southwest, on Poland (110 km) and the Kaliningrad region of the Russian Federation (303 km). The area of Lithuania (65 200 sq.km) is larger than that of Belgium, Denmark, the Netherlands and Switzerland
The climate of Lithuania is transitional between maritime and continental. The average temperature in January is -4.9C and +17.2C in July. It is characterized by moderate temperatures in the summer and adequate rainfall the year round. One unfavorable feature is the relatively short growing period (169-202 days).
Lithuania's major resources are timber, peat, gravel, construction sand, quartz sand, dolomite, clay, limestone, brick clay and mineral water. Amber is found on the coast of the Baltic Sea. Modest amounts of recoverable oil have been discovered in the western part of the country and in adjoining areas offshore. Lithuania's population is 3,715,400, of which 68% is urban. Ethnic Lithuanians predominate in the national composition of the population (81% of the total population).
Lithuania is administratively divided into 10 districts (apskritys), which are further subdivided into 56 local government units (savivaldybės). The capital of Lithuania is Vilnius (581 200 inhabitants). Other major cities include Kaunas (419 700), Klaipėda (203 900), Šiauliai (146 600) and Panevėžys (132 800).
The state holiday is February 16, which commemorates the Declaration of Independence in 1918.

EDUCATION AND SCIENCE

Basically all educational institutions are state or public. Schools of general education are of 3 kinds:

- primary (4 years, 836 schools, 141 preschools),

- basic (9 years, 592 schools) and

- secondary (12 years, 695 schools).

There are also 20 private schools. Children start school at the age of 6-7. A minimum of 9 years of education are compulsory. At present there are 14 institutions of higher education:

6 universities, 6 academies, two institutes of higher education and two Catholic seminaries with a total number of 55.728 students.

In addition, there is the Lithuanian Academy of Sciences, which has four divisions (social sciences; mathematics, physics and chemistry; biology, medicine, agriculture and technical sciences) and 17 research institutes.

GEOGRAPHY

The largest and most populous of the Baltic states, Lithuania is a generally maritime country with 60 miles of sandy coastline, of which only 24 miles face the open Baltic Sea. Lithuania's major warm-water port of Klaipeda lies at the narrow mouth of Kursiu Gulf, a shallow lagoon extending south to Kaliningrad. The Nemunas River and its dense network of tributaries connect the major inland cities and serve as a great asset to internal shipping. Between 56.27 and 53.54 latitude and 20.56 and 26.51 longitude, Lithuania is glacially flat, except for morainic hills in the western uplands and eastern highlands no higher than 300 meters. The terrain is marked by numerous small lakes and swamps, and a mixed forest zone covers 28% of the country. The growing season lasts 169 days in the east and 202 days in the west, with most farmland consisting of sandy- or clay loam soils. Limestone, clay, sand and gravel are Lithuania's primary natural resources, but the coastal shelf offers perhaps 10 million barrels' worth of oil deposits, and the southeast could provide high yields of iron ore and granite. Lithuania's capital, Vilnius, lies at the geographical center of Europe.

Border changes initiated by the U.S.S.R. from 1939-1945 have delayed a formal border agreement between Lithuania and Belarus, although a functional border exists based upon Soviet demarcations. The borders with Latvia, Poland and the Kaliningrad district are mutually recognized.

PEOPLE

The name "Lietuva" or Lithuania, might be derived from the word "lietava," for a small river, or "lietus," meaning rain (or land of rain). Lithuanian still retains the original sound system and morphological peculiarities of the prototypal Indo-European tongue and therefore is fascinating for linguistical study. Between 400-600 AD, the Lithuanian and Latvian languages split from the Eastern Baltic (Prussian) language group, which subsequently became extinct. The first known written Lithuanian text dates from a hymnal translation in 1545. Written with the Latin alphabet, Lithuanian has been the official language of Lithuania again since 1989. The Soviet era had imposed the official use of Russian, so most Lithuanians speak Russian as a second language while the resident Slavic populace generally speaks Russian as a first language.

Lithuanians are neither Slavic nor Germanic, although the union with Poland and Germanic colonization and settlement left cultural and religious influences. This highly literate society places strong emphasis upon education, which is free and compulsory until age 16. Most Lithuanians and ethnic Poles belong to the Roman Catholic Church, but a sizable minority are Russian Orthodox.

Enduring several border changes, Soviet deportations, a massacre of its Jewish population, and postwar German and Polish repatriations, Lithuania has maintained a fairly stable percentage of ethnic Lithuanians (from 84% in 1923 to 80% in 1993). Lithuania's citizenship law and constitution meet international and OSCE standards, guaranteeing universal human and civil rights.

HISTORICAL HIGHLIGHTS

The eastern shore of the Baltic Sea has been inhabited by Baltic tribes for approximately 4,000 years. The Roman historian Tacitus in his work Germania mentioned the existence of the Baltic tribes. However, the first recorded mention of Lithuania occurred in 1009, in the Quedlinburg

Annals. Over the course of several millennia, the Baltic tribes generally evolved into the major Lithuanian, Latvian and Prussian branches. Of these three, only the Lithuanians succeeded in establishing a state in the Middle Ages. The Latvians were subjected to the rule of Teutonic knights by the 13th century; the Prussians also were conquered by Teutonic forces, but during the subsequent centuries they were either annihilated or assimilated. The Lithuanian state was founded by Grand Duke Mindaugas in the middle of the 13th century. In 1251, Mindaugas adopted the Catholic faith, and in 1253 he was crowned King by dispensation of the Pope. During Grand Duke Vytautas' reign from 1392-1430, Lithuania became one of the largest states in Europe, extending over significant Eastern Slav lands. The Lithuanian state successfully resisted several centuries of expansion eastward by the Teutonic Knights as well as the sustained drive westward by the Mongol Tartar hordes. Facing growing pressure from the East, the Lithuanians found it necessary to ally themselves with the Kingdom of Poland. The period 1569-1795 was marked by the Lithuanian-Polish Commonwealth, during which Lithuania gradually lost its power. From 1795 to 1915, the major part of Lithuania was ruled by the Russian Empire, which had annexed Lithuanian territories during the partitions of the second half of the 18th century. Prussia controlled the smaller, western part of the country known as Lithuania Minor, which bordered on the Baltic Sea.

Independence was restored in the aftermath of World War I, which witnessed the collapse of the Czarist empire and the weakening of Germany. On February 16, 1918, the Lithuanian Council issued a declaration of independence, which was not immediately put into effect, since much of the country was still occupied by the German army. Real independence came after several years of fighting against a variety of hostile forces. In 1920, Poland seized the eastern part of Lithuania, including the capital Vilnius. Although Lithuania was a recognized member of the international community and a member of the League of Nations, it did not succeed in regaining these lost territories until World War II. Nevertheless, Lithuania managed to gain access to the Baltic Sea through Klaipeda harbor in 1923.

Beginning in the early 1920s, Lithuania began a steady economic and social recovery. Illiteracy was largely eliminated, and a sweeping reform of agriculture brought about a major redistribution of land away from large estates to small and medium-sized private farms. The expansion of agriculture, food processing, light industry, transportation and foreign trade created the basis for economic development, which unfortunately was interrupted by renewed occupation in 1940.

The loss of independence was a consequence of the 1939 Molotov-Ribbentrop Pact, a trade-off between Germany and Soviet Russia. The country was occupied by an extended process of coercion and take-over, ending in complete annexation. With the outbreak of the Nazi-Soviet war, an armed struggle against Soviet oppression rose up and spread over much of the countryside. Even after the end of World War II, the fighting continued for nearly ten years and claimed tens of thousands of lives. Meanwhile, the occupation authorities conducted mass deportation of the civilian population; several hundred thousand men, women and children were brutally uprooted from their homes and banished to outlying regions of the USSR, from which many did not return. Another major part of the nation was forced to flee Soviet repression, and wound up scattered around many Western countries. Nevertheless, Lithuania's diplomatic corps managed to survive, preserve Western recognition and work with the diaspora for the eventual restoration of independence. The tradition of resistance strengthened the commitment to the ideal of independence among those who remained inside Lithuania during 50 long years of Soviet control. The years spent inside the Soviet Union underscored for Lithuanians (as well as for Latvians and Estonians) their distinctiveness and helped them resist Sovietization. Many Western states refused to recognize the incorporation of the Baltic States into the Soviet Union.

Finally, on March 11, 1990, Lithuania's democratically-elected parliament declared the re-establishment of independence. Since August of 1991, Lithuania has joined the United Nations

(September 17, 1991), the Council of Europe (May 11, 1993), as well as becoming an associate member of the European Union (February 1, 1998). On October 21, 1997, Lithuania established diplomatic relations with the Ivory Coast, the 118th foreign entity with which it maintains diplomatic ties.

The earliest evidence of inhabitants in present-day Lithuania dates back to 10,000 BC. Between 3,000-2,000 BC, the cord-ware culture people spread over a vast region of Eastern Europe, between the Baltic Sea and the Vistula River in the west and the Moscow-Kursk line in the east. Merging with the indigenous population, they gave rise to the Balts, a distinct Indo-European ethnic group whose descendants are the present-day Lithuanian and Latvian nations and the now extinct Prussians.

The first written mention of Lithuania occurs in 1009 AD, although many centuries earlier the Roman historian Tacitus referred to the Lithuanians as excellent farmers. Spurred by the expansion into the Baltic lands of the Germanic monastic military orders (the Order of the Knights of the Sword and the Teutonic Order) Duke Mindaugas united the lands inhabited by the Lithuanians, the Samogitians, Yotvingians and Couranians into the Grand Duchy of Lithuania (GDL) in the 1230s and 40s. In 1251 Mindaugas adopted Catholicism and was crowned King of Lithuania on July 6, 1253; a decade later, civil war erupted upon his assassination until a ruler named Vitenis defeated the Teutonic Knights and restored order.

From 1316-41 Vitenis' brother and successor, Grand Duke Gediminas, expanded the empire as far as Kiev against the Tartars and Russians. He twice attempted to adopt Christianity in order to end the GDL's political and cultural isolation from Western Europe. To that purpose, he invited knights, merchants and artisans to settle in Lithuania and wrote letters to Pope John XXII and European cities maintaining that the Teutonic Order's purpose was to conquer lands rather than spread Christianity. Gediminas' dynasty ruled the GDL until 1572. In the 1300s through the early 1400s, the Lithuanian state expanded eastward. During the rule of Grand Duke Algirdas (1345-77), Lithuania almost doubled in size and achieved major victories over the Teutonic and Livonian Orders at the Battles of Saule (1236) and Durbe (1260). However, backed by the Pope and the Catholic West European countries, the Orders continued their aggression which greatly intensified in the 2nd half of the 14th century. During the period Algirdas' brother, Kestutis (Grand Duke in 1381-82) distinguished himself as the leader of the struggle against the Teutonic Order. The ongoing struggle precipitated the 1385 Kreva Union signed by the Grand Duke of Lithuania Jogaila (ruled in 1377-81 and 1382-92) and the Queen of Poland Jadwyga. Jogaila (Jagiello) married Jadwyga in 1386 and became the King of Poland. One of the conditions of the union was Lithuania's conversion to Christianity (1387) which intensified Lithuania's economic and cultural development, orienting it towards the West. The conversion invalidated the claims by the Teutonic Order and temporarily halted its wars against Lithuania.

Lithuania's independence under the union with Poland was restored by Grand Duke Vytautas. During his rule (1392-1430) the GDL turned into one of the largest states in Europe, encompassing present-day Belarus, most of Ukraine and the Smolensk region of western Russia. Led by Jogaila and Vytautas, the united Polish-Lithuanian army defeated the Teutonic Order in the Battle of Tannenberg (Gruenwald or Zalgiras) in 1410, terminating the medieval Germanic drive eastward.

The 16th century witnessed a number of wars against the growing Russian state over the Slavic lands ruled by the GDL. Coupled with the need for an ally in those wars, the wish of the middle and petty gentry to obtain more rights already granted to the Polish feudal lords drew Lithuania closer to Poland. The Union of Lublin in 1569 united Poland and Lithuania into a commonwealth in which the highest power belonged to the Sejm of the nobility and its elected King who was also the Grand Duke of Lithuania. Mid-16th century land reform strengthened serfdom and yet promoted the development of agriculture owing to the introduction of a regular three-field rotation system.

The 16th century saw a more rapid development of agriculture, growth of towns, spread of ideas of humanism and the Reformation, book printing, the emergence of Vilnius University in 1579 and the Lithuanian Codes of Law (the Statutes of Lithuania) which stimulated the development of culture both in Lithuania and in neighboring countries.

The rising domination of the big magnates, the 16-18th century wars against Russia and Sweden over Livonia, Ukraine and Byelorussia weakened the Polish-Lithuanian Republic. The end of the 18th century witnessed three divisions of the Commonwealth by Russia, Prussia and Austria; in 1795 most of Lithuania became part of the Russian Empire. Attempts to restore independence in the uprisings of 1794, 1830-31 and 1863 were suppressed and followed by a tightened police regime, increasing Russification, the closure of Vilnius University in 1832 and the 1864 ban on the printing of Lithuanian books in traditional Roman characters.

Because of his proclamation of liberation and self-rule, many Lithuanians gratefully volunteered for the French Army when Napoleon occupied Kaunas in 1812 during the fateful invasion of Russia. After the war, Russia imposed extra taxes on Catholic landowners and enserfed an increasing number of peasants. A market economy slowly developed with the abolition of serfdom in 1861. Lithuanian farmers grew stronger, contributing to an increase in the number of intellectuals of peasant origin which led to the growth of a Lithuanian national movement. In German-ruled Lithuania Minor (Königsberg or Kaliningrad), Lithuanian publications were printed in large numbers and then smuggled into Russian-ruled Lithuania. The most outstanding leaders of the national liberation movement were J. Basanavicius and V. Kudirka. The ban on the Lithuanian press finally was lifted in 1904.

During WW I, the German army occupied Lithuania in 1915, and the occupation administration allowed a Lithuanian Conference to convene in Vilnius in September 1917. The Conference adopted a resolution demanding the restoration of an independent Lithuanianstate and elected the Lithuanian Council, a standing body chaired by Antanas Smetona. On February 16, 1918, the Council declared Lithuania's independence. 1919-20 witnessed Lithuania's War for Independence against three factions: the Red Army, which in 1919 controlled territory ruled by a Bolshevist government headed by V. Kapsukas; the Polish army; and the Bermondt army, composed of Russian and German troops under the command of the Germans. Lithuania failed to regain the Polish-occupied Vilnius region.

In the Moscow Treaty of July 12, 1920, Russia recognized Lithuanian independence and renounced all previous claims to it. The Seimas (parliament) of Lithuania adopted a constitution on August 1, 1922, declaring Lithuania a parliamentary republic, and in 1923 Lithuania annexed the Klaipeda region, the northern part of Lithuania Minor. By then, most countries had recognized Lithuanian independence. After a military coup on December 17, 1926, Nationalist party leader Antanas Smetona became President and gradually introduced an authoritarian regime.

Lithuania's borders posed its major foreign policy problem. Poland's occupation (1920) and annexation (1922) of the Vilnius region strained bilateral relations, and in March 1939 Germany forced Lithuania to surrender the Klaipeda region (the Nürnberg trials declared the treaty null and void). Radical land reform in 1922 considerably reduced the number of estates, promoted the growth of small and middle farms and boosted agricultural production and exports, especially livestock. In particular, light industry and agriculture successfully adjusted to the new market situation and developed new structures.

The interwar period gave birth to a comprehensive system of education with Lithuanian as the language of instruction and the development of the press, literature, music, arts and theater. On August 23, 1939, the Molotov-Ribbentrop Pact pulled Lithuania first into German influence until the Soviet-German agreement of September 28, 1939 brought Lithuania under Soviet domination. Soviet pressure and a complicated international situation forced Lithuania to sign an agreement with the USSR on October 10, 1939, by which Lithuania was given back the city of Vilnius and the part of Vilnius region seized by the Red Army during the Soviet-Polish war; in return, some 20,000 Soviet soldiers were deployed in Lithuania.

On June 14, 1940 the Soviet Government issued an ultimatum to Lithuania, demanding the formation of a new Lithuanian government and permission to station additional Red Army troops. Lithuania succumbed to the Soviet demand, and 100,000 Soviet troops moved into the country the next day. Arriving in Kaunas, the Soviet government's special envoy began implementing the plan for Lithuania's incorporation into the U.S.S.R. On June 17 the alleged People's Government, headed by J. Paleckis, was formed; rump parliamentary elections one month later were held, whereupon Lithuania was proclaimed a Soviet Socialist Republic on August 3.

Totalitarian rule was established, Sovietization of the economy and culture began, and Lithuanian state employees and public figures were arrested and exiled to Russia. During the mass deportation campaign of June 14-18, 1941 about 7,439 families (12,600 people) were deported to Siberia without investigation or trial; 3,600 people were imprisoned and over 1,000 massacred.

Lithuanian revolt against the U.S.S.R. soon followed the outbreak of the war against Germany in 1941. Via Radio Kaunas on June 23, the rebels declared the restoration of Lithuania's independence and actively operated a Provisional Government, without German recognition, from June 24 to August 5. Lithuania became part of the German occupational administrative unit of Ostland. People were repressed and taken to forced labor camps in Germany. The Nazis and local collaborators deprived Lithuanian Jews of their civil rights and massacred about 200,000 of them. Together with Soviet partisans, supporters of independence put up a resistance movement to deflect Nazi recruitment of Lithuanians to the German army.

Forcing the Germans out of Lithuania by 1944, the Red Army reestablished control, and Sovietization continued with the arrival of Communist party leaders to create a local party administration. The mass deportation campaigns of 1941-52 exiled 29,923 families to Siberia and other remote parts of the Soviet Union. Official statistics state that over 120,000 people were deported from Lithuania during this period, while Lithuanian sources estimate the number of political prisoners and deportees at 300,000. In response to these events, an estimated several ten thousand resistance fighters participated in unsuccessful guerilla warfare against the Soviet regime from 1944-53. As a measure for integration and industrial development, Soviet authorities encouraged immigration of other Soviet workers, especially Russians.

Until mid-1988, all political, economical and cultural life was controlled by the Lithuanian Communist Party (LCP). First Secretary Antanas Snieckus ruled the LCP from 1940-74. The LCP, in turn, was responsible to the Communist party of the U.S.S.R. In 1947 Lithuanians comprised only 18% of total party membership in 1947 and continued to represent a minority until 1958; by 1986, they made up 70% of the party's 197,000-strong body. During the Khrushchev thaw in the 1950s, the leadership of the LCP acquired limited independence in decision-making.

The political and economic crisis that began in the U.S.S.R. in the mid-1980s also affected Lithuania, and Lithuanians as well as other Balts offered active support to Gorbachev's program of social and political reforms. Under the leadership of intellectuals, the Lithuanian reform movement Sajudis was formed in mid-1988 and declared a program of democratic and national rights, winning nation-wide popularity. On Sajudis' demand, the Lithuanian Supreme Soviet passed constitutional amendments on the supremacy of Lithuanian laws over Soviet legislation, annulled the 1940 decisions on proclaiming Lithuania a part of the U.S.S.R., legalized a multi-party system and adopted a number of other important decisions. A large number of LCP members also supported the ideas of Sajudis, and with Sajudis support, Algirdas Brazauskas was elected First Secretary of the Central Committee of the LCP in 1988. In December 1989, the Brazauskas-led LCP split from the CPSU and became an independent party, renaming itself in 1990 the Lithuanian Democratic Labor Party.

In 1990, Sajudis-backed candidates won the elections to the Lithuanian Supreme Soviet. On March 11, 1990, its chairman Vytautas Landsbergis proclaimed the restoration of Lithuanian independence, formed a new Cabinet of Ministers headed by Kazimiera Prunskiene, and adopted the Provisional Fundamental Law of the state and a number of by-laws. The U.S.S.R. demanded to revoke the act and began employing political and economic sanctions against Lithuania as well as demonstrating military force. On January 10, 1991, U.S.S.R. authorities seized the central publishing house and other premises in Vilnius and unsuccessfully attempted to overthrow the elected government by sponsoring a local "National Salvation Committee." Three days later the Soviets forcibly took over the TV tower, killing 14 civilians and injuring 700. During the national plebiscite on February 9, 91% of those who took part in the voting (76% of all eligible voters) voted in favor of an independent, democratic Lithuania. Led by the tenacious Landsbergis, Lithuania's leadership continued to seek Western diplomatic recognition of its independence. Soviet military-security forces continued forced conscription, occasional seizure of buildings, attacking customs posts, and sometimes killing customs and police officials.

During the August 19 coup against Gorbachev, Soviet military troops took over several communications and other government facilities in Vilnius and other cities, but returned to their barracks when the coup failed. The Lithuanian government banned the Communist Party and ordered confiscation of its property.

Despite Lithuania's achievement of complete independence, sizable numbers of Russian forces remained on its territory. Withdrawal of those forces was one of Lithuania's top foreign policy priorities. Lithuania and Russia signed an agreement on September 8, 1992 calling for Russian troop withdrawals by August 31, 1993, which now have been completed in full, despite unresolved issues such as Lithuania's compensation claims.

THE MOVE TOWARD INDEPENDENCE, 1987-91

The situation did not change until Mikhail S. Gorbachev came to power in 1985. Even then, Lithuania's communist party leadership hesitated to embrace Gorbachev's program of limited economic reforms under his policy of *perestroika* (see Glossary). The death of Petras Griskevicius, first secretary of the Communist Party of Lithuania, in 1987 did little to improve the atmosphere for reform. The new first secretary, Ringaudas Songaila, was a conservative functionary. But encouraged by new winds from Moscow, Baltic dissidents began in 1987 to hold public demonstrations in Riga, Tallinn, and Vilnius. In 1988, against the wishes of Songaila's regime, Lithuanian, engaged in widespread celebration of the February 16 Independence Day. Lithuanian intellectuals were pushed into taking more forceful action as well. Meeting at the Academy of Sciences on June 3, 1988, communist and noncommunist intellectuals formed "an initiative group" to organize a movement to support Gorbachev's program of *glasnost* (see Glossary), democratization, and *perestroika* . A council composed equally of communist party members and nonparty members was chosen to organize the Lithuanian Reconstruction Movement, which became known subsequently simply as Sajudis (Movement). The Communist Party of Lithuania leadership did not like this independent action but, knowing Gorbachev's limited acceptance of "informal" societies, did not interfere with the effort.

The movement supported Gorbachev's policies, but at the same time it promoted Lithuanian national issues such as restoration of the Lithuanian language as the "official" language. Its demands included revelations of the truth about the Stalinist years, protection of the environment, cessation of construction on a third nuclear reactor at the Ignalina nuclear power plant, and disclosure of secret protocols of the Nazi-Soviet Nonaggression Pact. Sajudis used mass meetings to advance its goals. At first, party leaders shunned these meetings, but by mid-1988 their participation became a political necessity. Thus, a Sajudis rally on June 24, 1988, was attended by Algirdas Brazauskas, then party secretary for industrial affairs.

In October 1988, Brazauskas was appointed first secretary of the party to replace Songaila, and Sajudis held its founding conference in Vilnius. It subsequently elected as its chairman Vytautas Landsbergis, a professor of musicology who was not a member of the communist party. In the elections to Moscow's newly authorized Congress of People's Deputies (see Glossary) in March-May 1989, Sajudis was victorious. From the communist party, the voters elected only Brazauskas and Vladimiras Beriozovas, his associate, whom Sajudis did not oppose. From that time, Brazauskas cooperated fully with Sajudis. Lithuanian sovereignty--as distinguished from Lithuanian independence, which had been declared on February 16, 1918--was proclaimed in May 1989, and Lithuania's incorporation into the Soviet Union was declared illegal. In August a human chain from Tallinn to Vilnius commemorated the fiftieth anniversary of the Nazi-Soviet Nonaggression Pact. In December Brazauskas forced the Communist Party of Lithuania to secede from the Communist Party of the Soviet Union and to give up its monopoly on power.

But even the separation of the Communist Party of Lithuania from Moscow did not save it in the electoral contest for the Supreme Soviet of the republic in March 1990. In the election, the Communist Party of Lithuania won only twenty-three of the 141 seats. On March 11, the newly elected parliament voted unanimously for independence. Brazauskas lost the election for chairman of the presidium of the Supreme Soviet to Landsbergis.

Moscow did not accept the legality of the independence vote, however; in April 1990, it imposed an economic blockade that lasted for three months, until the Lithuanian legislature, now known as the Supreme Council, agreed to a six-month moratorium on its independence declaration. Later, Moscow obstructed Lithuanian efforts to gain Western recognition, and on January 13, 1991, attempted to use force to remove the Lithuanian government in Vilnius and to reestablish Soviet rule. Although this attempted coup ended in a massacre of civilians--thirteen died, and hundreds were wounded--by the Soviet army, Lithuania's determination did not change. Finally, the failure of the August 1991 coup in Moscow permitted Lithuania to regain self-determination and prompted the international community to recognize it as an independent state. The United States extended recognition on September 2, and the Soviet Union did so on September 6. Lithuania was admitted to the United Nations on September 16, 1991.

GOVERNMENT AND POLITICAL CONDITIONS

For over a year after independence, political life was fettered by an unclear delineation of powers between parliament and government. Political polarization increased, and name recognition played a much more significant role in politics than party affiliation. Sajudis remained part of an unofficial ruling coalition with two other politically right-wing parties, but rivalries were heightened by personally divisive political attacks and bureaucratic gridlock.

In an effort to reduce the size and recalcitrance of a government bureaucracy allegedly impeding reform, in April 1992 then-Prime Minister Vagnorius unsuccessfully attempted to enact a measure permitting the dismissal of former Communist party members and of those unwilling to enforce government decrees.

Two deputies and a minister unsuccessfully tendered resignations in support of Vagnorius, but the rest of the cabinet wrote a letter to Chairman Landsbergis complaining of Vagnorius' confrontational governing style. Vagnorius unsuccessfully submitted his resignation in May. When a referendum in May to establish a permanent French-style office of president failed, Landsbergis also threatened to resign. Right-wing members of parliament boycotted legislative sessions to stall attempts to form a quorum and successfully forestalled Vagnorius' resignation until June, when a quorum passed a no-confidence motion. Landsbergis then chose Aleksandras Abisala as Prime Minister.

A constitution was approved by 53% of eligible voters (85% of those who actually voted) in an October 1992 referendum. The results of the October 25 and November 15 runoff elections handed the Democratic Labor Party (LDDP) headed by former Communist Party boss Algirdas Brazauskas a plurality of votes and a clear majority of parliamentary seats. February, 1993 presidential elections gave Brazauskas victory over a non-LDDP coalition led by independent candidate Stasys Lozoraitis, Lithuania's former ambassador to the U.S. Economic mismanagement and collapse, fueled by chronic energy shortages and political factionalism, played a decisive role in the election results.

Since then, the Lithuanian Government has worked steadily to improve relations with its neighbors and to implement necessary Western reforms. In August 1994, the Government, backed by the IMF, lobbied the public successfully to defeat a populist referendum backed by its own far left-wing as well as the opposition which called for the indexation of peoples' savings. However, LDDP candidates took a beating at the hands of the opposition in nationwide municipal elections held in March, 1995. Public perception that the government was not doing enough to promote prosperity and to combat corruption and organized crime again were significant issues,

Caused primarily by a lack of supervision and regulation over the banking sector, a long-simmering financial crisis boiled over in December 1995, leading to the resignation in February of Adolfas Slezevicius as Prime Minister and LDDP Chairman. The new LDDP Prime Minister, Mindaugas Stankevicius, instigated an IMF-backed, comprehensive banking sector bailout plan.

These measures were not enough to persuade voters in the October 25 and November 10, 1996 rounds of parliamentary elections. The Landsbergis-led Conservative Party, gained 70 out of 141 seats, and another 16 seats went to its coalition partner, the Christian Democrats. The new coalition established a new government in early December and won a significant majority in nationwide municipal elections held in March 1997. Valdas Adamkus was elected president in December 1997 and will be sworn in on February 25, 1998.

The seimas (parliament), a unicameral legislative body, is the highest organ of state authority. It initiates and approves legislation sponsored by the Prime Minister. The Prime Minister has full responsibility and control over his cabinet.

PRINCIPAL GOVERNMENT OFFICIALS

Ministry of Agriculture	Virginija Baltraitienė	Labour Party
Ministry of Culture	Šarūnas Birutis	Labour Party
Ministry of Economy	Evaldas Gustas	Social Democratic Party of Lithuania
Ministry of Education and Science	Dainius Pavalkis	Labour Party
Ministry of Energy	Rokas Masiulis	Independent
Ministry of Environment	Kęstutis Trečiokas	Order and Justice
Ministry of Finance	Rimantas Šadžius	Social Democratic Party of

		Lithuania
Ministry of Foreign Affairs	Linas Antanas Linkevičius	Social Democratic Party of Lithuania
Ministry of Health	Rimantė Šalaševičiūtė	Social Democratic Party of Lithuania
Ministry of the Interior	Saulius Skvernelis	Independent
Ministry of Justice	Juozas Bernatonis	Social Democratic Party of Lithuania
Ministry of National Defence	Juozas Olekas	Social Democratic Party of Lithuania
Ministry of Social Security and Labour	Algimanta Pabedinskienė	Labour Party
Ministry of Transport and Communications	Rimantas Sinkevičius	Social Democratic Party of Lithuania

Lithuania maintains an embassy in the United States, located at 2622 16th Street NW, Washington, DC 20009, tel: (202) 234-5860.

STATE STRUCTURE

The Republic of Lithuania is an independent democratic state expressing the common will and interests of its people. The foundations of the social system are enforced by the Constitution of the Republic of Lithuania adopted in 1992, by a referendum which also establishes the rights, freedoms and obligations of citizens. Under that law, sovereign state power is vested in the people of Lithuania and is exercised by the Seimas (Parliament), President of the Republic, Government and Courts.

The Seimas is a one-chamber parliament which deliberates on and enacts amendments to the Constitution; enacts laws; adopts resolutions regarding the organization of referenda; calls presidential elections; approves or rejects the candidacy of the Prime Minister proposed by the President of the Republic; reviews the programme of the Government submitted by the Prime Minister and decides whether to approve it or not; upon the recommendation of the Government, establishes or abolishes ministries of the Republic of Lithuania; supervises the activities of the Government; and may adopt a motion of no-confidence in the Prime Minister or individual Ministers; appoints judges to, and Chairpersons of, the Constitutional Court and the Supreme Court; appoints to, and dismisses from office, the State Controller as well as the Chairperson of the Board of the Bank of Lithuania; calls local government Council election; establishes the Central Electoral Committee and changes its composition; approves the State budget and supervises the implementation thereof; fixes State taxes and other obligatory payments; ratifies or denounces international treaties whereto the Republic of Lithuania is a party, and considers other issues of foreign policy.

The Seimas is composed of 141 members elected for a four-year term. The Seimas elects its Chairman (the Speaker) and Deputy Chairmen

MAJOR PARLIAMENTARY GROUPS: Liberals, New Union (Social Liberals), Social Democratic Coalition and Homeland Union - Conservatives.

THE PRESIDENT of the Republic is the head of State. The President represents the State of Lithuania and performs all the duties which he or she is charged with by the Constitution and laws.

The President of the Republic of Lithuania is elected by the citizens of the Republic of Lithuania on the basis of universal, equal, and direct suffrage by secret ballot for a term of five years.
The first democratically and directly elected President of the Republic was Algirdas Mykolas Brazauskas, who was elected on February 14, 1993. Recent presidential elections were held on December 21, 1997, resulting in the election of Valdas Adamkus, who took office on February 25, 1998.

THE GOVERNMENT is the highest authority of executive power. It comprises the Prime Minister and Ministers. The Prime Minister is appointed or dismissed by the President of the Republic, with the approval of the Seimas. Ministers are appointed by the President of the Republic on the nomination of the Prime Minister.

The Government administers the affairs of the country, protects the inviolability of the territory of the Republic of Lithuania, and ensures State security and public order; implements laws and resolutions of the Seimas, as well as the decrees of the President; coordinates the activities of the ministries and other governmental institutions; prepares the draft budget of the State and submits it to the Seimas; executes the State Budget and reports on the fulfilment of the budget to the Seimas; drafts bills and submits them to the Seimas for consideration; establishes diplomatic relations and maintains relations with foreign countries and international organizations; and discharges other duties prescribed to the Government by the Constitution and other laws.

LOCAL SELF-GOVERNMENT is organized on the basis of the administrative-territorial division of Lithuania. Apskritys (the largest local administrative units), urban settlements and district towns constitute the lower level of local self-government, which is represented by the municipal councils elected by the local population for a period of 2 years on the basis of universal, equal and direct suffrage by secret ballot.

COURTS AND PROSECUTION. Justice is exercised exclusively by courts. The court system in Lithuania comprises the Constitutional Court, the Supreme Court, the Court of Appeal, circuit courts and district courts, made up of elected judges and assessors. Judges of these courts and of the Supreme Court are elected by the Seimas for a term of 5 years. Legal assistance is rendered by the Bar, while cases of business disputes are heard in the Commercial Court of the Republic of Lithuania. Criminal prosecution is exercised by the Prosecutor General of the Republic of Lithuania and by local prosecutors under his subordination. The Prosecutor General and his deputies are appointed by the Seimas. Local prosecutors are appointed by the Prosecutor General of the Republic of Lithuania.

POLITICAL PARTIES. All political parties enjoy freedom and independence of action. Their organizational structure is based exclusively on the territorial principle. The activity of political parties of other states in Lithuania is forbidden by law. Political parties are registered by the Ministry of Justice.

ECONOMY

Currency	€ 1 Euro (EUR) = 100 cent
Fiscal year	1 January – 31 December
Trade organisations	EU, WTO and OSCE
	Statistics
GDP	▲$83.105 billion (PPP, 2015 est.)
GDP rank	87th (PPP, est.)
GDP growth	▲2.9% (Real, 2015 est.)
GDP per capita	▲$28,245 (PPP, 2015 est.)
GDP by sector	agriculture 3.3%, industry 28.4%, services 68.4% (2012 est.)
Inflation (CPI)	▼2.0% (CPI, est.)
Population below poverty line	▬4%
Labour force	▼1.587 million (
Labour force by occupation	services 72.5%, industry 19.6%, agriculture 7.9% (2012 est.)
Unemployment	▼11.3% (2014 est.)
Average gross salary	676 EUR / 879 $, monthly
Average net salary	527 EUR / 685 $, monthly
Main industries	metal-cutting machine tools, electric motors, television sets, refrigerators and freezers, petroleum refining, shipbuilding (small ships), furniture making, textiles, food processing, fertilizers, agricultural machinery, optical equipment, electronic components, computers, amber jewelry
Ease-of-doing-business rank	17th
	External
Exports	▲$29.01 billion
Export goods	mineral products, machinery and equipment, chemicals, textiles , foodstuffs, plastics
Main export partners	Russia 19.0% Latvia 11.0% Estonia 7.9% Germany 7.9% United Kingdom 6.4% Poland 6.1% Netherlands 5.9% Belarus 4.5% (2012 est.)
Imports	▲$31.41 billion (2012 est.)
Import goods	mineral products, machinery and equipment, transport equipment, chemicals, textiles and clothing, metals
Main import partners	Russia 32.5% Germany 9.8% Poland 9.8% Latvia 6.1% Netherlands 5.5%
FDI stock	▲$15.75 billion
Gross external debt	▲$31.37 billion
	Public finances
Revenues	$9.8 billion
Expenses	$10.1 billion
Economic aid	EU structural assistance: 2.286 Eur billion (est.), assistance from Switzerland: 9.09 Eur Mln.
Credit rating	Standard & Poor's: A- (Domestic) AA- (Foreign)

	A (T&C Assessment) Outlook: Stable Moody's: Baa1 Outlook: Stable Fitch: BBB Outlook: Positive
Foreign reserves	▲$8.821 billion

Lithuania is a member of the European Union and the biggest economy among the three Baltic states. GDP per capita reached USD 17,800 in 2008 and was higher than all of its neighbors – Latvia, Poland, Russia and Belarus.

GDP per capita in Lithuania is 70% above the world's average of US$10,500. Lithuania has a favorable legislative basis for business as the country is ranked the 3rd in the region of Eastern Europe and Central Asia and the 17th in the world by the Ease of Doing Business Index prepared by the World Bank Group. Lithuania is ranked the 22nd out of 177 countries in the Index of Economic Freedom, measured by The Heritage Foundation. According to the Human Development Report 2011, Lithuania belongs to the group of very high human development countries.

Having moved away from central planning system in the late 1980s, in 1990, Lithuania was the first to break away from the Soviet Union and become an independent capitalist economy. Lithuania soon implemented liberal reforms and became one of the fastest growing countries in the world last decade, as GDP growth rate was positive 9 years in a row till 2009. It enjoyed high growth rates after entering the European Union along with other Baltic states, leading to the notion of a Baltic Tiger. Current excellent telecommunication infrastructure and well-educated, multilingual workforce give the possibility to provide high quality business services and produce manufacturing products worldwide.

In 2005 the GDP grew by 7.5% and the inflation rate was 3%. GDP growth reached its height in 2007, increasing by 8.9%.Lithuania was the last among the Baltic states to be hit by the economic crisis because its GDP growth rate in 2008 was still positive. In the third quarter of 2009, compared to the previous quarter, GDP grew again by 6.9% after 5 quarters with negative numbers. Rebound in Lithuania's economy in the third quarter was the fastest in the EU. In the last quarter of 2009 Lithuanian economy rose moderately by 0.1%,.In 2011 real growth was higher than expected at first and reached 5.9%

The Soviet era brought Lithuania intensive industrialization and economic integration into the U.S.S.R., although the level of technology and State concern for environmental, health and labor issues sagged far behind Western standards. Urbanization increased from 39% in 1959 to 68% in 1989. From 1949-52 the Soviets abolished private ownership in agriculture, establishing collective and state farms. Production declined and did not reach pre-war levels until the early 1960s. The intensification of agricultural production through intense chemical use and mechanization eventually doubled production but created additional ecological problems.

Industry is Lithuania's largest economic sector. It is being privatized and most small firms are now under private ownership. Large industries, accounting for the bulk of Lithuania's capital investment, are still mainly under state control. Food-processing and light industries dominate but furniture, footwear, and textile manufacturing are important. Machine industries (tools, motors, computers, consumer durables) account for over one-third of the industrial work force but generally suffers from outdated plant and equipment. In agriculture, Lithuania produces for export cattle, hogs and poultry. The principal crops are wheat, feedgrains and rye. Farm production has dropped as a result of difficulties with agricultural privatization and poor weather.

The transportation infrastructure is adequate. Lithuania has one ice-free seaport with ferry services to German ports. There are operating commercial airports with scheduled international services at Vilnius and Kaunas. The road system is good but border crossings may be difficult due to inadequate border facilities at checkpoints with Poland. Telecommunications have improved greatly since independence as a result of heavy investment. The banking/financial sector is weak but improving.

Lithuania recorded a $369 million trade deficit in 1994. Its main trading partners are countries of the former Soviet Union (FSU) and Central Europe, and the main categories of imported products are energy, vehicles for transport and machinery. Exports consist mainly of machinery and food products.

Trade with Western countries increased from 8% of the total in 1992 to over 24% in 1994. In 1996, exports to European countries accounted for 94.3%, and exports to countries of the EU stood at 33.4% of Lithuania's export total.

Although gross national product (GNP) accounts comparable to Western figures are not yet fully available, real GDP has been declining since 1990 and finally broke even in 1994. Inflation is also high due to price deregulation and higher costs of imported energy and other inputs from the traditional suppliers in the FSU. The spread of private sector activity, not always reflected in national accounts statistics, is creating productive jobs and boosting consumer spending. Approximately 50% of Lithuanian workers are in the private sector, which accounts for half of Lithuania's GNP. The introduction in summer 1993, of a stable national currency backed by a currency board and pegged to the U.S. dollar has stimulated investment.

The government focuses its efforts on stabilizing the economy, taking measures to secure supplies of energy and other vital inputs, providing a social safety net to alleviate the worst consequences of the economic depression and combating economic crime. It has enacted legislation providing a reasonably transparent and favorable regulatory regime for private investment.

In 1996, Lithuania exported $34 million in goods to the U.S. and imported $63 million. In 1994, the Government privatized 70% of its state property, and to date has registered 5,300 foreign/joint ventures, whose authorized capital exceeds $400 million. Philip Morris is a major investor. As of January 1997, American companies have invested over $166 million (over 24% of total foreign direct investment) in Lithuania.

Over 139,000 enterprises now exist in Lithuania. State companies are now authorized to sell up to 50% of their shares for hard currency without cabinet approval, and many of over twenty commercial banks offer a full range of international banking services. Monthly inflation in 1996 was about 1%. In acceding to its European Union Association Agreement, the Government removed some restrictions on foreign ownership of land.

DEFENSE

Lithuania's defense system is based upon the Swedish-Finnish concept of a "total," rapid response force composed of a mobilization base and a small group of career professionals. The defense ministry is responsible for combat forces, border control, customs, civil defense, search/rescue and intelligence operations. The "Iron Wolf" Brigade consists of eight battalions of about 200 men each. The "SKAT," or home guard, consists of over 50-60 units varying in size from company to platoon strength. Perhaps the most prestigious arm of the military, SKAT was born during Lithuania's struggle to regain independence in the early 1990's and consists entirely of volunteers. The 500-man navy and coast guard use patrol boats and former Russian corvettes and frigates for coastal surveillance; the 800-man air force operates 20-30 helicopters and 35-45 planes used mostly for reconaissance and border patrol. There is a mandatory one-year active-duty draft period, and alternative service for conscientious objectors is available.

The 5,400 border guards fall under the Interior Ministry's supervision and are responsible for border protection, passport and customs duties, and share responsibility with the navy for smuggling/drug trafficking interdiction. A special security department handles VIP protection and communications security.

FOREIGN RELATIONS

Lithuania became a member of the United Nations on September 18, 1991 and is a signatory to a number of its organizations and other international agreements. It also is a member of the Organization on Security and Cooperation in Europe, the North Atlantic Coordinating Council and the Council of Europe. Lithuania is unaffiliated directly with any political alliance but welcomes membership in NATO, EU, WTO, OECD, and other Western organizations.

Lithuania maintains Embassies in the United States, Sweden, Finland, the Vatican, Belgium, Denmark, the EC, France, Germany, Poland, the United Kingdom, and Venezuela. It also operates missions in Estonia, Latvia, Russia, the Czech Republic, Italy, Ukraine, and in New York City, to the United Nations and a Consulate. Honorary consuls are located in Argentina, Australia, Canada, Iceland, Korea, Greece, Norway, the Philippines, and in the cities of Los Angeles and Chicago.

Lithuania's liberal "zero-option" citizenship law has substantially erased tensions with its neighbors. Lithuania's suspension of two strongly ethnic Polish district councils on charges of blocking reform or disloyalty during the August 1991 coup had cooled relations with Poland, but bilateral cooperation has markedly increased with the holding of elections in those districts and the signing of a bilateral Friendship Treaty in 1994. A similar agreement has been signed with Belarus in 1995.

The United States established diplomatic relations with Lithuania on July 28, 1922. U.S. representation accredited to Lithuania served from the legation in Riga, Latvia until May 31, 1930, when a legation in Kaunas was established. The Soviet invasion forced the closure of Legation Kaunas on September 5, 1940, but Lithuanian representation in the United States has continued uninterrupted for over 70 years. The U.S. never recognized the forcible incorporation of Lithuania into the U.S.S.R., and views the present Government of Lithuania as a legal continuation of the interwar republic. Lithuania has enjoyed Most-Favored-Nation (MFN) treatment with the U.S. since December, 1991. Through 1996, the U.S. has committed over $100 million to Lithuania's economic and political transformation and to address humanitarian needs. In 1994, the U.S. and Lithuania signed an agreement of bilateral trade and intellectual property protection, and in 1997 a bilateral investment treaty.

PRINCIPAL U.S. OFFICIALS

Ambassador: The Honorable John F. Tefft

Ambassador-- Deborah A. McCarthy

Deborah A. McCarthy, a career member of the Senior Foreign Service, is the current U.S. Ambassador to Lithuania. She was sworn into that office on February 5, 2013. Prior to holding this position, Ms. McCarthy was the Principal Deputy Assistant Secretary of State for Economic and Business Affairs, responsible for global economic engagement and negotiations (2010-2013).

Deputy Chief of Mission--Damian Leader
Political and Economic Section Chief--John Finkbeiner
Press and Cultural Attaché--William James
Defense Attaché--LTC David Millner (USA)
Defense Cooperation Officer--LTC Ron Hogan (USA)
Management Officer--Andrea Baker
Consular Officer--Bradley Norton

The U.S. Embassy in Lithuania is located at Akmenu 6, LT-03106 Vilnius [tel/fax: (370) 5-2665500]. The Embassy website is http://vilnius.usembassy.gov/

TRAVEL

Customs: Lithuania does not require visas for American, Canadian or British citizens. Visitors are encouraged to register at the U.S. Embassy. Polish border crossings have expanded and improved, but one can expect major delays.

Duty-exempt items include humanitarian aid, foreign currency and securities, goods and valuables unsuitable for consumption, and items temporarily imported and re-exported without "reworking or processing." Besides internationally banned or regulated items requiring special permission, import duties and restrictions are imposed on alcohol (40-100%), tobacco and sugar (30%), foodstuffs and metals (5%). Exports subject to duties are lumber, leather hides (10-15%) and metals (5%).

Climate and clothing: Vilnius's climate is temperately continental, with seasons of almost equal length. Summers are pleasant, but winters inland are very cold and snowy.

Health: Medical care does not meet Western standards, facing a shortage of basic medical supplies, including disposable needles, anesthetics and antibiotics. Take along your own personal medication. Sometimes heat and hot water are unavailable because of the occasional disruption of energy supplies. Raw fruits and vegetables are safe to eat, but avoid drinking unpasteurized milk and tapwater.

Transportation: SAS, LOT, Malev, Swissair, Austrian Air, Lithuanian Airlines and Lufthansa provide service between Vilnius

Airport and European cities. Two trains depart daily for Warsaw without crossing into Belarus, but take 12 hours. A bus line connects Warsaw, Vilnius, Riga and Tallinn. Bus and taxi services within the capital and its environs are good. Taxis are inexpensive and available at stands or may be ordered by phone. Rental cars are available. Gasoline prices are at market rates.

Telecommunications: Improved telephone and telegraph services are readily available at standard international rates. Vilnius is 7 hours ahead of Eastern Standard Time.

Work week: 40 hours. Offices are open 9am - 6pm on weekdays, and factories open/close two hours earlier. Food shops are open Monday-Saturday from 8am - 8pm, while other shops open two hours later. Stores and shops are closed on Sunday.

Tourist attractions: Over 550,000 tourists visited Lithuania in 1989. As Europe's geographic epicenter, Vilnius is the leading attraction, featuring beautiful Baroque churches and estates, 16 museums, fortress towers, and historic medieval castles nearby in Trakai and Medininkai. The seaside resorts of Palanga and Kursiu Nerija are famous for clean beaches and natural sand dunes. Ethnographic parks and museums depicting Lithuanian life through the centuries abound, as do scenic national preserves. Historic churches and castles dating to Lithuania's Great Power era are also readily accessible.

Currency, Weights and Measures: The national currency, the litas, is convertible with major Western monies. Major credit cards can be used primarily at large banks and Western hotels in Vilnius, but traveler's checks are not accepted everywhere. Lithuania uses the metric system.

Crime: By U.S. standards, Lithuania has a low rate of violent crime. However, the introduction of a market-oriented economy has resulted in an increase in street crime, especially at night near major hotels and restaurants frequented by foreigners. Take the same precautions that one would do in any major American city. Penalties for possession, use and dealing in illegal drugs are strict, and convicted offenders can expect jail sentences and fines.

LITHUANIA STRATEGIC INFORMATION

GEOGRAPHY

PHYSICAL ENVIRONMENT

Lithuania is situated on the eastern shore of the Baltic Sea. Lithuania's boundaries have changed several times since 1918, but they have been stable since 1945 (see fig. 2). Currently, Lithuania covers an area of about 65,200 square kilometers. About the size of West Virginia, it is larger than Belgium, Denmark, the Netherlands, or Switzerland.

Lithuania's northern neighbor is Latvia. The two countries share a border that extends 453 kilometers. Lithuania's eastern border with Belarus is longer, stretching 502 kilometers. The border with Poland on the south is relatively short, only ninety-one kilometers, but is very busy because of international traffic. Lithuania also has a 227-kilometer border with Russia. Russian territory adjacent to Lithuania is Kaliningrad Oblast, which is the northern part of the former German East Prussia, including the city of Kaliningrad. Finally, Lithuania has 108 kilometers of Baltic seashore with an ice-free harbor at Klaipeda. The Baltic coast offers sandy beaches and pine forests and attracts thousands of vacationers.

NATURAL RESOURCES

Lithuania's landscape is pleasing to the eye but modest in natural resources. The republic has an abundance of limestone, clay, quartz sand, gypsum sand, and dolomite, which are suitable for making high-quality cement, glass, and ceramics. There also is an ample supply of mineral water, but energy sources and industrial materials are all in short supply. Oil was discovered in Lithuania in the 1950s, but only a few wells operate, and all that do are located in the western part of the country. It is estimated that the Baltic Sea shelf and the western region of Lithuania hold commercially viable amounts of oil, but when exploited this oil will satisfy only about 20 percent of Lithuania's annual need for petroleum products for the next twenty years. Lithuania has a large amount of thermal energy along the Baltic Sea coast, however, which could be used to heat hundreds of thousands of homes, as is done in Iceland. In addition, iron ore deposits have been found in the southern region of Lithuania. But commercial exploitation of these deposits probably would require strip mining, which is environmentally unsound. Moreover, exploitation of these resources will depend on Lithuania's ability to attract capital and technology from abroad.

HISTORY

EARLY HISTORY

Lithuanians belong to the Baltic group of nations. Their ancestors moved to the Baltic region about 3000 B.C. from beyond the Volga region of central Russia. In Roman times, they traded amber with Rome and around A.D. 900-1000 split into different language groups, namely, Lithuanians, Prussians, Latvians, Semigallians, and others. The Prussians were conquered by the Teutonic Knights, and, ironically, the name "Prussia" was taken over by the conquerors, who destroyed or assimilated Prussia's original inhabitants. Other groups also died out or were assimilated by their neighbors. Only the Lithuanians and the Latvians survived the ravages of history.

Traditions of Lithuanian statehood date from the early Middle Ages. As a nation, Lithuania emerged about 1230 under the leadership of Duke Mindaugas. He united Lithuanian tribes to defend themselves against attacks by the Teutonic Knights, who had conquered the kindred tribes of Prussia and also parts of present-day Latvia. In 1251 Mindaugas accepted Latin Christianity, and in 1253 he became king. But his nobles disagreed with his policy of coexistence with the Teutonic Knights and with his search for access to western Europe. Mindaugas was killed, the monarchy was discontinued, and the country reverted to paganism. His successors looked for expansion toward the Slavic East. At that early stage of development, Lithuania had to face the historically recurring question dictated by its geopolitical position--whether to join western or eastern Europe.

At the end of the fourteenth century, Lithuania was already a large empire extending from the Baltic Sea to the shores of the Black Sea. Grand Duke Jogaila (r. 1377-81 and 1382-92) of the Gediminas Dynasty faced a problem similar to that faced by Mindaugas 150 years earlier: whether to look to the East or the West for political and cultural influences. Under pressure from the Teutonic Knights, Lithuania, a kingdom of Lithuanians and Slavs, pagans and Orthodox Christians, could no longer stand alone. Jogaila chose to open links to western Europe and to defeat the Teutonic Knights, who claimed that their mission was not to conquer the Lithuanians but to Christianize them. He was offered the crown of Poland, which he accepted in 1386. In return for the crown, Jogaila promised to Christianize Lithuania. He and his cousin Vytautas, who became Lithuania's grand duke, converted Lithuania to Christianity beginning in 1387. Lithuania was the last pagan country in Europe to become Christian. The cousins then defeated the Teutonic Knights in the Battle of Tannenberg in 1410, stopping Germanic expansion to the east.

Attempts by Vytautas to separate Lithuania from Poland (and to secure his own crown) failed because of the strength of the Polish nobility. Lithuania continued in a political union with Poland. In 1569 Lithuania and Poland united into a single state, the Polish-Lithuanian Commonwealth, whose capital was Kraków, and for the next 226 years Lithuania shared the fate of Poland. During this period, Lithuania's political elite was dominated by the Polish nobility and church, resulting in neglect of the Lithuanian language and introduction of Polish social and political institutions. It also opened the doors to Western models in education and culture.

In 1795 an alliance between the Germanic states--Prussia and Austria--and the Russian Empire ended Poland's independent existence. Lithuania became a Russian province. Two insurrections, initiated by the Poles in 1831 and again in 1863, failed to liberate the country. The Russian Empire eliminated Polish influence on Lithuanians and introduced Russian social and political institutions. Under tsarist rule, Lithuanian schools were forbidden, Lithuanian publications in the Latin script were outlawed, and the Roman Catholic Church was severely suppressed. However, the restrictive policies failed to extinguish indigenous cultural institutions and language.

A national awakening in the 1880s, led by the secular and clerical intelligentsia, produced demands for self-government. In 1905 Lithuania was the first of the Russian provinces to demand autonomy. Independence was not granted because the tsar firmly reestablished his rule after the Revolution of 1905. But the demand, articulated by the elected Grand Diet of Vilnius, was not abandoned. World War I led to the collapse of the two empires--the Russian and the German--making it possible for Lithuania to assert its statehood. Germany's attempt to persuade Lithuania to become a German protectorate was unsuccessful. On February 16, 1918, Lithuania declared its full independence, and the country still celebrates that day as its Independence Day.

INDEPENDENCE, 1918-40

During 1918-20 Lithuania successfully fought a war with newly independent Poland to defend its independence. At the end of 1920, however, Poland annexed Lithuania's capital city and province of Vilnius, which it held until World War II. Lithuania refused to have diplomatic relations with

Poland until 1938 on the grounds that Poland illegally held the Vilnius region. After declaring independence, Lithuania also fought against the Bermondt-Avalov army, a German-sponsored group of military adventurers that sought to preserve German influence in the Baltic region, and against Russia. In November 1918, the Red Army invaded the country but ultimately was repulsed by the forces of the young Lithuanian government. On July 9, 1920, Soviet leader Vladimir I. Lenin signed a peace treaty with Lithuania, "forever" denouncing Russia's claims to the territory and recognizing the Lithuanian state.

In the early 1920s, Lithuania had a border dispute with Germany. The city and region of Klaipeda (Memel in German) had been under German rule for 700 years. Originally inhabited by Lithuanians, it was detached from Germany in 1919 by the Treaty of Versailles and placed under French administration. In 1923 Lithuanians organized an insurrection and took over the Klaipeda region.

These conflicts burdened Lithuania's international diplomacy. Domestically, however, they fed the development of national identity and cultural awareness, displacing German and Polish influence.

Lithuania's early disorganization caused a delay in its recognition by Western powers; the last to do so was the United States in 1922. Washington recognized Lithuania's independence only after it had become clear that Western intervention in Russia could not restore the Russian Empire and that the communists were firmly entrenched in Moscow.

Independent Lithuania, led by political leaders mostly in their thirties or early forties, became a democratic republic with a strong legislature, a weak executive, a multiparty system, and a proportional system of representation. Christian Democratic coalitions dominated the democratic period. However, almost a third of the country was illiterate, and farmers--87 percent of the population--were conservative and unfamiliar with democratic processes. In 1926 the Socialist-Populist coalition government was removed by a military coup. Antanas Smetona, a former acting president, was elected to the presidency by a rump parliament. Within three years, he established an authoritarian regime. Political parties were outlawed and the press censored, but Smetona did not completely suppress civil rights. Smetona established Tautininkai, a nationalist political party, which reappeared in the parliament in 1991 after Lithuania regained independence from the Soviet Union.

From 1920 to 1940, independent Lithuania made great strides in nation building and development. A progressive land reform program was introduced in 1922, a cooperative movement was organized, and a strong currency and conservative fiscal management were maintained. Schools and universities were established (there had been no institutions of higher education and very few secondary schools under Russian rule), and illiteracy was substantially reduced. Artists and writers of the period produced works that have become classics.

THE SOVIET REPUBLIC

On August 23, 1939, Joseph V. Stalin and Adolf Hitler concluded the notorious Nazi-Soviet Nonaggression Pact (also known as the Molotov-Ribbentrop Pact). The agreement had a secret protocol that divided Poland, much of Central Europe, and the Baltic states between Germany and the Soviet Union. Lithuania, at first assigned to the German sphere of influence, in September was transferred to the Soviet Union. In October 1939, the Soviet Union forced on Lithuania a nonaggression pact that allowed Moscow to garrison 20,000 troops in the country. In return, the city of Vilnius, now occupied by Soviet troops, was granted to Lithuania. On June 15, 1940, Lithuania was overrun by the Red Army. At first a procommunist, so-called people's government was installed, and elections to a new parliament were organized. The elections were noncompetitive; a single approved list of candidates was presented to the voters. The parliament met on July 21, declared Soviet rule, and "joined" the Soviet Union as the Lithuanian Soviet Socialist Republic on August 6, 1940. The United States and many other countries refused to recognize the Soviet occupation.

Soviet rule brought about radical political and economic changes and Stalinist terror, which culminated in deportations to Siberia of more than 30,000 people on the night of June 14-15, 1941. Germany interrupted the Stalinist terror by attacking the Soviet Union on June 22, 1941. The next day, the Lithuanian Activist Front, an organization of anti-Soviet resistance groups, revolted against the Soviet occupiers. Partisans took over the largest cities--Kaunas and Vilnius--and declared restoration of Lithuanian independence. The Germans replaced the provisional government with a Lithuanian Vertrauensrat (Council of Trustees), which was headed by an ethnic Lithuanian, General Petras Kubiliunas, and was given some autonomy in local affairs.

The Lithuanian leadership went underground. An anti-Nazi resistance movement developed, publishing underground newspapers, organizing economic boycotts, and gathering arms. The resistance hoped that after victory the Western allies would insist on the restoration of Lithuanian statehood.

A Soviet-sponsored underground also existed in Lithuania beginning in 1942. It staged military raids against German transportation, administrative, and economic enterprises. The Soviet forces were aided by the remnants of the Communist Party of Lithuania, now barely surviving in the underground.

The nationalist Lithuanian resistance was supported by many Lithuanian political parties and resistance groups, including the Social Democrats and a coalition known as the Supreme Committee for the Liberation of Lithuania, which continued its activities many years after Lithuania was retaken by the Red Army. In 1943 this resistance frustrated German efforts at organizing a Lithuanian Schutz-Staffel (SS) legion. The Nazis responded by arresting Lithuanian nationalists and by closing universities. Moreover, occupation authorities succeeded, in the period 1941-44, in recruiting or capturing tens of thousands of people to work in Germany or to serve in the German military. Many perished in prisons or concentration camps. The main victims, however, were members of Lithuania's Jewish community. About 185,000 Jews, or 85 percent of the community's population, were massacred by Nazi squads, which were helped by Lithuanian collaborators in a number of localities.

Soviet armies recaptured Lithuania in the summer of 1944, although Klaipeda did not fall until January 1945. Antanas Snieckus, the Communist Party of Lithuania leader, returned from Moscow with the other officials who had fled before the advancing German armies. Lithuania's full Sovietization, however, was obstructed from 1944 to 1952 by an armed partisan resistance movement, which cost an estimated 20,000 to 30,000 partisan casualties.

Soviet rule in Lithuania displayed well-known features of communist rule. The party had a monopoly on power, and the management of the economy was centralized. The regime collectivized agriculture from 1947 to 1951. Secret police terrorized the society and attempted to transfer Lithuanian nation-alist loyalties to the communists. Deportations to Siberia were resumed. Religion was brutally suppressed. One Roman Catholic bishop was shot, one perished in prison, two died shortly after release, and two were banished for more than thirty years, leaving only one in office. Almost one-third of the clergy was deported, although survivors were allowed to return after Stalin's death in 1953. Eventually, the training of new priests was essentially stopped.

Institutions of power--the party, the secret police, and the government--at first were mainly in Russian hands. In the postwar period, ethnic Lithuanians constituted only 18.4 percent of the republic's communist party members. Beginning in the 1950s, college graduates and those who wanted to make careers in economic, cultural, or political life realized that the Soviet system was not transitory, so they joined the communist party. The party swelled to a membership of 205,000 by 1989, but most of these members were opportunists, very different from the few revolutionary fanatics who had administered Lithuania in the immediate postwar period. Still others joined the party in the expectation that they would be of better use to the preservation of Lithuanian traditions, language, and culture in the ranks of the ruling group. There developed a stratum of communists who wanted to promote not only Moscow's but also Lithuania's advantage.

Underground resistance never disappeared, although the armed underground was destroyed. As a movement, resistance was first sparked by efforts to defend the Roman Catholic Church. After the Soviet invasion of Czechoslovakia in 1968, which led to increased repression in the Soviet Union, the dissident movement spread. In the 1970s, Lithuania had numerous underground publications. The most significant and regularly published among them was *The Chronicle of the Catholic Church of Lithuania* . It was never uncovered by the Soviet secret police, the Committee for State Security (Komitet gosudarstvennoy bezopasnosti--KGB), and was published for twenty years. In 1972 a young student, Romas Kalanta, immolated himself in protest against Soviet rule. Army units had to be sent in to quell a street rebellion by students that followed the self-immolation. The Committee for the Defense of Religious Rights and the Helsinki Watch Committee were established in the underground. Dissident work brought arrests and imprisonment. At the same time, the Lithuanian intelligentsia, especially writers and artists, demanded greater freedom of creative expression and protection of the Lithuanian language, traditions, and cultural values from the pressure to Russify that intensified during the administration of Leonid I. Brezhnev (1964-82).

THE MOVE TOWARD INDEPENDENCE, 1987-91

The situation did not change until Mikhail S. Gorbachev came to power in 1985. Even then, Lithuania's communist party leadership hesitated to embrace Gorbachev's program of limited economic reforms under his policy of *perestroika* (see Glossary). The death of Petras Griskevicius, first secretary of the Communist Party of Lithuania, in 1987 did little to improve the atmosphere for reform. The new first secretary, Ringaudas Songaila, was a conservative functionary. But encouraged by new winds from Moscow, Baltic dissidents began in 1987 to hold public demonstrations in Riga, Tallinn, and Vilnius. In 1988, against the wishes of Songaila's regime, Lithuanian, engaged in widespread celebration of the February 16 Independence Day. Lithuanian intellectuals were pushed into taking more forceful action as well. Meeting at the Academy of Sciences on June 3, 1988, communist and noncommunist intellectuals formed "an initiative group" to organize a movement to support Gorbachev's program of *glasnost* (see Glossary), democratization, and *perestroika* . A council composed equally of communist party members and nonparty members was chosen to organize the Lithuanian Reconstruction Movement, which became known subsequently simply as Sajudis (Movement). The Communist Party of Lithuania leadership did not like this independent action but, knowing Gorbachev's limited acceptance of "informal" societies, did not interfere with the effort.

The movement supported Gorbachev's policies, but at the same time it promoted Lithuanian national issues such as restoration of the Lithuanian language as the "official" language. Its demands included revelations of the truth about the Stalinist years, protection of the environment, cessation of construction on a third nuclear reactor at the Ignalina nuclear power plant, and disclosure of secret protocols of the Nazi-Soviet Nonaggression Pact. Sajudis used mass meetings to advance its goals. At first, party leaders shunned these meetings, but by mid-1988 their participation became a political necessity. Thus, a Sajudis rally on June 24, 1988, was attended by Algirdas Brazauskas, then party secretary for industrial affairs.

In October 1988, Brazauskas was appointed first secretary of the party to replace Songaila, and Sajudis held its founding conference in Vilnius. It subsequently elected as its chairman Vytautas Landsbergis, a professor of musicology who was not a member of the communist party. In the elections to Moscow's newly authorized Congress of People's Deputies (see Glossary) in March-May 1989, Sajudis was victorious. From the communist party, the voters elected only Brazauskas and Vladimiras Beriozovas, his associate, whom Sajudis did not oppose. From that time, Brazauskas cooperated fully with Sajudis. Lithuanian sovereignty--as distinguished from Lithuanian independence, which had been declared on February 16, 1918--was proclaimed in May 1989, and Lithuania's incorporation into the Soviet Union was declared illegal. In August a human chain from Tallinn to Vilnius commemorated the fiftieth anniversary of the Nazi-Soviet Nonaggression Pact. In December Brazauskas forced the Communist Party of Lithuania to secede from the Communist Party of the Soviet Union and to give up its monopoly on power.

But even the separation of the Communist Party of Lithuania from Moscow did not save it in the electoral contest for the Supreme Soviet of the republic in March 1990. In the election, the Communist Party of Lithuania won only twenty-three of the 141 seats. On March 11, the newly elected parliament voted unanimously for independence. Brazauskas lost the election for chairman of the presidium of the Supreme Soviet to Landsbergis.

Moscow did not accept the legality of the independence vote, however; in April 1990, it imposed an economic blockade that lasted for three months, until the Lithuanian legislature, now known as the Supreme Council, agreed to a six-month moratorium on its independence declaration. Later, Moscow obstructed Lithuanian efforts to gain Western recognition, and on January 13, 1991, attempted to use force to remove the Lithuanian government in Vilnius and to reestablish Soviet rule. Although this attempted coup ended in a massacre of civilians--thirteen died, and hundreds were wounded--by the Soviet army, Lithuania's determination did not change. Finally, the failure of the August 1991 coup in Moscow permitted Lithuania to regain self-determination and prompted the international community to recognize it as an independent state. The United States extended recognition on September 2, and the Soviet Union did so on September 6. Lithuania was admitted to the United Nations on September 16, 1991.

20TH AND 21ST CENTURIES

The original 20 members of the Council of Lithuania after signing the Act of Independence of Lithuania, 16 February 1918.

During World War I, the Council of Lithuania (Lietuvos Taryba) declared the independence of Lithuania on 16 February 1918, and the re-establishment of the Lithuanian State. Lithuania's foreign policy was dominated by territorial disputes with Poland and Germany. The Vilnius Region, and Vilnius, the historical capital of Lithuania, (and so designated in the Constitution of Lithuania) were seized by the Polish army during Żeligowski's Mutiny in October 1920 and annexed two years later by Poland. For 19 years Kaunas became the Temporary capital of Lithuania. The Polish occupation of Vilnius was greatly resented by Lithuania; there were no diplomatic relations between the two states for most of the period between the two world wars.

Acquired during the Klaipėda Revolt of 1923, the Klaipėda Region was ceded to Germany after a German ultimatum in March 1939. During the interwar period, the domestic affairs of Lithuania were controlled by the authoritarian President, Antanas Smetona and his party, the Lithuanian Nationalist Union, who came to power after the coup d'état of 1926.

The Soviet Union returned Vilnius to Lithuania after the Soviet invasion of Eastern Poland in September 1939. In June 1940, the Soviet Union occupied and annexed Lithuania in accordance to the secret protocols of Molotov–Ribbentrop Pact. A year later the Soviet Union was attacked by Nazi Germany, leading to the Nazi occupation of Lithuania. The Nazis and their collaborators murdered around 190,000 Jews of Lithuania (91% of the pre-war Jewish community) during the Holocaust.

After the retreat of the German armed forces, the Soviets re-established the annexation of Lithuania in 1944. Under border changes promulgated at the Potsdam Conference in 1945, the former German Memelland, with its Baltic port Memel (Lithuanian: Klaipėda), was again transferred to Lithuania, or as it was after 1945 the Lithuanian SSR. Most German residents of the area had fled in the final months of World War II.

The Soviets engaged in massive deportations of Lithuanians to Siberia, complete nationalisation and collectivisation and general sovietization of everyday life. From 1944 to 1952 approximately 100,000 Lithuanian partisans fought a guerrilla war against the Soviet system. An estimated 30,000 partisans and their supporters were killed, and many more were arrested and deported to Siberian gulags. It is estimated that Lithuania lost 780,000 people during World War II.

The advent of perestroika and glasnost in the late 1980s allowed the establishment of Sąjūdis, an anti-communist independence movement. After a landslide victory in elections to the Supreme Soviet, members of Sąjūdis proclaimed Lithuania's independence on 11 March 1990, becoming the first Soviet republic to do so. The Soviet Union attempted to suppress the secession by imposing an economic blockade. Soviet troops attacked the Vilnius TV Tower, killing 14 Lithuanian civilians and wounding 600 others on the night of 13 January 1991 (January Events). On 31 July 1991 Soviet paramilitaries killed seven Lithuanian border guards on the Belarusian border in what became known as the Medininkai Massacre.

On 4 February 1991, Iceland became the first country to recognise Lithuanian independence. After the Soviet August Coup, independent Lithuania received wide official recognition and joined the United Nations on 17 September 1991. The last Soviet troops left Lithuania on 31 August 1993 – even earlier than they departed from East Germany. Lithuania, seeking closer ties with the West, applied for NATO membership in 1994. After a transition from a planned economy to a free market one, Lithuania became a full member of NATO and the European Union in the spring of 2004 and a member of the Schengen Agreement on 21 December 2007.

POPULATION AND SOCIETY

In 1995 Lithuania had an estimated population of 3,717,000, which was 44,000 fewer people than in 1992. Of the total, females were in the majority, as in most Central European countries and in Russia. The population group that has increased most quickly in Lithuania, as in many other relatively developed countries, consists of senior citizens and pensioners (those over age sixty) (see fig. 12). For example, pensioners grew in number from 546,000 to 906,000 between 1970 and 1991. This group grew from 17.3 percent of the population in 1980 to 19.5 percent in 1992. The zero-to-fifteen-year-old age-group, by comparison, diminished slightly from 25.2 percent in 1980 to 23.9 in 1992, not as a result of increased mortality but as a result of a continuing decline in the birth rate.

The group of working-age people (aged sixteen to fifty-nine for men and fifteen to fifty-four for women) also decreased, from 57.5 percent to 56.6 percent. The birth rate decreased from 17.6 per 1,000 population in 1970 to 12.5 per 1,000 population in 1993 and 12.0 per 1,000 population in 1994. Mortality increased from 10.5 per 1,000 population in 1980 to 10.9 in 1991 and 12.8 in 1994. Life expectancy in 1993 was 63.3 years for males and 75.0 years for females, or an average of 69.1 years. This, too, was on the decline from the peak years of 1986-87, when the average was 72.5 years (67.9 years for males and 76.6 years for females). The decrease coincides with the worsening economic situation and the decline in the quality of health services during the postindependence economic transition.

The average Lithuanian family is still somewhat larger than families in the neighboring Baltic states, but it has been declining. The average family size shrank to 3.2 by 1989. People marry young, but their marriages are often quickly dissolved. The divorce rate has been increasing. In 1989, of 9.3 marriages per 1,000 population, there were 3.3 divorces. The highest divorce rate is among ethnic Russians and in ethnically mixed families. These statistics indicate the existence of social problems with which society has been ill equipped to deal. Churches are not allowed to intervene to address these problems, and the profession of social work is still virtually nonexistent. The postcommunist government must face the formidable task of developing a social work sector.

Under Soviet rule, especially in the last decade, one-half or more of the annual population increase resulted from immigration, primarily from Russia. But this situation has changed. More people emigrate to former Soviet republics than arrive from them, and more people leave for the West than come from there. In 1990 Lithuania's net migration loss to former Soviet republics was 6,345. Loss to the West includes Jewish emigration. Gains from the West include returning Americans and Canadians of Lithuanian descent.

Soviet industrialization brought about fast and sustained urban development. Annually, almost 1 percent of the rural population has moved to cities since the early 1950s. In 1939 only 23 percent of the population lived in cities; in 1992 the urban percentage was 69. Lithuania has five cities with a population of more than 100,000. The largest is the capital, Vilnius, established in 1321 (1994 population 584,000); Kaunas, the capital between the two world wars, founded in 1361 (1994 population 424,000); the port city of Klaipeda, established in 1252 (1994 population 205,000); the center of the electronics industry, Siauliai, founded in 1236 (1994 population 147,000); and the city of chemical and automobile parts industries, Panevezys, founded in 1548 (1994 population 132,000).

In 1994, according to official estimates, 81.1 percent of Lithuania's population consisted of ethnic Lithuanians. The remaining 18.9 percent was divided among Russians (8.5 percent), Poles (7.0 percent), Belarusians (1.5 percent), Ukrainians (1.0 percent), and others, including Jews, Latvians, Tatars, Gypsies, Germans, and Estonians (0.9 percent). Altogether, people of more than 100 nationalities live in Lithuania.

The proportion of the ethnic Lithuanian population--more than 90 percent of whom speak Lithuanian--stayed at 80 percent or a fraction higher until 1989, when it dropped slightly below 80 percent. The decrease resulted in fears that a pattern of decline would develop as a result of increasing Russian immigration, which might endanger the survival of Lithuania's culture and national identity as it did in Estonia and Latvia.

The Russian minority consists of old and new immigrants. Many Russians settled in Lithuania in the nineteenth century or in the early twentieth century, shortly after the Bolsheviks came to power in Moscow. Two-thirds of the Russian minority, however, are immigrants--or their descendants--of the Soviet era, many of whom regard Lithuania as their homeland. They usually live in larger cities. In Vilnius 20.2 percent of the population was Russian in 1989. The same year, in Klaipeda, 28.2 percent of the inhabitants were Russians; in Siauliai, 10.5 percent. Ignalina, where the nuclear power plant is located, had a Russian majority of 64.2 percent. Less than 10 percent of the population in Kaunas and the resort towns of Druskininkai, Palanga, or Neringa was Russian, however. These percentages most likely will decline slightly in the 1990s because some Russians, finding it difficult to accept that they live in a "foreign" country, are leaving Lithuania. The majority of Russians, however, have shown little inclination to leave; 88 percent of those polled in the fall of 1993 described relations between their group and the ethnic Lithuanian population as good, and more than 60 percent felt that economic conditions for people like themselves would be worse in Russia than in Lithuania.

Poles live primarily in the city of Vilnius (18.8 percent of Vilnius's population in 1989) and in three adjacent rural districts. In 1989 the ethnic Polish population in the Salcininkai district constituted 79.6 percent; in the rural district of Vilnius, it was 63.5 percent; and in the district of Trakai, it was 23.8 percent. Small Polish groups also live in a number of other localities. Since the late 1940s, the Polish presence in Lithuania has declined considerably. About 200,000 Poles left Lithuania for Poland in 1946, under an agreement signed between Warsaw and Vilnius. Afterward, the Polish percentage of Lithuania's population declined from 8.5 percent in 1959 to 7.0 percent in 1989, primarily as a result of the influx of Russians. The Polish population of eastern Lithuania is composed of inhabitants whose families settled there centuries ago, of immigrants who came from Poland in the nineteenth and early twentieth centuries when the region was part of Poland, and of many assimilated Lithuanians and Belarusians.

Jews began settling in Lithuania in the fourteenth century. In time, Vilnius and some other cities became centers of Jewish learning, and Vilnius was internationally known as the Jerusalem of the North. Between the two world wars, Jews developed an active educational and cultural life. The Jewish community, which did not experience large-scale persecution until World War II, was almost entirely liquidated during the Nazi occupation. In 1989 only 12,400 Jews were left in Lithuania, and emigration after independence had cut their number to an estimated 6,500 by 1994.

For centuries, Vilnius has been an ethnically diverse city. Historically, the city has served as a cultural center for Lithuanians, Poles, Jews, and Belorussians. In the sixteenth and early seventeenth centuries, it also was a center of Ukrainian religious and cultural life. At the turn of the century, the largest minority ethnic group was Jewish. After World War II, the largest minority ethnic group was Polish. The population of Vilnius in 1989 was 50.5 percent Lithuanian, 20.2 percent Russian, 18.8 percent Polish, and 5.3 percent Belorussian.

HEALTH AND WELFARE

The Lithuanian constitution of 1992 provides guarantees of social rights that were earlier provided by the Soviet regime. The constitution puts special emphasis on the maintenance and care of the family. It expresses in detail, for example, the guarantee for working mothers to receive paid leave before and after childbirth (Article 39). The constitution provides for free public education in all state schools, including schools of higher education (Article 41). The constitution forbids forced labor (Article 48); legalizes labor unions and the right to strike (Articles 50 and 51); guarantees annual paid vacations (Article 49); and guarantees old-age and disability pensions, unemployment and sick leave compensation, and support for widows and families that have lost their head of household, as well as for others in situations as defined by law (Article 52). Finally, the constitution guarantees free medical care (Article 53).

All political groups support these guarantees--considered more or less inviolable--although it is not clear to what extent the government will be able to fund the promised services during the continuing economic transition. The amounts of support and the quality of services have declined from the modest, but always predictable, level first established in the Soviet period.

The national system of social security consists of programs of social insurance and social benefits designed to continue the benefits provided by the Soviet system. Social insurance includes old-age retirement; survivor and disability pensions; unemployment compensation; pregnancy, childbirth, and child supplements; certain welfare support; and free medical care. It is cradle-to-grave insurance. According to a 1990 law, payments cannot be lower than necessary for a "minimal" living standard. In 1990 old-age and disability pensions in Lithuania were slightly more generous than in Estonia and Latvia. The budget for the program is separate from the national and local budgets. Only military pensions and some other special pensions are paid from the national budget.

Social insurance is financed, according to a law passed in 1991, from required payments by workers and employers, from income generated by the management of state social insurance activities, and from budgetary supplements by the state if the program threatens to run a deficit. To be eligible for an old-age pension, a male worker must be at least sixty years of age and have at least a twenty-five-year record of employment. A woman must be fifty-five and have a record of twenty years of employment. This category of recipients includes not only factory and government workers but also farmers and farm workers.

A program of social benefits is financed by local governments. It includes support payments for women during pregnancy and childbirth and for expenses after the child's birth. The program features single payments for each newly born child, as well as child support for single parents or families. These latter payments continue up to age limits established by law. The state also maintains a number of orphanages, sanatoriums, and old-age homes.

In the medical field, Lithuania has sufficient facilities to fulfill the guarantee of free medical care. In 1990 the country had more than 14,700 physicians and 2,300 dentists; its ratio of forty-six physicians and dentists combined per 10,000 inhabitants compared favorably with that of most advanced countries. In addition, in 1990 Lithuania had more than 47,000 paramedical personnel, or 127 per 10,000 population and 46,200 hospital beds, or 124 beds per 10,000 population. In the medical profession, Lithuania's cardiologists are among the most advanced in the former Soviet Union. In 1987 the first heart transplant operation was performed at the cardiac surgery clinic of Vilnius University. Hundreds of kidney transplants have been performed as well. One reasonably reliable and generally used indicator of the quality of a country's health services system is infant mortality. In 1990 Lithuania's infant mortality rate of 10.3 per 1,000 population was among the lowest of the Soviet republics but higher than that of many West European countries.

Special features of Lithuania's health status are high alcoholism (191 cases per 100,000 persons), low drug abuse (3.1 cases per 100,000), and few cases of human immunodeficiency virus (HIV) infection. Reported cases of HIV in 1992 were under 100. The main causes of death are cardiovascular diseases, cancer, accidents, and respiratory diseases. In addition to alcoholism, important risk factors for disease are smoking, a diet high in saturated fat, hypertension, and environmental pollution.

Notwithstanding efficient ambulance service and emergency care, medical services and facilities in Lithuania suffer from a lack of equipment, supplies, and drugs, as well as from inertia in the operation and administration of health services. The system is mainly state owned and state run. Private medical practice, begun only in the late 1980s, has not progressed appreciably because of the economic crisis. Since 1989 the government has encouraged church groups and others to enter the field of welfare services and medicine. The best-known such group is the Roman Catholic charitable organization Caritas.

Health care expenditures increased from 3.3 percent of the gross national product (GNP--see Glossary) in 1960 to 4.9 percent of GNP in 1990, but this figure is still low by world standards. Lithuania is unable to afford investments to improve its health care infrastructure at this time. Lithuania needs humanitarian assistance from the world community in importing the most critically needed drugs and vaccines. Disease prevention needs to be emphasized, especially with regard to prenatal, pediatric, and dental care. To reduce the occurrence of prevalent risk factors, the government needs to make fundamental improvements in public education and health programs.

Lithuania's standard of living in the early 1990s was slightly below Estonia's and Latvia's but higher than in the rest of the former Soviet Union. At the end of 1992, the standard of living had declined substantially, however. Energy shortages caused severe limitations in heating apartments and providing hot water and electricity. Before the post-Soviet economic transition, Lithuanians had abundant food supplies and consumed 3,400 calories a day per capita, compared with 2,805 calories for Finns and 3,454 calories for Swedes. But an average Lithuanian had only 19.1 square meters of apartment living space (less in the cities, more in rural areas), which was much less than the 30.5 square meters Finns had in the late 1980s. Housing, moreover, had fewer amenities than in the Scandinavian countries; 75 percent of Lithuanian urban housing had running water in 1989, 62 percent had hot water, 74 percent had central heating, 70 percent had flush toilets, and 64 percent had bathing facilities. Formerly low utility rates skyrocketed in the 1990s. Rents also increased, although by the end of 1992 almost 90 percent of all state-owned housing (there was some privately owned housing under Soviet rule) had been privatized--bought from the state, mostly by those who lived there. In 1989 families were well equipped with radios and televisions (109 and 107 sets, respectively, per 100 families). Most had refrigerators (ninety-one per 100 families), and many had washing machines (seventy), bicycles (eighty-four), vacuum cleaners (sixty), sewing machines (forty-eight), and tape re-corders (forty-four). Every third family had a private automobile (thirty-six automobiles per 100 families). Detracting from the quality of life, however, was the increasing rate of violent crime, especially in the larger cities

RELIGION

Traditionally, Lithuania has been a Roman Catholic country. Although severely affected by Soviet repression, the Roman Catholic Church remains the dominant and the most influential denomination. However, Lithuania in the past has had two small but active Protestant denominations, the Evangelical Reformed (Calvinist) and the Evangelical Lutheran. In addition, Orthodox Christianity as well as Judaism have roots at least as old as those of Roman Catholicism. In 1991 a Western poll found that 69 percent of respondents in Lithuania identified themselves as Roman Catholics (in 1939 the percentage was 85), 4 percent identified themselves as Orthodox, and 1 percent professed Evangelical Christian beliefs. New in this self-identification was a large category--25 percent--who did not profess any religion. Lithuanian journalists have also noted that twenty-one out of the 141 new members of parliament elected in 1992 left out "so help me God" from the oath when sworn in as deputies.

In 1992 Lithuania's Roman Catholic Church consisted of two archdioceses (Vilnius and Kaunas) and four dioceses (Kaisiadorys, Panevezys, Vilkaviskis, and Telsiai). The church is presided over by Cardinal Vincentas Sladkevicius in Kaunas. For thirty years, Sladkevicius, then a bishop, was held by Soviet authorities in internal exile. The church has 688 parishes, two theological seminaries (one reestablished in 1990), and several con-vents and monasteries. There is also one Uniate, or Eastern-Rite Catholic, congregation.

The archeparchy (archdiocese) of the Russian Orthodox Church has forty-five parishes and two monasteries. Archbishop Chrisostom and his archeparchy are under the jurisdiction of the Patriarch of Moscow. The Old Believers (see Glossary) have fifty-one congregations. The Lithuanian Evangelical Lutheran Church under Bishop Jonas Kalvanas has thirty-three congregations, and the Evangelical Reformed Church (Calvinist) has eight. Other Christian denominations include Baptists, Seventh-Day Adventists, and Pentecostals. The non-Christian religious groups include Jews (two communities), Muslims (four communities), Krishna followers (two communities), and one Karaite (see Glossary) group.

Traditionally, most Roman Catholics in Lithuania were either Lithuanians or Poles, and the Orthodox and Old Believer adherents were predominantly Russians. This division has not changed, although currently it is no longer possible to assume religious affiliation on the basis of ethnic identity. The Calvinist and Evangelical Lutheran groups are very small--an estimated 15,000 Calvinists and 35,000 Lutherans. The younger Protestant denominations are even smaller but are intensely active. Generally, Lithuanian society in the 1990s is secularized, although, as in many postcommunist countries, younger people are searching for some sort of spiritual fulfillment.

The Roman Catholic Church is the oldest continuously surviving Lithuanian institution. As such, it has played a dominant role in the development of Lithuanian society, especially crucial during those long stretches of time when Lithuanians had no state of their own. At first highly influenced by the Polish community, the church under Bishop Motiejus Valancius in the nineteenth century promoted Lithuanian language and publications, which prepared the country for the national awakening of the 1880s. Because Russian imperial authorities had forbidden the publication of Lithuanian books in the Latin alphabet, Valancius had them printed in German-ruled, Protestant East Prussia and then smuggled into Lithuania. The bishop also organized a network of secret Lithuanian schools. In 1918 the church supported the establishment of Lithuania as an independent and democratic republic. Years later, it endorsed land reform, and in the 1930s the bishops opposed and restrained Smetona's authoritarian rule. Under Soviet rule, the church served as a focal point of resistance and dissident activities. Its theological outlook, however, has been conservative.

Protestants also have contributed significantly to Lithuania's cultural development. The first book printed in Lithuanian was a Lutheran catechism, published by Martynas Mazvydas in East Prussia in 1547. Protestant Lithuanians from this region published the literature of national awakening. Later, Protestants--both Lutheran and Calvinist--supplied political leadership out of proportion to their numbers in the population.

In Lithuania between the two world wars, the Roman Catholic Church and other denominations had a constitutionally guaranteed monopoly over registration of marriages, births, and deaths. Religious education in public schools was compulsory. Although there was no established religion, all denominations received some state support in rough proportion to their size. The Soviet authorities totally separated churches not only from the state but also from individual support. On June 12, 1990, Lithuania's newly elected independent parliament adopted an act of restitution of the Roman Catholic Church's condition status quo ante but promised compensation for the losses suffered under Soviet rule and pledged cooperation on a parity basis. The constitution of 1992 guarantees "freedom of thought, religion, and conscience" to all and "recognizes traditional churches and religious organizations of Lithuania." Other religious organizations have to pass a test to ensure that their teachings do not "contradict the law and morality." All recognized churches are guaranteed the rights of legal persons and can govern themselves without state interference. Religious teaching in public schools is allowed if parents desire it. Religious marriage registration also is legally valid, as in the United States. The government maintains an office of counselor on religious affairs.

Language and Culture

Like Latvian and Old Prussian, the Lithuanian language belongs to the Baltic branch of the Indo-European language family. The size of the territory in which Lithuanian was spoken shrank considerably through the ages. Today it is roughly coterminous with the boundaries of Lithuania except for some areas of Lithuanian speakers in Poland and Belarus, and except for the diaspora living in the United States, Canada, Western Europe, Latin America, Australia, and even Siberia.

The medieval Lithuanian rulers did not develop a written form of the Lithuanian language. The literary Lithuanian language, based on a southwestern Lithuanian dialect, came into use during the last quarter of the nineteenth century, replacing the use of the Samogitian, or western Lithuanian, dialect. At the beginning of the twentieth century, the use of Lithuanian was confined mainly to the peasantry, but the language was revived subsequently. In 1988 it was declared the official language of Lithuania, as it had been during 1918-40 and the early years of Soviet rule.

Unlike Estonia and Latvia, Lithuania's cultural development was affected by Poland rather than Germany. The imperial Russian regime had an enormous impact on Lithuania from 1795 to 1915, and the Soviet Union had similar influence from 1940 to 1991. Direct contacts with western Europe also made significant contributions beginning in the sixteenth century. Lithuanian nobility in the sixteenth to eighteenth centuries and Lithuanian intellectuals since the turn of the twentieth century brought back ideas and experiences from Italy, Germany, and France. Also, between the two world wars independent Lithuania's direct communication with western Europe affected the development of educational and religious institutions, the arts and literature, architecture, and social thought. Lithuania's historical heritage and the imprint of the Western outlook acquired in the twentieth century were strong enough to make Soviet citizens feel that by going to Lithuania they were going abroad, to the West.

Lithuanian folk art, especially woodcarving and weaving, contributed to the growth of Lithuanian artistic development. Traditionally, Lithuanian folk artists carved mostly crosses, wayside chapels, and figures of a sorrowful Christ--very symbolic and characteristic of Lithuanian crossroads. Under Soviet rule, which outlawed religious subjects, woodcarvings became sec-ular. Today, Lithuania's roads and gardens are dotted with wooden crosses, poles, and other carvings.

Among Lithuanian artists, probably the best known is Mikalojus Ciurlionis (1875-1911), an originator of abstract painting and a composer whose music became the main subject of study by Professor Vytautas Landsbergis, Lithuania's de facto president 1990-92 and a leader of the independence movement. During the Soviet period, Lithuanian art was best known for graphic arts and for stained glass windows, but the most prominent art forms included abstract painting, sculpture, commercial art, and amber jewelry.

Lithuanian music is as ancient as its art. Folk music has had great influence on its development, and choral singing--periodically demonstrated in huge singing festivals--remains extremely popular. Lithuanian composers write not only choral but also symphonic, ballet, chamber, and opera music. A conservatory, established in 1933, has contributed much to the development of musical culture. In addition to the conservatory, Lithuania supports four higher music schools, three art schools, two pedagogical music schools, eighty music schools for children, five symphony orchestras, ensembles for medieval and contemporary music, and an internationally known string quartet. Many instrumentalists and soloists are winners of international prizes. Folk music ensembles also abound.

Opera and ballet are important elements of Lithuania's national culture. Dancers are trained at the Vilnius School of Choreography and the Kaunas School of Music, as well as in Russia.

All of these activities were state supported under the Soviet system. Membership in artistic associations usually assured work in the profession. All of this now has to be reorganized on a private basis, and both the state and the artists are struggling to find satisfactory working arrangements. Many supporters of the arts believe that art should be state-supported but not state controlled.

The movie industry was established in the late 1940s. Lithuanian filmmakers released four full-length films in 1989 and five in 1990; they also released twenty-eight short films, twenty-four newsreels, and four documentaries. Artistic photography has roots that are older than the Soviet regime in Lithuania.

Sports are also a prevalent national pastime. Lithuania's most popular game is basketball, and a few Lithuanians play professionally in the United States and in European countries. Lithuania's individual athletes have won Olympic medals and routinely compete in European events.

RELIGION

Traditionally, Lithuania has been a Roman Catholic country. Although severely affected by Soviet repression, the Roman Catholic Church remains the dominant and the most influential denomination. However, Lithuania in the past has had two small but active Protestant denominations, the Evangelical Reformed (Calvinist) and the Evangelical Lutheran. In addition, Orthodox Christianity as well as Judaism have roots at least as old as those of Roman Catholicism. In 1991 a Western poll found that 69 percent of respondents in Lithuania identified themselves as Roman Catholics (in 1939 the percentage was 85), 4 percent identified themselves as Orthodox, and 1 percent professed Evangelical Christian beliefs. New in this self-identification was a large category--25 percent--who did not profess any religion. Lithuanian journalists have also noted that twenty-one out of the 141 new members of parliament elected in 1992 left out "so help me God" from the oath when sworn in as deputies.

In 1992 Lithuania's Roman Catholic Church consisted of two archdioceses (Vilnius and Kaunas) and four dioceses (Kaisiadorys, Panevezys, Vilkaviskis, and Telsiai). The church is presided over by Cardinal Vincentas Sladkevicius in Kaunas. For thirty years, Sladkevicius, then a bishop, was held by Soviet authorities in internal exile. The church has 688 parishes, two theological seminaries (one reestablished in 1990), and several con-vents and monasteries. There is also one Uniate, or Eastern-Rite Catholic, congregation.

The archeparchy (archdiocese) of the Russian Orthodox Church has forty-five parishes and two monasteries. Archbishop Chrisostom and his archeparchy are under the jurisdiction of the Patriarch of Moscow. The Old Believers (see Glossary) have fifty-one congregations. The Lithuanian Evangelical Lutheran Church under Bishop Jonas Kalvanas has thirty-three congregations, and the Evangelical Reformed Church (Calvinist) has eight. Other Christian denominations include Baptists, Seventh-Day Adventists, and Pentecostals. The non-Christian religious groups include Jews (two communities), Muslims (four communities), Krishna followers (two communities), and one Karaite (see Glossary) group.

Traditionally, most Roman Catholics in Lithuania were either Lithuanians or Poles, and the Orthodox and Old Believer adherents were predominantly Russians. This division has not changed, although currently it is no longer possible to assume religious affiliation on the basis of ethnic identity. The Calvinist and Evangelical Lutheran groups are very small--an estimated 15,000 Calvinists and 35,000 Lutherans. The younger Protestant denominations are even smaller but are intensely active. Generally, Lithuanian society in the 1990s is secularized, although, as in many postcommunist countries, younger people are searching for some sort of spiritual fulfillment.

The Roman Catholic Church is the oldest continuously surviving Lithuanian institution. As such, it has played a dominant role in the development of Lithuanian society, especially crucial during those long stretches of time when Lithuanians had no state of their own. At first highly influenced by the Polish community, the church under Bishop Motiejus Valancius in the nineteenth century promoted Lithuanian language and publications, which prepared the country for the national awakening of the 1880s. Because Russian imperial authorities had forbidden the publication of Lithuanian books in the Latin alphabet, Valancius had them printed in German-ruled, Protestant East Prussia and then smuggled into Lithuania. The bishop also organized a network of secret Lithuanian schools. In 1918 the church supported the establishment of Lithuania as an independent and democratic republic. Years later, it endorsed land reform, and in the 1930s the bishops opposed and restrained Smetona's authoritarian rule. Under Soviet rule, the church served as a focal point of resistance and dissident activities. Its theological outlook, however, has been conservative.

Protestants also have contributed significantly to Lithuania's cultural development. The first book printed in Lithuanian was a Lutheran catechism, published by Martynas Mazvydas in East Prussia in 1547. Protestant Lithuanians from this region published the literature of national awakening. Later, Protestants--both Lutheran and Calvinist--supplied political leadership out of proportion to their numbers in the population.

In Lithuania between the two world wars, the Roman Catholic Church and other denominations had a constitutionally guaranteed monopoly over registration of marriages, births, and deaths. Religious education in public schools was compulsory. Although there was no established religion, all denominations received some state support in rough proportion to their size. The Soviet authorities totally separated churches not only from the state but also from individual support. On June 12, 1990, Lithuania's newly elected independent parliament adopted an act of restitution of the Roman Catholic Church's condition status quo ante but promised compensation for the losses suffered under Soviet rule and pledged cooperation on a parity basis. The constitution of 1992 guarantees "freedom of thought, religion, and conscience" to all and "recognizes traditional churches and religious organizations of Lithuania." Other religious organizations have to pass a test to ensure that their teachings do not "contradict the law and morality." All recognized churches are guaranteed the rights of legal persons and can govern themselves without state interference. Religious teaching in public schools is allowed if parents desire it. Religious marriage registration also is legally valid, as in the United States. The government maintains an office of counselor on religious affairs.

Language and Culture

Like Latvian and Old Prussian, the Lithuanian language belongs to the Baltic branch of the Indo-European language family. The size of the territory in which Lithuanian was spoken shrank considerably through the ages. Today it is roughly coterminous with the boundaries of Lithuania except for some areas of Lithuanian speakers in Poland and Belarus, and except for the diaspora living in the United States, Canada, Western Europe, Latin America, Australia, and even Siberia.

The medieval Lithuanian rulers did not develop a written form of the Lithuanian language. The literary Lithuanian language, based on a southwestern Lithuanian dialect, came into use during the last quarter of the nineteenth century, replacing the use of the Samogitian, or western Lithuanian, dialect. At the beginning of the twentieth century, the use of Lithuanian was confined mainly to the peasantry, but the language was revived subsequently. In 1988 it was declared the official language of Lithuania, as it had been during 1918-40 and the early years of Soviet rule.

Unlike Estonia and Latvia, Lithuania's cultural development was affected by Poland rather than Germany. The imperial Russian regime had an enormous impact on Lithuania from 1795 to 1915, and the Soviet Union had similar influence from 1940 to 1991. Direct contacts with western Europe also made significant contributions beginning in the sixteenth century. Lithuanian nobility in the sixteenth to eighteenth centuries and Lithuanian intellectuals since the turn of the twentieth century brought back ideas and experiences from Italy, Germany, and France. Also, between the two world wars independent Lithuania's direct communication with western Europe affected the development of educational and religious institutions, the arts and literature, architecture, and social thought. Lithuania's historical heritage and the imprint of the Western outlook acquired in the twentieth century were strong enough to make Soviet citizens feel that by going to Lithuania they were going abroad, to the West.

Lithuanian folk art, especially woodcarving and weaving, contributed to the growth of Lithuanian artistic development. Traditionally, Lithuanian folk artists carved mostly crosses, wayside chapels, and figures of a sorrowful Christ--very symbolic and characteristic of Lithuanian crossroads. Under Soviet rule, which outlawed religious subjects, woodcarvings became sec-ular. Today, Lithuania's roads and gardens are dotted with wooden crosses, poles, and other carvings.

Among Lithuanian artists, probably the best known is Mikalojus Ciurlionis (1875-1911), an originator of abstract painting and a composer whose music became the main subject of study by Professor Vytautas Landsbergis, Lithuania's de facto president 1990-92 and a leader of the independence movement. During the Soviet period, Lithuanian art was best known for graphic arts and for stained glass windows, but the most prominent art forms included abstract painting, sculpture, commercial art, and amber jewelry.

Lithuanian music is as ancient as its art. Folk music has had great influence on its development, and choral singing--periodically demonstrated in huge singing festivals--remains extremely popular. Lithuanian composers write not only choral but also symphonic, ballet, chamber, and opera music. A conservatory, established in 1933, has contributed much to the development of musical culture. In addition to the conservatory, Lithuania supports four higher music schools, three art schools, two pedagogical music schools, eighty music schools for children, five symphony orchestras, ensembles for medieval and contemporary music, and an internationally known string quartet. Many instrumentalists and soloists are winners of international prizes. Folk music ensembles also abound.

Opera and ballet are important elements of Lithuania's national culture. Dancers are trained at the Vilnius School of Choreography and the Kaunas School of Music, as well as in Russia.

All of these activities were state supported under the Soviet system. Membership in artistic associations usually assured work in the profession. All of this now has to be reorganized on a private basis, and both the state and the artists are struggling to find satisfactory working arrangements. Many supporters of the arts believe that art should be state-supported but not state controlled.

The movie industry was established in the late 1940s. Lithuanian filmmakers released four full-length films in 1989 and five in 1990; they also released twenty-eight short films, twenty-four newsreels, and four documentaries. Artistic photography has roots that are older than the Soviet regime in Lithuania.

Sports are also a prevalent national pastime. Lithuania's most popular game is basketball, and a few Lithuanians play professionally in the United States and in European countries. Lithuania's individual athletes have won Olympic medals and routinely compete in European events.

EDUCATION

The population of Lithuania is highly educated. Virtually all those in the age-group fifteen to thirty-nine have completed basic schooling. The average level of education, however, gradually drops for those older than forty. Large numbers of students attend special schools and schools of higher education. In 1993 Lithuania had 67.3 students per 1,000 population in universities and other institutions of higher education, and 46.4 in vocational schools. These numbers compared with 25.9 and 49.0, respectively, for Estonian and Latvian university students and 18.6 and 36.1 for vocational school students. Lithuania had 106 university graduates per 1,000 population. Enrollment rates compared favorably with those in Western Europe. Lithuania had a literacy rate of 99 percent in 1994.

Schools using Lithuanian as the language of instruction are a product of the twentieth century. The system of education--primary, secondary, and higher--was developed between the two world wars. Soviet officials further expanded it, added adult education, and severely ideologized and politicized the philosophy of education and the teaching process. Independent Lithuania has replaced a "Soviet school" with a "national school" philosophy, although the system still maintains some Soviet organizational features. Primary and secondary education together last twelve years. Three types of schools exist: schools that include grades one to four, those that include grades one to nine, and those that include grades one to twelve. Schooling begins at age six. Since 1978 secondary education has been compulsory. In 1993-94 there were 2,317 primary and secondary schools, 108 secondary specialized institu-tions, and fifteen higher education institutions in the country. Separate schools exist with Russian or Polish as the language of instruction.

Lithuania's "flagship" institution of higher learning is Vilnius University. Others include Vytautas Magnus University in Kaunas, founded by the Lithuanian diaspora of the United States and based on the American model, and the new university in Klaipeda. Unlike the Soviet universities, Lithuanian universities are self-governing and have their autonomy guaranteed by law. The entire system of education is administered by the Ministry of Education and Culture.

Following Soviet practice, research and teaching functions in Lithuania are institutionally separated. Research is mainly conducted by the seventeen institutes of the Academy of Sciences. Altogether, in 1990 forty-six research institutes em-ployed 15,400 scientists. Research is relatively weak in the humanities and the social sciences. Probably the most internationally distinguished activity in these fields is the study of Baltic linguistics under the aegis of the center for such studies in Vilnius. Studies in probability theory by the faculty of Vilnius University are internationally known, and important advances have been made in semiconductor physics and chemistry, biochemistry and genetics, studies related to various aspects of environmental protection, and other fields of the natural sciences and technology. Distinguished advanced research has been carried out in the fields of medicine (especially in cardiovascular disease) and agriculture. Internationally, the best recognized Lithuanian contribution is in biotechnology.

GOVERNMENT AND POLITICS

PRESIDENT

Dalia Grybauskaitė born 1 March 1956) is a Lithuanian politician and the current President of Lithuania inaugurated on July 12, 2009. She was previously Lithuania's Vice-Minister of Foreign Affairs, Finance Minister, and European Commissioner for Financial Programming & the Budget. Often referred to as the "Iron Lady", Grybauskaitė is Lithuania's first female head of state

2009 PRESIDENTIAL ELECTIONS

On 26 February 2009, Grybauskaitė officially announced her candidacy for the 2009 presidential election. In her declaration speech, she said:

> I decided to return to Lithuania if the Lithuanian people decide I am needed there now. I think that we all long for the truth, transparency and responsibility for our country. We all want to live without fear, with confidence in ourselves, in each other, and in tomorrow.
>
> I can and I want to contribute with my experience, knowledge and skills to expel shadows from morality, politics, and economics to create a citizen-ruled Lithuania - a state of citizens. Therefore, I will run for the Lithuanian presidency.

Opinion polls taken in February 2009 showed that Grybauskaitė was the undisputed leader in the race. She ran as an independent, although she was supported by the dominant Conservative Party as well as by NGOs, including Sąjūdis.

Her campaign was primarily focused on domestic issues. After years of strong economic growth, Lithuania faced a deep recession with double-digit declines in economic indicators. The unemployment rate rose to 15.5% in March, and a January street protest against the government's response to the recession turned violent. During the campaign, Grybauskaitė stressed the need to combat the financial troubles by protecting those with the lowest incomes, simplifying the Lithuanian bureaucratic apparatus, and reviewing the government's investment program. She also promised a more balanced approach in conducting foreign policy, the primary constitutional role of the Lithuanian presidency.

The election was held on 17 May 2009. Dalia Grybauskaitė won in a landslide, receiving 68.18% of the vote. The 51.6% turnout was just above the threshold needed to avoid a runoff election. In winning the election, Grybauskaitė became not only the first female president of Lithuania, but won by the largest margin recorded in presidential elections.
Political analysts attributed the easy victory to Grybauskaitė's financial competence and her ability to avoid domestic scandals. The international press was quick to dub her the "Lithuanian Iron Lady" for her outspoken speech and her black belt in karate. Grybauskaitė, who speaks Lithuanian, English, Russian, French and Polish, has mentioned Margaret Thatcher and Mahatma Gandhi as her political role models.

Grybauskaitė assumed presidential duties on 12 July 2009. She accepted half of her presidential salary (312,000 litas) as well. Her first presidential visits abroad were made to Sweden and Latvia

PRIME MINISTER

Assumed office
13 December 2012

President	Dalia Grybauskaitė
Preceded by	Andrius Kubilius

Leader of the Social Democratic Party
Incumbent
Assumed office
7 March 2009

Preceded by	Gediminas Kirkilas

Minister of Finance
In office
1 May 2004 – 14 May 2005

Prime Minister	Algirdas Brazauskas
Preceded by	Dalia Grybauskaitė
Succeeded by	Zigmantas Balčytis

Personal details	
Born	19 November 1958 (age 54) Radviliškis district municipality, Lithuania
Political party	Social Democratic Party

Algirdas Butkevičius (born 19 November 1958) is a Lithuanian politician who has been Prime Minister of Lithuania since December 2012. Previously he was Minister of Finance from 2004 to 2005 and Minister of Transport and Communications from 2006 to 2008. He has led the Social Democratic Party of Lithuania since 2009

Butkevičius was born at Paežeriai village in Radviliškis district municipality. Since 1992 he is member of the Social Democratic Party of Lithuania (SDPL). He was Chairman of Vilkaviškis Department of the SDPL in 1995-1997, Deputy Chairman of the SDPL in 1999-2005 (re-elected in 2001), and Chairman of the SDPL since 2009.

In 1996 and 2000, he was elected to the Seimas (parliament). From 2004 to 2005 he served as Minister of Finance and from 2006 to 2008 as Minister of Transport and Communications.

Butkevičius was the SDPL candidate in the 2009 presidential election, placing second with 11.83% of the votes. As of 2010, he is the chairman of the SDPL.

During the 2012 parliamentary election, Butkevičius was among the few candidates who were elected in the first round of the popular vote.

On 22 November 2012 he was elected by the Seimas to be Prime Minister-designate. He was appointed as Prime Minister by presidential decree on 7 December 2012 and his cabinet was sworn on 13 December, following the approval of the governmental program by Parliament

MINISTRIES

Ministry of Agriculture	Kazimieras Starkevičius	Homeland Union – Lithuanian Christian Democrats
Ministry of Culture	Arūnas Gelūnas	Independent
Ministry of Economy	Rimantas Žylius	Independent
Ministry of Education and Science	Gintaras Steponavičius	Liberal Movement
Ministry of Energy	Arvydas Sekmokas	Independent
Ministry of Environment	Gediminas Kazlauskas	Independent
Ministry of Finance	Ingrida Šimonytė	Independent
Ministry of Foreign Affairs	Audronius Ažubalis	Homeland Union – Lithuanian Christian Democrats
Ministry of Health	Raimondas Šukys	Liberal and Centre Union
Ministry of the Interior	Raimundas Palaitis	Liberal and Centre Union
Ministry of Justice	Remigijus Šimašius	Liberal Movement
Ministry of Defence	Rasa Juknevičienė	Homeland Union – Lithuanian Christian Democrats

Ministry of Social Security and Labour	Donatas Jankauskas	Homeland Union – Lithuanian Christian Democrats
Ministry of Transport and Communications	Eligijus Masiulis	Liberal Movement

INSTITUTIONS UNDER THE GOVERNMENT OF LR

Information Society Development Committee
Department of Physical Education and Sports
Lithuanian Archives Department
Weaponry Fund of the Republic of Lithuania
Drug Control Department
Department of Statistics
The Department of National minorities and Lithuanians living abroad
State Nuclear Power Safety Inspectorate
State Data Protection Inspectorate
State Food and Veterinary Service
State Tobacco and Alcohol Control Service
Public Procurement Office

IMPORTANT POLITICAL DEVELOPMENTS

Since Lithuania declared independence on 11 March 1990, it has maintained strong democratic traditions. In the first general elections after the independence on 25 October 1992, 56.75% of the total number of voters supported the new constitution There were intense debates concerning the constitution, especially the role of the president. A separate referendum was held on 23 May 1992 to gauge public opinion on the matter and 41% of all the eligible voters supported the restoration of the President of Lithuania. Eventually a semi-presidential system was agreed upon.

The Lithuanian head of state is the President, elected directly for a five-year term, serving a maximum of two consecutive terms. The post of president is largely ceremonial; main policy functions however include foreign affairs and national security policy. The president is also the military commander-in-chief. The President, with the approval of the parliamentary body, the Seimas, also appoints the Prime Minister and, on the latter's nomination, the rest of the cabinet, as well as a number of other top civil servants and the judges for all courts. The judges of the Constitutional Court (*Konstitucinis Teismas*), who serve nine-year terms, are appointed by the President (three judges), the Chairman of the Seimas (three judges) and the Chairman of the Supreme Court (three judges). The unicameral Lithuanian parliament, the Seimas, has 141 members who are elected to four-year terms. 71 of the members of this legislative body are elected in single constituencies, and the other 70 are elected in a nationwide vote by proportional representation. A party must receive at least 5% of the national vote to be represented in the Seimas

Politics of Lithuania takes place in a framework of a parliamentary representative democratic republic, whereby the Prime Minister of Lithuania is the head of government, and of a multi-party system. Executive power is exercised by the government, which is headed by the Prime Minister. Federal legislative power is vested in both the government and the unicameral Seimas (Lithuanian Parliament). Judicial power is vested in judges appointed by the President of Lithuania and is independent of executive and legislature power. The judiciary consists of the Constitutional Court, the Supreme Court, and the Court of Appeal as well as the separate administrative courts. The Constitution of the Republic of Lithuania established these powers upon its approval on October 25, 1992. Being a multi-party system, the government of Lithuania is not dominated by any single political party, rather it consists of numerous parties that must work with each other to form coalition governments.

POLITICAL PARTIES AND ELECTIONS

SUMMARY OF THE 17 MAY 2009 LITHUANIAN PRESIDENTIAL ELECTION RESULTS

Candidate	Party	Votes	%
Dalia Grybauskaite	Independent	949,357	69.08%
Algirdas Butkevičius	Social Democratic Party of Lithuania	162,549	11.83%
Valentinas Mazuronis	Order and Justice	84,629	6.16%
Waldemar Tomaszewski	Electoral Action of Poles in Lithuania	65,161	4.74%
Kazimira Prunskienė	Lithuanian Peasant Popular Union	53,686	3.91%
Loreta Graužinienė	Labour Party	49,667	3.61%
Česlovas Jezerskas	Independent	9,176	0.67%
Valid votes		1,374,216	98.73%
Invalid votes		17,634	1.27%
Total votes (turnout 51.71%)		1,391,850	—
Source: VRK			

LITHUANIAN PARLIAMENTARY ELECTION, 2012

Parliamentary elections were held in Lithuania on 14 and 28 October 2012, alongside a referendum on the construction of a new power plant. All 141 seats in the Seimas were up for election, 71 of them were filled through a two round race, one from each constituency; the remaining 70, through proportional representation from the results of the first round.

The Lithuanian Social Democratic Party became the largest party in the Seimas and defeated the centre-right coalition of Andrius Kubilius. The Social Democrats announced to form a government coalition with the populist Labour Party and Order and Justice. President Dalia Grybauskaitė, however, refuses to appoint a government with participation of the Labour Party due to allegations of electoral fraud.

Party	Proportional			Constituency seats	Total seats	+/–
	Votes	%	Seats			
Social Democrats	251,610	18.37	15	23	38	▲13
Homeland Union	206,590	15.08	13	20	33	▼12
Labour Party	271,520	19.82	17	12	29	▲19
Order and Justice	100,120	7.31	6	5	11	▼4
Liberal Movement	117,476	8.57	7	3	10	▼1
Electoral Action of Poles in Lithuania	79,840	5.83	5	3	8	▲5
The Way of Courage	109,448	7.99	7	–	7	New

Peasant and Greens Union	53,141	3.88	–	1	1	▼2
Liberal and Centre Union	28,263	2.06	–	–	–	▼8
YES	24,129	1.76	–	–	–	New
Socialist People's Front	16,515	1.21	–	–	–	–
Christian Party	16,494	1.20	–	–	–	New
For Lithuania in Lithuania	12,854	0.94	–	–	–	New
Young Lithuania	8,632	0.63	–	–	–	–
Democratic Labour and Unity Party	4,383	0.32	–	–	–	New
Emigrants Party	4,015	0.29	–	–	–	New
Republican Party	3,661	0.27	–	–	–	New
Lithuanian People's Party	3,399	0.25	–	–	–	New
Independents	–	–	–	3	3	▼1
Invalid/blank votes	57,924	–	–	–	–	–
Total	1,370,014	100	70	70 (1 to go)	140	–
Registered voters/turnout	2,588,418	52.93	–	–	–	–

SUMMARY OF THE RESULTS OF LITHUANIA'S 7 JUNE 2009 ELECTION TO THE EUROPEAN PARLIAMENT

Party	Votes	%	Seats	Change
Homeland Union – Lithuanian Christian Democrats	147,756	26.16%	4	+2
Social Democratic Party of Lithuania	102,347	18.12%	3	+1
Order and Justice	67,237	11.90%	2	+1
Labour Party	48,368	8.56%	1	−4
Electoral Action of Poles in Lithuania	46,293	8.20%	1	+1
Liberals' Movement of the Republic of Lithuania	40,502	7.17%	1	+1
Liberal and Centre Union	19,105	3.38%	0	−2
Centre Party of Lithuania	17,004	3.01%	0	
Christian Conservative Social Union	16,108	2.85%	0	
FRONTAS	13,341	2.36%	0	
Lithuanian Peasant Popular Union	10,285	1.82%	0	−1
Civic Democratic Party	7,425	1.31%	0	
Samogitian Party	6,961	1.23%	0	
National Resurrection Party	5,717	1.01%	0	
National Party Lithuanian Way	1,568	0.28%	0	
Total	550,017	100.0	12	−1

POLITICAL ENVIRONMENT

Lithuania is an independent democratic republic. Its new constitution is that of a presidential democracy with separation of powers and a system of checks and balances. In some ways, the institutional structure of the government is similar to that of the United States; however, it is closer to the system former French president Charles de Gaulle gave to the Fifth Republic of France--a strong presidency leading a parliament divided into many factions.

Lithuania has very good bilateral relations with the U.S., and the Lithuanian government and Parliament generally support American business interests. The current President is a Lithuanian-American who enjoys great popularity with the Lithuanian electorate. Their parliamentary system is vigorous, however, the governing coalitions can be quite tenuous which results in frequent personnel changes at the cabinet level. The United States strongly supports Lithuania's efforts to join European and Trans-Atlantic institutions. Lithuania has made notable progress towards membership in the WTO and the EU and hopes to join NATO in the future. While the Lithuanian Government and all major political parties support a free-market system, there are still visible traces of the Soviet methodology and regulatory traditions at the lower levels of bureaucracy.

THE CONSTITUTIONAL SYSTEM

On the same day that Lithuania declared independence on March 11, 1990, its parliament adopted a provisional constitution, called the "provisional basic law," which established a framework for the new state's government. The constitution comprehensively listed guarantees of democratic rights and rules of democratic process, but basic elements of the Soviet-style government were maintained. Thus, legislative and executive functions were combined under the leadership of parliament, and the court system was kept totally dependent on legislative definitions and appointments. The legislature's name--Supreme Soviet--also was maintained. Its presidium became the foremost leadership body, and the chairman of the presidium became the chief of parliament, of state, and, in effect, of the executive. The provisional basic law, too, was made relatively easy to change.

Despite its democratization, the Soviet model quickly proved that it was not suitable for a new, substantively democratic system of government. It took two years of conflict and frustration, however, before contending parties agreed to a compro-mise between a parliamentary system of legislative superiority with a figurehead president and a very strong presidential system in which the legislature would be at best coequal with the president.

The constitution was approved by the voters in a referendum on October 25, 1992. Seventy-five percent of those voting favored the document. Thus, it was adopted by a solid majority, although the percentage of voters participating in the referendum was smaller (57 percent) than had been the case in most elections until then.

The constitution of 1992 reflects the institutions and experiences of the United States, France, and Germany as integrated into Lithuanian tradition. It also incorporates guarantees of a social safety network inherited from the Soviet Union. In its introductory provisions, the document not only places a high value on democracy but also asserts the right of defense against attempts by force to encroach upon or overthrow "state independence, territorial integrity, or the constitutional system" (Article 3). It also disallows division of Lithuanian territory into any "statelike structures"--an obvious reference to territorial autonomy as a solution to ethnic minority problems in the country. Furthermore, the status of Lithuania as an "independent democratic republic" can be changed only by a referendum and only if three-fourths of Lithuanian citizens approve it. Similarly, the first seventeen articles (which define the characteristics of the state, citizenship, state language, and symbols) and Articles 147, 148, and 149 (which determine the methods for constitutional changes or amendments) can be altered only by a referendum. Article 150 of the constitution forbids Lithuania from joining the Commonwealth of Independent States (CIS--see Glossary). Finally, the constitution incorporates the declaration of independence of March 11, 1990.

Fundamental human rights and democratic values, including freedom of "thought, faith, and conscience," are enshrined in the constitution, which also guarantees the status of legal person to religious denominations and allows religious teaching in public schools. In addition to personal, political, and religious rights, the constitution secures social rights. As al-ready noted, these include free medical care, old-age pensions, unemployment compensation, and support for families and children.

The power to govern is divided between the legislative and executive branches, with an independent judiciary acting as interpreter of the constitution and of the branches' jurisdictions, as well as arbiter of conflicts between them. The constitution clearly acknowledges the danger of concentration of power in a single person or institution. The legislature has regained its old name, Seimas, which was used in the interwar years. The executive consists of a president and a prime minister with a cabinet, known as the Council of Ministers. The judiciary is composed of the Supreme Court and subordinate courts (the Court of Appeals, district courts, and local courts), as well as the Constitutional Court, which decides on the constitutionality of acts of the Seimas, the president, and the government.The Office of the Procurator General is an autono-mous institution of the judiciary. Creation of special courts, such as administrative or family courts, is allowed, although establishing courts with "special powers" is forbidden in peacetime.

The parliament consists of 141 members, seventy elected from party lists on the basis of proportional representation and seventy-one from single-member districts. To be seated in the Seimas on the basis of proportional representation, a party must receive at least 4 percent of the votes cast. An exception is made for ethnic minority groups, however, which do not need to pass the 4 percent threshold. The legislature is elected for four years. Candidates for the legislature must be at least twenty-five years old. Members of the Seimas may serve as prime minister or cabinet member, but they may not hold any other position in either central or local government or in private enterprises or organizations. The parliament must approve the prime minister, as well as his or her government and program. It also may force the government's resignation by rejecting twice in sequence its program or by expressing no confidence by a majority of legislators in secret ballot.

The powers of the legislature are checked by a number of devices: first, by certain constitutional limitations; second, by the president as defined under the constitution; and third, by the Constitutional Court. Articles 64, 131, and 132 of the constitution circumscribe the ability of the Seimas to control the government, especially the budget. Article 64 specifies the times of parliamentary sessions. Although extension is possible, ordinarily the legislature cannot sit longer than seven months and three days, divided into two sessions. The budget submitted by the government can be increased by the legislature only if the latter indicates the sources of financing for additional expenditures. If the budget is not approved before the start of the budget year, proposed expenditures cannot be higher than those of the previous year. Finally, the legislature is not entrusted with making decisions concerning the basic characteristics of Lithuanian statehood and democracy. These are left to the citizens by means of referendum. Similarly, the initiative for making laws is not limited to the legislature but also belongs to the citizens, who can force the legislature to consider a law by submitting a petition with 50,000 signatures.

The powers of the legislature are further checked by those of the president, who may veto legislation, both ordinary and constitutional, passed by the legislature. Normally, laws are not promulgated without the signature of the president. A presidential veto can be overridden, but only by an absolute majority of the Seimas membership. The president can also dissolve the parliament if it refuses to approve the government's budget within sixty days or if it directly votes no confidence in the government. However, the next elected parliament may retaliate by calling for an earlier presidential election.

The president is elected directly by the people for a term of five years and a maximum of two consecutive terms. The president is not, strictly speaking, the chief of the executive branch or the chief administrator. The Lithuanians borrowed the French model of the presidency, then adapted it to their needs. Candidates must be at least forty years old. To be elected in the first round, 50 percent of the voters must participate and a candidate must receive more than half of the total votes cast. If 50 percent of the voters do not participate, a plurality wins the presidency unless it constitutes less than one-third of the total vote. If the first round does not produce a president, a second round is held within two weeks between the two top candidates. A plurality vote is sufficient to win.

The president is the head of state. The president also selects the prime minister (with the approval of the Seimas), approves ministerial candidates, and appoints the commander in chief of the armed forces--with legislative confirmation. The president resolves basic foreign policy issues and can confer military and diplomatic ranks, appoint diplomats without legislative approval, and issue decrees subject to the legislature's right to later overturn a decree by legislative action.

Finally, the president has considerable powers to influence the judicial branch. The president has the right to nominate (and the Seimas to approve the nomination of) three justices to the Constitutional Court and all justices to the Supreme Court. The president also appoints, with legislative approval, judges of the Court of Appeals. However, legislative confirmation is not required for the appointment or transfer of judges in local, district, and special courts.

The Constitutional Court checks both the legislative and the executive branches of government by ruling on whether their legislation and/or actions are constitutional. The court consists of nine justices appointed by the legislature, three each from the nominees of the president, the parliamentary chairman, and the chief justice of the Supreme Court. The president nominates the chief justice of the Constitutional Court. Cases for consideration by the Constitutional Court, however, may be brought only by one-fifth of the membership of the Seimas, the ordinary courts, or the president of the republic.

POLITICS

The new system of government became operative with the election of President Algirdas Brazauskas in February 1993. Brazauskas came from the Lithuanian Democratic Labor Party (LDLP), successor to the Communist Party of Lithuania. The Brazauskas government surprised many of its critics during 1994 by its continued commitment to rapid economic reform and to Lithuania's independence. Rural interests, which formed the bedrock of support for the LDLP, were unhappy with the failure to roll back implementation of the free market in agriculture and with the breakup of centralized state farms and cooperatives.

Since the declaration of independence, Lithuanian politics have been stormy, especially the struggle between the former Communist Party of Lithuania and the movement for independence, Sajudis. On its own, the Communist Party of Lithuania had won only twenty-three seats out of the 141 seats in the March 1990 parliamentary elections. Sajudis and other political parties that supported independence had won a majority. In addition, the Lithuanian Social Democratic Party (LSDP) won nine seats; the Christian Democratic Party of Lithuania (CDPL), two; the Lithuanian Democratic Party (LDP), two; and the Lithuanian Green Party, four. Noncommunist parties were in their infancy--small and weak. Seventy members of parliament did not belong formally to any party, although virtually all of them were ideologically close to Sajudis.

Parliamentary organization was complicated by the numerous parliamentary factions, unrelated to party strength or differentiation in society. Parliamentary factions had no fixed constituencies to which they were accountable. In 1992 there were nine parliamentary factions and a nonfaction group consisting of twenty independent deputies. The largest was the Center faction (eighteen members), followed by the Moderates (sixteen), the LDLP (twelve), the Liberals (ten), the Poles (eight), and the Nationalists (nine). The United Sajudis faction had sixteen members, and the Santara faction of Sajudis had ten.

The weakness of the LDLP was deceptive. This group had lost adherents in the parliament, but in April 1990, while still known as the Communist Party of Lithuania, it won approximately 40 percent of the votes--and offices--in local elections. It was strong in small towns and rural areas. Later in 1990, these reformist communists adopted a new name and an essentially social democratic program, gaining a new lease on political life.

In this political landscape, the position of chairman of the presidium of the Supreme Soviet (de facto president) was won in May 1990 by Vytautas Landsbergis, the president of Sajudis and a professor of musicology who had never been a member of the Communist Party of Lithuania. Landsbergis defeated the former leader, Brazauskas, by two-thirds of the vote. Brazauskas refused to accept the position of deputy chairman. Kazimiera Prunskiene, an economist, was chosen as prime minister, whereupon she immediately quit the Communist Party of Lithuania. Brazauskas agreed to serve as one of the deputy prime ministers. The other deputy prime minister was Romualdas Ozolas, a philosopher and former communist who eventually joined the Center faction in the parliament.

Soon, however, a conflict developed between Landsbergis and Prunskiene, primarily over Lithuania's response to the 1990 Soviet blockade. Landsbergis stood firm and defiant. Prunskiene, after visiting Western leaders, pursued compromise with the Soviet Union, as suggested by these leaders. In early 1991, Prunskiene took the first radical steps in economic reform, but the Sajudis forces used that action to unseat her. A fellow economist, Albertas Simenas, was chosen as her successor, but he temporarily disappeared during the turmoil created by the Soviet army, which staged a putsch against the Lithuanian government and on January 13, 1991, massacred un-armed civilians. Landsbergis summoned the people to defend the parliament. His heroic determination and leadership won him further domestic recognition as a national leader and a favorable international reputation abroad. For a moment, all political groups united against Soviet aggression. Lithuanians refused to participate in Gorbachev's referendum on the continuation of a federal union and instead held their own "national poll," which confirmed overwhelming support for independence. However, unity did not last long.

In Simenas's absence, Gediminas Vagnorius became prime minister. He initiated economic reforms and continued the political struggle against Brazauskas's party that Landsbergis had begun in the spring of 1990. Vagnorius's efforts frequently were frustrated by the parliament, and the LDLP formally declared opposition to the government in the fall of 1991. Reform measures, especially in agriculture, were not successful. His struggle with the leadership of the Bank of Lithuania over the introduction of a Lithuanian currency, the litas, was unsuccessful because neither the bank nor a majority in parliament supported his program.

In the meantime, the strength of the Sajudis group and of the coalition in parliament that supported Vagnorius was withering. The leadership of the independence movement, furthermore, was gradually shifting to more conservative nationalist positions after the third conference of the movement in December 1991. Anticommunist activities were facilitated by access to KGB archives, and past collaboration with the KGB was made a political issue. The atmosphere was not improved by the ultimately unsuccessful attempts by Sajudis to pass a law that would temporarily bar from public office certain categories of former officeholders in the communist party power structure. The attempt sharpened confrontation between the nationalist and former communist party forces. Landsbergis sought to strengthen the powers of the executive branch and his own position by establishing an executive presidency. But on May 23, 1992, his proposal failed in a referendum.

After several attempts in parliament to remove the unpopular prime minister in the summer of 1992, Vagnorius had to resign in July, and new parliamentary elections were agreed upon for October. Aleksandras Abisala, another Sajudis leader, took over from Vagnorius with the acquiescence of the opposition. However, neither his attempts to correct the economic situation nor his conciliatory politics improved Sajudis's chances in the upcoming elections of October 25, 1992.

Seventeen groups or coalitions ran candidates for the 141 seats of the new parliament, the Seimas, but some did not muster enough votes for the 4 percent threshold. Against everyone's expectations--and even to Brazauskas's own surprise--the LDLP and its satellites won an absolute majority of seventy-three seats (51 percent). Landsbergis's forces still hoped for a strong showing of their coalition, but the Sajudis-Santara coalition succeeded in winning only sixteen seats, including three contested ones. The Social Democratic representation de-creased to eight seats, the Christian Democrats increased to ten, and the Center barely squeaked through with two victories in single-member districts but did not meet the 4 percent threshold for seats elected by party lists. Three new groups entered the parliament--the Citizens Charter with ten seats; Political Prisoners and Exiles with twelve; and the Christian Democratic Association, a splinter of the Christian Democratic Party with one. One seat was won by an independent. The Polish minority, however, was able to win four seats because it was not required to reach the 4 percent threshold.

The significance of the parliamentary elections result was threefold: the nationalist forces of Landsbergis were crushed, the postcommunist politicians led by Brazauskas made an amazing comeback, and the political center in the parliament was destroyed. Neither the Center nor the Liberal faction met the 4 percent threshold for seats elected by party lists. Political polarization of the country was confirmed: there was a strong and well-organized left, and there was a weak, shattered, and splintered right.

The polarization was even more conspicuously demonstrated in the direct presidential election of February 14, 1993. The Lithuanian ambassador to the United States, Stasys Lozoraitis, lost to Brazauskas, who won majorities everywhere except in the urban district of Kaunas. The final vote was 61.1 percent for Brazauskas and 38.2 percent for Lozoraitis. Brazauskas was catapulted to office by the rural population. His majority was increased by the vote from urban districts with Polish or Russian majorities. Brazauskas won for the same reasons his party earlier captured the majority in the parliament: economic crisis, disappointment with Sajudis, dislike of the once very popular Landsbergis, and, most of all, the electorate's trust in Brazauskas as a well-known and popular candidate whose campaign succeeded in portraying the ambassador as a "foreigner" ignorant of Lithuania's concerns.

The Western press saw the election as a victory for former communist party members who would stop reform and return Lithuania to some sort of association with the former Soviet Union. However, the LDLP was no longer communist, and, although sympathetic to Russia, it was committed to Lithuania's independence. The new president stated repeatedly that he would preserve Lithuania's independence, although Landsbergis, now in the role of opposition leader, continued to warn of threats to Lithuania's status as an independent state. Brazauskas resigned as leader of the LDLP, as required by the constitution.

Shortly after the election, President Brazauskas appointed Raimundas Rajeckas, a distinguished economist with an academic background, as his special counsel. Rajeckas had been associated with Harvard and other Western universities and had served as Brazauskas's campaign manager. He functioned as a "deputy president." Brazauskas also accepted the resignation of Prime Minister Bronislovas Lubys and chose as his successor an economist, Adolfas Slezevicius, president of a private joint Lithuanian-Norwegian company and former deputy minister of agriculture for dairy and meat production. Slezevicius continued to implement Lithuania's political and economic reforms while pursuing an improved relationship with Russia.

MASS MEDIA

The collapse of the communist system brought about the privatization of most publishing. Although the government still plays a role in book publishing, all newspapers and journals are privately owned, usually by limited stock companies or by private individuals. The number of periodicals has increased dramatically, and competition is intense. There are several main dailies. *Lietuvos aidas* was first published by the Landsbergis government but is now private, although editorially it supports Landsbergis and Sajudis. *Lietuvos rytas* , an independent daily, leans slightly to the left and is very conscious of the power and responsibility of the press. It is edited by the former editor of *Komjaunimo tiesa* , the largest daily in Lithuania, and has a circulation of more than 100,000. *Tiesa* now is the voice of the Democratic Labor Party after previously being published by the Communist Party of Lithuania. *Respublika* , founded and owned by a prize-winning journalist and former member of the Soviet Union's Congress of People's Deputies, specializes in "investigative journalism" and leans to the left.

In 1990 Lithuanian newspaper circulation and book publishing suffered a decline because of a shortage of paper, a result of the Soviet economic blockade. In 1989 Lithuanian newspaper circulation per 1,000 inhabitants was 1,223--higher than in Latvia (1,032) but lower than in Estonia (1,620). Annual circulation of magazines and other periodicals was eleven copies per inhabitant (compared with twenty-eight in Latvia and twenty-six in Estonia). Annual book and booklet publication was six copies per inhabitant (compared with six in Latvia and twelve in Estonia).

Library statistics indicate that newly published books and current periodicals are accessible to readers in remote rural areas. Lithuania had 1,885 libraries in the early 1990s, compared with 1,318 for Latvia and 629 for Estonia.

FOREIGN RELATIONS

The course of Lithuania's foreign policy in the 1990s has been more stable than its domestic politics. This has been demonstrated by the fact that between March 1990 and November 1992 it had five prime ministers but only one minister of foreign affairs. Since independence the cornerstone of Lithuanian foreign policy has been integration with European security institutions: the Organization for Security and Cooperation in Europe (OSCE; until January 1995 known as the Conference on Security and Cooperation in Europe--see Glos-sary), the Council of Europe (COE), the European Union (EU), the North Atlantic Cooperation Council (NACC), the World Trade Organization (WTO), and ultimately, the North Atlantic Treaty Organization (NATO). Lithuania is a member of the OSCE, the COE, and the NACC and is an associate member of the EU. It hopes eventually to join the EU, the WTO, and NATO, and progress was made toward these goals in 1994.

In the beginning, Lithuania's aims were more fundamental. Lithuania's sole foreign policy concern in 1990 was to gain international recognition of the restored Lithuanian state. However, efforts directed at Gorbachev on the one hand and the Western powers on the other hand bore no fruit. Gorbachev could not afford the political cost of recognizing Lithuanian independence, nor did he believe in Lithuania's right to statehood. The West's attitude, according to Egon Bahr, a German foreign policy expert, was "We'll throw you a life preserver after you learn how to swim."

Gorbachev informally agreed not to use force, and the West did not push him to permit Lithuanian independence.

However, after the Vilnius massacre of January 13, 1991, which revealed that Gorbachev had authorized attempts to overthrow Lithuania's government, Western states broke ranks. The first was Iceland, which declared that it recognized Lithuania's sovereignty. Iceland had extended recognition in 1922 and had never reneged on it. Next, Denmark expressed its commitment to early recognition. Paradoxically, the greatest appreciation of Lithuania's needs came from Russia. After learning about the Vilnius massacre, Russian president Boris N. Yeltsin met with Baltic leaders in Tallinn and expressed solidarity with Lithuania. This expression gained legal status on July 29, 1991. On that day, United States President George H.W. Bush signed the Strategic Arms Reduction Talks (START) treaty with Gorbachev in Moscow, and Yeltsin and Landsbergis signed a treaty "on the basis of relations" between the Republic of Lithuania and the Russian Soviet Federated Socialist Republic. The crucial item of the treaty was Article 1, which stated that "The High Contracting Parties recognize one another as full-fledged subjects of international law and as sovereign states according to their state status as established by the fundamental acts adopted by the Republic of Lithuania on 11 March 1990 and by the Russian Soviet Federated Socialist Republic on 12 June 1990." Lithuanians hastily ratified the treaty on August 19, 1991, the same day as a coup was carried out by conservative forces in Moscow against Gorbachev. It was not until January 17, 1992, however, that Russia ratified the agreement.

After the coup failed, the international community quickly recognized the independence of Lithuania and the other Baltic states. In September 1991, President Bush renewed the United States recognition of Lithuania of 1922 and announced that an ambassador would be sent to Vilnius. The Soviet Union recognized Lithuania's independence on September 6, 1991. On the recommendation of the United States and the Soviet Union, Lithuania was admitted to the United Nations (UN) on September 16. Then on December 21, the Soviet Union collapsed as a legal entity, and on December 24 Yeltsin informed UN secretary general Javier Pérez de Cuellar that the Russian Federation had assumed "all rights and obligations of the USSR." Thus, Russia still was, for all practical purposes, the Soviet Union, only under different leadership.

Once Lithuania joined the UN, Landsbergis indicated the next priorities of Lithuania's foreign policy: to join all accessible international organizations, and to legally strengthen the status of the new state while working toward the withdrawal of Russian troops, regarded by Lithuanians as an occupying force, from Lithuania. The Russian military strongly opposed this demand, claiming that the troops had no place to go. The commander of the Baltic Military District believed the troops would leave only after several years. Russian foreign minister Andrey Kozyrev suggested a "status of forces" agreement to legalize the Russian troop presence. In June 1992, the Baltic Council, a consultative body of Baltic leaders, appealed to the CSCE, the UN, and the Group of Seven (Canada, France, Germany, Italy, Japan, Britain, and the United States). The Group of Seven, the CSCE, and the UN, as well as NATO, counseled the Russians to set a definite withdrawal date. After protracted negotiations, Russia agreed to withdraw its troops from Lithuania. An agreement was signed in Moscow on September 8, 1992, setting the deadline for withdrawal at August 31, 1993, a year earlier than expected.

The withdrawal of Russian troops was completed on time, opening a new chapter between Russia and Lithuania and encouraging closer economic and other relations. When Lithuania first declared independence from the Soviet Union and tried to negotiate its status with the Gorbachev administration, it did not achieve its goals. But after the dissolution of the Soviet Union, Moscow and Vilnius tried to put the past behind them, even though the Soviet Union had imposed an economic blockade and had used violence to force Lithuania to renounce independence. Although diplomatic relations between the two countries were established in 1991, Russia did not send an ambassador to Lithuania until 1992, and Lithuania reciprocated only in March 1993.

Relations between Vilnius and Moscow were often unsettled by press reports of violations of Lithuanian airspace throughout the first half of the 1990s. Despite a desire to control air traffic within its borders, Lithuania has been unable to come to an agreement with Russia to regulate air transit. The two countries did, however, sign an economic cooperation agreement in November 1993.

Preoccupied with Russia and with the West, Lithuanian policy makers had somewhat neglected Lithuania's other neighbors, especially Belarus and Ukraine. Nevertheless, trade with Belarus expanded, and a border agreement was reached. Ukrainian president Leonid Kuchma's administration was supportive of Lithuanian sovereignty, and the two countries signed an economic cooperation agreement in February 1994. Vilnius focused on a rapprochement with Poland, which resulted in a treaty of cooperation covering various fields, including de-fense, and providing even for joint maneuvers of their armed forces. The agreement was signed during a visit to Lithuania by Polish president Lech Walesa in April 1994 and was ratified by Lithuania in October 1994.

Lithuania seeks closer relations with Scandinavia. The Swedish king and the Danish queen have visited Lithuania. Close economic ties are being developed with Norway and Denmark. Denmark cooperates closely with Lithuania in military affairs and has agreed to train Lithuanian military units to serve as UN peacekeepers in the former Yugoslavia.

In relations with Western Europe and the United States, Lithuania has two main objectives. The first is economic cooperation and attracting Western capital to boost Lithuania's economy and to help with the transition to a free market and democracy. The second objective is to gain security guarantees so that Lithuania and the other Baltic states would not be left alone to face any threat from Russia. Vilnius has pursued these objectives by demonstrating its respect for Western values and by negotiating bilateral trade agreements, tax treaties, and consular and other agreements with West European countries and the United States.

NATIONAL SECURITY

If permanence of policy-making personnel is an indication of policy continuity, Lithuania's defense policy in the early 1990s has been even more consistent than its foreign policy. Audrius Butkevicius, a young physician, was appointed minister of defense in Prunskiene's government in 1990 and served several years under five prime ministers.

Lithuania's struggle for independence was a peaceful revolution in which violence was not used. Thus, Lithuania's government did not inherit guerrilla forces or special troops, only the regular law enforcement agencies that chose to support independence. Following the declaration of independence, however, the Sajudis governments paid attention to the develop-ment of some defensive capability, and budgetary appropriations increased until 1993 when they stabilized at 1 percent of the budget, or at least 1 percent less than appropriations for education and culture and 3 percent less than those for medical care and other health services.

Butkevicius maintained that Lithuanian defense policy has the goal of responding to three threats to Lithuania's national security. First, Lithuania is highly vulnerable to threats from beyond its borders because of its location. Second, Lithuania's internal security and the defense of its borders are also challenged by instability within the former Soviet Union and by authoritarianism and nationalism expressed by certain political parties and movements in Russia. Finally, Lithuania's domestic peace is threatened by the growing problem of organized crime, which destabilizes social institutions and is accompanied by smuggling--of drugs, weapons, and aliens--as well as by violent crime. These threats are countered in part by participating in the activities of the NACC, the OSCE, and the Western European Union (WEU). Moreover, Lithuania is developing good bilateral relations with the other Baltic states and with Poland and Belarus, and it is improving its relations with Russia. Another important forum in which threats to Lithuania's national security can be countered is the Nordic Council (see Glossary). Butkevicius has coordinated policies and enhanced ties with the Nordic countries, especially with Denmark.

Lithuania's main defense accomplishments so far have been the withdrawal of Russian military forces, the establishment of an army, and association with NATO. An agreement signed with Russia in September 1992 committed Russia to removing its troops by August 31, 1993. Withdrawal was completed on time. The Lithuanian army slowly began taking shape in the fall of 1991 but was not formally established until November 19, 1992.

Lithuania's contacts with NATO have been numerous. Most important, Lithuania joined NATO's Partnership for Peace program. Reciprocal visits by officials have been supplemented by NATO naval unit visits to Klaipeda, Lithuania's only major port. An American frigate was among the visitors in 1992. Together with Poland, Lithuania has participated in several NATO war exercises, the first of which was "Baltops 1993," held in June in the Baltic Sea. Baltops continued in subsequent summers.

Lithuania remains especially concerned about the Russian presence in the Baltic region, which will be permanently based in the exclave of Kaliningrad. Although Russia has said it will gradually reduce the numbers of its military forces there, there are currently tens of thousands of military personnel in Kaliningrad Oblast.

ARMED FORCES

The information available on Lithuania's defense establishment indicates that Lithuania's "security structure" includes armed forces run by the Ministry of Defense; a domestic police force subordinate to the Ministry of Interior; and a Parliamentary Defense Service that protects the parliament and the president of the republic. The chief of the Internal Security Agency insists that the agency--successor to some of the KGB's functions--has no security force, although he thinks that there ought to be a budget to establish a force to deal with criminal and subversive elements. Under Soviet rule, the KGB had its own army and also controlled the border guard.

The president of the republic chairs the State Defense Council, consisting of the prime minister, the speaker of the parliament, the minister of defense, and the chief of the armed forces. All of those people, except the speaker, are appointed by the president; therefore, the State Defense Council is likely to be dominated by the president. The council considers and coordinates the most important questions of national defense. The government, the minister of defense, and the chief of the armed forces are responsible to the Seimas for the management and leadership of the armed forces. The minister of defense must be a civilian or a retired military officer.

Total armed forces in 1994 numbered about 8,900, including a 4,300-member army, 350-member navy, 250-member air force, and 4,000-member border guard. A coast guard, which is modeled on the United States Coast Guard, is being established. There is also a 12,000-member Home Guard force. The army's equipment includes fifteen BTR-60 armored personnel carriers. The navy has two small Soviet Grisha-III frigates, one Swedish and two Soviet patrol craft, and four converted civilian vessels. The air force's equipment includes twenty-four Soviet An-2, two Czechoslovak L-410 and four L-39 aircraft, and three Soviet Mi-8 helicopters. Germany has donated jeeps and uniforms for Lithuania's armed forces.

The Home Guard is organized on the Scandinavian model and protects borders, strategic facilities, and natural resources. Lithuania's military structure also includes civil defense forces, which provide administrative control of hazardous facilities, transportation, and special rescue services. The national security service is part of the Ministry of Interior and is responsible for the fight against organized crime.

The constitution calls for one year of compulsory military training or alternative service (for conscientious objectors). Conscription for defense forces started in December 1991. However, of the 20,000 annually eligible and legally obligated young men, only 6,000 were inducted in 1992. This rate is expected to continue. Women are not called to duty, and there are no plans for them to serve in the military.

In the opinion of the commander of NATO forces in Northern Europe, Lithuanian troops are well trained by Western standards. In the past, Lithuanians trained in France's military antiterrorism school, and some Lithuanian officers and noncommissioned officers have attended military schools in the United States, France, and Denmark.

CRIME AND LAW ENFORCEMENT

Crime increased dramatically in Lithuania in the 1990s. The number of reported crimes per 100,000 inhabitants in 1990 was 992. This number increased to 1,197 in 1991, to 1,507 in 1992, and to 1,612 in 1993. Both violent crimes and crimes against property increased substantially over this period. So far, law enforcement bodies, such as the Ministry of Interior, have been ineffective in combating this problem because information about their repressive activities during the Soviet period has discouraged public support. The law enforcement bodies have difficulty combining respect for the rule of law with aggressive intervention against crime, and criminals have expanded their activities.

The Ministry of Interior is responsible, along with local police forces, for fighting crime in Lithuania. Retraining, cooperation with foreign and international police forces, and a concentrated effort to rebuild public support have been emphasized to achieve a more effective police force. The Ministry of Interior was expected to claim 20 percent of the state budget in 1995, according to a parliamentary deputy. In August 1994, the cabinet decried widespread corruption in the customs service. A commodity exchange president claimed later that year that 70 percent of imports into Lithuania were sold on the black market.

While violent crime continued to increase in 1994, property crime decreased. Overall crime dropped 19 percent in the first quarter of 1994 compared with the same period in 1993. Premeditated murder and attempted murder increased about 59 percent, and theft increased about 83 percent.

Organized crime is a serious problem in Lithuania. It en-.gages in violent crime as well as in smuggling aliens, drugs, radioactive materials, and weapons. The son of Georgi Deka-nidze, head of the notorious Vilnius Brigade, an organized crime ring, was to be executed in 1995 for the murder of a journalist who had been investigating organized crime. Dekanidze reportedly threatened in November 1994 to blow up the Ignalina nuclear power plant if his son were executed.

PENAL CODE AND PRISONS

The Office of the Procurator General is an independent institution responsible for enforcing the penal code and ensuring that detention of criminal suspects is based on reliable evidence of criminal activity. A magistrate must approve detention after seventy-two hours, and the right to counsel is guaranteed by law. Shortages of qualified attorneys limit this right in practice, however. Capital punishment is still legal but is rarely used.

Prison conditions in Lithuania are primitive, a legacy of the Soviet period, but have not been the subject of international concern or criticism to the same extent as in Russia and other former Soviet republics. Human rights organizations are active in the country, and their right to exist and operate is not challenged by the government. Lithuania, as part of its accession to the Council of Europe, submitted to an intensive investigation of its human rights practices and respect for democratic values. The UN High Commissioner for Human Rights, José Ayala Lasso, visited Lithuania in 1994 and stated that human rights and democratic values are respected in Lithuania. He suggested, however, that Vilnius needs to ratify conventions concerning racial discrimination, torture, and protocols on capital punishment, refugees, and persons without citizenship.

STUDYING COUNTRY THROUGH THE CONSTITUTION

CONSTITUTION[1]

CHAPTER 1 THE STATE OF LITHUANIA

Article 1
The State of Lithuania shall be an independent and democratic republic.

Article 2
The State of Lithuania shall be created by the People. Sovereignty shall be vested in the People.

Article 3
(1) No one may limit or restrict the sovereignty of the People or make claims to the sovereign powers of the People.
(2) The People and each citizen shall have the right to oppose anyone who encroaches on the independence, territorial integrity, or constitutional order of the State of Lithuania by force.

Article 4
The People shall exercise the supreme sovereign power vested in them either directly or through their democratically elected representatives.

Article 5
(1) In Lithuania, the powers of the State shall be exercised by the Parliament, the President of the Republic and Government, and the Judiciary.
(2) The scope of powers shall be defined by the Constitution.
(3) Institutions of power shall serve the people.

Article 6
(1) The Constitution shall be an integral and directly applicable statute.
(2) Every person may defend his or her rights on the basis of the Constitution.

Article 7
(1) Any law or other statute which contradicts the Constitution shall be invalid.
(2) Only laws which are promulgated shall be valid.
(3) Ignorance of the law shall not exempt a person from responsibility.

Article 8
The forced seizure of State power or any of its institutions shall be considered an anti-constitutional action, which is illegal and invalid.

Article 9
(1) The most significant issues concerning the life of the State and the People shall be decided by referendum.
(2) In the cases established by law, referendums shall be announced by the Parliament.
(3) Referendums shall also be announced if no less than 300,000 of the electorate so request.
(4) The procedure for the announcement and execution of a referendum shall be established by law.

[1] *Adopted: 25 Oct 1992 / Status: 25 Oct 1992*

Article 10
(1) The territory of the State of Lithuania shall be integral and shall not be divided into any state derivatives.
(2) The State borders may only be realigned by an international treaty of the Republic of Lithuania which has been ratified by four-fifths of all the Parliament members.

Article 11
The administrative divisions of the territory of the State of Lithuania and their boundaries shall be determined by law.

Article 12
(1) Citizenship of the Republic of Lithuania shall be acquired by birth or on other bases established by law.
(2) With the exception of cases established by law, no person may be a citizen of the Republic of Lithuania and another state at the same time.
(3) The procedure for the acquisition and loss of citizenship of the Republic of Lithuania shall be established by law.

Article 13
(1) The State of Lithuania shall protect its citizens abroad.
(2) It shall be prohibited to extradite a citizen of the Republic of Lithuania to another state unless an international agreement whereto the Republic of Lithuania is a party establishes otherwise.

Article 14
Lithuanian shall be the State language.

Article 15
(1) The colors of the State flag shall be yellow, green, and red.
(2) The State emblem shall be a white Vytis on a red background.
(3) The State flag and emblem and their use shall be established by law.

Article 16
The national anthem shall be Vincas Kudirka's *"Tautiska Giesmes"*.

Article 17
The capital of the Republic of Lithuania shall be the city of Vilnius, the long-standing historical capital of Lithuania.

CHAPTER 2 THE INDIVIDUAL AND THE STATE

Article 18
The rights and freedoms of individuals shall be inborn.

Article 19
The right to life of individuals shall be protected by law.

Article 20
(1) Personal freedom shall be inviolable.
(2) No person may be arbitrarily arrested or detained. No person may be deprived of freedom except on the bases, and according to the procedures, which have been established in laws.
(3) A person detained in flagrante delicto must, within 48 hours, be brought to court for the purpose of determining, in the presence of the detainee, the validity of the detention. In the event

that the court does not pass a decision to arrest the person, the detained individual shall be released immediately.

Article 21
(1) The person shall be inviolable.
(2) Human dignity shall be protected by law.
(3) It shall be prohibited to torture, injure, degrade, or maltreat a person, as well as to establish such punishments.
(4) No person may be subjected to scientific or medical testing without his or her knowledge thereof and consent thereto.

Article 22
(1) The private life of an individual shall be inviolable.
(2) Personal correspondence, telephone conversations, telegraph messages, and other intercommunications shall be inviolable.
(3) Information concerning the private life of an individual may be collected only upon a justified court order and in accordance with the law.
(4) The law and the court shall protect individuals from arbitrary or unlawful interference in their private or family life, and from encroachment upon their honor and dignity.

Article 23
(1) Property shall be inviolable.
(2) The rights of ownership shall be protected by law.
(3) Property may only be seized for the needs of society according to the procedure established by law and must be adequately compensated for.

Article 24
(1) A person's dwelling place shall be inviolable.
(2) Without the consent of the resident(s), entrance into a dwelling place shall only be permitted upon a corresponding court order, or according to the procedure established by law when the objective of such an action is to protect public order, apprehend a criminal, or save a person's life, health, or property.

Article 25
(1) Individuals shall have the right to have their own convictions and freely express them.
(2) Individuals must not be hindered from seeking, obtaining, or disseminating information or ideas.
(3) Freedom to express convictions, as well as to obtain and disseminate information, may not be restricted in any way other than as established by law, when it is necessary for the safeguard of the health, honor and dignity, private life, or morals of a person, or for the protection of constitutional order.
(4) Freedom to express convictions or impart information shall be incompatible with criminal actions - the instigation of national, racial, religious, or social hatred, violence, or discrimination, the dissemination of slander, or misinformation.
(5) Citizens shall have the right to obtain any available information which concerns them from State agencies in the manner established by law.

Article 26
(1) Freedom of thought, conscience, and religion shall not be restricted.
(2) Every person shall have the right to freely choose any religion or faith and, either individually or with others, in public or in private, to manifest his or her religion or faith in worship, observance, practice or teaching.
(3) No person may coerce another person or be subject to coercion to adopt or profess any

religion or faith.
(4) A person's freedom to profess and propagate his or her religion or faith may be subject only to those limitations prescribed by law and only when such restrictions are necessary to protect the safety of society, public order, a person's health or morals, or the fundamental rights and freedoms of others.
(5) Parents and legal guardians shall have the liberty to ensure the religious and moral education of their children in conformity with their own convictions.

Article 27
A person's convictions, professed religion or faith may justify neither the commission of a crime nor the violation of law.

Article 28
While exercising their rights and freedoms, persons must observe the Constitution and the laws of the Republic of Lithuania, and must not impair the rights and interests of other people.

Article 29
(1) All people shall be equal before the law, the court, and other State institutions and officers.
(2) A person may not have his rights restricted in any way, or be granted any privileges, on the basis of his or her sex, race, nationality, language, origin, social status, religion, convictions, or opinions.

Article 30
(1) Any person whose constitutional rights or freedoms are violated shall have the right to appeal to court.
(2) The law shall establish the procedure for compensating material and moral damage inflicted on a person.

Article 31
(1) Every person shall be presumed innocent until proven guilty according to the procedure established by law and until declared guilty by an effective court sentence.
(2) Every indicted person shall have the right to a fair and public hearing by an independent and impartial court. Persons cannot be compelled to give evidence against themselves or against their family members or close relatives.
(3) Punishments may only be administered or applied on the basis of law.
(4) No person may be punished for the same offence twice.
(5) From the moment of arrest or first interrogation, persons suspected or accused of a crime shall be guaranteed the right to defence and legal counsel.

Article 32
(1) Citizens may move and choose their place of residence in Lithuania freely, and may leave Lithuania at their own will.
(2) This right may not be restricted except as provided by law and if it is necessary for the protection of State security or the health of the people, or to administer justice.
(3) A citizen may not be prohibited from returning to Lithuania.
(4) Every Lithuanian person may settle in Lithuania.

Article 33
(1) Citizens shall have the right to participate in the government of their State both directly and through their freely elected representatives, and shall have the equal opportunity to serve in a State office of the Republic of Lithuania.
(2) Each citizen shall be guaranteed the right to criticize the work of State institutions and their

officers, and to appeal against their decisions. It shall be prohibited to persecute people for criticism.
(3) Citizens shall be guaranteed the right to petition; the procedure for implementing this right shall be established by law.

Article 34
(1) Citizens who, on the day of election, are 18 years of age or over, shall have the right to vote in the election.
(2) The right to be elected shall be established by the Constitution of the Republic of Lithuania and by the election laws.
(3) Citizens who are declared legally incapable by court shall not participate in elections.

Article 35
(1) Citizens shall be guaranteed the right to freely form societies, political parties, and associations, provided that the aims and activities thereof do not contradict the Constitution and laws.
(2) No person may be forced to belong to any society, political party, or association.
(3) The founding and functioning of political parties and other political and public organization shall be regulated by law.

Article 36
(1) Citizens may not be prohibited or hindered from assembling in unarmed peaceful meetings.
(2) This right may not be subjected to any restrictions except those which are provided by law and are necessary to protect the security of the State or the community, public order, people's health or morals, or the rights and freedoms of other persons.

Article 37
Citizens who belong to ethnic communities shall have the right to foster their language, culture, and customs.

CHAPTER 3 SOCIETY AND THE STATE

Article 38
(1) The family shall be the basis of society and the State.
(2) Family, motherhood, fatherhood, and childhood shall be under the care and protection of the State.
(3) Marriage shall be entered into upon the free consent of man and woman.
(4) The State shall register marriages, births, and deaths. The State shall also recognize marriages registered in church.
(5) In the family, spouses shall have equal rights.
(6) The right and duty of parents is to bring up their children to be honest individuals and loyal citizens, as well as to support them until they come of age.
(7) The duty of children is to respect their parents, to care for them in old age, and to preserve their heritage.

Article 39
(1) The State shall take care of families bringing up children at home, and shall render them support in the manner established by law.
(2) The law shall provide for paid maternity leave before and after childbirth, as well as for favorable working conditions and other privileges.
(3) Children who are under age shall be protected by law.

Article 40
(1) State and local government establishments of teaching and education shall be secular. At the request of parents, they shall offer classes in religious instruction.
(2) Non-governmental teaching and educational institutions may be established according to the procedure established by law.
(3) Institutions of higher learning shall be granted autonomy.
(4) The State shall supervise the activities of establishments of teaching and education.

Article 41
(1) Education shall be compulsory for persons under the age of 16.
(2) Education at State and local government secondary, vocational, and higher schools shall be free of charge.
(3) Everyone shall have an equal opportunity to attain higher education according to their individual abilities. Citizens who demonstrate suitable academic progress shall be guaranteed education at establishments of higher education free of charge.

Article 42
(1) Culture, science, research and teaching shall be unrestricted.
(2) The State shall support culture and science, and shall be concerned with the protection of Lithuanian history, art, and other cultural monuments and valuables.
(3) The law shall protect and defend the spiritual and material interests of authors which are related to scientific, technical, cultural, and artistic work.

Article 43
(1) The State shall recognize traditional Lithuanian churches and religious organizations, as well as other churches and religious organizations provided that they have a basis in society and their teaching and rituals do not contradict morality or the law.
(2) Churches and religious organizations recognized by the State shall have the rights of legal persons.
(3) Churches and religious organizations shall freely proclaim the teaching of their faith, perform the rituals of their belief, and have houses of prayer, charity institutions, and educational institutions for the training of priests of their faith.
(4) Churches and religious organizations shall function freely according to their canons and statutes.
(5) The status of churches and other religious organizations in the State shall be established by agreement or by law.
(6) The teachings proclaimed by churches and other religious organizations, other religious activities, and houses of prayer may not be used for purposes which contradict the Constitution and the law.
(7) There shall not be a State religion in Lithuania.

Article 44
(1) Censorship of mass media shall be prohibited.
(2) The State, political parties, political and public organizations, and other institutions or persons may not monopolize means of mass media.

Article 45
Ethnic communities of citizens shall independently administer the affairs of their ethnic culture, education, organizations, charity, and mutual assistance. The State shall support ethnic communities.

CHAPTER 4 NATIONAL ECONOMY AND LABOR

Article 46
(1) Lithuania's economy shall be based on the right to private ownership, freedom of individual economic activity, and initiative.
(2) The State shall support economic efforts and initiative which are useful to the community.
(3) The State shall regulate economic activity so that it serves the general welfare of the people.
(4) The law shall prohibit monopolization of production and the market, and shall protect freedom of fair competition.
(5) The State shall defend the interests of the consumers.

Article 47
(1) Land, internal waters, forests, and parks may only belong to the citizens and the State of the Republic of Lithuania by the right of ownership.
(2) Plots of land may belong to a foreign state by the right of ownership for the establishment of its diplomatic and consular missions in accordance with the procedure and conditions established by law.
(3) The right of ownership of entrails of the earth, as well as nationally significant internal waters, forests, parks, roads, and historical, archaeological and cultural facilities shall exclusively belong to the Republic of Lithuania
(4) The Republic of Lithuania shall have the exclusive ownership right to the air-space over its territory, its continental shelf, and the economic zone in the Baltic Sea.

Article 48
(1) Every person may freely choose an occupation or business, and shall have the right to adequate, safe and healthy working conditions, adequate compensation for work, and social security in the event of unemployment.
(2) The employment of foreigners in the Republic of Lithuania shall be regulated by law.
(3) Forced labor shall be prohibited.
(4) Military service or alternative service, as well as labor which is executed during war, natural calamity, epidemic, or other urgent circumstances, shall not be deemed as forced labor.
(5) Labor which is performed by convicts in places of confinement and which is regulated by law shall not be deemed as forced labor either.

Article 49
(1) Every person shall have the right to rest and leisure, as well as to annual paid holidays.
(2) Working hours shall be established by law.

Article 50
(1) Trade unions shall be freely established and shall function independently. They shall defend the professional, economic, and social rights and interests of employees.
(2) All trade unions shall have equal rights.

Article 51
(1) Employees shall have the right to strike in order to protect their economic and social interests.
(2) The restrictions of this right, and the conditions and procedures for the implementation thereof shall be established by law.

Article 52
The State shall guarantee the right of citizens to old age and disability pension, as well as to social assistance in the event of unemployment, sickness, widowhood, loss of breadwinner, and other cases provided by law.

Article 53
(1) The State shall take care of people's health and shall guarantee medical aid and services in the event of sickness. The procedure for providing medical aid to citizens free of charge at State medical facilities shall be established by law.
(2) The State shall promote physical culture of the society and shall support sports.
(3) The State and each individual must protect the environment from harmful influences.

Article 54
(1) The State shall concern itself with the protection of the natural environment, its fauna and flora, separate objects of nature and particularly valuable districts, and shall supervise the moderate utilization of natural resources as well as their restoration and augmentation.
(2) The exhaustion of land and entrails of the earth, the pollution of waters and air, the production of radioactive impact, as well as the impoverishment of fauna and flora, shall be prohibited by law.

CHAPTER 5 THE PARLIAMENT

Article 55
(1) The Parliament shall consist of 141 Parliament members -
- representatives of the People, who shall be elected for a four-year term on the basis of universal, equal, and direct suffrage by secret ballot.
(2) The Parliament shall be deemed elected when at least three-fifths of the Parliament members have been elected.
(3) The electoral procedure shall be established by law.

Article 56
(1) Any citizen of the Republic of Lithuania who is not bound by an oath or pledge to a foreign state, and who, on the election day, is 25 years of age or over and has permanently been residing in Lithuania, may be elected a Parliament member.
(2) Persons who have not served their court-imposed sentence, as well as persons declared legally incapable by court, may not be elected members of the Parliament.

Article 57
Regular elections to the Parliament shall be held no earlier than 2 months, and no later than 1 month, prior to the expiration of the powers of the Parliament members.

Article 58
(1) Pre-term elections to the Parliament may be held on the decision of the Parliament adopted by three-fifths majority vote of all the Parliament members.
(2) The President of the Republic of Lithuania may also announce pre-term elections to the Parliament:
1) if the Parliament fails to adopt a decision on the new program of the Government within 30 days of its presentation, or if the Parliament twice in succession disapproves of the Government program within 60 days of its initial presentation; or
2) on the proposal of the Government, if the Parliament expresses direct non-confidence in the Government.
(3) The President of the Republic may not announce pre-term elections to the Parliament if the term of office of the President of the Republic expires within less than six months, or if six months have not passed since the pre-term elections to the Parliament.
(4) The day of elections to the new Parliament shall be specified in the resolution of the Parliament or in the decree of the President of the Republic concerning the pre-term elections to the Parliament. The election to the new Parliament must be organized within three months from the adoption of the decision on the pre-term elections.

Article 59

(1) The term of office of Parliament members shall commence from the day that the newly-elected Parliament convenes for the first sitting. The powers of the previously elected Parliament members shall expire as from the opening of the sitting.
(2) Newly-elected Parliament members shall acquire all the rights of a People's representative only after swearing in the Parliament to be loyal to the Republic of Lithuania.
(3) Parliament members who either do not take an oath in the manner prescribed by law, or who take a conditional oath, shall lose the mandate of a Parliament member. The Parliament shall adopt a corresponding resolution thereon.
(4) In office, Parliament members shall act in accordance with the Constitution of the Republic of Lithuania, the interests of the State, as well as their own consciences, and may not be restricted by any mandates.

Article 60

(1) The duties of Parliament members, with the exception of their duties in the Parliament, shall be incompatible with any other duties in State institutions or organizations, as well as with work in trade, commercial and other private institutions or enterprises. For term of office, Parliament members shall be exempt from the duty to perform national defence service.
(2) A Parliament member may be appointed only as Prime Minister or Minister.
(3) The service of a Parliament member shall be remunerated, and all expenses incurred from parliamentary activities shall be reimbursed with funds from the State Budget. A Parliament member may not receive any other salary, with the exception of payment for creative activities.
(4) The duties, rights and guarantees of the activities of Parliament members shall be established by law.

Article 61

(1) Parliament members shall have the right to submit inquiries to the Prime Minister, the individual Ministers, and the heads of other State institutions formed or elected by the Parliament. Said persons or bodies must respond orally or in writing at the Parliaments session in the manner established by the Parliament.
(2) At sessions of the Parliament, a group of no less than one-fifth of the Parliament members may interpellate the Prime Minister or a Minister.
(3) Upon considering the response of the Prime Minister or Minister to the interpellation, the Parliament may decide that the response is not satisfactory, and, by a majority vote of half of all the Parliament members, express non-confidence in the Prime Minister or a Minister.
(4) The voting procedure shall be established by law.

Article 62

(1) The person of a Parliament member shall be inviolable.
(2) Parliament members may not be found criminally responsible, may not be arrested, and may not be subjected to any other restriction of personal freedom without the consent of the Parliament.
(3) Parliament members may not be persecuted for voting or speeches in the Parliament. However, legal actions may be instituted against Parliament members according to the general procedure if they are guilty of personal insult or slander.

Article 63

The powers of a Parliament member shall be terminated:
1) on the expiration of the term of his or her powers, or when the Parliament, elected in pre-term elections, convenes for the first sitting;
2) upon his or her death;
3) upon his or her resignation;
4) when he or she is declared legally incapable by the court;

5) when the Parliament revokes his or her mandate in accordance with impeachment proceedings;
6) when the election is recognized as invalid, or if the law on election is grossly violated;
7) if he or she takes up, or does not resign from, employment which is incompatible with the duties of a Parliament member; and
8) if he or she loses citizenship of the Republic of Lithuania.

Article 64
(1) Every year, the Parliament shall convene for two regular sessions - one in spring and one in fall. The spring session shall commence on March 10th and shall end on June 30th. The fall session shall commence on September 10th and shall end on December 23rd. The Parliament may resolve to prolong a session.
(2) Extraordinary sessions shall be convened by the Parliament Chairperson upon the proposal of at least one-third of all the Parliament members, and, in cases provided for in the Constitution, by the President of the Republic.

Article 65
The President of the Republic shall convene the first sitting of the newly-elected Parliament which must be held within 15 days of the Parliament election. If the President of the Republic fails to convene the sitting of the Parliament, the members of the Parliament shall assemble the day following the expiration of the 15-day period.

Article 66
(1) The Chairperson or Assistant Chairperson of the Parliament shall preside over sittings of the Parliament.
(2) The sitting directly following elections of the Parliament shall be opened by the eldest member of the Parliament.

Article 67
The Parliament shall:
1) consider and enact amendments to the Constitution;
2) enact laws;
3) adopt resolutions for the organization of referendums;
4) announce presidential elections of the Republic of Lithuania;
5) form State institutions provided by law, and shall appoint and dismiss their chief officers;
6) approve or reject the candidature of the Prime Minister proposed by the President of the Republic;
7) consider the program of the Government submitted by the Prime Minister, and decide whether to approve it or not;
8) upon the recommendation of the Government, establish or abolish ministries of the Republic of Lithuania;
9) supervise the activities of the Government, and may express non-confidence in the Prime Minister or individual Ministers;
10) appoint judges to, and Chairpersons of, the Constitutional Court and the Supreme Court;
11) appoint to, and dismiss from, office the State Controller as well as the Chairperson of the Board of the Bank of Lithuania;
12) announce local government Council election;
13) form the Central Electoral Committee and change its composition;
14) approve the State Budget and supervise the implementation thereof;
15) establish State taxes and other obligatory payments;
16) ratify or denounce international treaties whereto the Republic of Lithuania is a party, and consider other issues of foreign policy;
17) establish administrative divisions of the Republic;

18) establish State awards of the Republic of Lithuania;
19) issue acts of amnesty; and
20) impose direct administration and martial law, declare states of emergency, announce mobilization, and adopt decisions to use the Armed Forces.

Article 68
(1) The right of legislative initiative in the Parliament shall belong to the members of the Parliament, the President of the Republic, and the Government.
(2) Citizens of the Republic of Lithuania shall also have the right of legislative initiative. A draft law may be submitted to the Parliament by 50,000 citizens of the Republic of Lithuania who have the right to vote. The Parliament must consider this draft law.

Article 69
(1) Laws shall be enacted in the Parliament in accordance with the procedure established by law.
(2) Laws shall be deemed adopted if the majority of the Parliament members participating in the sitting vote in favor thereof.
(3) Constitutional laws of the Republic of Lithuania shall be deemed adopted if more than half of all the members of the Parliament vote in the affirmative. Constitutional laws shall be amended by at least a three-fifths majority vote of all the Parliament members. The Parliament shall establish a list of constitutional laws by a three-fifths majority vote of the Parliament members.
(4) Provisions of the laws of the Republic of Lithuania may also be adopted by referendum.

Article 70
(1) The laws enacted by the Parliament shall be enforced after the signing and official promulgation thereof by the President of the Republic, unless the laws themselves establish a later enforcement date.
(2) Other acts adopted by the Parliament and the Statute of the Parliament shall be signed by the Chairperson of the Parliament. Said acts shall become effective the day following the promulgation thereof, unless the acts themselves provide for another procedure of enforcement.

Article 71
(1) Within ten days of receiving a law passed by the Parliament, the President of the Republic shall either sign and officially promulgate said law, or shall refer it back to the Parliament together with relevant reasons for reconsideration.
(2) In the event that the law enacted by the Parliament is not referred back or signed by the President of the Republic within the established period, the law shall become effective upon the signing and official promulgation thereof by the Chairperson of the Parliament.
(3) The President of the Republic must, within five days, sign and officially promulgate laws and other acts adopted by referendum.
(4) In the event that the President of the Republic does not sign and promulgate such laws within the established period. said laws shall become effective upon being signed and officially promulgated by the Chairperson of the Parliament.

Article 72
(1) The Parliament may reconsider and enact laws which have been referred back by the President of the Republic.
(2) After reconsideration by the Parliament, a law shall be deemed enacted if the amendments and supplements submitted by the President of the Republic were adopted, or if more than half of all the Parliament members vote in the affirmative, and if it is a constitutional law - if at least three-fifths of all the Parliament members vote in the affirmative.
(3) The President of the Republic must, within three days, sign and forthwith officially promulgate laws re-enacted by the Parliament.

Article 73
(1) Parliament controllers shall examine complaints of citizens concerning the abuse of powers by, and bureaucracy of, State and local government officers (with the exception of judges). Controllers shall have the right to submit proposals to the court to dismiss guilty officers from their posts.
(2) The powers of the Parliament controllers shall be established by law.
(3) As necessary, the Parliament shall also establish other institutions of control. The system and powers of said institutions shall be established by law.

Article 74
For gross violation of the Constitution, breach of oath, or upon the disclosure of the commitment of felony, the Parliament may, by three-fifths majority vote of all the Parliament members, remove from office the President of the Republic, the Chairperson and judges of the Constitutional Court, the Chairperson and judges of the Supreme Court, the Chairperson and judges of the Court of Appeals, as well as Parliament members, or may revoke their mandate of a Parliament member. Such actions shall be carried out in accordance with impeachment proceedings which shall be established by the Statute of the Parliament.

Article 75
Officers appointed or chosen by the Parliament (with the exception of persons specified in Article 74) shall be removed from office when the Parliament, by majority vote of all the members, expresses non-confidence in the officer in question.

Article 76
The structure and procedure of activities of the Parliament shall be determined by the Statute of the Parliament. The Statute of the Parliament shall have the power of law.

CHAPTER 6 THE PRESIDENT OF THE REPUBLIC

Article 77
(1) The President of the Republic is the Head of State.
(2) The President shall represent the State of Lithuania and shall perform all the duties which he or she is charged with by the Constitution and laws.

Article 78
(1) Any person who is a citizen of the Republic of Lithuania by birth, who has lived in Lithuania for at least the past three years, who has reached the age of 40 prior to the election day, and who is eligible for election to a Parliament member may be elected President of the Republic.
(2) The President of the Republic shall be elected by the citizens of the Republic of Lithuania on the basis of universal, equal, and direct suffrage by secret ballot for a term of five years.
(3) The same person may not be elected President of the Republic of Lithuania for more than two consecutive terms.

Article 79
(1) Any citizen who meets the requirements set forth in Article 78 (1) and has collected the signatures of at least 20,000 voters shall be registered as a presidential candidate.
(2) The number of presidential candidates shall not be limited.

Article 80
Regular presidential elections shall be held on the last Sunday two months before the expiration of the term of office of the President of the Republic.

Article 81
(1) The candidate for the post of President of the Republic who, during the first election round in which at least a half of the voters participate, receives the votes of more than half of all the voters who voted in the election, shall be deemed the elected candidate. If less than a half of the registered voters participate in the election, the candidate who receives the greatest number of votes, but no less than one-third of votes of all the voters, shall be deemed the elected candidate. If, during the first election round, no single candidate gets the requisite number of votes, a repeat election shall be organized after two weeks between the two candidates who received the greatest number of votes. The candidate who receives more votes thereafter shall be deemed elected.
(2) If no more than two candidates take part in the first election round, and not one of them receives the requisite number of votes, a repeat election shall be held.

Article 82
(1) The elected President of the Republic shall begin his duties on the day following the expiration of the term of office of the President of the Republic, after, in Vilnius and in the presence of the representatives of the People - members of the Parliament, taking an oath to the People, swearing to be loyal to the Republic of Lithuania and the Constitution, to conscientiously fulfill the duties of President, and to be equally just to all. The President of the Republic, upon being re-elected, shall take the oath as well.
(2) The act of oath of the President of the Republic shall be signed by the President and by the Chairperson of the Constitutional Court, or, in the absence of the Chairperson, by a judge of the Constitutional Court.

Article 83
(1) The President of the Republic may not be a member of the Parliament or hold any other office, and may not receive any remuneration other than the salary established for the President as well as compensation for creative activities.
(2) A person elected President of the Republic must suspend his or her activities in political parties and political organizations until a new presidential election campaign begins.

Article 84
The President of the Republic shall:
1) settle basic foreign policy issues and, together with the Government, implement foreign policy;
2) sign international treaties of the Republic of Lithuania and submit them to the Parliament for ratification;
3) appoint or recall, upon the recommendation of the Government, diplomatic representatives of the Republic of Lithuania in foreign states and international organizations; receive letters of credence and recall of diplomatic representatives of foreign states; confer highest diplomatic ranks and special titles;
4) appoint, upon approval of the Parliament, the Prime Minister, charge him or her to form the Government, and approve its composition;
5) remove, upon approval of the Parliament, the Prime Minister from office;
6) accept the powers returned by the Government upon the election of a new Parliament, and charge it to continue exercising its functions until a new Government is formed;
7) accept resignations of the Government and, as necessary, charge it to continue exercising its functions or charge one of the Ministers to exercise the functions of the Prime Minister until a new Government is formed; accept resignations of individual Ministers and commission them to continue in office until a new Minister is appointed;
8) submit to the Parliament, upon the resignation of the Government or after it returns its powers and no later than within 15 days, the candidature of a new Prime Minister for consideration;
9) appoint or dismiss individual Ministers upon the recommendation of the Prime Minister;
10) appoint or dismiss, according to the established procedure, state officers provided by law;

11) propose Supreme Court judge candidates to the Parliament, and, upon the appointment of all the Supreme Court judges, recommend from among them a Supreme Court Chairperson to the Parliament; appoint, with the approval of the Parliament, Court of Appeal judges, and from among them - the Court of Appeal Chairperson; appoint judges and chairpersons of district and local district courts, and change their places of office; in cases provided by Law, propose the dismissal of judges to the Parliament;
12) propose to the Parliament the candidatures of three Constitutional Court judges, and, upon appointing all the judges of the Constitutional Court, propose, from among them, a candidate for Constitutional Court Chairperson to the Parliament;
13) propose to the Parliament candidates for State Controller and Chairperson of the Board of the Bank of Lithuania; if necessary, propose to the Parliament to express non-confidence in said officials;
14) appoint or dismiss, upon the approval of the Parliament, the chief commander of the Army and the head of the Security Service; 15) confer highest military ranks;
16) adopt, in the event of an armed attack which threatens State sovereignty or territorial integrity, decisions concerning defence against such armed aggression, the imposition of martial law, and mobilization, and submit these decisions to the next sitting of the Parliament for approval;
17) declare states of emergency according to the procedures and situations established by law, and submit these decisions to the next sitting of the Parliament for approval;
18) make annual reports in the Parliament about the situation in Lithuania and the domestic and foreign policies of the Republic of Lithuania;
19) call, in cases provided in the Constitution, extraordinary sessions of the Parliament;
20) announce regular elections to the Parliament, and, in cases set forth in Article 58 (2), announce pre-term elections to the Parliament;
21) grant citizenship of the Republic of Lithuania according to the procedure established by law;
22) confer State awards;
23) grant pardons to sentenced persons; and
24) sign and promulgate laws enacted by the Parliament or refer them back to the Parliament according to the procedure provided for in Article 71.

Article 85
The President of the Republic, implementing the powers vested in him or her, shall issue acts-decrees. Decrees of the President, specified in Article 84 Nr. 3 & 15 & 17 & 21, shall be valid only if they bear the signature of the Prime Minister or an appropriate Minister. Responsibility for such decrees shall lie with the Prime Minister or the Minister who signed it.

Article 86
(1) The person of the President of the Republic shall be inviolable: while in office, the President may neither be arrested nor charged with criminal or administrative proceedings.
(2) The President of the Republic may be prematurely removed from office only for gross violation of the Constitution, breach of the oath of office, or conviction of an offence. The Parliament shall resolve issues concerning the dismissal of the President of the Republic from office according to impeachment proceedings.

Article 87
(1) When, in cases specified in Article 58 (2), the President of the Republic announces pre-term elections to the Parliament, the newly-elected Parliament may, by three-fifths majority vote of all the Parliament members and within 30 days of the first sitting, announce a pre-term election of the President of the Republic.
(2) If the President of the Republic wishes to compete in the election, he or she shall immediately be registered as a candidate.
(3) If the President of the Republic is re-elected in such an election, he or she shall be deemed elected for a second term, provided that more than three years of the first term had expired prior

to the election. If the expired period of the first term is less than three years, the President of the Republic shall only be elected for the remainder of the first term, which shall not be considered a second term.
(4) If a pre-term election for the President of the Republic is announced during the President's second term, the current President of the Republic may only be elected for the remainder of the second term.

Article 88
The powers of the President of the Republic shall be terminated:
1) upon the expiration of the term of office;
2) upon holding a pre-term presidential election;
3) upon resignation from office;
4) upon the death of the President of the Republic;
5) when the Parliament removes the President from office according to impeachment proceedings; and
6) when the Parliament, taking into consideration the conclusion of the Constitutional Court and by three-fifths majority vote of all the Parliament members, adopts a resolution stating that the President of the Republic is unable to fulfill the duties of office for reasons of health.

Article 89
(1) In the event that the President dies or is removed from office according to impeachment proceedings, or if the Parliament resolves that the President of the Republic is unable to fulfill the duties of office for reasons of health, the duties of President shall temporarily be passed over to the Parliament Chairperson. In such a case, the Chairperson of the Parliament shall lose his or her powers in the Parliament, and at the behest of the Parliament, the duties of Chairperson shall temporarily be carried out by the Assistant Chairperson. In said cases, the Parliament shall announce, within 10 days, an election for the President of the Republic which must be held within two months. If the Parliament cannot convene and announce the election for the President of the Republic, the election shall be announced by the Government.
(2) The Chairperson of the Parliament shall act for the President of the Republic when the President is temporarily absent beyond the boundaries of the country or has fallen ill and by reason thereof is temporarily unable to fulfill the duties of office.
(3) While temporarily acting for the President of the Republic, the Chairperson of the Parliament may neither announce pre-term elections of the Parliament nor dismiss or appoint Ministers without the agreement of the Parliament. During the said period, the Parliament may not consider the issue of lack of confidence in the Chairperson of the Parliament.
(4) The powers of the President of the Republic may not be executed in any other cases, or by any other persons or institutions.

Article 90
The President of the Republic shall have residence. The financing of the President of the Republic and of the President's residence shall be established by law.

CHAPTER 7 THE GOVERNMENT OF THE REPUBLIC OF LITHUANIA

Article 91
The Government of the Republic of Lithuania shall consist of the Prime Minister and Ministers.

Article 92
(1) The Prime Minister shall, with the approval of the Parliament, be appointed or dismissed by the President of the Republic. The Ministers shall be appointed by the President of the Republic on the nomination of the Prime Minister.
(2) The Prime Minister, within 15 days of being appointed, shall present the Government which he

or she has formed and which has been approved by the President of the Republic to the Parliament and shall submit the program of its activities to the Parliament for consideration.
(3) The Government shall return its powers to the President of the Republic after the Parliament elections or upon electing the President of the Republic.
(4) A new Government shall be empowered to act after the Parliament approves its program by majority vote of the Parliament members participating in the sitting.

Article 93
On entering upon their duties, the Prime Minister and the individual Ministers shall, in the Parliament, take an oath to be loyal to the Republic of Lithuania and to observe the Constitution and laws. The text of the oath shall be established by the Law on the Government.

Article 94
The Government of the Republic of Lithuania shall:
1) administer the affairs of the country, protect the inviolability of the territory of the Republic of Lithuania, and ensure State security and public order;
2) implement laws and resolutions of the Parliament concerning the implementation of laws, as well as the decrees of the President;
3) Coordinate the activities of the ministries and other governmental institutions;
4) prepare the draft Budget of the State and submit it to the Parliament; execute the State Budget and report on the fulfillment of the Budget to the Parliament;
5) draft bills and submit them to the Parliament for consideration;
6) establish diplomatic relations and maintain relations with foreign countries and international organizations; and
7) discharge other duties prescribed to the Government by the Constitution and other laws.

Article 95
(1) The Government of the Republic of Lithuania shall resolve the affairs of State administration at its sittings by issuing directives which must be passed by a majority vote of all members of the Government. The State Controller may also participate in the sittings of the Government.
(2) Government directives shall be signed by the Prime Minister and the appropriate Minister.

Article 96
(1) The Government of the Republic of Lithuania shall be jointly responsible to the Parliament for the general activities of the Government.
(2) The Ministers, in directing the spheres of administration entrusted to them, shall be responsible to the Parliament, the President of the Republic, and directly subordinate to the Prime Minister.

Article 97
(1) The Prime Minister shall represent the Government of the Republic of Lithuania and shall direct its activities.
(2) In the absence of the Prime Minister, or when the Prime Minister is unable to fulfill his or her duties, the President of the Republic of Lithuania, upon the recommendation of the Prime Minister, shall charge one of the Ministers to substitute for the Prime Minister during a period not exceeding 60 days; when there is no recommendation, the President of the Republic shall charge one of the Ministers to substitute for the Prime Minister.

Article 98
(1) Ministers shall head their respective ministries, shall resolve issues assigned to the competence of their ministries, and shall also discharge other functions prescribed by laws.
(2) A Minister may be temporarily substituted only by another member of the Government appointed by the Prime Minister.

Article 99
The Prime Minister and Ministers may not hold any other office subject to nomination or election, may not be employed in business, commercial or other private institutions or companies, and may not receive any remuneration other than the salary established for their respective Government offices and compensation for creative activities.

Article 100
The Prime Minister and Ministers may not be prosecuted, arrested or have their freedoms restricted in any other way without the preliminary consent of the Parliament, or, if the Parliament is not in session, of the President of the Republic.

Article 101
(1) Upon the request of the Parliament, the Government or individual Ministers must give an account of their activities to the Parliament.
(2) When more than half of the Ministers are changed, the Government must be re-invested with authority by the Parliament. Otherwise, the Government must resign.
(3) The Government must also resign if:
1) the Parliament disapproves two times in succession of the program of the newly-formed Government;
2) the majority of all the Parliament deputies express a lack of confidence in the Government or in the Prime Minister in a secret ballot vote;
3) the Prime Minister resigns or dies; or
4) after Parliament elections, when a new Government is formed.
(4) A Minister must resign if more than a half of all the Parliament members express, in a secret ballot vote, a lack of confidence in him or her.
(5) The President of the Republic shall accept resignations of the Government or individual Ministers.

CHAPTER 8 THE CONSTITUTIONAL COURT

Article 102
(1) The Constitutional Court shall decide whether the laws and other legal acts adopted by the Parliament are in conformity with the Constitution and legal acts adopted by the President and the Government, do not violate the Constitution or laws.
(2) The status of the Constitutional Court and the procedure for the execution of powers thereof shall be established by the Law on the Constitutional Court of the Republic of Lithuania.

Article 103
(1) The Constitutional Court shall consist of 9 judges appointed for an non-renewable term of 9 years. Every three years, one-third of the Constitutional Court shall be reconstituted. The Parliament shall choose 3 candidates for Constitutional Court judges from the candidates nominated by the President of the Republic of Lithuania, 3 candidates from those nominated by the Chairperson of the Parliament, and 3 candidates from those nominated by the Chairperson of the Supreme Court; the Parliament shall appoint the candidates that they choose as judges.
(2) The Parliament shall appoint the Chairperson of the Constitutional Court from among the judges thereof and on the nomination of the President of the Republic of Lithuania.
(3) Citizens of the Republic of Lithuania who have an impeccable reputation, who are trained in law, and who have served, for at least 10 years, in the legal profession or in an area of education related to his or her qualifications as a lawyer, shall be eligible for appointment as judges of the Constitutional Court.

Article 104
(1) In fulfilling their duties, judges of the Constitutional Court shall act independently of any other

State institution, person or organization and shall observe only the Constitution of the Republic of Lithuania.
(2) Before entering office, judges of the Constitutional Court shall, in the Parliament, swear to be faithful to the Republic of Lithuania and the Constitution.
(3) The restrictions on work and political activities which are imposed on court judges shall also apply to judges of the Constitutional Court.
(4) Judges of the Constitutional Court shall have the same rights concerning the inviolability of their person as shall members of the Parliament.

Article 105
(1) The Constitutional Court shall consider and adopt decisions concerning the conformity of laws of the Republic of Lithuania and legal acts adopted by the Parliament with the Constitution of the Republic of Lithuania.
(2) The Constitutional Court shall also consider the conformity with the Constitution of:
1) legal acts of the President; and
2) legal acts of the Government.
(3) The Constitutional Court shall present conclusions concerning:
1) the violation of election laws during presidential elections or elections to the Parliament;
2) whether the President of the Republic of Lithuania's health is not limiting his or her capacity to continue in office;
3) the conformity of international agreements of the Republic of Lithuania with the Constitution; and
4) the compliance with the Constitution of concrete actions of Parliament members or other State officers against whom impeachment proceedings have been instituted.

Article 106
(1) The Government, no less than 1/5 of the members of the Parliament, and the courts shall have the right to address the Constitutional Court concerning legal acts specified in Article 105 (1).
(2) No less than 1/5 of the members of the Parliament and the courts shall have the right to address the Constitutional Court concerning the conformity of acts of the President with the Constitution and the laws.
(3) No less than 1/5 of the members of the Parliament, the courts, and the President of the Republic of Lithuania shall have the right to address the Constitutional Court concerning the conformity of an act of the Government with the Constitution and the laws.
(4) Upon the proposal of the President or the decision of the Parliament to investigate the conformity of an act with the Constitution, the applicability of the act shall be suspended.
(5) The Parliament may request a conclusion from the Constitutional Court, and in cases concerning Parliament elections and international agreements, the President of the Republic of Lithuania may also request a conclusion.
(6) The Constitutional Court shall have the right to refuse to accept cases for investigation or to prepare conclusions if the appeal is not based on legal motives.

Article 107
(1) Laws (or parts thereof) of the Republic of Lithuania or any other acts (or parts thereof) of the Parliament, acts of the President of the Republic of Lithuania, and acts (or parts thereof) of the Government may not be applied from the day of official promulgation of the decision of the Constitutional Court that the act in question (or part thereof) is inconsistent with the Constitution of the Republic of Lithuania.
(2) The decisions of the Constitutional Court on issues assigned to its jurisdiction by the Constitution shall be final and may not be appealed.
(3) On the basis of the conclusions of the Constitutional Court, the Parliament shall have a final decision on the issues set forth in Article 105 (3).

Article 108
The powers of a judge of the Constitutional Court shall be terminated:
1) on the expiration of the term of office;
2) upon the death of the judge;
3) upon voluntary resignation;
4) when the judge is incapable to fulfill his or her duties for health reasons; and
5) upon being removed from office by the Parliament according to the impeachment proceedings.

CHAPTER 9 THE COURTS

Article 109
(1) In the Republic of Lithuania, the courts shall have the exclusive right to administer justice.
(2) While administering justice, judges, and courts shall be independent.
(3) While investigating cases, judges shall obey only the law.
(4) The court shall adopt decisions on behalf of the Republic of Lithuania.

Article 110
(1) Judges may not apply laws which contradict the Constitution.
(2) In cases, when there are grounds to believe that the law or other legal act applicable in a certain case contradicts the Constitution, the judge shall suspend the investigation and shall appeal to the Constitutional Court to decide whether the law or other legal act in question complies with the Constitution.

Article 111
(1) The court system of the Republic of Lithuania shall consist of the Supreme Court, the Court of Appeal, district courts, and local courts.
(2) For the investigation of administrative, labor, family and other litigations, specialized courts may be established pursuant to law.
(3) Courts with special powers may not be established in the Republic of Lithuania in times of peace.
(4) The formation and competence of courts shall be determined by the Law on Courts of the Republic of Lithuania.

Article 112
(1) In Lithuania only citizens of the Republic of Lithuania may be judges.
(2) Supreme Court judges, as well as the Chairperson of the Supreme Court, who shall be chosen from among them, shall be appointed and dismissed by the Parliament upon the recommendation of the President of the Republic of Lithuania.
(3) Judges of the Court of Appeals, as well as the Chairperson, who shall be chosen from among them, shall be appointed by the President of the Republic of Lithuania upon the approval of the Parliament.
(4) Judges and chairpersons of district courts, local courts, and other specialized courts shall be appointed, and if necessary, transferred to other places of office, by the President of the Republic of Lithuania.
(5) A special institution of judges provided by law shall submit recommendations to the President concerning the appointment of judges, as well as their promotion, transference, or dismissal from office.
(6) A person appointed as judge shall swear, according to the procedure established by law, to be faithful to the Republic of Lithuania and to administer justice only pursuant to law.

Article 113
(1) Judges may not hold any other elected or appointed posts, and may not be employed in any business, commercial, or other private institution or company. They are also not permitted to

receive any remuneration other than the salary established for judges as well as payments for educational, scientific, or creative activities.
(2) Judges may not participate in the activities of political parties and other political organizations.

Article 114
(1) Institutions of State power and administration, members of the Parliament and other officers, political parties, public organizations, and citizens shall be prohibited from interfering with the activities of a judge or the court, and violation of this shall incur liability.
(2) Judges may not have legal actions instituted against them, nor may they be arrested or restricted of personal freedom without the consent of the Parliament, or in the period between sessions of the Parliament, of the President of the Republic of Lithuania.

Article 115
Court judges of the Republic of Lithuania shall be dismissed from office according to the procedure established by law in the following cases:
1) at their own will;
2) upon expiration of their powers or upon reaching pensionable age as determined by law;
3) for reasons of health;
4) upon appointment to another office or upon voluntary transference to another place of office;
5) if their behavior discredits their position as judge; and
6) when judgment imposed on them by court comes into force.

Article 116
If the Chairperson or judges of the Supreme Court or of the Court of Appeals grossly violate the Constitution, break their oath, or are found guilty of an offence, the Parliament may remove them from office according to impeachment proceedings.

Article 117
(1) In all courts the investigation of cases shall be open to the public. Closed court sittings may be held in order to protect the secrecy of a citizen's or the citizen's family's private life, or to prevent the disclosure of State, professional, or commercial secrets.
(2) In the Republic of Lithuania court trials shall be conducted in the State language.
(3) Persons who do not speak Lithuanian shall be guaranteed the right to participate in investigation and court proceedings through an interpreter.

Article 118
(1) Public prosecutors shall prosecute criminal cases on behalf of the State, shall carry out criminal prosecutions, and shall supervise the activities of the interrogative bodies.
(2) Pretrial interrogation shall be carried out by investigators.
(3) The procedure for the appointment of public prosecutors and judges and their status shall be established by law.

CHAPTER 10 LOCAL GOVERNMENTS AND ADMINISTRATION

Article 119
(1) Administrative units provided by law on State territory shall be entitled to the right of self-government. This right shall be implemented through local government Councils.
(2) Members of local government Councils shall be elected for a two-year term on the basis of universal, equal and direct suffrage by secret ballot by the residents of their administrative unit who are citizens of the Republic of Lithuania.
(3) The procedure for the organization and activities of self-government institutions shall be established by law.

(4) Local government Councils shall form executive bodies which are accountable to them for the direct implementation of the laws of the Republic of Lithuania and the decisions of the Government and the local government Council.

Article 120
(1) The State shall support local governments.
(2) Local governments shall act freely and independently within the limits of their competence which shall be established by the Constitution and laws.

Article 121
(1) Local governments shall draft and approve their own Budget.
(2) Local government Councils shall have the right within the established limits and according to the procedure provided by law to establish local dues, and to provide for the leverage of taxes and duties at the expense of their own Budget.

Article 122
Local government Councils shall have the right to appeal to court regarding the violation of their rights.

Article 123
(1) In higher level administrative units, the administration shall be organized by the Government according to the procedure established by law.
(2) Representatives shall be appointed by the Government to supervise that the Constitution and the laws are observed, and that the decisions of the Government are implemented.
(3) The powers of Government representatives and the procedures of their implementation shall be established by law.
(4) In cases and according to procedures provided by law, the Parliament may introduce direct administration on local government territory.

Article 124
Deeds and actions of local government Councils as well as of their executive bodies and officers which violate the rights of citizens and organizations may be appealed against in court.

CHAPTER 11 FINANCES, STATE BUDGET

Article 125
(1) In the Republic of Lithuania the central bank shall be the Bank of Lithuania, which is owned by the State.
(2) The Bank of Lithuania shall have the exclusive right to issue bank notes.
(3) The procedures for the organization and activities of the Bank of Lithuania as well as its powers shall be established by law.

Article 126
(1) The Bank of Lithuania shall be directed by the Bank Board, which shall consist of the Board Chairperson, the deputies to the Chairperson, and the Board members.
(2) The Board Chairperson of the Bank of Lithuania shall be appointed for a five-year term by the Parliament on the nomination of the President of the Republic of Lithuania.

Article 127
(1) The Budgetary system of the Republic of Lithuania shall consist of the independent State Budget of the Republic of Lithuania and the independent local governments Budgets.
(2) State Budget revenues shall be accrued from taxes, compulsory payments, dues, receipts

from State property, and other income.
(3) Taxes, other Budgetary payments, and dues shall be established by the laws of the Republic of Lithuania.

Article 128
(1) Decisions concerning State loans and other basic property liabilities of the State shall be adopted by the Parliament on the recommendation of the Government.
(2) Procedures concerning the management, utilization, and disposal of State property shall be established by law.

Article 129
The Budget year shall begin on the first of January and shall end on the thirty-first of December.

Article 130
The Government of the Republic of Lithuania shall prepare a draft Budget of the State, and shall submit it to the Parliament no later than 75 days before the end of the Budget year.

Article 131
(1) The draft Budget of the State shall be considered by the Parliament, and shall be approved by law by the beginning of the new Budget year.
(2) Upon considering the draft Budget, the Parliament may only increase expenditures upon specifying financial sources for said expenditures. Expenditures established by law may not be reduced as long as said laws are not amended.

Article 132
(1) If the State Budget is not approved by the prescribed date, monthly Budget expenditures at the beginning of the Budget year may not exceed one-twelfth of the State Budget expenditures of the previous Budget year.
(2) During the Budget year the Parliament may change the Budget. It shall be changed according to the same procedure by which it was drafted, adopted and approved. As necessary, the Parliament may approve an additional Budget.

CHAPTER 12 CONTROL OF THE STATE

Article 133
(1) The system and powers of State Control shall be established by law.
(2) State control shall be directed by the State Controller who shall be appointed for a five-year term by the Parliament upon the nomination of the President of the Republic of Lithuania.
(3) Before taking office, the State Controller shall take an oath. The oath shall be established by law.

Article 134
(1) State control shall supervise the legality of the management and utilization of State property and the realization of the State Budget.
(2) The State Controller shall give an account to the Parliament on the annual execution of the State Budget.

CHAPTER 13 FOREIGN POLICY AND NATIONAL DEFENCE

Article 135
(1) In conducting foreign policy, the Republic of Lithuania shall pursue the universally recognized principles and norms of international law, shall strive to safeguard national security and

independence as well as the basic rights, freedoms and welfare of its citizens, and shall take part in the creation of sound international order based on law and justice.
(2) In the Republic of Lithuania, war propaganda shall be prohibited.

Article 136
The Republic of Lithuania shall participate in international organizations provided that they do not contradict the interests and independence of the State.

Article 137
Weapons of mass destruction and foreign military bases may not be stationed on the territory of the Republic of Lithuania.

Article 138
(1) The Parliament shall either ratify or denounce international treaties of the Republic of Lithuania which concern:
1) the realignment of the State borders of the Republic of Lithuania;
2) political cooperation with foreign countries, mutual assistance, or treaties related to national defence;
3) the renunciation of the utilization of, or threatening by, force, as well as peace treaties;
4) the stationing and status of the Armed Forces of the Republic of Lithuania on the territory of a foreign state;
5) the participation of Lithuania in universal or regional international organizations; and
6) multilateral or long-term economic agreements.
(2) Laws and international treaties may provide for other cases in which the Parliament shall ratify international treaties of the Republic of Lithuania.
(3) International agreements which are ratified by the Parliament of the Republic of Lithuania shall be the constituent part of the legal system of the Republic of Lithuania.

Article 139
(1) The defence of the state of Lithuania from foreign armed attack shall be the right and duty of every citizen of the Republic of Lithuania.
(2) Citizens of the Republic of Lithuania are obliged to serve in the national defence service or to perform alternative service in the manner established by law.
(3) The organization of national defence shall be established by laws.

Article 140
(1) The main issues of national defence shall be considered and coordinated by the State Defence Council which consists of the President of the Republic of Lithuania, the Prime Minister, the Parliament Chairperson, the Minister of National Defence, and the Chief Commander of the Army. The State Defence Council shall be headed by the President of the Republic of Lithuania. Procedures for its formation, activities and powers shall be established by law.
(2) The Chief Commander of the Armed Forces shall be the President of the Republic of Lithuania.
(3) The Government, the Minister of National Defence, and the Chief Commander of the Army shall be responsible to the Parliament for the provision and command of State Armed Forces. The Minister of National Defence may not be a serviceman who has not yet retired from active service.

Article 141
Soldiers in active military service or alternative service, officers of the national defence, the police and the internal service, non-commissioned officers, re-enlistees who have not retired from service, and other paid officers of military and security services may not be members of the Parliament or of local government Councils. They may not hold elected or appointed posts in

State civil service, and may not take part in the activities of political parties and political organizations.

Article 142
(1) The Parliament shall impose martial law, shall announce mobilization or demobilization, and shall adopt decisions to use the Armed Forces in defence of the homeland or for the fulfillment of the international obligations of Lithuania.
(2) In the event of an armed attack which threatens the sovereignty of the State or territorial integrity, the President of the Republic of Lithuania shall immediately pass a decision concerning defence against such armed aggression, shall impose martial law throughout the country or in separate parts thereof, shall declare mobilization, and shall submit these decisions to the next sitting of the Parliament; in the period between sessions, the President shall immediately convene an unscheduled session of the Parliament. The Parliament shall approve or abolish the decision of the President of the Republic of Lithuania.

Article 143
In the event that a regular election must be held in time of military actions, either the Parliament or the President shall adopt a decision to extend the terms of the Parliament, the President, and local government Councils. In such cases, elections must be held within three months of the end of the war.

Article 144
(1) In the event that the constitutional system or public order of the State is threatened, the Parliament may declare a state of emergency throughout the country, or in separate parts thereof, for a period not exceeding six months.
(2) In the event of emergency, and if the Parliament is not in session, the President of the Republic shall have the right to pass such a decision, and shall, at the same time, convene an unscheduled session of the Parliament for the consideration of this issue. The Parliament shall approve or abolish the decision of the President of the Republic of Lithuania.
(3) States of emergency shall be regulated by law.

Article 145
During martial law or a state of emergency, the rights and freedoms specified in Articles 22, 24, 25, 32, 35, and 36 may be temporarily restricted.

Article 146
(1) The State shall provide and care for soldiers whose health is damaged during military service, as well as for the families of soldiers who lose their lives during military service.
(2) The State shall also provide for citizens whose health is damaged while defending the homeland, and for the families of citizens who lose their lives in defence of the State.

CHAPTER 14 AMENDING THE CONSTITUTION

Article 147
(1) In order to amend or append the Constitution of the Republic of Lithuania, a proposal must be submitted to the Parliament by either no less than one-fourth of the members of the Parliament, or by at least 300,000 voters.
(2) During a state of emergency or martial law, amendments to the Constitution may not be made.

Article 148
(1) The provision of Article 1 that the State of Lithuania is an independent democratic republic

may only be amended by a referendum in which at least three-fourths of the electorate of Lithuania vote in favor thereof.
(2) The provisions of Chapter 1 and Chapter 14 may be amended only by referendum.
(3) Amendments of other chapters of the Constitution must be considered and voted upon in the Parliament twice. There must be a lapse of at least three months between each vote. Bills for constitutional amendments shall be deemed adopted by the Parliament if, in each of the votes, at least two-thirds of all the members of the Parliament vote in favor of the enactment.
(4) An amendment to the Constitution which is rejected by the Parliament may not be submitted to the Parliament for reconsideration for the period of one year.

Article 149
(1) The adopted law on an amendment to the Constitution shall be signed by the President of the Republic of Lithuania and officially promulgated within 5 days.
(2) If the President of the Republic of Lithuania does not sign and promulgate such a law in due time, this law shall become effective when the Chairperson of the Parliament signs and promulgates it.
(3) The law on an amendment to the Constitution shall become effective no earlier than one month after the adoption thereof.

CHAPTER 15 FINAL PROVISIONS

Article 150
(1) The constituent parts of the Constitution of the Republic of Lithuania shall be:
(2) The 11 Feb 1991 Constitutional Law *"On the State of Lithuania"*;
(3) The 8 June 1992 Constitutional Act *"On the Non-Alignment of the Republic of Lithuania with Post-Soviet Eastern Alliances"*.

Article 151
This Constitution of the Republic of Lithuania shall become effective the day following the official promulgation of the results of the Referendum, provided that in the Referendum more than half of the electorate of Lithuania voted in favor thereof.

Article 152
The procedure for the enforcement of this Constitution and separate provisions thereof shall be regulated by Law of the Republic of Lithuania *"On the Procedure for the Enforcement of the Constitution of the Republic of Lithuania"*, which, together with this Constitution of the Republic of Lithuania, shall be adopted by referendum.

Article 153
Upon the adoption of this Constitution in the Referendum, the Parliament of the Republic of Lithuania may, by 25 Oct 1993, amend by three-fifths majority vote of all the Parliament members the provisions of the Constitution of the Republic of Lithuania set forth in Articles 47, 55, 56, 58 (2) Nr. 2, 65, 68, 69, 84 Nr. 11 & 12, 87 (1), 96, 103, 118 and 119 (4).

Article 154
Upon their adoption by referendum, the Constitution of the Republic of Lithuania and the Law of the Republic of Lithuania *"On the Procedure for the Enforcement of the Constitution of the Republic of Lithuania"* shall be signed and promulgated within 15 days by the President of the Supreme Council of the Republic of Lithuania.

LITHUANIA FOREIGN POLICY

MINISTRY OF FOREIGN AFFAIRS

Linas Antanas Linkevičius

Linas Antanas Linkevičius (born 6 January 1961) is a Lithuanian politician of the Social Democratic Party.

Linkevičius served as minister of National Defence from 1993-1996 and 2000-2004. He was the Lithuanian Permanent Representative to NATO from 2005 until 2011. In December 2012 he was appointed minister of Foreign Affairs.

MISSION OF THE MINISTRY OF FOREIGN AFFAIRS

The Ministry of Foreign Affairs of the Republic of Lithuania is the main body of the Executive, responsible for the implementation of Lithuania's Foreign Policy and co-ordination of activities of other public institutions in this field. The Mission of the Ministry includes the representation of State interests in the international arena, based on foreign policy goals. In representing the national interests, the Ministry works to ensure maintenance of diplomatic relations with foreign countries, seek the integration of Lithuania into international political, economic and military structures and organisations, consolidate Lithuania's economic contacts abroad, promote export and investments, and form a positive image of Lithuania abroad.

LEGAL FRAMEWORK

In implementing Lithuania's Foreign Policy priorities, the Ministry works within the framework set by the Constitution of the Republic of Lithuania, the Law, strategic objectives (priorities) and programs established by the Government of the Republic of Lithuania. It also follows acts and documents of international law on diplomatic relations, as well as other regulations.

STRATEGIC FOREIGN POLICY OBJECTIVES

1. Seek speedy accession to the European Union by using political and diplomatic means.
2. Join NATO by using political and diplomatic means.
3. Maintain and develop good neighbourly relations.
4. Intensify Lithuania's economic diplomacy.
5. Contribute to international community efforts in ensuring democracy, human rights, peace and stability.

VICE-MINISTER, STATE SECRETARY AND UNDERSECRETARIES OF THE MINISTRY

Justas Vincas Paleckis
Vice-Minister
(b. 1942 01 01)

Graduated from Vilnius University Faculty of Journalism and the Higher Diplomatic School of the MFA of the USSR. Signatory to the Independence Act Justas Vincas Paleckis worked as Advisor to the President of the Republic of Lithuania on Matters of Foreign Policy during 1993-1996; held the office of the Ambassador Extraordinary and Plenipotentiary of the Republic of Lithuania to the United Kingdom of Great Britain and Northern Ireland during 1996-2001; since 9 January 2002, the Foreign Vice-Minister of the Republic of Lithuania. Foreign Vice-Minister Paleckis speaks English, German, Russian; married, has two sons and a daughter.

Neris Germanas
MFA Undersecretary
(b. 1946 12 07)

Graduated from Faculty of Radio-Electronics of Leningrad Institute of Polytechnics in 1970; elected Member of Parliament (the Seimas) in 1992; an Advisor to the President of the Republic of Lithuania on Matters of Foreign Policy during 1996-1998; the Ambassador Extraordinary and Plenipotentiary of the Republic of Lithuania to the Republic of Finland during 1998-2001; a Vice-Minister of the MFA during 2001-2002; since 8 May 2002, an Undersecretary of the MFA. Undersecretary of the MFA Germanas speaks English, Russian and Polish; married, has a daughter and a son.

Evaldas Ignatavičius
MFA State Secretary
(b. 1967 02 08)

Graduated from Vilnius University Faculty of Philology in 1992; worked in the Division of Eastern and Central Europe of the MFA of the Republic of Lithuania during 1991-1995; took diplomatic courses at the Leeds Institute of International Relations (Great Britain) in 1994; held the office of Counsellor to the Embassy of the Republic of Lithuania in Poland during 1995-1998; the Head of Eastern Europe and Central Asia Division in 1998-2000; the Consul General of the Republic of Lithuania to the Kaliningrad Region of Russia in 2000; a Vice-Minister of the MFA during 2001-2002; since 8 May 2002, the State Secretary of the MFA. State Secretary of the MFA Ignatavičius speaks English, Polish, German, Russian; married, has a son and a daughter.

Darius Jurgelevičius
MFA Undersecretary
(b. 1966 04 08)

Graduated from Vilnius University Faculty of Law in 1991; worked in the Department of Law and International Treaties of the MFA during 1991-1993; the Director of the Department of Law and International Treaties of the MFA during 1993-1999; a Deputy Director for Political Affairs of the OSCE Mission in Moldova during 1999-2001; a Vice-Minister of the MFA during 2001-2002; since 8 May 2002, an Undersecretary of the MFA. Undersecretary of the MFA Jurgelevičius speaks English, Polish, Russian; single.

Giedrius Čekuolis
MFA Undersecretary
(b. 1959 03 29)

Graduated from Moscow State Institute of International Relations in 1982; worked as Chief Reviewer of the Society of Lithuania's Friendship and Cultural Ties with Foreign Countries during

1982-1990; the First Secretary of the Division of Nordic European Countries of the MFA of the Republic of Lithuania during 1990-1992; a Counsellor to the Lithuanian Embassy in Stockholm during 1992-1994; the Charge d'Affaires ai of the Lithuanian Embassy to France in 1994; the Charge d'Affaires ai of the Lithuanian Embassy to the Kingdom of Spain during 1994-1995; the Ambassador Extraordinary and Plenipotentiary of the Republic of Lithuania to the Kingdom of Spain during 1995-1999; the Director of the Department of Multilateral Relations of the MFA during 1999 – 2000; a Vice-Minister of the MFA during 2000-2002; since 8 May 2002, an Undersecretary of the MFA. Undersecretary of the MFA Čekuolis speaks English, French, Spanish, Swedish and Russian; married, has a daughter.

Rytis Martikonis
MFA Undersecretary
(b. 1967 02 08)

Graduated from Vilnius University Faculty of Law in 1993; studied at the Bowdoin Colledge (USA) during 1989-1990, Orhus University (Denmark) during 1991-1992, the Royal Institute of International Relations in the Hague in 1993; worked at the Multilateral Relations Department, European Integration Department and West European Division of the MFA during 1992-1995; a Counsellor to the Mission of the Republic of Lithuania to the European Communities (Brussels) during 1995-1999; the Director of the European Integration Department during 1999-2001; a member of the Delegation for Negotiations on EU Accession 2000-2001; a Vice-Minister of the MFA during 2001-2002; on 30 January 2002 appointed Representative of the Lithuanian Government to the Convention on the Future of the European Union; an Undersecretary of the MFA since 8 May 2002. Undersecretary of the MFA Martikonis speaks English and Russian; married, has two daughters.

FUNCTIONS OF FOREIGN VICE-MINISTER, STATE SECRETARY OF THE MINISTRY AND MFA UNDERSECRETARIES

In accordance with the Government of the Republic of Lithuania Decision No 1155 of 25 September 1998 on adoption of regulations of the MFA and Foreign Minister's Order No 92 of 17 May 2002 on definition of functions for the Vice-Minister, the State Secretary of the Ministry and assignment of fields of administration for the Undersecretaries of the Ministry pursuant to Sub-Clause 12 of Clause 3 of Article 26, Sub-Clauses 5 and 8 of Clause 2 of Article 31 of the Law on Government of the Republic of Lithuania (Official Gazette, 1994, No. 43-772),

The Foreign Vice-Minister is a civil servant of political (personal) confidence, who helps the Foreign Minister to form the Ministry's political guidelines and priorities, to make and implement decisions. The Vice-Minister supervises drafting of acts of law and programmes within the field of his/ her responsibility ensuring their compliance with the Minister's political stance. The Foreign Vice-Minister coordinates activities of civil servants of the Minister's political (personal) confidence; on the Minister's commission, represents the Minister in delivering and clarifying the Minister's political position to the public, at sittings of parliamentary committees and the Government of the Republic of Lithuania. The Foreign Vice-Minister participates in agreeing draft acts of law and programmes of the Ministry with institutions concerned; performs other functions assigned by the Minister.

Vice-Minister Justas Vincas Paleckis is assigned to oversee diplomatic activities of the Republic of Lithuania under organisational networks of the UNO, the ESCO and the Council of Europe, to organise shaping of information policy; to set tasks within Vice-Minister's competence for the Department of Information and Culture, the Department of Multilateral Relations, diplomatic missions of the Republic of Lithuania and for the Group of Regional Cooperation; to coordinate relations with international Jewish communities, matters of Holocaust and Jewish cultural heritage.

The State Secretary of the MFA is a career civil servant subordinate to the Foreign Minister. The State Secretary of the MFA coordinates and supervises activities of the Ministry's administrative units ensuring optimal management and usage of financial, material, intellectual and informational resources during implementation of strategic action plans. The State Secretary of the Ministry coordinates execution of tasks received from the Prime Minister and the Government in accordance with the Ministry's strategic action plans and measures for implementation of the Programme of the Government of the Republic of Lithuania and ensures consistency of the Ministry's decisions; coordinates and supervises drafting and adjustment of legal acts and programmes; passes ordinances within his/ her competence; organises drafting of regulations for administration and units of the Ministry, lists of civil servant tenures and orders of the Minister; under the Minister's direction and provisions of the Law on Civil Service, appoints and dismisses civil servants of the Ministry's administration, except those appointed by the Minister; keeps the Ministry's stamp and is responsible for its usage; performs other duties assigned by the Minister.

State Secretary of the Ministry Evaldas Ignatavičius has been given the responsibility to coordinate personnel management of the Ministry and diplomatic missions; to head the Ministry's Attestation Commission; to appoint and dismiss officers of the Ministry's administration under the terms of the Law on Civil Service; to oversee bilateral relations (except those with the EU countries); within his competence, to set tasks for the Undersecretaries of the Ministry, the 1st and 2nd Departments of Bilateral Relations, the Department of Personnel and for diplomatic missions of the Republic of Lithuania; to perform the functions of National Coordinator of the Lithuanian-Polish Intergovernmental Cooperation Council and Chair of Lithuania-Kaliningrad Cooperation Council.

The Undersecretaries of the MFA are career civil servants directly subordinate to the State Secretary of the Ministry and held accountable to the Foreign Minister. The Undersecretaries of the Ministry within their field of administration determined by the Minister organise and supervise drafting and implementation of programmes, which comply with the Ministry's strategic objectives and the guidelines of the Lithuanian Government's Programme; organise drafting and adjustment of legal acts in line with the Ministry's strategic objectives and the guidelines of the Government's Programme; organise and supervise execution of assignments received from the Prime Minister and the Government of the Republic of Lithuania, the Minister and the State Secretary of the MFA; in accordance with their competence, ensure implementation of adopted acts of law; perform other functions assigned by the Minister.

Undersecretary of the Ministry Giedrius Čekuolis oversees integration into NATO, coordinates the formation of national security policy objectives; within his competence, sets tasks for the Multilateral Relations Department and for diplomatic missions of the Republic of Lithuania; organises shaping of information policy on the issues of integration into NATO.

Undersecretary of the Ministry Neris Germanas organises ministerial activities related to the Ministry's maintenance and finance; within his remit, sets tasks for the Administrative

Department, the IT Department, the Department of Finance and for diplomatic missions of the Republic of Lithuania.

Undersecretary of the Ministry Darius Jurgelevičius coordinates formation and implementation of consular policy; oversees state border issues; organises formation of foreign economic policy; within his competence, sets tasks for the Law and International Treaties Department, the Economics Department, the Consular Department, the State Border Group and for diplomatic missions of the Republic of Lithuania; oversees legal aspects of Lithuania's integration into NATO; organises signature of international treaties and supervision of their implementation.

Undersecretary of the Ministry Rytis Martikonis oversees integration into the EU, relations with EU member states and EU institutions; within his capacity and competence as Deputy Head of Negotiations Delegation of Lithuania and the MFA, coordinates negotiations on EU accession and implementation of the Lithuania-EU Association (Europe) Agreement; sets tasks for the European Integration Department, the 1st Department of Bilateral Relations and for Lithuanian diplomatic missions; represents the MFA at the Centre of European Integration Studies.

EUROPEAN UNION

BACKGROUND OF THE EUROPEAN UNION AND LITHUANIAN RELATIONS

On 27 August 1991 the European Communities have recognised the independence of Lithuania. Diplomatic relations were established with the all member states of the European Communities separately.

On 8 December 1995 Lithuania has submitted the official application for the membership of the EU.

On 15 February 2000 Lithuania has started the EU accession negotiations.

Legal Foundation

Agreement on Trade and Commercial and Economic Co-operation between Lithuania and the European Communities was signed on 11 May 1992, and came into force on 1 February 1993. Simultaneously with signing the Agreement, Declaration on Political Dialogue between the European Communities and its member states, on the one side, and the Republic of Lithuania, on the other side, was adopted, thus creating favourable conditions for political co-operation.
Agreement on Free Trade and Trade - Related Matters between Lithuania and the European Communities was signed on 18 July 1994, and came into force on 1 January 1995. The Agreement provides that the Community and Lithuania shall gradually establish a free trade area during a transitional period lasting a maximum of six years starting from 1 January 1995. Customs duties, quantitative restrictions and measures having an equivalent effect on imports applicable in the Community to industrial products originating in Lithuania are abolished from 1 January 1995. Customs duties, quantitative restrictions and measures having an equivalent effect on imports applicable in Lithuania to industrial products originating in the Community other than those listed in the Annexes II, III and IV are abolished from the enforcement of the Agreement. Free trade regime is not foreseen for trade in agricultural products, processed agricultural products, fish and fisheries products, as well as textile products.

The Europe (Association) Agreement was signed on 12 June 1995, and came into force on 1 February 1998. The Europe Agreement changed the Agreement on Trade and Commercial and Economic Co-operation. The Agreement on Free Trade and Trade - Related Matters became a part of the Europe Agreement. The Europe Agreement recognised Lithuania's aspiration to become a member of the European Union and created conditions for Lithuania's participation in the Pre-accession Strategy for candidate countries. It also provides for regulations, according to which movement of goods, services, capital and persons is being liberalised, as well as regulations on co-operation in law harmonisation, finance, environmental protection, culture and other areas. The following institutions are responsible for the implementation of the Europe Agreement: Association Council (Ministerial level, Council's decisions are binding for both parties), Association Committee (senior official level, provides for in-depth discussion of and finds solutions to issues arising under the Europe agreement), Sub-committees (meetings of the experts at working level) and Joint Parliamentary Committee (meetings of the groups of European Parliament and the Seimas).

List of treaties between Lithuania and the European Union.

Implementation of the Europe Agreement

The meetings of the Association Council, the Association Committee, Sub-committees and the Joint Parliamentary Committee are taking place in order to monitor the implementation of Europe Agreement.

Association Council

The first meeting of the Association Council was held on 23 February 1998 in Brussels.
The second meeting of the Association Council was held on 23 February 1999 in Luxembourg.
The third meeting of the Association Council was held on 15 February 2000 in Brussels.
The fourth meeting of the Association Council was held on 27 February 2001 in Brussels.
The fifth meeting of the Association Council was held on 19 February 2002 in Brussels. Joint press release of the Association Council.

Association Committee

The first meeting of the Association Committee was held on 25 June 1998 in Brussels.
The second meeting of the Association Committee was held on 18 June 1999 in Vilnius.
The third meeting of the Association Committee was held on 15 June 2000 in Brussels.
The fourth meeting of the Association Committee was held on 11 June 2001 in Vilnius.
The fifth meeting of the Association Committee was held on 14 June 2002 in Brussels. Joint press release.

Joint Parliamentary Committee

The Meetings of Joint Parliamentary Committee are taking place twice a year.
The first meeting of the Joint Parliamentary Committee was held on 6 - 8 October 1997 in Vilnius.
The second meeting of the Joint Parliamentary Committee was held on 26 - 27 January 1998 in Brussels.
The third meeting of the Joint Parliamentary Committee was held on 21 - 22 September 1998 in Vilnius.
The fourth meeting of the Joint Parliamentary Committee was held on 22 - 23 February 1999 in

Brussels.
The fifth meeting of the Joint Parliamentary Committee was held on 6 - 7 December 1999 in Vilnius.
The sixth meeting of the Joint Parliamentary Committee was held on 5 - 7 June 2000 in Vilnius and Neringa.
The seventh meeting of the Joint Parliamentary Committee was held on 22 - 23 November 2000 in Brussels. Declaration and recommendations.
The eighth meeting of the Joint Parliamentary Committee was held on 25 - 26 June 2001 in Vilnius and Visaginas. Declaration and recommendations.
The ninth meeting of Joint Parliamentary Committee was held on 20 –21 November 2001 in Brussels. Declaration and recommendations
The tenth meeting of Joint Parliamentary Committee was held on 27 –28 May 2002 in Vilnius and Kaunas. Declaration and recommendations

Since the enforcement of the Europe Agreement, changes were made in a number of its Annexes and Protocols.

On 18 December 1998, Lithuania and the European Community signed the Additional Protocol which approved trade liberalisation in textile. On 11 May 1999, the Seimas has ratified the Additional Protocol. By the mutual agreement, the provisions of the Additional Protocol have been applied since 1 January 1998.

On 16 July 1998, the European Community and Lithuania signed the Protocol adjusting trade aspects of the Europe Agreement taking into account the accession of the Republic of Austria, the Republic of Finland and the Kingdom of Sweden to the European Union and the outcome of the Uruguay Round negotiations on agriculture, including improvements to the existing preferential arrangements. This Protocol has changed the annexes of the Europe Agreement regulating bilateral trade in agricultural products, processed agricultural products and fisheries products. On 11 May 1999, the Seimas has ratified the Protocol. By the mutual agreement, the provisions of the Additional Protocol have been applied since 1 January 1999.

On 1 April 1997, a new Protocol allowing for pan-European cumulation of rules of origin entered into force. The Association Council decision amending Protocol 3 to the Europe Agreement (including Turkey in pan-Euroepan cumulation) was signed on 27 January 1999. It has entered into force since 1 January 1999. The Association Council decision amending Protocol 3 on the definition of the concept of "originating products" and methods of administrative co-operation to the Europe Agreement was signed on 23 December 1999. It has entered into force since 1 January 2000.

The Europe Agreement provided for a transition period in a number of clearly specified areas. This transitional period, referred to in article 3 of the Agreement, came to an end on 31 December 1999. However, Lithuania requested for the extension of transitional periods concerning state aids (until the end of 2004) and the right of establishment in the field of telecommunications (until the end of 2002).

Since the year 2001, the trade in industrial products between Lithuania and the EU was fully liberalised.

On July 5, 2002 Protocol on European Conformity Assessment to the Europe Agreement was ratified. Since the entering into force of this Protocol, quality certificates granted by the notified Lithuanian conformity assessment bodies are recognised in all the EU Member States.

POSITION OF THE GOVERNMENT OF LITHUANIA ON THE EU INSTITUTIONAL REFORM

Equality of Member States of the European Union, democratic legitimacy and efficiency of the EU institutions should be the cornerstones of the institutional reform of the EU. The institutional balance of the EU should be upheld.

Community method, which reflects a dual nature of the EU as the Union of Member States and citizens – should be consistently preserved and strengthened.

Proposals concerning reform of the particular EU institution should be assessed only in the light of the entirety of the institutional reform. The existing institutions of the EU should be reformed in such way, that the whole institutional system would not become more complicated. The establishment of the new EU institutions would contribute to the structural and decision making-making complication of the EU.

Council

Rotating Presidency (in the European Council and the key formations of the Council of Ministers) should be maintained. It ensures the equality of the Member States and their direct participation in the EU governance. Rotating Presidency of the Council is an important link between the citizens of Member States and EU institutions.

Continuity and coherence of the work of the Council should be ensured by strengthening of strategic planning as well as by closer co-operation among the Presidencies and EU institutions.

Current state of discussions on the permanent President of the European Council (to be elected for a longer period than six months) does not provide enough convincing arguments for the necessity of such a post. Permanent President of the European Council would change the institutional balance of the EU, lead to the competition with Commission's President and bring confusion with regard to political accountability.

The possibility of team Presidencies could be considered, but it should be viewed in a context of interaction amongst all EU institutions.

The scope of application of the qualified majority voting in the EU legislation should be extended, but decisions concerning this extension of scope should be taken on a case-by-case basis taking into account financial consequences and capabilities to implement the decisions taken by the qualified majority.

Commission

Proposal that the President of the Commission would be elected by the European Parliament and then approved by the European Council could be supported. It would increase the legitimacy of the Commission.

Composition of the Commission - if Nice treaty provisions are revised, the principle of one commissioner per Member State should be maintained. Otherwise, when the Union consists of 27 Member States, the number of Members of the Commission should be less than the number of Member States. The Members of the Commission should be chosen according to a rotation system based on the principle of equality.

Current positions of the High Representative for CFSP and the External Relations Commissioner should be merged into a position of the EU Minister of Foreign Affairs, who at the same time would be a Vice-president of the Commission. Minister of Foreign Affairs should be appointed by the European Council in consultation with the President of the Commission.

European Parliament

Support the proposal concerning the extension of co-decision procedure. This would strengthen the role of European Parliament in the process of the EU's legislation.

The role of European Parliament would be strengthened by introducing the right to elect the President of the Commission.

National Parliaments

National parliaments should be more involved in the political surveillance of the application of the principle of subsidiarity before the European legal act enters into force. The review of the application of the subsidiarity principle after the act enters into force should remain within the competence of the Court of Justice.

POSITIONS OF LITHUANIA AND THE EUROPEAN UNION ON ENLARGEMENT

Lithuania's Position on Enlargement

The Annual Address of the President of the Republic of Lithuania, the Resolutions of the Seimas and the Programme of the Government reveal Lithuania's position on enlargement.

Excerpts from the Annual Address of the President of the Republic of Lithuania, Vilnius, 2002

"Today we can state with full responsibility that a crucial period of consolidation of the Independent Lithuania is nearing completion. I link its completion with the strategic goals of today - Lithuania's invitation to join NATO and conclusion of the accession negotiations for the EU membership. To secure the achievement of these goals we need well co-ordinated action of politicians and society.
Today we must ask ourselves how we shall build our prosperity and all aspects of our life as a full-fledged member of the Western democratic hemisphere. What key objectives shall we set for ourselves while planning a new stage of development of our state?

<..>

It is not possible to see a creative Lithuania without individual initiative and responsibility. The path to such Lithuania unavoidably will be based on the new public agreement on the priorities for our future as well as our national development.
Such agreement was reached on our foreign policy and national defence. But regardless of the success in these areas which was largely determined, most probably, by broad endorsement of all our society, Lithuania faces difficult tasks ahead.

Ladies and Gentlemen,
During the next stage of national development Lithuania must establish itself in the world as a solid and responsible community and as a reliable and constructive power dedicated to the betterment of mankind. These are the attributes that will lead to a successful and active role of Lithuania in the community of Western nations.
After joining NATO and the European Union, we will have to expand and strengthen the broad spectrum of relations with Western nations. Lithuania will have to increase substantially its participation in the development and implementation of the common policy of the North Atlantic Alliance and Europe. Together with other countries we shall build our common house of Europe and strengthen NATO as our security umbrella.
Membership of the European Union will transform our life. We shall act according to the common rules, encouraging us to consult and seek a common agreement. However, this does not mean that someone else will make decisions for us. On the contrary, we shall have to make decisions with responsibility for ourselves and for other nations. We shall seek to create Europe as a community of sovereign states, which respects the rights and freedoms of every individual and each nation.
Common rules will be our rules. And the sense of responsibility will be genuine if the moral foundation of our society is firm and if we share the common values with other European nations.

<..>

We, with the help of our neighbours, must strive that Lithuania, having properly developed its infrastructure, becomes a bridge connecting the Central and Northern Europe. These regions can be brought closer together by joint multilateral projects in the areas of transport, energy and other sectors of economy. It is essential to secure political support of the European Union and funding from structural funds for the implementation of such projects.
The future of the infrastructure of our region is much more than an issue of local concern. It will largely determine not only the progress of our own country and that of our neighbours, but also free movement of people in the future territory of the enlarged European Union. The condition of our roads, pipelines and airports will have an impact on the European Union's trade with the East, consequently, on the overall development of the European economy.

<..>

In order to receive allocations from the European Union structural funds, we must ensure their transparent and effective management. This seems to be clear. But why is it that no steps have been taken so far to ensure a likewise transparent and effective management of our public funds? Is the money earned through our citizens' work and sweat less valuable than the funds extended to us by others that we can afford to spend them on ill-founded projects, not requiring stricter accountability and assessment of results?
We as politicians bear direct responsibility for establishing, without further delay, a modern civil service system, dedicated to serve our citizens conscientiously and professionally.
Lithuania needs such a system in view of the approaching European Union membership. Indeed, in the near future we shall have to post a number of qualified civil servants to common EU bodies. Therefore we must think about their replacement already today. Lithuania will need competent administrators capable of acting at the state level and defend its national interests. To a large

extent, their professional proficiency and integrity will decide whether billions of litas that will be channelled from the European funds into Lithuania will be used with the greatest effectiveness for the modernisation of the country and long term well-being of our people.

<..>

I would like to draw your attention to another paradox. The government draws national and regional development programmes not so much because the country and the people need them, but more so because of the demand of Brussels. Indeed, Lithuania has to produce those plans and programmes in order to get access to European Union funds. That is clear. But again the question arises: how can we spend money earned by our taxpayers on the development of plans that were not evaluated by experts and discussed with the people? Why can millions of litas from our budget be spent on a whim of politicians? Shouldn't the case of the Šiauliai free economic zone be the last of many problematic examples of this policy? Even last year I emphasised that the regional and national development plans should be viewed as essential instruments for our nation to grow rather than a formal report intended for submission to foreign officials.

<..>

In 2000, in Lisbon the European Union member states rose to the challenge of transforming Europe into a region of most competitive and dynamic economy over the next decade. The recent Summit of the EU member states and candidate countries in Barcelona addressed ways to achieve this goal. Regrettably, now Lithuania, together with Bulgaria and Romania, is dangerously behind other associate members of the European Union in terms of the level of knowledge economy. Only by taking immediate and tailor-made actions can we bridge this gap. First of all, our government has to improve the co-ordination of the activities aimed at advancement of knowledge society. At present, even several institutions are competing in this area, which leads to repetitive work.

It is about time we started concentrating state and private capital on sectors that offer a higher, though slower, return on capital - firstly, on people and their education. At the same time the state must, without any further delay, embark on the development of knowledge economy as its strategic goal.

<..>

Further reform of the taxation system calls for your special attention, as we are currently patching our national system of taxation based on the models of the European Union. It is unavoidable at times. However, it is not always sufficient as the EU members themselves are reforming their own economic policies by improving rules regulating economic activity.

<..>

In order to smoothly decommission the 1st and 2nd units of Ignalina Nuclear Power Plant we have to secure the needed financial support of European states. However, Lithuania must not reject an opportunity of being a nuclear state. Our economic independence will be largely determined by our access to different energy resources.

<..>

The Lithuanian countryside must not be left standing by the road leading to Europe. Its interests must be consistently defended during the EU accession negotiations. Adequate agricultural production quotas should be guaranteed; not only direct aid to farmers should be taken care of but also investments into promoting various businesses in the countryside. What is even more important is to enhance the capacities of our countryside so that it could get the maximum benefit offered by the enlargement and the presence in the common European area. To achieve that we do not have to wrestle with Brussels but rather with our inertia and sluggishness.

Amendments of our Constitution will provide the right to legal entities of Lithuania and foreign nationals, with certain safeguards, to buy agricultural land. This will give further impulses to a credit market in agriculture and will promote more rational land use. It is my hope that the future Law on the Development of Agriculture and Countryside which the Seimas has to pass soon will set forth new instruments of economic regulation which are already in place in the European Union."

<..>

Annual Addresses of the President of the Republic of Lithuania (1999, 2000, 2001 and 2002).

The Resolution of the Seimas regarding the Integration of the Republic of Lithuania into the European Union

On 19 January 2001 the joint statement on common actions in order to speed up Lithuania's integration into the EU was signed by the Seimas factions. On 23 January 2001 the Seimas adopted a resolution which lists laws necessary for Lithuania's EU membership negotiations as priority legislation. The Seimas confirmed an agreement to make common efforts for Lithuania's becoming EU member state with the first group of candidate countries. The Seimas committed itself to adopt legal acts necessary for EU integration during the 1st half of 2001, which would demonstrate Lithuania's progress in EU talks during Sweden's presidency. The Seimas agreed to establish a permanent commission, which will prepare necessary amendments of the Constitution.

Excerpt from the Programme of the Government of the Republic of Lithuania

"To aim at maintaining the momentum gained in the pace of negotiations and to complete negotiations on EU membership in 2002 providing Lithuania with a possibility to become a full-fledged Member State of the European Union in 2004 and enabling the Lithuanian citizens to participate on equal terms in European Parliament elections in 2004.

To pursue the policy of active relations with all Member States of the European Union thereby ensuring adequate safeguarding of the Lithuanian national interests in the process of the negotiations and accession.

To participate in the structures of Common Foreign and Security Policy and Common Security and Defence Policy on the grounds that this participation is an inseparable part of the European integration process and with full awareness that the strengthening of CESDP and the establishment of European Crises Management Forces will contribute to the reinforcement of the transatlantic relations, which represents the basis of European security.

To aim at the widest possible participation of the public in the discussions on the future vision of the European Union; to strengthen the processes of disseminating information among the people and pursuing a dialogue on the most critical issues of EU integration.

To endeavour to make the enlargement of the European Union a stimulus for the development of Lithuania's relations with its neighbours and other countries of the region as well as the implementation of cross-border cooperation projects."

The Programme of the Government of the Republic of Lithuania for 2001 – 2004.

Conference on Accession to the European Union. An Opening Statement of the Minister of Foreign Affairs of the Republic of Lithuania, Brussels, 15 February 2000.

Position of the European Union on Enlargement

European Council

The European Council defines main guidelines of the activities and development of the European Union by meeting at least four times a year.

The Copenhagen European Council held on 21-22 June 1993 agreed "that the associated countries in Central and Eastern Europe that so desire shall become members of the European Union. Accession shall take place as soon as an associated country is able to assume the obligations of membership by satisfying the economic and political conditions required".

The Luxembourg European Council held on 12-13 December 1997 taking into account the European Commission's Opinions on the Associated Countries' Applications for Membership of the European Union decided to begin accession negotiations with Cyprus, Hungary, Poland, Estonia, the Czech Republic and Slovenia. Meanwhile, the preparation of negotiations with Romania, Slovakia, Latvia, Lithuania and Bulgaria will be speeded up in particular through an analytical examination of the Union *acquis*.

The Helsinki European Council held on 15-16 December 1999 decided to begin accession negotiations with Romania, Slovakia, Latvia, Lithuania, Bulgaria and Malta on the conditions for their entry into the Union and the ensuing Treaty adjustments. In the negotiations, each candidate country will be judged on its own merits. Candidate countries, which have now been brought into the negotiating process, will have the possibility to catch up with those already in negotiations. These decisions were taken on the basis of the Commission's Progress Reports. The adoption of the Lithuanian National Energy Strategy which provides for decommissioning of Ignalina NPP was assessed by the European Commission as an important development in Lithuania's way to the European Union.

The Santa Maria da Feira European Council held on 19-20 June 2000 noted that it should be feasible to open negotiations in all areas of the acquis with the most advanced candidates countries which started accession negotiations in 2000 as early as possible in 2001.

The Nice European Council held on 7-10 December 2000 confirmed the Enlargement Strategy prepared by the European Commission. The European Council also decided on the institutional reform of the EU which placed the Union in a position to welcome those new member states which are ready as from the end of 2002, in the hope that they will be able to take part in the next European Parliament elections in 2004.

The Göteborg European Concil held on 16 June 2001 stated that the process of enlargement is irreversible. European Council noted significant breakthroughs, which have been achieved in the accession negotiations. Determined efforts by all parties have made it possible to meet and surpass the objectives set out at Nice for the first half of 2001. European Council has reaffirmed the road map as the framework for the successful completion of the enlargement negotiations. The road map should make it possible to complete negotiations by the end of 2002 for those candidate countries that are ready.

The Laeken European Council held on 14-15 December 2001 named the candidate countries, including Lithuania, which have potential to be ready for membership in 2004. The Council stated, that it is necessary to keep the pace of negotiations with candidate countries and the pace of reforms in these countries. Position of the Ministry of Foreign Affairs of Lithuania on the Conclusions of the European Council Meeting.

The Seville European Council held on 21-22 June 2002 noted that during the last semester crucial progress has been achieved and now the negotiations were entering the concluding phase. The EU reaffirmed its determination to conclude accession negotiations with the "Laeken group": Cyprus, Malta, Hungary, Poland, Slovakia, Lithuania, Latvia, Estonia, the Czech Republic and Slovenia by the end of 2002, if those countries are ready. The EU leaders also noted that it was reasonable to expect that the Treaty of Accession would be signed in spring 2003 with the aim that these countries should participate in the elections for the European Parliament in 2004 as full members.

Criteria for Membership

The Copenhagen European Council in 1993 decided that associated countries shall become members of the European Union as soon as they will be able to assume the membership criteria:

Stability of institutions guaranteeing democracy, the rule of law, human rights and respect for and protection of minorities;
Existence of a functioning market economy as well as the capacity to cope with competitive pressure and market forces within the Union;
Ability to take on the obligations of membership including adherence to the aims of political, economic and monetary union.

Political criteria: free and fair elections; alteration of power in proper conditions; implementation of principal of separation of powers; effectiveness and operation of different institutions; fight against corruption; respect of political, civil, economic, social and cultural human rights; protection of minorities; and ensuring of equal rights of men and women.

Economic criteria:
a) The existence of a market economy requires: equilibrium between supply and demand which is established by the free interplay of market forces; price and trade liberalisation; an absence of significant barriers to market entry and exit; legal system, including the regulation of property rights; implementation of national law and treaties; macroeconomic stability, including stability of prices and public financial sector; co-ordinated economic policy; and strong financial sector.

b) The capacity to cope with competitive pressure and market forces requires: a stable macroeconomic framework within which individual economic agents can make decisions in a climate of a reasonable degree of predictability; sufficient amount of human and physical capital, including infrastructure, science and research and development of these areas in the future; restructuring of economy; access of firms to investment finance; and competitiveness.

Third criterion - **ability to take on the obligations of membership** – includes alignment of national legislation with the EU acquis and implementation of the acquis.

The Madrid European Council in 1995 noted the importance of restructuring and adjustment of candidate countries' administrative structures in line with the requirements of the EU. Since Madrid European Council, candidate countries' administrative capacity to implement acquis is another criterion for membership.

The European Commission has applied and further developed the criteria for membership drafting Opinions on Candidate Countries' Applications for Membership of the EU and Regular Reports.

Regular Reports of the European Commission

In 1997 European Commission published Opinions on Candidate Countries' Applications for membership of the European Union. Since 1998 European Commission presents annual Progress Reports on the progress towards accession of candidate countries.

European Commission's Opinion on Lithuania's Application for Membership of the European Union, 15 July 1997.

European Commission's **Progress Reports** on Lithuania's Progress towards Accession:

4 November 1998,
13 October 1999,
8 November 2000,
13 November 2001, Position of the Ministry of Foreign Affairs of Lithuania on the Commission's Regular report 2001 and on the Strategy paper.

Accession Partnership

The purpose of the Accession Partnership is to set out in a single framework the priority areas for further work implementing reforms in candidate country and the financial means available to help implement these priorities. The Accession Partnership is a programme decided by the European Commission after consulting candidate country. The present Accession Partnership on Lithuania was published on 13 October 1999 and revised in February 2000. Short- and medium-term priorities listed in this programme were reviewed in the new Accession Partnership document, which was released on 13 November 2001.

NEGOTIATIONS

Position Papers of the Republic of Lithuania (European Committee under the Government of the Republic of Lithuania)

Organisation of the Negotiations

Principles of the Negotiations

The principle of independence of the negotiating chapters. The views and opinions of the negotiating countries expressed in one negotiating chapter do not and cannot have any

influence over the negotiations carried out in other chapters and do not influence them beforehand in any way.
The principle of universality or "nothing is agreed till everything is agreed". Full and partial agreements reached negotiating in one negotiating chapter cannot be considered as final till agreements in all the chapters will be reached.

Procedure of Organisation of the Negotiations

The negotiations are conducted in the Accession Conference. 15 EU member states, the candidate country and the European Commission are taking part in this Conference. The meetings are presided over by the head of the delegation of the EU presidency.

The Accession Conference meetings are held at ministerial (usually twice a year) and Chief Negotiators (not less than four times a year) level. The negotiations may be held at working parties (expert) level if this is necessary and if both sides agree. The working parties operate under the authority of the Chief Negotiators.

Before the start of the negotiations the European Commission organises screening exercises. During these meetings the EU requests to present the updated information on the progress of the "acquis" acceptance in each negotiating chapter.

The "opening" of the negotiating chapter marks the beginning of the negotiations on a specific subject. The EU decides to open the chapter when the candidate's progress in the acceptance and implementation of the "acquis" is sufficient for the conclusion of negotiations in the nearest future.

The "closing" of the negotiating chapter is a preliminary agreement that all the questions raised are co-ordinated enough, and there is no need for further negotiations. If the obligations are not implemented the chapter can be "reopened".

Taking into account the screening report and referring to the position paper of the candidate country, the European Commission prepares the Draft Common Position of the EU, which is presented to all the member states. At first, it is considered by the Enlargement Working Group of the Council, and the final decision is made by the COREPER (Council of Permanent Representatives). The approved Draft Common Position becomes the Common Position of the EU, which is officially presented to the candidate country during the Accession Conference.

The subject of the negotiations is not the EU acquis but the conditions and terms of its acceptance, i.e. the transitional periods, exceptions and technical adaptations.

Having reached the agreement in all negotiating chapters, the Accession Treaty is prepared, which includes all the agreed transitional periods, exceptions and technical adaptations. The Accession Treaty is signed in the state and government leaders' meeting, and then it is presented for the ratification.

LITHUANIAN DELEGATION FOR THE EU ACCESSION NEGOTIATIONS

<table>
<tr><td colspan="2" align="center">H. E. ANTANAS VALIONIS
MINISTER OF FOREIGN AFFAIRS
HEAD OF THE DELEGATION</td></tr>
<tr><td align="center">Mr. PETRAS AUŠTREVIČIUS</td><td align="center">Mr. RYTIS MARTIKONIS</td></tr>
</table>

<table>
<tr><td colspan="2">Deputy Head of the delegation
Chief Negotiator
Director General of the European Committee under the Government
Tel: 370 2 661760
Fax: 370 2 612178
E-mail: a.petras@euro.lt</td><td colspan="2">Deputy Head of the Delegation
Undersecretary of the Ministry of Foreign Affairs
Tel: 370 2 362 418
Fax: 370 2 313090
E-mail: rytis.martikonis@urm.lt</td></tr>
<tr><td>Mr. KLAUDIJUS MANIOKAS
Deputy Chief Negotiator
Deputy Director General, European Committee under the Government

Tel: 370 2 661760
Fax: 370 2 612178
E-mail:klaud@euro.lt</td><td colspan="2">H. E. OSKARAS JUSYS
Deputy Chief negotiator
Head of the Lithuanian Permanent Mission to the European Communities

Tel: 32 2 775 9083
Fax: 32 2 771 4597
E-mail:

oskaras.jusys@lt-mission-eu.be</td><td>Mr. ŽYGIMANTAS PAVILIONIS
Deputy Chief Negotiator
Director, European Integration Department of the Ministry of Foreign Affairs

Tel: 370 2 362570
Fax: 370 2 362552

E-mail:
zygimantas.pavilionis@urm.lt</td></tr>
<tr><td></td><td colspan="2">Core Group of the Delegation

o Head of the Delegation
o Deputy Heads of delegation
o Deputy Chief Negotiators
o Director General of European Law Department
o Adviser on Economic Issues of EU Accession Negotiations, MFA
o Secretary of the Delegation

Main functions:

o Strategy
o Policy planning</td><td></td></tr>
<tr><td colspan="2">SECRETARIAT OF THE DELEGATION
EUROPEAN COMMITTEE UNDER THE GOVERNMENT
Mr. PETRAS AUŠTREVIČIUS,
Director General
Mr. VIDMANTAS PURLYS
Secretary of the Delegation
Head of Integration Policy Division</td><td colspan="2">EUROPEAN INTEGRATION DEPARTMENT OF THE MINISTRY OF FOREIGN AFFAIRS
Mr. ŽYGIMANTAS PAVILIONIS
Director

Main functions:

o Diplomatic support to the Delegation
o Policy input
o Bilateral affairs in support of EU integration
o Contacts with the Accession</td></tr>
</table>

Tel: 370 2 661748 · fax: 370 2 612178 E-mail: vidma@euro.lt **Main functions:** ○ Political and technical support to the Delegation and the Chief Negotiator ○ Co-ordination of the preparation and reporting of additional information to the Accession Conference ○ Co-ordination of acquis transposition and implementation	Conference

	30 HEADS OF WORKING GROUPS MEMBERS OF THE DELEGATION ○ **Main function: preparation of additional information to the Accession Conference**	

COURSE OF THE NEGOTIATIONS

By the end of the year 2000 all the position papers were prepared and approved by the Government of the Republic of Lithuania. By the beginning of the year 2001 all of them were handed over to the Accession Conference.

Since the beginning of the negotiations following Accession Conference meetings between Lithuania and European Union took place:

15 February 2000 – the negotiations on Lithuania's accession to the EU were officially opened at ministerial level in Brussels.
28 March 2000 – Chief Negotiator of Lithuania presented eight position papers of Lithuania to the European Union.
25 May 2000 – in the meeting of the EU and Lithuania at Chief Negotiators' level the European Union officially presented its eight position papers.
14 June 2000 – five negotiating chapters were preliminary closed in the second meeting at ministerial level.
24 October 2000 – it was recommended to close two chapters at Chief Negotiators' level.
16 November 2000 – seven negotiating chapters were opened at Chief Negotiators' level.

20 November 2000 – the results of the negotiations of the 2nd half of the year 2000 were confirmed at ministerial level.
30 March 2001 - six negotiating chapters were opened at Chief Negotiators' level and it was also recommended to preliminary close six chapters.
17 May 2001 – three negotiating chapters were opened at Chief Negotiators' level and it was recommended to preliminary close two chapters.
11 June 2001 - the results of the negotiations of the 1st half of the year 2001 were confirmed at ministerial level, as well as three negotiating chapters were opened and two – preliminary closed.
27 June 2001 - one negotiating chapter was opened at Chief Negotiators' level and it was recommended to preliminary close another chapter.
28 November 2001 – three negotiating chapters were closed at Chief Negotiators' level.
12 December 2001 – the results of the negotiations of 2nd half of 2001 were confirmed at ministerial level. Statement by Minister of Foreign affairs of Lithuania A.Valionis.
21 December 2001 – two negotiating chapters were closed at Chief Negotiators' level.
21 March 2002 – one negotiating chapter was closed at Chief Negotiators' level, and progress was achieved in Energy chapter (one transitional period was agreed).
22 April 2002 - two negotiating chapters were closed at Chief Negotiators' level.
11 June 2002 - the results of the negotiations of 1st half of 2002 were confirmed at ministerial level as well as two more chapters were closed.
28 June 2002 - at the Chief Negotiators' meeting the EU presented its negotiating position on agriculture production quotas and reference periods.

28 negotiating chapters was preliminary closed since the beginning of the negotiations: Freedom to Provide Services, Fisheries, Statistics, Industrial Policy, Small and Medium-Sized Enterprises, Science and Research, Education and training, External Relations, Common Foreign and Security Policy, Free Movement of Capital, Telecommunications and Information Technology, Social Policy and Employment, Culture and Audiovisual policy, Economic and Monetary Union, Consumers and Health Protection, Free Movement of Goods, Company Law, Environment, Free movement of persons, Competition policy, Customs union, Transport policy, Financial control, Taxation, Energy, Regional Policy and Structural Instruments, Justice and Home Affairs and Institutions.

CO-OPERATION BETWEEN LITHUANIA AND THE EUROPEAN UNION

Political Dialogue between Lithuania and the EU

Lithuania participates in the political dialogue with the EU in the framework of Common Foreign and Security Policy (CFSP).

The preliminary stage of political dialogue has started since the enforcement of Agreement on Trade and Commercial and Economic Co-operation between Lithuania and the European Communities which includes the declaration on political dialogue. This declaration provides for concrete frameworks of co-operation: meetings at ministerial and senior official level and exchange of information on foreign policy issues.

According to the Title II of the Europe Agreement on political dialogue, the purpose of the political dialogue is to develop co-operation in the area of CFSP. The structure of the political dialogue is as follows:
Multilateral meetings;
Meetings at ministerial level;

Meetings at Political Directors level;
Co-operation in third countries and international organisations;
Meetings at parliamentary level.

The major forms of the Lithuanian participation in the political dialogue are:
Participation in the EU and candidate countries' meetings;
Alignment with the EU statements, demarches, common positions and common actions;
Co-operation in the third countries and international organisations.

During every EU Presidency Lithuania participates in the political dialogue meetings on the level of Foreign Ministers, Political Directors, European Correspondents and experts. The political dialogue meetings concentrate on issues such as:
Security,
Non-proliferation,
Analysis and Planning,
Eastern Europe and Central Asia,
Disarmament,
United Nations,
OSCE,
Human Rights,
Terrorism,
Western Balkans,
Drugs,
Conventional Arms Export.

Another example of Lithuania's participation in the political dialogue is the alignment with the EU statements, demarches, common positions and common actions. During the 4th quarter of 2000 Lithuania aligned itself with 202 EU statements, demarches and common positions through the Council's Secretariat in Brussels, in the framework of the United Nations and its agencies, in the framework of OSCE. Lithuanian representatives also participate in the regular political dialogue meetings in the third countries and international organisations.

The secure communication system between EU Council Secretariat and candidate countries in the area of CFSP functions since 6 December 1999. The system ensures secure transfer of documents in the area of CFSP between Lithuanian and the EU Council Secretariat. The EU Capabilities Commitment Conference has taken place on 20 November 2000, where the EU Foreign and Defence Ministers announced their countries' contributions to the European Security and defence Policy. The EU candidate countries were also invited to the Conference. Lithuania's contribution was as follows: 3 infantry battalions, combat support platoon, combat service support section, 2 aircraft, one helicopter, two naval vessels and training areas in Pabrad? and Rukla.

Trade with the European Union

The European Union is the main Lithuania's trade partner. During year 2001, Lithuanian exports to the EU amounted to LTL 8782 million and imports LTL 12150 million. The annual trade turnover with the EU was 48% of the total trade turnover, and imports and exports amounted 48% of their total figures.

Lithuanian Trade with the European Union, 1995-2001, mln LTL

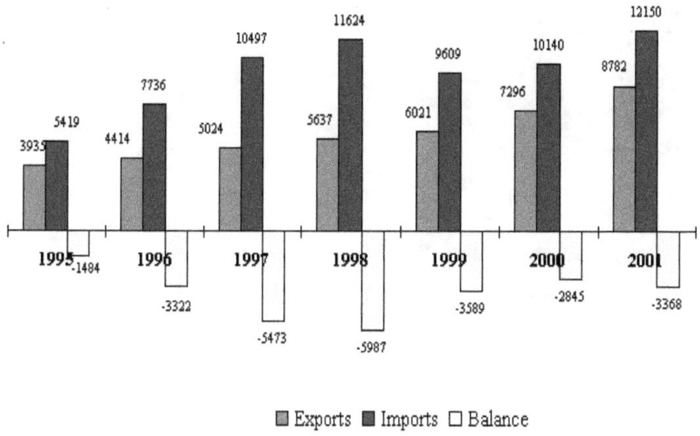

Source: Lithuanian Statistical Department

Since the Free Trade Agreement came into force in 1995, the share of EU in Lithuania's trade has constantly increased. However, the trade turnover with EU did not grow proportionally over the period. The growth of imports was significantly larger than the growth of exports. Only starting with 1998 increase in exports exceeded increase in imports: exports compared with the same figure of 1997, increased by 12.2%, whereas imports increased by only 10.7%. In 1999, this trend was even more significant: imports compared with the figure of 1998, decreased by 17.3%, and exports increased by 6.8%. In 2001, the growth of both imports and exports grew uniform - imports rose by 19.8%, and exports by 20.4%.

In 2001, Germany remained the main Lithuania's trade partner. Lithuanian exports to Germany were 12% of the total exports, and imports were 19% of the total imports. The other largest trade partners among the EU countries were the United Kingdom (14% of the total exports and 3% of the total imports), Denmark (4% of exports an 4% of imports), Netherlands (3% of exports and 4% imports), Sweden (4% of exports and 3% of imports), France (3% of exports and 3% of imports) and Italy (2% of exports and 8% of imports).

EU Member States - the Main Lithuania's Trade Partners, 2001

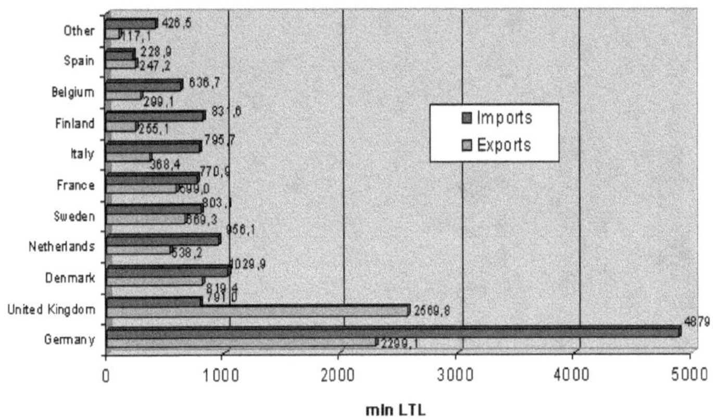

Source: Lithuanian Statistical Department

In 2001, as compared to 2000, Lithuania's exports considerably increased to the United Kingdom (117%), Finland (31%), Belgium (24%), and decreased to Netherlands (26%), Austria (21%), France (10%).

Lithuania's imports from the most EU countries increased in 2001, in comparison to 2000. The most remarkable growth of imports was from Portugal (78%), Austria (41%0, Belgium (35%), Ireland (32%).

In 2001, the main groups of goods exported to the EU were textile, mineral products, machinery and equipment, chemicals, various manufactured articles and wood. These product groups together constituted 79% of the total Lithuania's exports to the EU.

Exports of mineral products, food, vegetable products, textile increased in 2001, as compared to 2000, while exports of chemicals and wood decreased.

Lithuania's Exports to the EU Structure, 2001

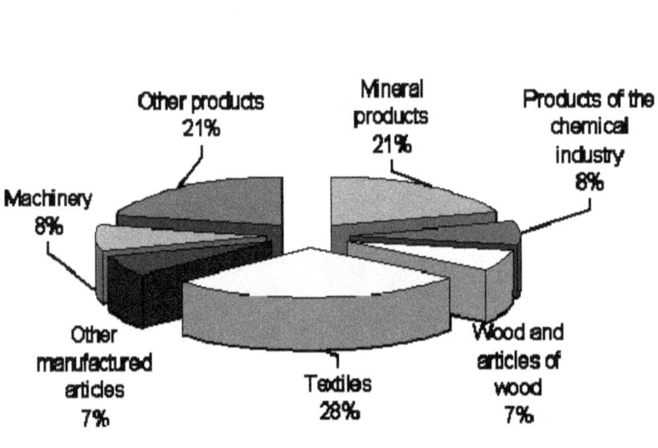

Source: Lithuanian Statistical Department

The leading groups of goods imported from the EU in 2001 were machinery and equipment, transport equipment, textile and its products, products of chemical industry and plastics. These groups amounted to 72% of the total imports from the EU.
In 2001, as compared to 2000, there was growth of imports of vehicles, food products, products of chemical industry, machinery and mechanical equipment. Imports from the EU of mineral products and vegetable products has decreased.

Lithuania's Imports from the EU Structure,2001

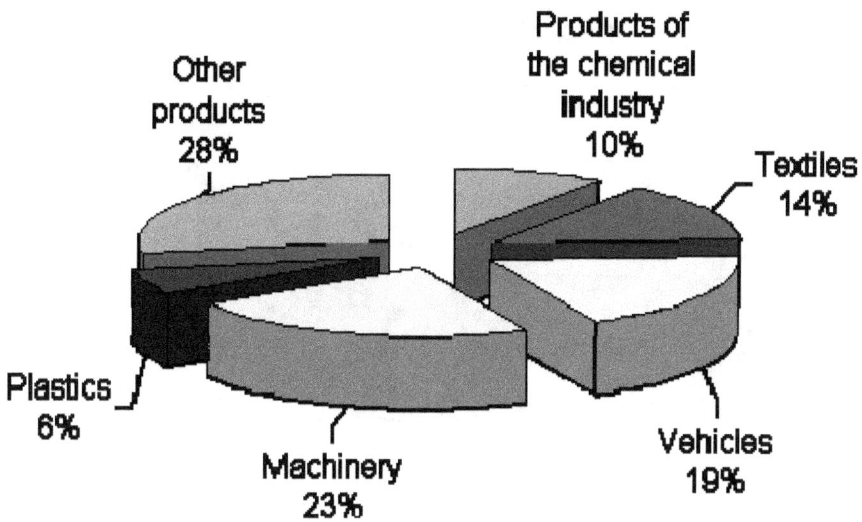

Source: Lithuanian Statistical Department

Foreign Direct Investment from the European Union to Lithuania

The Dynamics of Foreign Direct Investment to Lithuania, mln LTL

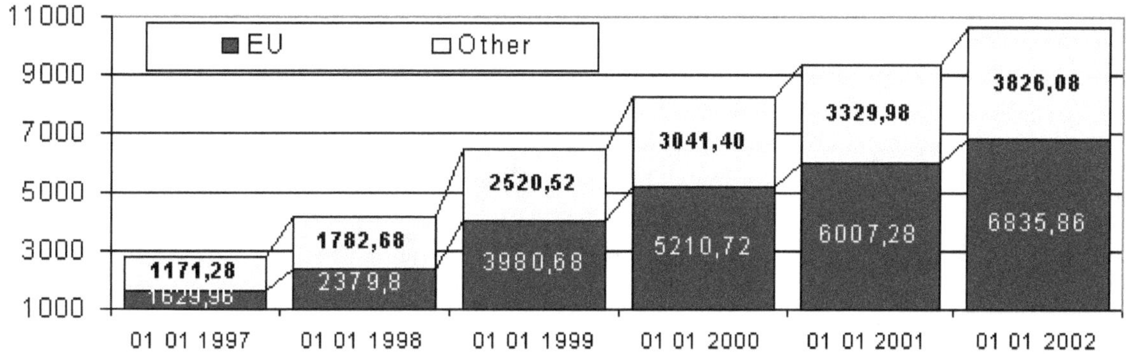

Sour

On 1 January 2002, total foreign direct investment to Lithuania was LTL 10661.9 million. The share of the EU in foreign direct investment to Lithuania amounted to 64% of the total foreign direct investment.

Foreign Direct Investment by Country Group, 1 January 2002

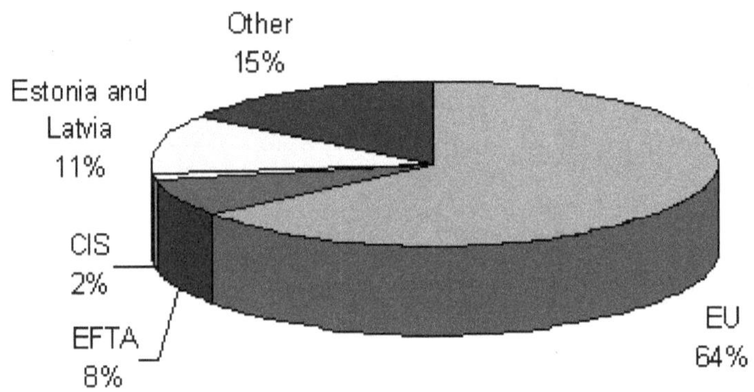

The greatest share of investment among the EU countries was from Denmark (18% of total investment), Sweden (17% of total investment), Germany (7% of total investment), the United Kingdom (7% of total investment), and Finland (6% of total investment).

Foreign Direct Investment to Lithuania by EU Country, 1998-2002

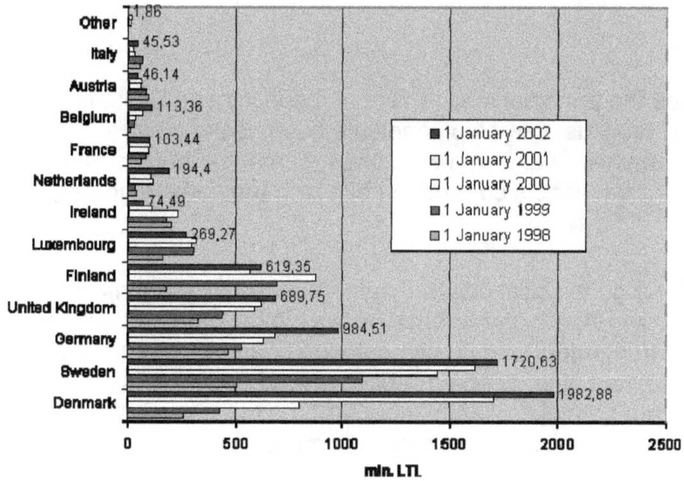

Source: Lithuanian Statistical Department

EU Financial Assistance

PHARE programme is one of the three European Community financial instruments supporting the preparation of the candidate countries for the EU accession. The other two instruments – the Instrument for Structural Policies for Pre-Accession (ISPA) and Special Action for Pre-Accession for Agriculture and Rural Development (SAPARD) are focusing on environment, transport and rural development, while PHARE will continue to provide broader support for accession across all sectors.

EU allocations to Lithuania in 2000:
43 MEUR for PHARE;
50 MEUR for ISPA;
29 MEUR for SAPARD.

PHARE

Lithuania has been a beneficiary of the PHARE programme since 1991. The total amount received by Lithuania through the National PHARE Programme in 1991 – 1999 is 342 MEUR.

The main objective of PHARE is to assist the Central and Eastern European countries in their preparation for the accession by focusing on the priorities identified in the Community acquis, especially in the Accession Partnership and National Programme for the Adoption of the Acquis.

National PHARE Programme allocations, in MEUR:

Year	1991	1992	1993	1994	1995	1996	1997	1998	1999	2000	Total

Total	6	20	25	34	38	47	46	29,1	30	43	318,1

Twinning

Twinning was launched in May 1998 as the principal mechanism of the Institution Building projects. The objective of the Twinning projects is to help candidate countries in their development of modern and efficient administrations with structures, human resources and management skills needed to implement the acquis communautaire with the same standards as the Member States.

The Twinning provides the framework for administrations and semi-public organisations in the candidate countries to work with their counterparts in Member States top develop and implement a projects involves the transposition, enforcement and implementation of a specific part of the acquis communautaire. Twinning project has at least on pre-accession advisor who is an individual seconded from a Member State administration to work full time in the correspondent ministry in a candidate country for a minimum of 12 months to implement the project.

5 projects of 1998 PHARE National Programme, 12 projects of 1999 PHARE National Programme and 2 projects of the Pre-Ins Facility, 8 projects of 2000 PHARE programme are under the implementation by means of 'Twinning' instrument.

Since 1 September 2001, the Ministry of Finance of the Republic of Lithuania and the Central Financing and Contracting Unit coordinate the use of PHARE funds.

ISPA

Since 2000 Lithuania has been benefiting from the new EU pre-accession instrument – ISPA (Instrument for Structural Policies for Pre-Accession), which is transitional from the financial support to candidate countries (PHARE) to the financial support to Member States (Cohesion Fund). ISPA is guided by the Accession Partnership and the National Programme for the Adoption of the Acquis, follows an approach similar to that of the Cohesion Fund, and operates in the fields of environment and transport.

Although ISPA is an instrument designed for project financing, it requires strategies, which were completed in 2000 by the Ministry of Transport and the Ministry of Environment in co-ordination with the Ministry of Foreign Affairs.

Over a period of seven years starting from 2000 up to 1 billion EUR will be granted to applicant countries. The annual appropriations for Lithuania will be approximately 50 MEUR until its accession to EU. ISPA support is granted to the projects, which cost not less than 5 MEUR, and rate of the Community assistance may be up to 75 %. A balance shall be struck between projects in the field of environment and projects relating to transport infrastructure.

ISPA makes an emphasis on the environmental directives that are very costly to implement. These concern drinking water supply, waste water treatment, management of solid waste and hazardous waste, air pollution.

As for transport sector, ISPA promotes the projects aimed at extending the trans-European Transport Networks to provide good connections between the Union and the applicant countries and interconnections between national networks and links from these to the Trans-European Transport Networks, in particular those that constitute projects of common interest based on the criteria of Decision No 1692/96/EC. In this context, the TINA (Transport Infrastructure Needs Assessment) network is an important reference for identifying projects. ISPA priorities in transport sector include railways, roads, ports and airports.

With regard to project applications, in 2000 a total of 7 official applications have been submitted to the European Commission by the National ISPA Co-ordinator (at that time – Ministry of Foreign Affairs): 2 in the environmental sector and 5 in the transport sector.

Since 1 September 2001, the Ministry of Finance of the Republic of Lithuania coordinates the use of ISPA funds in Lithuania.

SAPARD

SAPARD (Special Accession Programme for Agriculture and Rural Development) follows an approach similar to that of the EAGGF (European Agricultural Guidance and Guarantee Fund) and FIFG (Financial Instrument for Fisheries Guidance).

SAPARD is aimed at supporting the efforts being made by the applicant countries to run up to accession as they prepare for their participation in the Common Agricultural Policy (CAP), familiarise with policies and procedures of the EU. SAPARD will fund a wide range of structural adjustment and rural development priorities.

SAPARD funds amount to 520 MEUR for each year, including allocations of 29,829 MEUR for Lithuania until Lithuania's accession to EU. Under the SAPARD programme, the Community contributes up to 75 % of the total eligible expenditures. The rest of financing should come from national sources.

In order to achieve the effective use of SAPARD programme, National Paying Agency under the Ministry of Agriculture has been set up. The Agency will assume the responsibility for the administrating of the programme.

In preparation for SAPARD, Lithuania has drafted a Rural Development Plan in accordance with the programming requirements of Council Regulation (EC) No 1268/1999 and Commission Regulation (EC) No 2759/1999.

The Plan presents the objectives and instruments for the Lithuania's agricultural and rural development in order to qualify for SAPARD assistance. The Plan is based on the Programme of Government of Lithuania, the Lithuanian Agricultural Strategy, the Preliminary National Development Plan and the National Agri-Environmental Programme. The aid measures are in conformity with the obligations assumed in the Accession Partnership and are in line with the National Programme for the Adoption of the acquis. In addition, the measures are consistent with the objectives of the EU Common Agricultural Policy.

The Plan comprises ten chapters and eleven annexes, which include rural development context, strengths and weaknesses, strategy, objectives, priorities and financial plan.

The Plan foresees the following priority measures for agriculture and rural development:
1. Investment in agricultural holdings
2. Improving processing and marketing of agricultural and fisheries products
3. Development and diversification of economic activities, providing for multiple activities and alternative income
4. Improvement of rural infrastructure

5. Afforestation of agricultural land and improvement of forestry infrastructure
6. Environmentally friendly agricultural methods
7. Vocational training
8. Technical assistance.

The preparation of the Rural Development Plan, which has received a positive opinion in the European Commission, and the establishing of the National Paying Agency provide a sound basis for programming.

According to decision of F.Fischler, member of European Commission, responsible for Agriculture, of 26 November 2001, institutions of the Republic of Lithuania have received the function of administration of SAPARD funds. In Lithuania this function is implemented by the National Paying Agency.

EU Northern Dimension

Northern Dimension is the initiative of Finland, the outline of which was first officially presented by the Prime Minister of Finland - Paavo Lipponen - in 1997. The European Council in Feira confirmed the Northern Dimension Action Plan.

The Northern Dimension geographically covers the regions of the Baltic Sea, the North-Barents and the Arctic. Thematically it covers the following subjects: energy, security of nuclear power stations, transport infrastructure, forest and nature security, trade and economic co-operation, justice, work force, social and health protection and other.

The goal of the Northern Dimension is to direct the attention and strategic interests of the EU at Northern Europe balancing two European political-economical axes: the southern and the northern. This can be achieved inter alia through a more active involvement of Russia, especially its northern-western region, into co-operation. The Northern Dimension also seeks to use the northern-western natural and other resources of Russia for meeting the needs of the EU states.

When putting into practice the Northern Dimension projects it would be important to co-ordinate effectively the activities of the financial instruments of the EU – PHARE, TACIS, INTERREG.

Lithuania's contribution to the Northern Dimension is its relations and co-operation with Kaliningrad. In this sense the bilateral Nida initiative of Lithuania and Russia announced in 2000 is important. This initiative comprises the agreements reached on certain bilateral projects. The Nida initiative was included into the Northern Dimension Action Plan.

The European Conference

The conclusions drawn at the Luxembourg European Council (December 1997) assert that the European Conference is "a multilateral forum of political consultations, where the participants can discuss common problems and extend co-operation in the spheres of foreign and security policy, justice and home affairs, and others, including economic problems and regional co-operation." The states of Central and Eastern Europe that are striving for the EU membership, Cyprus, Malta, Turkey and Switzerland are taking part in the Conference.

The first meeting of the European Conference took place in London on 12 March 1998 on the level of heads of states. The following questions were discussed during the meeting: prevention of crime, common foreign and security policy, environment protection, stimulation of competition economy, extension of regional co-operation. The meeting of the Ministers of Foreign Affairs took place in Luxembourg on 6 October 1998, as well as four meetings at expert level in the framework of the Pact against organised crime. The second meeting of the European Conference at ministerial level in the framework of General Affairs Council took place in Brussels on 19 June 1999. (The question of the Western Balkans was considered). The other meeting took place in the town of Sochaux-Montbelliard, in France, on 23 November 2000. The meeting was held at ministerial level on the affairs of Europe; the institutional structure of the EU was discussed.

It was expected that the Conference would become one of the enlargement instruments that would cover all the candidate countries and would be a mechanism for inclusion of Turkey. The European Conference did not become an instrument of the preparation for accession.

The European Commission's Enlargement Strategy of 2000 suggests using the European Conference as the forum for the discussion of the future of the EU with the candidate countries in the future.

THE EUROPEAN UNION INTERGOVERNMENTAL CONFERENCE

Decisions of the European Council in Nice

The Intergovernmental Conference (IGC) on the institutional reform of the EU was concluded on 10 December 2000 in Nice. The following most important decisions were made:

On the size and composition of the European Commission. The European Commission formed in 2005 will be composed of one Commissionerfrom every member state. When the number of the EU member states reaches 27, the number of the members of the Commission will be reduced, and the posts of the Commissioners will be allocated among the member states on equal bases under the procedure of rotation. The powers of the President of the Commission will be strengthened and he will be able to determine the internal structure of the Commission at his own discretion;

On the weighting of votes in the Council of the European Union. According to the new arrangement of votes in the Council, Germany, France, Great Britain and Italy will possess the largest number of votes – 29, Malta will own least – 3; Lithuania will have 7 votes, Latvia and Estonia – 4 each. Alongside with the number of mandates, the counting by the number of population is foreseen. [For instance, to make a decision there should be not only the qualified majority of votes but also the approval of the countries representing not less than 62 % of the EU inhabitants.] ;

On the extension of qualified majority voting in the Council. The qualified majority voting in the Council is extended to 29 spheres. The right of veto will remain on some of the questions of fiscal (taxation) security, social security, immigration and border security (refugee and asylum including), health and education. The qualified majority voting will be applied for structural policy (since the year 2007), the nominations of the Secretary of the Council and the nominations of the representatives of the EU Common Foreign and Security Policy, for services of trade with foreign countries (except the audio-visual sector), and for other questions;

On enhanced co-operation. According to a certain procedure 8 member states will be able to start intensified co-operation; it will be open to the EU member states that want and are able to take part in it;

On the EU Charter of Fundamental Rights. This is a document of political, but not of legal character yet, concerning the main human rights. The EU practically has not yet had any competence in this area.

Representation in the EU institutions according to the decisions of the European Council in Nice

Country	Votes in the Council of the European Union	Seats in the European Parliament	Representatives in the Committee of Economic and Social Issues	Representatives in the Regional Committee
Germany	29	99	24	24
United Kingdom	29	72	24	24
France	29	72	24	24
Italy	29	72	24	24
Spain	27	50	21	21
Poland	27	50	21	21
Romania	14	33	15	15
Netherlands	13	25	12	12
Greece	12	22	12	12
Czech Republic	12	20	12	12
Belgium	12	22	12	12
Hungary	12	20	12	12
Portugal	12	22	12	12
Sweden	10	18	12	12
Bulgaria	10	17	12	12
Austria	10	17	12	12
Slovakia	7	13	9	9
Denmark	7	13	9	9
Finland	7	13	9	9
Ireland	7	12	9	9
Lithuania	**7**	**12**	**9**	**9**

Latvia	4	8	7	7
Slovenia	4	7	7	7
Estonia	4	6	7	7
Cyprus	4	6	6	6
Luxembourg	4	6	6	6
Malta	3	5	5	5
Total	**345**	**732**	**344**	**344**

SMILING ABOUT LITHUANIA AND THE EUROPEAN UNION

The European Union and European integration are not just a matter of complicated wording and piles of documentation. These processes are the ones that can make us smile as well.

In order to prove this the Ministry of Foreign Affairs of Lithuania arranged an exhibition "Smiling about Lithuania and the European Union" in July 2001. The exhibition included cartoons by more than twenty Lithuanian artists who have accepted the invitation from European integration department at the Ministry of Foreign Affairs of Lithuania and Cartoonists section at the Lithuanian Artists' Association to present their cartoons on the topic of Lithuania's integration into the EU. Some of these cartoons are brand new, some of them are older and reflect previous years of country's integration into the EU.

After the exhibition at MFA cartoons started their journey to EU member states and candidate countries, as well as various cities and towns of Lithuania.

The exhibition is accompanied by a colourful booklet. By clicking on the banner CARTOONS CATALOGUE (.pdf) you can view the electronic version of this booklet.

We are very grateful to all the artists who have sent their cartoons for this exhibition. Our special thanks to Jonas Varnas, Head of Cartoonists section, who was very helpful in arranging the exhibition. We are also grateful to the EC Delegation in Vilnius for the support.

LITHUANIA AND NATO

LITHUANIAN CONTRIBUTION TO THE EURO-ATLANTIC STABILITY

Lithuania supports the Alliance's goal to strengthen and further project Euro-Atlantic security and stability. Lithuania contributes to these objectives by:
· maintaining good neighbourly relations and stability in the region,
· participating in the global antiterrorist coalition,
· developing its military capabilities for participation in Article 5 and non-Article 5 operations of the Alliance,
· and participating in international peace missions.

GOOD NEIGHBOURLY RELATIONS AND STABILITY IN THE REGION

One of Lithuania's foreign and security policy strategic objectives - to maintain and develop good neighbourly relations – strengthens confidence, stability and security in the whole Baltic Sea region.

Lithuania addresses economic, social, and environmental issues within the framework of the Council of the Baltic Sea States.

Among other areas of co-operation with Latvia and Estonia Lithuania actively participates in trilateral co-operative projects in the field of defence. The BALTBAT, BALTRON, BALTNET, and BALTDEFCOL projects strengthen Baltic military ties and ensure confidence among partners. New "Balt" project BALTCISS (Baltic Command, Control and Information System) is on the way.

Lithuania continues to develop the joint Lithuanian-Polish Battalion LITPOLBAT for international security and peace support missions and its strategic partnership with Poland. Lithuania also has close contacts with other NATO allies through active political-military consultations and practical co-operation.

Lithuania constructs its relations with Russia as an integral element of NATO-Russia and EU-Russia partnership and co-operation. Lithuania also develops economic, financial, commercial, cultural, and other relations with Russia's Kaliningrad region. Co-operation takes place on various levels and in different frameworks.

Lithuania adheres to a policy of "selective engagement" vis-a-vis Belarus and is interested in strengthening the foundation of the civil society in this country.

With the purpose of enhancing military transparency and predictability with its neighbours, Lithuania has initiated and developed bilateral Confidence and Security Building Measures (CSBMs) with Russia and Belarus in accordance with the 1999 Vienna document of OSCE and CFE Treaty requirements.

Lithuania is exporting security and stability by working with the countries of Central Asia and the Caucasus in areas of military education and training and defence planning. Attention is also given to co-operation building with Ukraine.

PARTICIPATION IN THE GLOBAL COALITION AGAINST TERRORISM

In September 2001, authorisation has been issued for US Governmental and military aircrafts to use the Lithuanian air space and land in Lithuanian airports during the antiterrorist campaign. Four Lithuanian military medical personnel are deployed as a part of the 6th Czech military field hospital in Kabul, Afghanistan (UN-led ISAF operation). In October 2002, Lithuania also plans to send its Special Force (40 soldiers) for participation in the Operation "Enduring Freedom."

The Government of Lithuania adopted a Resolution on the measures for the implementation of the UN Security Council Resolutions 1333 and 1373. A report on the actual implementation of the Security Council resolution 1373 has been submitted to the UN Counter-Terrorism Committee.

On 16 January 2002, the Lithuanian Government adopted the Counter-Terrorism Program in order to effectively fight terrorism. The Program foresees complex antiterrorist measures and activities, which have a fixed time of implementation from 3 months to 2 years.

The Government has allocated an additional amount of LTL 7 million (Euro 2.03 million) in 2002 state budget to fight terrorism.

DEVELOPMENT OF DEFENCE CAPABILITIES

On 23 May 2001, Lithuanian parliamentary parties signed The Agreement on the Defence Policy, 2001-2004. The document highlights the political consensus to strengthen Lithuania's military capabilities in order to be prepared for collective defence and participation in NATO and EU international operations as well as in crisis and conflict prevention. The agreement sets clear guidelines and ensures appropriate defence spending for our integration into NATO. Lithuania's defence expenditures for the period of 2002-2004 will amount to 2 per cent of GDP.

On 15 January 2002, the Seimas approved the Law on International Operations, Military and Other Events. The Law foresees transparent and effective procedures to send military units to Article 5 and other operations, as well as receive foreign units on Lithuanian soil. The Law came into force on 6 February 2002.

The main thrust of Lithuanian defence reform is the implementation of revised defence structures, which reflects the balance between the resources available and the international security environment. The main directions are these: the development of self-defence capabilities, abilities to contribute to the NATO-led operations and host nation support. In developing Lithuanian defence capabilities priority is given to the Land Forces. Military units of the Land Forces will be small, mobile, deployable, well trained and equipped with modern armament.

A comprehensive National Security Strategy has been drafted in a co-ordinated cross-agency effort. The draft, which currently awaits confirmation, marks a strategic drift from the post-Soviet recovery tasks to Lithuania functioning as a mature modern Western-type democracy with a free-market economy, observing fully human and minority rights, fulfilling reliably its international commitments and integrating purposefully into the strategic communities of nations with shared values, NATO and the EU.

In October 2002, a NATO compatible battalion available for deployment on Article 5 operations and capable of operating as an organic part of the Allied force for operation outside Lithuania is ready as planned.

The highest priority is given to the establishment and development of a fully NATO-interoperable Reaction Brigade, which by the end of 2006 will be able to conduct Article 5 operations together with NATO forces on Lithuanian soil.

Building of an effective air space monitoring and control system and an infrastructure for host nation support (HNS) is a top priority.

The BALTNET (Baltic Air Surveillance System) provides a recognised air picture over the territory of the Baltic States, creating an effective air space monitoring and control system. BALTNET is interoperable with NATO Integrated Air Defence System.

In the meantime, the airfield at Šiauliai and the seaport at Klaipėda have been identified as an airport and a seaport of debarkation of the Allied forces. Upgraded military airports and a seaport can fully serve NATO needs. Alternatively, there are three civil airports in Vilnius, Kaunas and Palanga that could be used for the same purpose. It has been three years, since Lithuania started providing HNS to Allied troops that conducted PfP and "In the Spirit of PfP" exercises in Lithuania.

The air defence systems, radars, tactical communications equipment, anti-tank systems, transport and logistics are the main procurement projects in the period from 2001 to 2003. The expenditure for procurement projects increased from 9,8 per cent at the overall defence budget in 2000 to 20.4 per cent in 2001 and 21,4 per cent in 2002. The last acquisition agreements are the Javelin Anti-Tank System and 3D air surveillance radars (EADS). Lithuania is the first European country to purchase the Javelin Anti-Tank System. Stinger missiles' acquisition is on the way.

For NATO international peace operations conducted in peacetime, Lithuania plans to deploy one motorised infantry company, one infantry company as a part of BALTBAT, an engineer platoon, a medical section, two light transport aircrafts, two light transport helicopters, a mine countermeasures vessel, and a mine-hunter as a part of BALTRON.

PARTICIPATION AND FUTURE PLANS IN INTERNATIONAL PEACE MISSIONS

Shortly after the restoration of independence in 1990, the Government of Lithuania has joined the efforts of the international community in peace building. The idea of our participation in international peace operations has received a broad national support and is still regarded as Lithuania's direct contribution to stability and security building in the Euro-Atlantic area.

Since 1994, over 1000 Lithuanian peacekeepers and civilian policemen have continuously served in UN, OSCE, and NATO-led missions, including UNPROFOR II, UNTAES, UNMIBH, UNMIK, IFOR, AFOR, SFOR, KFOR and ISAF missions. Lithuania has also shown its determination to contribute to the Petersberg tasks within European Security and Defence Policy.

Currently, Lithuanian officers and soldiers are serving in KFOR (30 military personnel) and SFOR (2 military personnel) missions in the Balkans. Lithuania has also provided military aircraft and crew maintenance personnel to the NATO-led KFOR/SFOR operations. Lithuanian policemen are serving in the UN Interim Administration mission in Kosovo (UNMIK).

Along with troops, since 1996 Lithuanian civilian police have served with UNTAES mission in Eastern Slavonia (later, the OSCE monitoring group), UNMIBH in Bosnia and Herzegovina, and UNMIK in Kosovo. About 30 policemen were on duties at UN civilian police and at OSCE verifications, acted as WEU instructors.

Lithuania is a member of the UN Special Committee on Peacekeeping Operations and a member of the UN Stand-by Arrangement system. Currently Lithuania has a participant status of the Multinational Stand-by High Readiness Brigade for United Nations Operations (SHIRBRIG). On May 22, 2002 Lithuania signed Letter of Intent and Memoranda of Understanding (MOU) for the Steering Committee, SHIRBRIG, and has pledged to contribute a medical evacuation section comprising of two squads to SHIRBRIG. MOU for SHIRBRIG is being staffed, and will be signed as soon as internal legal procedures will be over.

To further develop peacekeeping capabilities Lithuania takes part in Lithuanian–Polish Battalion (LITPOLBAT) and Baltic Battalion (BALTBAT) projects. LITPOLBAT is fully prepared for the peacekeeping missions. Recently, two Lithuanian platoons of LITPOLBAT took part in KFOR operations. BALTBAT, having received the assistance of partner countries under Danish chairmanship, has enhanced its capabilities. That enables Lithuania to participate in a full spectrum of peace operations and to sustain long-term deployment of its forces outside the territory of our country. Since 1998, BALTBAT has been contributing to SFOR operation in Bosnia. Presently, Lithuanian soldiers form a basis of BALTSQN-5 in SFOR mission.

TABLE NO.1 Participation of the Lithuanian Armed Forces in International Peace Support Operations

OPERATION	Period	Participating Force	Remarks
UN Operations			
UNPROFOR II (Croatia)	22/ 08/ 1994 - 16/ 10/ 1995	One platoon (32/32/26 personnel) on a half year rotation basis	Within Danish Battalion LITPLA-1, LITPLA-2, LITPLA-3
UN-led ISAF (Afghanistan)	14/ 10/ 2002 – until now	4 military medical officers	Within the Czech Military Hospital
NATO-led operations			
NATO IFOR operation "Joint Endeavor" (Bosnia)	19/ 02/ 1996 - 27/ 08/ 1996	34 personnel - LITPLA-4	Within Danish Battalion/ Nordic–Polish Brigade. 1st Lt Normundas Valteris died on 17/ 04/ 1996 in a mine accident
	02/ 10/ 1996 - 19/ 12/ 1996	141 personnel - LITCOY-1	
NATO SFOR operation "Joint Guard" (Bosnia)	20/ 12/ 1996 - 07/ 04/ 1997	141 personnel - LITCOY-1	Within Danish Battalion/ Nordic–Polish Brigade
	18/ 04/ 1997 - 13/ 10/ 1997	41 personnel - LITPLA-5	
	12/ 10/ 1997 - 21/ 04/ 1998	41 personnel - LITPLA-6	
	16/ 04/ 1998 - 23/ 10/ 1998	41 personnel - LITPLA-7	
	20/ 10/ 1998 - 15/ 03/ 1999	41 personnel - BALTCON-1	
	15/ 03/ 1999 - 13/ 10/ 1999	147 personnel - BALTCON-2	
	13/ 10/ 1999 - 20/ 03/ 2000	19 personnel - BALTCON-3	
	20/ 03/ 2000 - 27/ 08/ 2000	2 personnel - BALTSQN-1	Within Danish Battalion /NORDPOL Battle Group
	21/ 08/ 2000 - 15/ 02/ 2001	74 personnel - BALTSQN-2	
	15/ 02/ 2001 -14/ 08/ 2001	2 personnel - BALTSQN-3	
	14/ 08/ 2001- 17/ 02/ 2002	2 personnel - BALTSQN-4	
	17/ 02/ 2002 – 16/ 08/ 2002	95 personnel - BALTSQN-5	

	16/ 08/ 2002 – until now	2 personnel - BALTSQN-6	
NATO–led humanitarian aid operation "Allied Harbour" (Albania)	02/ 05/ 1999 - 01/ 09/ 1999	10 personnel - Military Medical Team	Within Czech 6th Military Hospital
NATO–led KFOR operation "Joint Guardian" (Kosovo)	18/ 09/ 1999 - until now	30 personnel on rotation basis every 6 month	KFOR-1, KFOR-2, KFOR-3, KFOR-4, KFOR-5, KFOR-6 within Polish Battalion/ US Area of Responsibility
NATO-led execution of KFOR/SFOR tasks	04/ 04/ 2001 - until now	Aircraft An-26 with crew and maintenance personnel (7 personnel)	
Participation in anticipated NATO-led operations			
NATO SFOR operation "Joint Guard" (Bosnia)	02/2003 - 08/2003	2 personnel - BALTSQN-7	Within Danish Battalion /NORDPOL Battle Group
	08/2003 - 02/2004	up to 99 personnel - BALTSQN-8	
	02/2004 - 08/2004	2 personnel - BALTSQN-9	
Participation in anticipated US-led operations			
"Enduring Freedom" (Afghanistan)	11/2002	Special Forces (up to 40 soldiers)	
OSCE operations			
OSCE Verification Mission in Kosovo	03/ 12/ 1998 - 29/ 03/ 1999	3 military observers	
OSCE Border Monitoring Mission in Georgia	24/ 02/ 2000 - 15/ 11/ 2000	1 military observer	
	05/ 06/ 2000 - 15/ 09/ 2000	1 military observer	
	18/ 05/ 2001 – 16/ 04/ 2002	1 military observer	
	08/ 04/ 2002 - until now	1 military observer	
More than 1000 Lithuanian military personnel have participated in PSO since 1994.			

INTERNATIONAL RELATIONS

LITHUANIA'S CO-OPERATION WITH LATVIA, ESTONIA AND THE NORDIC COUNTRIES

During the recent years the Baltic and Nordic countries have developed a cohesive network of co-operation activities in political, military, economic, environmental, cultural and other aspects. Co-operation is intensifying in all public and private levels thereby activating the vast potential for development in the region.

COOPERATION WITH LATVIA AND ESTONIA

The Council of the Baltic States (CBS) was established on May 12, 1990. The CBS included the Heads of the three states and the Heads of Government. The CBS later on was transformed into regular summits of the Presidents of the three states.
In 1990, the first joint session of the parliaments of Estonia, Latvia and Lithuania was held in Vilnius. In 1991 the Baltic Assembly, comprised of 60 parliamentarians of the Baltic states was founded.
In 1994, the Baltic Council of Ministers (BCM) was established (http://www.bcmvs.net). In this framework the Prime Ministers of the Baltic states meet at least twice a year. Committees of Senior Officials of the BCM co-ordinate the co-operative activities of the three states in the fields of their competence.
The main activities of the BCM and priorities of Lithuania during it's presidency are as follows:

Trade

Ensuring smooth and efficient implementation of the free trade agreement between the Baltic States is among the major tasks of the BCM. Latvia is Lithuania's export partner No1. During the year 2000 14.9% of Lithuanian export went to Latvia and 2% to Estonia.

Cooperation in the field of energy

Lithuania, Latvia and Estonia parallelly operate their power systems. The creation of a common Baltic electricity market is on the agenda.

Implementation of the transport infrastructure projects

Lithuania continues developing infrastructure projects, in particular the Via Baltica and the Rail Baltica - the First Crete Corridor.

Cooperation in the field of defence

Lithuania stresses the importance of enhancing defence-related co-operation by developing common projects:
BALTBAT - common Baltic Battalion formed for participation in international peace keeping operations. Recently BALTBAT was upgraded to a full-power infantry battalion.
BALTRON - Baltic Naval Squadron consists of ships, designated by Lithuania, Latvia and Estonia. Works according to annual plans which provide for personnel training and participation in international exercises and in the naval mine counter-measure operations.
BALTNET - Baltic Air Surveillance Network system consists of national air surveillance centres in Lithuania, Latvia and Estonia and allows the Baltic States to effectively survail and co-ordinate their sovereign air space and to ensure safety of air traffic.
BALTDEFCOL - Baltic Defence College has the task to train staff officers from the Baltic States for future service in the national Ministries of defence, national and international headquarters from the regiment/brigade level upwards, as defence attaches or military academy instructors.
It is in the interest of Lithuania to co-ordinate actions in the field of defence procurement.

Creation of the common Baltic education area

Lithuania, Latvia and Estonia have the agreements on the creation of a common secondary and vocational education area; on academic recognition of educational qualifications in the Baltic Educational space; and on the common Baltic higher education area. Implementation of the agreements is on the agenda. The exchange of students among the Baltic States is scheduled for 2002-2003.

Cooperation in Home and Justice Affairs

major recent agreementss:
The Baltic countries aim to intensify mutual relations in performing the functions of crime prevention and control. The trilateral agreement on consular cooperation among the Baltic States was signed on 5 February 1999 in Vilnius, and is of the utmost importance for facilitating consular assistance to Lithuanian, Latvian and Estonian citizens in foreign countries.
The agreement on co-operation in protecting victims and witnesses among the Baltic States was signed on 17 March 2000.

COOPERATION WITH THE NORDIC COUNTRIES

Lithuania has a variety of bilateral ties with all Nordic countries – Sweden, Denmark, Finland, Norway and Iceland.

Lithuania's cooperation with the Nordic countries develops in several ways, e.g. intensive bilateral contacts and consultations, cooperation according to the Nordic-Baltic 8 (NB 8) formula, working relations between the Baltic Council of Ministers (BCM) and the Nordic Council of Ministers (NCM), collaboration in the framework of regional and international organisations as well as co-operation between regions.
Practical cooperation with the Nordic countries involves culture, education, environmental protection, infrastructure, social security, people-to-people contacts, etc.
The Nordic countries are among the major investors to Lithuania: by October 2000, direct investment of these countries to Lithuania was 919.79 million USD, which made 41.7 % of the total direct investment to Lithuania. Trade turnover between Lithuania and the Nordic countries during 9 months of 2000 was 729.66 million USD, which made 10.74 % of the total annual trade turnover between Lithuania and other countries.
On the political level the Nordic countries remain among the main supporters of Lithuania's accession to EU and NATO.

NORDIC-BALTIC 8 (5+3)

5+3 meetings started in 1992 on the Prime Ministerial level. The Prime Ministers now meet annually to discuss common foreign policy and regional issues. The Ministers of Foreign Affairs have met annually since 1993, the Ministers of Defence since 1994 and the Ministers for Regional Cooperation (Baltic States are represented by Ministers of Foreign Affairs) since 1996. Cooperation according to formula 5+3 has got a new impetus through frequent consultations on the level of Political Directors. Ad hoc meetings with the participation of one guest country are also being held e.g. EU High Commissioner Javier Solana participated in the last meeting of the Ministers of Foreign Affairs in Middelfart, Denmark (2000.08.29-30). At the given meeting Ministers have come to a consensus that forthcoming meetings are to be called Nordic Baltic 8.

THE COUNCIL OF THE BALTIC SEA STATES

The Council of the Baltic Sea States (CBSS), established in 1992, is the regional economic, cultural and human rights cooperation forum which, aside from the Baltic and Nordic countries also includes Poland, Germany and Russia.

Lithuania was holding the presidency of the CBSS for one year from July 1998 till July 1999. Continuation of the work in the core areas of cooperation such as assistance to democratic institutions and human rights, economic integration and trade, civic security, education and nuclear safety, as well as greater inclusion of the Kaliningrad region of Russia into the activities of the CBSS were the priorities of Lithuanian presidency.
The establishment of the permanent CBSS Secretariat during Lithuania's presidency was one of the most important factors achieving a higher level of efficiency in the work of the CBSS. The document regarding the participation of the third countries in the activities of the CBSS was adopted during the Lithuanian presidency.

BALTIC COUNCIL OF MINISTERS GUIDELINES FOR THE LITHUANIAN CHAIRMANSHIP

(1 JULY 2001 – 30 JUNE 2002)

I. PREPARATION FOR EU MEMBERSHIP

One of the top priorities of the Lithuanian, Latvian, and Estonian foreign and domestic policy is the integration into the European Union. In pursuing the common goal the countries should engage in more intensive consultations on the matters of the negotiation process and seek to better prepare for the membership of the European Union through active trilateral co-operation and deeper regional integration.

ECONOMIC CO-OPERATION

Energy
In the process of the regional integration and with a view to joining the single European energy market it becomes essential that the Baltic Energy Strategy would be implemented. It is necessary to harmonise actions among the Nordic and Baltic countries for the co-operation in the energy area and also to present common positions in the BASREC activities.
The establishment of the Common Baltic Electricity Market and the construction of the power transmission mains connecting the power systems of the Baltic States, Poland, and Finland further remain priority projects. In compliance with the tasks formulated in the Prime Ministers' Resolution of the BCM Lithuania will seek to ensure the fulfillment of the obligations that predetermine the beginning of the functioning of the Common Baltic Electricity Market at the agreed time.

Transport
It is important to further develop the transport infrastructure of the Baltic States thereby contributing to the acceleration of the integration process both on the regional and European levels. The main focus should be placed on the road and railway transport in the direction South-North.

VIA BALTICA
The first investment Via Baltica programme for the years 1996-2000 was completed in December 2000. Its priority was the reconstruction of the main roads in the Via Baltica network. The second investment programme will also be launched to extend the first programme and to merge both programmes into a single development process of the road infrastructure.

There are still road sections that do not comply with the norms and present serious problems for the increasing traffic flow in the Via Baltica road. Therefore, Lithuania will seek to accelerate and bring to the fore the solution of this problem, i.e. to accelerate the implementation of unified

standards at the whole length of the main corridor.
RAIL BALTICA

Lithuania attaches priority to the modernisation of the railway infrastructure in the direction North-South in the Baltic region. This direction has recently been neglected due to a variety of reasons.

It is necessary to shape as soon as possible a vision of common standards and gradual implementation of the railway development to be acceptable to all the countries that take part at the corridor operation. It is extremely important to identify future railway border crossing points, which would facilitate fundamentally the preparation of all pre-project activities and would help to draft in due time applications to receive financing from EU support funds. It would also compliment proposals drafted during the TINA process.
The initial stage in the railway development of the North-South transport corridor calls for the initiation of:

- the establishment of uniform transport legislation;
- the improvement of passenger carriage;
- shaping a long-term infrastructure development vision within the TINA context.

Environmental Protection
Having assessed the complexity of the current environmental situation and in view of a huge importance of environmental projects for the region, Lithuania during its chairmanship will place a lot of focus on the enforcement and supervision of the signed bilateral and trilateral agreements as well as the initiation and drafting of new agreements.

A number of seminars and meetings are scheduled within the framework of the Baltic Environmental Forum on the matters of EU integration (common policy, implementation of the Basic Directive on Waters, issues of waste and emissions), control of chemicals in the Baltic region as well as nature conservation.

Trade, improvement of business climate
During its chairmanship the Lithuanian side is ready to intensify work in enforcing provisions of the following trilateral agreements: free trade, agreement on the abolition of non-tariff barriers to trade, and the avoidance of double taxation.
On 1 January 2001 the Agreement on the Common Transit Procedure came into force. Lithuania is going to encourage all economic entities concerned to take the best possible advantage of the possibilities offered by the Agreement.

Resolution of border crossing issues
Lithuania will aim at the highest possible capacity of borders crossing and will at the same time devote its attention to the re-enforcement of the future external borders of the EU.

With a view to enhancing mutual co-operation in the customs area an attempt will be made to review the trilateral intergovernmental agreement on mutual co-operation in the customs area.

A common customs control system in the Estonian-Latvian and Latvian-Lithuanian border crossing points should be created by way of co-operation.
Preparatory work for the implementation of the ASYCUDA system should take place in line with the exchange of data among the Baltic customs administrations.

CO-OPERATION IN THE AREA OF HOME AND JUSTICE AFFAIRS

Co-operation in the area of home affairs to fight against organised crime.
The Baltic countries will aim to intensify mutual relations in performing the functions of crime prevention and control. There is a strong intention to draft a trilateral agreement "On the Co-operation in Recognising the Procedures for the Exaction of Fines on the Violation of Road Traffic Rules". Moreover, further actions will be taken to enforce the trilateral agreement "On the Protection of Witnesses and Victims".

Attention should be given to the types of crime most rapidly spreading in the Baltic States, i.e. computer crimes, drug trafficking and proliferation, and trafficking in persons. To this end, the co-operation field will be expanded, new sub-committees will be set up.
The integration into the EU calls for further co-operation in implementing EU and Schengen acquis. With this in view the following steps will be made:

- preparation for the entry into the Schengen Information System;
- ensuring the implementation of legal as well as practical aspects of cross-border surveillance and persecution.

Co-operation to resolve migration problems
During the Lithuanian chairmanship special attention will be given to the resolution of issues pertinent to the repatriation and integration into the society as well as the implementation of the migration and asylum policy.

Co-operation in the area of justice
During its chairmanship Lithuania will seek to co-ordinate the agreement on common representation of interests of the Baltic law enforcement agencies in third countries through the position of the law enforcement attaché (police communications officers) to follow the Nordic example.

II. PREPARATION FOR NATO MEMBERSHIP

The preparation of the Baltic States for NATO accession remains of immense importance during the Lithuanian chairmanship due to the fact that in the Prague NATO Summit in 2002 further NATO enlargement is to take place. The Baltic States aim at seeing NATO enlargement become an on-going process in building a single and unified Europe. The Baltic co-operation is an important factor in ensuring stability of the Baltic Sea region.

During its chairmanship Lithuania will strive to bring the Baltic dimension to the wave of NATO enlargement to be proclaimed in Prague.

Lithuania wants to highlight the following key areas of co-operation:

Political solidarity and support for one another in pursuing NATO membership, particulary within the framework of the Vilnius Processs. Mutual consultations on all levels on the implementation of the Membership Action Plan and the Planning and Review Process
Development of joint military units, infrastructure elements and military training institutions (BALTBAT, BALTRON, BALTNET, and BALTDEFCOL). The integration of these projects into common NATO military structures as well as their involvement in peacekeeping operations headed by NATO.
"Baltification" of Baltic projects supported on the international level (gradual taking over of political responsibility for the success of projects as well as financial burden from supporting partners).

Further joint participation at the NATO-headed peacekeeping mission in Bosnia according to the BALTSQN plan co-ordinated with Denmark in the capacity of an intelligence company within the Danish battalion.
Examination of possibilities and preconditions for joint procurement of weaponry, also, if possible, signing of joint procurement contracts.
Exchange of experience in the following specific areas of activity of defence ministries and armies: personnel management, budget planning, environmental protection in an army, formation of public opinion, international weapon control, etc.

III. CULTURE, EDUCATION, INFORMATION TECHNOLOGIES

During Lithuania's chairmanship at the BCM special attention will be given to:

Co-operation in the Area of Information Technologies,

- by way of creating the Baltic network of common databases (customs, police, border protection, registers, establishment of classifiers, their upgrading).
- by way of continuing activities in the area of publishing an information technologies magazine of the BS (publishing the magazine Baltic IT Review).
- by way of solving problems of information protection in computer networks, legal issues of the electronic signature, creating necessary infrastructure
- by way of standardising information technologies.

Co-operation in the Cultural Area:
It is important to facilitate direct personal contacts, to initiate joint events as well as implement trilateral projects already devised out of which the following should be highlighted as the most important:

- a joint event to be organised in the Nordic countries in autumn 2001, i.e. the Baltic Culture Festival.
- The Forth Song Festival of the Baltic and Nordic Countries to be organised in June–July 2002 in Klaip?da.

Co-operation in the Area of Education:
The Baltic States have created all necessary conditions for the establishment of the common Baltic education area. The exchange of students among the Baltic States is scheduled for 2002-2003. With a view to affecting a common general and higher education area a number of mechanisms and measures for the accomplishment of goals set in signed agreements are being devised. Consultations with the Nordic countries have been launched to help create the common Baltic general and higher education area. As soon as this model is realised the Nordic countries are ready to assist in creating a model of the common Baltic and Nordic education area.

IV. REGIONAL CO-OPERATION

Co-operation with the Nordic Countries
The co-operation of the Nordic and Baltic States in the NB 8 format calls for the extended geography of joint projects. Increased attention should be devoted to the co-operation in the areas of energy, transport, fight against crime, environmental protection, education, information technologies, and defence.

Council of the Baltic Sea States
Lithuania is of the opinion that the Baltic States have to support one another's as well as trilateral interests in the international formats. It is, therefore, worthwhile committing country representatives at the Senior Officials Committee and the working groups to represent together the trilateral interests and harmonise positions to maintain a single Baltic initiative.

Northern Dimension
Within the context of the European integration it is essential to proceed with joint projects of Lithuania, Latvia, and Estonia. It is equally important to develop cross-border co-operation in line with the implementation of the large-scale infrastructure projects (RAIL BALTICA, the Baltic Power Grid, etc.). Joint efforts should be targeted at the consistency of EU PHARE and TACIS mechanisms for the implementation of joint Baltic and Russian Federation projects.

V. TECHNICAL/FUNCTIONAL MATTERS

It is necessary to analyse and assess the activities of the Senior Officials Committees of the Baltic Council of Ministers and accordingly modify the structure of the BCM.
Having assessed the insufficiently active use of possibilities offered by the Virtual Secretariat of the BCM (www.bcmvs.net), attempts should be made to encourage the use of the virtual secretariat on all levels.

LITHUANIA AND THE COUNCIL OF THE BALTIC SEA STATES

Lithuania is an active participant of the Council of the Baltic Sea States since its establishment in 1992. CBSS is a regional political forum covering the whole range of co-operation areas excluding military co-operation issues. In 1998-1999 Lithuania was holding the presidency of the CBSS. While continuing the work in the core areas such as civil security, economic integration, environment protection and nuclear safety Lithuania focused on activating co-operation with the Kaliningrad region of the Russian Federation. Since then issues related to the Kaliningrad area are constantly on the agenda of the CBSS.

Lithuania welcomes the initiative of the German presidency of the CBSS to draw up a list of regional priority projects and propose them as a contribution to the Action plan of the EU's Northern Dimension initiative. Lithuania's contribution to the list of regional priorities include Rail Baltica project, modernization of the Transport corridor IXD, short distance sea transport in the Baltic Sea, Construction of Tourist terminal in Klaipeda port, project on management of of the Nemunas river basin, development of communicable disease control programmes, joint projects with the Kaliningrad region of the RF and trilateral (Polish-Lithuanian-Russian) cross-border training programmes.

LIST OF CONTACTS INVOLVED IN CBSS CO-OPERATION

Baltic Agenda 21

Member of the SOG	Mr. Evaldas Vebra Head of Section Ministry of Environment A.Jaksto 4/9 LT-2694 Vilnius	tel. +370 2 62 36 92 fax. +370 2 62 35 29 e-mail: E.Vebra@aplinkuma.lt
Education	Ms. Aurelija Remeikiene International co-operation	tel. +370 2 74 31 79 fax. +370 2 61 20 77

	and European integration division Ministry of Education and Science A.Volano 2/7 LT-2691 Vilnius	e-mail: aurelija@smm.lt
Children at risk	Ms. Audrone Mikalauskaite Head of Section Ministry of Social Security and Labour A.Vivulskio 11 LT-2693 Vilnius	tel. +370 2 60 37 88 fax. +370 2 60 38 13 e-mail: audram@socmin.lt
Civil security	Mr. Arunas Siuksta Deputy director Civil protection department Ministry of Defence Pamenkalnio 30 LT-2000 Vilnius	tel. +370 2 61 19 31 fax. +370 2 22 06 35 fax. +370 2 62 45 64 e-mail: csd@csd.lt e-mail: siukstaa@lt.pims.org
Committee of Senior officials (CSO)	Ms. Skaiste Aniuliene Counsellor 1st Bilateral Relations Department Ministry of Foreign Affairs J.Tumo Vaizganto 2 LT-2600 Vilnius	tel.+370 2 36 24 80 fax. +370 2 36 24 90 e-mail:cbss@urm.lt
Culture Co-operation	Ms. Vida Graziene Head of International Co-operation Division Ministry of Culture Basanaviciaus 5 LT-2600 Vilnius	tel. +370 2 22 00 55 fax. +370 2 62 31 20 e-mail:vida@muza.lt
Customs co-operation	Ms. Alvyda Jovaisiene Head of Section Customs department Ministry of Finance Jaksto 1/25 LT-2600 Vilnius	tel. + 370 2 62 56 06 fax. + 370 2 22 66 31 e-mail:al.jovaisiene@matheus.cust.lt
Democratic Institutions (WGDI)	Ms. Skaiste Aniuliene Counsellor 1st Bilateral Relations Department Ministry of Foreign Affairs J.Tumo Vaizganto 2 LT-2600 Vilnius	tel. +370 2 36 24 80 fax. +370 2 36 24 90 e-mail:cbss@urm.lt
Economic co-operation (WGEC)	Ms. Rasa Adomaitiene International Economic Organizations Division Ministry of Foreign Affairs J.Tumo Vaizganto 2 LT-2600 Vilnius	tel. +370 2 36 25 96 fax. +370 2 36 25 86 e-mail:teo.ed@urm.lt
Education (EuroFaculty)	Mr. Rimantas Vaitkus Head of Section	tel. +370 2 22 22 51 fax. + 370 2 31 22 95

	Ministry of Education and Science Zygimantu g. 9 LT-2600 Vilnius	e-mail:vaitkus@mokslas.lt
Health	Mr. Viktoras Meizis Head of Foreign Relations and European Integration Division Ministry of Health Vilniaus 33 LT-2001 Vilnius	tel. +370 2 61 17 24 fax. +370 2 22 46 01 e-mail:viktoras.meizis@sam.lt
Labour Market	Ms. Rita Zemaityte Head of Section Ministry of Social Security and Labour A.Vivulskio g. 11 LT-2693 Vilnius	tel. +370 2 60 37 93 fax. +370 2 60 37 98 e-mail:RitaZ@socmin.lt
Organised Crime (Task Force)	Mr. Laimonas Vasiliauskas Senior Commissioner National bureau of Interpol Saltoniskiu 19 LT-2034 Vilnius	tel. +370 2 71 99 02 tel. +370 2 71 99 01 tel. +370 2 71 99 00 fax. +370 2 72 54 61 e-mail:office@ilnb.lt
Spatial Planning (VASAB)	Mr. Aleksandras Gordevicius Spacial Planning and Regional Development Division Ministry of Environment A.Jaksto 4/9 LT-2694 Vilnius	tel. +370 2 61 66 40 fax. +370 2 61 53 39 e-mail:A.Gordevicius@aplinkuma.lt
Taxes	Mr. Gediminas Mudenas International co-operation Division State Taxation Inspection Ministry of Finance Vasario 16-osios g. 15 LT-2600 Vilnius	tel. +370 2 68 78 59 fax. +370 2 22 56 04 e-mail:g.mudenas@vmi.lt

TREATIES

Treaties valid for the Republic of Lithuania

BILATERAL AGREEMENTS

- **ARGENTINA**
- **ARMENIA**
- **AUSTRALIA**
- **AUSTRIA**
- **AZERBAIJAN**
- **BELARUS**
- **BELGO-LUXEMBOURG ECONOMIC UNION**
- **BULGARIA**
- **THE CZECH REPUBLIC**
- **FLANDERS**
- **FRANCE**
- **GEORGIA**
- **GERMANY**
- **GREECE**
- **THE HOLY SEE**
- **HUNGARY**
- **ICELAND**
- **INDIA**
- **IRELAND**
- **NORWAY**
- **PHILIPPINES**
- **POLAND**
- **PORTUGAL**
- **ROMANIA**
- **RUSSIA**
- **SLOVAKIA**
- **SLOVENIA**
- **SPAIN**
- **SWEDEN**

- □ CANADA
- □ CHILE
- □ CHINA
- □ COLOMBIA
- □ CROATIA
- □ CUBA
- □ CYPRUS
- □ DENMARK
- □ EGYPT
- □ ESTONIA
- □ FINLAND
- □ ITALY
- □ ISRAEL
- □ JAPAN
- □ KAZAKSTAN
- □ KUWAIT
- □ REPUBLIC OF KOREA
- □ LATVIA
- □ MALTA
- □ MEXICO
- □ MOLDOVA
- □ THE NETHERLANDS
- □ SWITZERLAND
- □ TATARSTAN
- □ TUNISIA
- □ TURKEY
- □ UKRAINE
- □ UNITED KINGDOM
- □ URUGUAY
- □ USA
- □ UZBEKISTAN
- □ VENEZUELA
- □ VIETNAM

TRILATERAL AGREEMENTS

TRIŠALĖS SUTARTYS
TRILATERAL AGREEMENTS

BALTARUSIJA IR LATVIJA
BELARUS AND LATVIA

1. Lietuvos Respublikos Vyriausybės, Baltarusijos Respublikos Vyriausybės ir Latvijos Respublikos Vyriausybės susitarimas dėl
valstybių sienų sankirtos taško paženklinimo tvarkos
Agreement between the Government of the Republic of Lithuania, the Government of the Republic of Belarus and the Government of
the Republic of Latvia on the procedure of the marking the the point of intersection of the national borders
Vilnius, 1998.03.25
Įsigaliojo 1999.03.17
"V.Ž." - 1999 Nr.25

ESTIJA IR LATVIJA
ESTONIA AND LATVIA

1. Deklaracija dėl Lietuvos Respublikos, Latvijos Respublikos ir Estijos Respublikos santarvės ir bendradarbiavimo
Šia deklaracija buvo atnaujinta 1934 09 12 Ženevoje sudaryta Sutartis bei Deklaracija dėl Lietuvos, Latvijos ir Estijos santarvės ir
bendradarbiavimo
Declaration on Unity and Cooperation by the Republic of Lithuania, the Republic of Latvia and the Republic of Estonia
By this Declaration the Treaty on Unity and Cooperation and the resulting Declaration signed by Lithuania, Latvia and Estonia in
Geneva on September 12, 1934 have been renewed
Talinas, 1990.05.12

2. Lietuvos Respublikos, Estijos Respublikos ir Latvijos Respublikos sutartis dėl teisinės pagalbos ir teisinių santykių
Agreement between the Republic of Lithuania, the Republic of Estonia, the Republic of Latvia on legal assistance and legal relations

Talinas, 1992.11.11
Įsigaliojo 1994.04.03
"V.Ž." - 1994 Nr.28

3. Estijos Respublikos, Latvijos Respublikos ir Lietuvos Respublikos laisvos prekybos sutartis
Free Trade Agreement between the Republic of Estonia, the Republic of Latvia and the Republic of Lithuania
Talinas, 1993.09.13
Įsigaliojo 1994.04.01
"V.Ž." - 1994 Nr.66, 67, atitaisymas Nr.69, papildymai 1995 Nr.13
Rezoliucija Nr.1/97 dėl Laisvosios prekybos sutarties tarp Estijos Respublikos, Latvijos Respublikos ir Lietuvos Respublikos,
pasirašytos 1993 m. rugsėjo 13 d., Protokolo A pataisų
Resolution No.1/97 on the changes to Protocol A to the Free Trade Agreement between the Republic of Estonia, the Republic of
Latvia and the Republic of Lithuania signed on 13 September, 1993
Talinas, 1997.02.06
Įsigaliojo 1997.06.01
"V.Ž." - 1997 Nr.52

4. Estijos Respublikos, Latvijos Respublikos ir Lietuvos Respublikos susitarimas dėl Baltijos šalių tarpparlamentinio ir
tarpvyriausybinio bendradarbiavimo
Agreement on Baltic Parliamentary and Governmental cooperation between the Republic of Estonia, the Republic of Latvia and the
Republic of Lithuania
Talinas, 1994.06.13
Įsigaliojo 1994.12.24
"V.Ž." - 1995 Nr.11

5. Estijos Respublikos Vyriausybės, Latvijos Respublikos Vyriausybės ir Lietuvos Respublikos Vyriausybės susitarimas dėl
tarpusavio pagalbos muitinės veiklos srityje
Agreement between the Government of the Republic of Latvia, the Government of the Republic of Estonia and the Government of the
Republic of Lithuania regarding mutual assistance in customs matters
Palanga, 1994.08.30
Įsigaliojo 1995.11.17
"V.Ž." - 1995 Nr.97

6. Estijos Respublikos, Latvijos Respublikos ir Lietuvos Respublikos sutartis dėl Jungtinio taikos palaikymo dalinio kūrimo ir
formavimo
Agreement between the Republic of Estonia, the Republic of Latvia and the Republic of Lithuania concerning the establishment and
formation of joint peacekeeping unit
Ryga, 1994.09.13
Įsigaliojo 1997.03.14
"V.Ž." - 1997 Nr.37

7. Lietuvos Respublikos Vyriausybės, Estijos Respublikos Vyriausybės ir Latvijos Respublikos Vyriausybės susitarimas dėl
bendradarbiavimo valstybių sienos apsaugos srityje

Agreement between the Government of the Republic of Lithuania, Government of the Republic of Latvia and the Government of the
Republic of Estonia on cooperation in the field of state border protection
Ryga, 1994.11.23
Įsigaliojo 1994.11.23
"V.Ž." - 1995 Nr.11

8. Lietuvos Respublikos Vyriausybės, Estijos Respublikos Vyriausybės ir Latvijos Respublikos Vyriausybės sutartis dėl bevizinio
vykimo tvarkos
Agreement between the Government of the Republic of Lithuania, the Government of the Republic of Estonia and the Government of
the Republic of Latvia on the mutual visa free traveling procedure
Ryga, 1995.06.09
Įsigaliojo 1995.07.01
"V.Ž." - 1995 Nr.55

9. Lietuvos Respublikos Vyriausybės, Estijos Respublikos Vyriausybės ir Latvijos Respublikos Vyriausybės sutartis dėl nelegaliai
gyvenančių asmenų grąžinimo
Agreement between the Government of the Republic of Lithuania, the Government of the Republic of Estonia and the Government of
the Republic of Latvia on the readmission of persons residing illegally
Vilnius, 1995.06.30
Įsigaliojo 1995.06.30
"V.Ž." - 1995 Nr.62

10. Lietuvos Respublikos Vyriausybės, Estijos Respublikos Vyriausybės ir Latvijos Respublikos Vyriausybės bendradarbiavimo
aplinkos apsaugos srityje
Agreement between the Government of the Republic of Lithuania, the Government of the Republic of Estonia and the Government of
the Republic of Latvia on cooperation in the field of Environmental Protection
Talinas, 1995.07.21
Įsigaliojo 1995.07.21
"V.Ž." - 1996 Nr.14

11. Baltijos šalių prezidentų Bendra deklaracija dėl bendradarbiavimo integracijos srityje
Joint Declaration of the Presidents on Partnership for integration
Vilnius, 1996.05.28

12. Sutartis dėl laisvosios prekybos žemės ūkio prekėmis tarp Estijos Respublikos ir Latvijos Respublikos ir Lietuvos Respublikos
Free Trade Agreement between the Republic of Estonia and the Republic of Latvia and the Republic of Lithuania on trade in
agricultural products
Vilnius, 1996.06.16
Įsigaliojo 1997.01.01
"V.Ž." - 1996 Nr.124

13. Rygos deklaracija dėl kovos prieš pinigų plovimą
Riga Declaration on the fight against money laundering
Ryga, 1996.11.14

14. Sutartis dėl netarifinių barjerų prekyboje panaikinimo tarp Estijos Respublikos, Latvijos Respublikos ir Lietuvos Respublikos
Agreement on the abolition of non-tariff barriers to trade between the Republic of Estonia, the Republic of Latvia and the Republic of Lithuania
Ryga, 1997.11.20
Įsigaliojo 1998.07.01
"V.Ž." - 1998 Nr.29

15. Lietuvos Respublikos Vyriausybės, Estijos Respublikos Vyriausybės ir Latvijos Respublikos Vyriausybės sutartis dėl Baltijos bataliono
Agreement between the Government of the Republic of Lithuania, the Government of the Republic of Estonia and the Government of the Republic of Latvia concerning the Baltic Battalion
Talinas, 1997.12.10
Įsigaliojo 1999.03.07
"V.Ž." - 1998 Nr.53

16. Estijos Respublikos Vyriausybės, Latvijos Respublikos Vyriausybės ir Lietuvos Respublikos Vyriausybės sutartis dėl Baltijos oro erdvės stebėjimo sistemos sukūrimo
Agreement between the Government of the Republic of Estonia, the Government of the Republic of Latvia and the Government of the Republic of Lithuania on the establishment of the Baltic air surveillance network
Ryga, 1998.04.16
Įsigaliojo 1999.06.27
"V.Ž." - 1999 Nr.35

17. Lietuvos Respublikos Vyriausybės, Estijos Respublikos Vyriausybės ir Latvijos Respublikos Vyriausybės susitarimas dėl Baltijos jūrų eskadros įkūrimo
Agreement between the Government of the Republic of Lithuania, The Government of the Republic of Estonia and the Government of the Republic of Latvia concerning the establishment of the Baltic Naval Squadron
Ryga, 1998.04.16
Įsigaliojo 1999.06.26
"V.Ž." - 1999 Nr.35

18. Lietuvos Respublikos Vyriausybės, Estijos Respublikos Vyriausybės ir Latvijos Respublikos Vyriausybės protokolas dėl Baltijos bataliono vadaviečių ir Baltijos bataliono personalo statuso
Protocol between the Government of the Republic of Latvia, the Government of the Republic of Estonia and the Government of the Republic of Lithuania concerning the status of the Baltic Battalion Headquarters and the Personnel of the Baltic Battalion
Ryga, 1998.04.16
Įsigaliojo 2000.08.18
"V.Ž." - 1999 Nr.35

19. Baltijos šalių Tarybos deklaracija
Declaration of the Baltic Council
Venspilis, 1998.05.09

20. Lietuvos Respublikos Vyriausybės, Estijos Respublikos Vyriausybės ir Latvijos Respublikos Vyriausybės sutartis dėl Baltijos gynybos koledžo
Agreement between the Government of the Republic of Estonia, the Government of the Republic of Latvia and the Government of the Republic of Lithuania concerning the Baltic defence college
Briuselis, 1998.06.12
Įsigaliojo 2000.02.18
"V.Ž." - 1999 Nr.35

21. Sutartis dėl Baltijos valstybių bendrosios tranzito procedūros
Agreement on the Baltic common transit procedure
Sigulda, 1998.07.10
Įsigaliojo 1999.06.01
"V.Ž." - 1999 Nr.17

Baltijos valstybių bendrojo tranzito Jungtinio komiteto sprendimas Nr.1/2000 dėl nuostatų, reglamentuojančių Jungtinio komiteto, atsakingo už sutarties dėl Baltijos valstybių bendrosios tranzito procedūros administravimą ir įgyvendinimą, ir darbo grupės Baltijos valstybių bendrosios tranzito procedūros taikymo klausimais nagrinėti veiklą
Decision No 1/2000 of the Joint Committee on the Baltic Common Transit on the Provisions regarding Operation of the Joint Committee responsible for Administration and Implementation of the Agreement and the Working Party on the Baltic Common Transit Procedure
Ryga, 2000.09.27
Įsigaliojo 2000.09.27
"V.Ž." - 2001 Nr.40

Baltijos valstybių bendrojo tranzito Jungtinio komiteto rekomendacija Nr.1/2000 dėl sutarties dėl Baltijos valstybių bendrosios tranzito procedūros, pasirašytos 1998 m. liepos 10 d., dalinio pakeitimo
Recomendation No 1/2000 of the Joint Committee on the Baltic Common Transit for the amendment of the Agreement of 10 July 1998 on the Baltic Common Transit Procedure
Ryga, 2000.09.27
Pakeitimai įsigaliojo 2001.01.01

Baltijos valstybių bendrojo tranzito Jungtinio komiteto sprendimas Nr.2/2000 dėl darbo grupės
Decision No 2/2000 of the Joint Committee on the Baltic Common Transit on Working Party
Ryga, 2000.09.27
Įsigaliojo 2000.10.01
"V.Ž." - 2001 Nr.40

Baltijos valstybių bendrojo tranzito Jungtinio komiteto sprendimas Nr.3/2000 dėl sutarties dėl Baltijos valstybių bendrosios tranzito procedūros, pasirašytos 1998 m. liepos 10 d., II ir IV priedų dalinio pakeitimo
Decision No 3/2000 of the Joint Committee on the Baltic Common Transit for the amendment of the Appendices II and IV of Agreement of 10 July 1998 on the Baltic Common Transit Procedure
Ryga, 2000.09.27
Įsigaliojo 2001.01.01

Baltijos valstybių bendrojo tranzito Jungtinio komiteto sprendimas Nr.4/2000 dėl sutarties dėl Baltijos valstybių bendrosios tranzito
procedūros taikymo
Decision No 4/2000 of the Joint Committee on the Baltic Common Transit on Implementation the Agreement on the Baltic Common
Transit Procedure
Ryga, 2000.09.27
Įsigaliojo 2000.10.01
"V.Ž." - 2001 Nr.40

Baltijos valstybių bendrojo tranzito Jungtinio komiteto 2001 m. gruodžio 3 d. sprendimas Nr. 1/2001 dėl sutarties dėl Baltijos
valstybių bendrosios tranzito procedūros, pasirašytos 1998 m. liepos 10 d., II priedo 34 B straipsnio taikymo
Decision No 1/2001 of the Joint Committee on the Baltic Common Transit of 3 December 2001 on Implementing Article 34 of
Appendix II of the Agreement of July on the Baltic Common Transit Procedure
Vilnius, 2001.12.03
Įsigaliojo 2002.01.01

22. Estijos Respublikos, Latvijos Respublikos ir Lietuvos Respublikos Vyriausybių vadovų rezoliucija
Resolution of the Heads of Government of the Republic of Estonia, the Republic of latvia and the Republic Lithuania
Sigulda, 1998.07.10

23. Lietuvos Respublikos Vyriausybės, Estijos Respublikos Vyriausybės ir Latvijos Respublikos Vyriausybės sutartis dėl bendros
švietimo erdvės Baltijos šalyse sukūrimo vidurinio bendrojo lavinimo paskutinės pakopos ir profesinio mokymo lygiu (neapimant
aukštojo mokslo)
Agreement among the Government of the Republic of Lithuania, the Government of the Republic of Estonia and the Government of
the Republic of Latvia on the creation of a common educational space in general upper secondary education and vocational (up to
higher education level) education within the Baltic States
Sigulda, 1998.07.10
Įsigaliojo 2000.07.16
"V.Ž." - 2000 Nr.53

24. Estijos Respublikos Vyriausybės, Latvijos Respublikos Vyriausybės ir Lietuvos Respublikos Vyriausybės susitarimas dėl
konsulinės pagalbos ir bendradarbiavimo
Agreement on the consular assistance and co-operation between the Government of the Republic of Estonia, the Government of the
Republic of Latvia and the Government of the Republic of Lithuania
Vilnius, 1999.02.05
Įsigaliojo 1999.09.23
"V.Ž." - 1999 Nr.82

25. Lietuvos Respublikos Vyriausybės, Latvijos Respublikos Vyriausybės ir Estijos Respublikos Vyriausybės sutartis dėl prekybinės
laivybos

Agreement on merchant shipping between the Government of the Republic of Lithuania, the Government of the Republic of Latvia
and the Government of the Republic of Estonia
Klaipėda, 1999.04.15
Įsigaliojo 2000.01.19
"V.Ž." - 1999 Nr.103

26. Estijos Respublikos Vyriausybės, Latvijos Respublikos Vyriausybės ir Lietuvos Respublikos Vyriausybės protokolas dėl Baltijos
gynybos koledžo ir jo personalo statuso
Protocol between the Government of the Republic of Estonia, the Government of the Republic of Latvia and the Government of the
Republic of Lithuania concerning the status of the Baltic Defence College and its personnel
Ryga, 1999.06.14
Įsigaliojo 2000.02.17
"V.Ž." - 1999 Nr.103

27. Lietuvos Respublikos Vyriausybės, Estijos Respublikos Vyriausybės ir Latvijos Respublikos Vyriausybės sutartis dėl
išsimokslinimo pripažinimo Baltijos valstybių aukštojo mokslo erdvėje
Agreement among the Government of the Republic of Lithuania, the Government of the Republic of Estonia and the Government of
the Republic of Latvia on the academic recognition of educational qualifications in the Baltic educational space
Talinas, 2000.02.18
Įsigaliojo: 2001.04.01
"V.Ž." - 2001 Nr.4

28. Lietuvos Respublikos Vyriausybės, Estijos Respublikos Vyriausybės ir Latvijos Respublikos Vyriausybės sutartis dėl
bendradarbiavimo vykdant liudytojų ir nukentėjusiųjų apsaugą
Agreement between the Government of the Republic of Lithuania, the Government of the Republic of Estonia and the Government of
the Republic of Latvia on co-operation in protection of witness and victims
Talinas, 2000.03.17
Įsigaliojo 2001.06.08
"V.Ž." - 2001 Nr. 49

29. Lietuvos Respublikos Vyriausybės, Estijos Respublikos Vyriausybės ir Latvijos Respublikos Vyriausybės sutartis dėl bendros
aukštojo mokslo erdvės sukūrimo Baltijos šalyse
Agreement between the Government of the Republic of Lithuania, the Government of the Republic of Estonia and the Government of
the Republic of Latvia on the creation of a common educational space in the higher education within the Baltic States
Kretinga, 2000.12.08
Įsigaliojo 2001.07.06
"V.Ž." - 2001 Nr.73

30. Estijos Respublikos, Latvijos Respublikos ir Lietuvos Respublikos laisvosios prekybos sutarties Jungtinio komiteto Sprendimas Nr.1/2000 dėl Estijos Respublikos, Latvijos Respublikos ir Lietuvos Respublikos laisvosios prekybos sutarties A protokolo pakeitimų
Resolution No.1/2000 of the Joint Committee of the Free trade agreement between the Republic

of Estonia, the Republic of Latvia and the Republic of Lithuania on Amendments to the Protocol A to the Free trade agreement between the Republic of Estonia and the Republic of Latvia and the Republic of Lithuania
2000.12.28
Įsigaliojo 2002.05.01
"V.Ž." - 2001 Nr.38

31. Lietuvos Respublikos Vyriausybės, Estijos Respublikos Vyriausybės ir Latvijos Respublikos Vyriausybės susitarimas dėl bendradarbiavimo turizmo srityje
Agreement among the Government of the Republic of Lithuania, the Government of the Republic of Estonia and the Government of the the Republic of Latvia on Co-operation in the Field of Tourism
Visaginas, 2002.06.26
Įsigaliojo 2002.06.26
"V.Ž." - 2002 Nr.75

MULTILATERAL AGREEMENTS

MULTILATERAL AGREEMENTS

1. Lietuvos Respublikos, Estijos Respublikos, Latvijos Respublikos, Belgijos Karalystės, Liuksemburgo Didžiosios Hercogystės ir Nyderlandų Karalystės susitarimas dėl kelių transporto
Agreement between the Government of the Republic of Lithuania, the Government of the Republic of Estonia, the Government of the Republic of Latvia, the Government of the Kingdom of Belgium, the Government of the Kingdom of Netherlands and the Government of the Grand Duchy of Luxembourg on international road transport
Atėnai, 1992.06.08
Įsigaliojo 1995.01.01
"V.Ž." - 2000 Nr.96

2. Tarpusavio supratimo memorandumas tarp Lietuvos Respublikos ir Šiaurės Ministrų Tarybos dėl Šiaurės Šalių informacijos biuro įkūrimo Vilniuje
Memorandum of Understanding between the Republic of Lithuania and the Nordic Council of Ministers regarding the establishment of a Nordic information office in Vilnius
Kopenhaga, 1992.08.13

3. Sutartis tarp Danijos Karalystės Vyriausybės ir Estijos Respublikos, Suomijos Respublikos, Vokietijos Federacinės Respublikos, Latvijos Respublikos, Lietuvos Respublikos, Norvegijos Karalystės, Lenkijos Respublikos, Rusijos Federacijos, Švedijos Karalystės vyriausybių bei Europos Bendrijų Komisijos dėl Baltijos Jūros Valstybių Tarybos Komisaro demokratinėms institucijoms ir žmogaus teisėms, taip pat teisėms asmenų, priklausančių mažumoms, sekretoriato Kopenhagoje
Agreement between the Government of the Kingdom of Denmark and the Governments of the Republic of Estonia, the Republic of Finland, the Federal Republic of Germany, the Republic of Latvia, the Republic of Lithuania, the Kingdom of Norway, the Republic of Poland, the Russian Federation, the Kingdom of Sweden and the Commission of the European Communities relating to the secretariat in Copenhagen of the Commissioner of the Council of the Baltic Sea States on democratic institutions and human rights, including the rights of persons belonging to minorities
1995.06.02
Įsigaliojo 1995.07.02

AGREEMENTS WITH INTERNATIONAL ORGANIZATIONS

□ EFTA
□ EUROPEAN BANK FOR RECONSTRUCTION AND DEVELOPMENT
□ EUROPEAN COMMUNITY
□ EUROPEAN COUNCIL
□ EUROPEAN INVESTMENT BANK
□ EUROPEAN PATENT ORGANIZATION
□ EUROPEAN UNION
□ INTERNATIONAL ATOMIC ENERGY AGENCY
□ MULTILATERAL INVESTMENT GUARANTEE AGENCY
□ NATO
□ OECD
□ UNITED NATIONS
□ WESTERN EUROPEAN UNION
□ WORLD BANK
□ WORLD TRADE ORGANIZATION

CONVENTIONS

□ CONVENTIONS OF THE COUNCIL OF EUROPE
□ GENEVA CONVENTIONS (CONCERNING WAR VICTIMS)
□ HAGUE CONFERENCE ON PRIVATE INTERNATIONAL LAW
□ CONVENTIONS OF THE INTERNATIONAL ATOMIC ENERGY AGENCY
□ CONVENTIONS ON INTERNATIONAL CIVIL AVIATION
□ CONVENTIONS OF INTERNATIONAL LABOUR ORGANIZATION
□ IMO CONVENTIONS
□ UNESCO CONVENTIONS
□ CONVENTIONS OF UNITED NATIONS
□ WIPO CONVENTIONS
□ OTHER CONVENTIONS

FOREIGN ECONOMIC RELATIONS

LITHUANIA'S ECONOMY

· **Gross Domestic Product (GDP)** According to the data of the Department of Statistics, Gross Domestic Product (GDP) in 2001 went up by 5.9 %, if compared to the year 2000, and made up to EUR 13.38 billion (at current prices). In 2001 GDP per capita equalled to EUR 3836.1.

· Based on the data released by National accounts, Gross Domestic Product (GDP) over the 3rd quarter of 2002 against the respective period of 2001 grew by 6.8 % and made up EUR 3.89 bn at current prices. Over the nine months of 2002 against the January-September period in 2001 GDP ascended by 6.1 %. GDP at current prices generated over the three quarters of 2002 equalled EUR 10.79 billion. The per capita GDP totalled EUR 3.10 thousand (EUR 1.1 thousand over the third quarter).

· The GDP growth over the 3rd quarter of 2002 like during the previous quarters was determined by the growth in value added generated in all economic activities except fishery, mining and quarrying and health care services. The bulk growth rate against the July-September period of 2001 fell per enterprises engaged in agriculture and forestry (15.3 %), construction (9.1 %), trade (6.9 %), hotels and restaurants (7.1 %) and financial intermediation (9.9 %).

More information –*Department of Statistics* – http://www.std.lt/

· **Inflation** Annual deflation in 2002 (December 2002 against December 2001) made up 1.0 % (in December 2001 against December 2000 annual inflation was 2.0 %).

· The annual inflation level was determined by a 5.3 % yearly (December 2002 against December 2001) decline in prices for food products and non-alcoholic beverages. The fall in prices for consumer goods and services was partially offset by a 9.4 % increase in prices for transport, 1.5 % for housing, water, electricity, gas and other fuel group commodities and services. The influence of other groups' commodities and services on the total CPI was not substantial.

· Average annual inflation in 2002 (2002 as compared to 2001) totalled 0.3 % (in 2001 against 2000 it was 1.3 %).

More information –*Department of Statistics* – http://www.std.lt/

· **Unemployment** According to the Lithuanian Labour Exchange, as of 1st January 2003, there were 191.2 thousand unemployed. In December 2002 the unemployed women accounted for 50.3 % of all unemployed. The unemployment rate in December 2002 was 10.9 % (in December 2001 – 12.9 %).

More information – *Lithuanian Labour Exchange* – http://www.is.lt/rdb/

· **Privatisation** According to the figures of the State Property Fund, 963 entities were sold for EUR 101.1 mill. in 2002. 510 objects of the sate ownership were privatised for EUR 77.2 mill. as well as 453 of the municipality ownership were privatised for EUR 23.9 mill.

· In 2002, two important privatisation deals were signed. The consortium of "Ruhrgas AG" and "E.ON Energie AG " acquired the 34 % stake of the Lithuanian Gas and "Nordeutsche Landesbank Girocentrale" acquired the 76.01 % stake of the Lithuanian Agricultural Bank. This contract completed the Lithuanian financial sector privatisation.

· Transport, energy entities and spirits manufactories must be privatised during the last phase of the privatisation process. Privatisation of such state monopolies as Lithuanian Energy, Lithuanian Railways, which are currently undergoing the reorganisation, is on its way. Currently the tender of the 34 % stake of the state ownership in the Lithuanian Gas for gas supplier is going on.

More information – *State Property Fund* – http://www.vtf.lt/

· **Foreign Direct Investment** Foreign direct investment as of 1st October 2002 equalled EUR 3644,9 million and comparing with the 1st January 2002 increased by 18.0 %. The per capita FDI in Lithuania was EUR 1051.

· The main countries investors were: Sweden (EUR 601.8 million or 16.6 %), Denmark (EUR 581.8 million or 16.0 %), Estonia (EUR 364.5 million or 10.0 %), Germany (EUR 356.6 million or 9.8 %), the United States (EUR 320.4 million or 8.8 %), Finland (EUR 229.4 million or 6.3 %), Russia (EUR 220.3 million or 6.1 %) and the United Kingdom (EUR 193.8 million or 5.3 %).

· The biggest share of total FDI fell per manufacturing industry, i.e. 29.3 %, financial intermediation enterprises (19.7 %), trade (17.3 %) and communication services (14.0 %).

· **Foreign Trade** According to the data of the Lithuanian Customs declarations, the turnover of the foreign trade over January -November 2002 accounted for EUR 12.9 billion:

exports – EUR 5.4 billion, imports – EUR 7.5 billion. Exports increased by 10.2 % and imports - by 12.4 %. The balance of foreign trade was negative and equal to EUR 2.1 billion.

· Main part of Lithuanian exports over January- November 2002 was directed to the EU countries - 48.9 % of the total exports. Exports to the CIS made up 19.3 % of the total exports. The biggest part of imports also came from the EU – 45.3 % of the total imports. Imports from the CIS reached 26.2 %. Imports from the EU increased by 16.7 %, meanwhile imports from the CIS decreased by 1.5 %, if compared to the corresponding period of 2001. Exports to the EU countries increased by 11.7 %, to the CIS countries - by 11.1 %, if compared to the same period of 2001.

· Main Lithuanian export partners: United Kingdom (14.2 %), Russia (12.3 %), Germany (10.4 %), Latvia (9.4 %), and import partners - Russia (21.5 %), Germany (17.3 %), Italy (4.9 %) and Poland (4.8 %).

· **Current** Account According to the Bank of Lithuania, in 2001 the Current Account Deficit amounted to EUR 0.64 billion or 4.8 % of GDP. It was by EUR 112.86 mill. or by 15 % lower than in 2000. The Current Account deficit in 2000 made up 6.0 % of GDP.

· In January-September 2002, the Current Account Deficit (CAD) stood at EUR 401.0 mill. or 3.7 % of GDP.

· **State Debt** According to the figures of the Ministry of Finance, total public debt stood at EUR 3.66 billion at the end of the year 2001. During the year 2001 it increased by EUR 4.92 mill. Long-term debt made up 93.8 % or EUR 3.4 billion of the total debt. As on 31st December 2001, foreign debt stood at EUR 2.8 billion or 76.4 % of the total state debt. The foreign debt accounted for 20.6 % of GDP.

· Total public debt during November 2002 decreased by EUR 8.5 mill. and at the end of this month stood at EUR 3.84 billion or 26.4 % of estimated GDP. Foreign debt during November 2002 decreased by EUR 40.8 mill. and amounted to EUR 2.7 billion or 70.6 % of the total public debt. Total long-term debt accounted for EUR 3.63 billion or 94.6 % of the total debt.

· **State Budget** According to the final data of the Ministry of Finance, for the first time during the last four years the plan of national budget revenues was exceeded, municipality budgets also received more revenues than planned. The state budget deficit was only symbolic and the lowest since the year 1997. In 2002 the state budget revenues increased by EUR 0.74 billion if compared to the year 2001.

· The national budget collected by EUR 8.7 million more than expected. The plan of revenues was EUR 3.03 billion. Successful revenues collection was caused by the growing Lithuanian economy despite the internal and external pressing.

· **Banking Sector** At the end of third quarter of 2002, there were 10 banks operating under a license from the Bank of Lithuania, 4 foreign bank branches and 2 foreign bank representative offices.

· As of 1st October 2002, in seven out of ten operating commercial banks foreign investors held more than one half of the share capital.

· On 1st October 2002 the total profit of the banking system was EUR 40.9 million, while during the same period last year banks suffered a total loss of EUR 11.3 million. Seven banks and two foreign bank branches earned a profit of EUR 44.8 million, while three banks (Agricultural Bank of Lithuania, Sampo Bank and VB Mortgage Bank) and two foreign bank branches incurred a total loss of EUR 3.9 million over the nine months.

· According to the financial statements for 1st October 2002 presented by the banks, operating domestic commercial banks were characterised by the following: assets totalled EUR 4.7 billion, increasing over the third quarter by EUR 0.3 billion (6.4%); total loans granted to clients amounted to nearly EUR 2.1 billion, increasing in comparison with the beginning of July by 0.17 million (8.7%); deposits totalled EUR 3.3 billion, increasing over the quarter by EUR 251.7 million (8.2%).

· **Agriculture** According to the Department of Statistics, over January-September 2002 agriculture, hunting and forestry sectors created the added value for EUR 0.76 billion at current prices or 7.0 % of GDP. If compared to the same period of 2001 (at constant prices), the created added value of this economic activity increased by 10.4 %.

· In the third quarter of 2002, 17.1 % of total employed worked in this sectors.

· **Transportation** According to the figures of the Department of Statistics, over January-September 2002 the added value in transportation, storage and communications sectors accounted for EUR 1.33 billion (at current prices) or 12.3 % of GDP. The annual growth of the added value of this sector was 9.2 %.

· In 2002, the transportation of goods by rail increased by 26.1 %, by transport of Lithuanian air companies – 1.5 %, by waterways decreased by 5.2 %, if compared to 2001.

· **Domestic Trade** According to the data of the Department of Statistics, over January-September 2002 wholesales and retail trade created the added value for EUR 1.53 billion at current prices or 14.2 % of GDP. If compared to the same period of 2001 (at constant prices), the created added value of this sector increased by 7.5 %.

· Over January-November 2002 the turnover (without VAT) of the retail trade, including sales of motor vehicles and motorcycles, their maintenance and repair, retail sales of automotive fuel, increased by 13.5 %, if compared to the corresponding period of 2001. The retail sales of the motor vehicles and motorcycles (increased by 35.2 %), their maintenance and repair (30.3 %), clothing (42.4 %), footwear and leather goods (35.6 %) in specialized stores mostly increased during the period in question.

COOPERATION WITH INTERNATIONAL ECONOMIC ORGANIZATIONS

WORLD TRADE ORGANIZATION (WTO)

On May 31, 2001 the Republic of Lithuania became the 141st full-fledged member of the World Trade Organization (WTO). In this way the accession to the WTO process that has started in 1995 has been completed. On April 24, 2001 after the Parliament has ratified the results of Lithuania's negotiations for membership in the World Trade Organization (WTO), and notified the WTO Secretariat, Lithuania has completed all the legal procedures necessary to become a member of the WTO.

The process of Lithuania's accession to this organization began in 1995, when, understanding the importance of international political changes in the region and paying particular attention to very intensive and beneficial international economic and trade relations, in its programme for 1995, Lithuanian Government included an objective to start the negotiations for joining the *General Agreement on Tariffs and Trade* (GATT). When, on the basis of GATT, the WTO was established, Lithuania strove for membership in the WTO. It is necessary to note that Lithuania's integration into the WTO and EU was and is a complementary and inter-related process. The screening of national legislation regulating domestic and foreign trade and related areas has shown that membership in the WTO is indispensable because one of the basic requirements for Lithuania's integration into EU is de facto application of the WTO agreements' rules in Lithuania's domestic and foreign trade policy.

Membership in the WTO commits Lithuania to pursue its trade regime under the transparent and well-known rules and, consequently, Lithuania becomes a reliable and attractive partner in foreign trade. Lithuanian trade policy gains predictability and transparency, thus FDI flows into the country might be positively influenced. Membership in the WTO also has an enormous effect on the promotion of exports as well as it makes impact in such spheres on the application of the WTO trade measures and improvement of business environment - membership in the WTO opens new foreign markets of 144 WTO members for domestic producers (after Lithuania, such countries as Moldova, China and Chinese Taipei have joined the WTO). Lithuanian producers of goods and services gain more possibilities to export their production because WTO members would have to apply equal treatment to goods of Lithuanian origin in the domestic market.

The World Trade Organization was established in 1995 and replaced GATT which was created in 1947 with an objective to regulate global trade. Being one of the most significant global international organizations, the WTO has an objective to insure that all members of the organization will pursue certain commonly agreed rules being constructed on two basic non-discriminative principles of international trade - namely, most-favored nation (MFN) and national treatment - in their international trade policy. Every WTO member commits itself to harmonize its national legislation regulating international trade and trade policy with the rules of the WTO agreements, as well as to comply fully with the principles of the WTO rules. The WTO agreements focus on two major objectives: (1) to eliminate all kinds of obstacles hindering the development of free trade and (2) to create a mechanism that would allow to solve trade disputes among countries effectively.

The topmost decision-making body of the WTO is the Ministerial Conference which has to meet at least every two years. The Ministerial Conference takes decisions on all matters under any of the multilateral trade agreements and foresees trade liberalization agenda for the coming period. It is within the powers of the Ministerial Conference to start a new WTO negotiation round. As a result of the Uruguay Round held in 1986 -1994 the WTO was established. Currently the new round has started, it has been opened in Doha, Qatar, during the fourth WTO Ministerial Conference held in November 2001 (initially the round was planned to be announced in the third WTO Ministerial Conference held in Seattle, 30 November – 3 December 1999, but it failed; in spite of that the negotiations in two sectors, namely agriculture and services have started already in 2000).

Membership in the WTO provides for Lithuania more instruments to defend country's interests in the area of trade by participating in further world trade liberalization process, negotiating for more favorable trade conditions with acceding countries (first of all with Russia, Ukraine and Belarus), and using the possibility to appeal to relevant WTO bodies for adjustment of the situation in WTO member countries were omitting of non-discrimination principles can be observed. It is important that the membership in the WTO allows Lithuania to negotiate for the better trade conditions with Russia, and to seek the elimination from the Russian side of discriminative trade regime, if there is such. Russian accession to WTO is also a good opportunity to improve the conditions of business-making with Russia and to make in this way the Russian trade regime more stable and predictable. Lithuania has already prepared and submitted its negotiating position on the conditions of liberalization of Lithuanian export to Russia, i.e. on the review of Russian import and export tariffs, as well on the liberalization of Russian services market.

It should be noted that the WTO is not merely a set of trade rules and regulations. It also has an effective mechanism which insures that the WTO trade rules and regulations are strictly followed - it is a *Dispute Settlement Mechanism* which provides the real possibility to defend their interests because the WTO is based on principles of consensus and equality.

It is also important that membership in the WTO enhances Lithuania's possibilities to contribute to the world globalization process. Lithuania as the full-fledged member of the WTO has recently participated in the fourth WTO Ministerial Conference, held in November 2001 in Doha, Qatar. In the Conference after the adoption of the Ministerial Declaration, new round of negotiations on the world trade liberalization was announced. This Ministerial Declaration, taking it as a negotiation plan, would guide the organizational work of the new WTO negotiations round in preparing the negotiations positions of every member state on each trade or trade-related sphere. The negotiations of the new round would cover such issues as the reduction of import tariffs, review of agricultural policies, liberalization of services market, also the incorporation of such questions as competition, investments, e-commerce, etc. in to the sphere of the WTO regulation.

Lithuanian delegation headed by Deputy Minister of Foreign Affairs Mr. E. Ignatavičius actively participated in Doha Conference as well as in the pre-Doha negotiations. Lithuania managed to form the group of 8 recently acceded countries and managed to reach that the special attention was paid to the extensive commitments of recently acceded countries regarding market access. This provision is already taken into account in the undergoing new round negotiations. Lithuania supports the new round of negotiations and is in favor of balanced liberalization considering it as a key principle of globalization. At the same time, Lithuania together with the other recently acceded countries expressed a common concern regarding negotiations leading to the new commitments and their interaction with the commitments made recently during the accession process. As it is noted in the WTO Ministerial Declaration, newly acceded countries during their accession have made extensive commitments in the market-access, domestic support, export subsidies, services market opening and etc., often more broader than that of old GATT-WTO Members. Taking into consideration all these different starting positions, Lithuania with the other countries, referred in the 9 paragraph of the WTO Ministerial Declaration, requests for the adequate (appropriate) flexibility in the light of new commitments, particularly in agriculture sector.

After becoming the WTO member, Lithuania committed itself to implement adequately the commitments in a range of areas (such as market access for goods, services, agricultural support policy; customs valuation; protection of intellectual property rights (TRIPS) and etc.) undertaken during the accession process and also the requirements and provisions of all the WTO agreements. Therefore, the control of the implementations of all Lithuanian commitments and the adequate fulfillment of all WTO requirements is executed – all trade measures taken as well as all newly adopted legal acts that directly or indirectly influence Lithuanian foreign trade should be in conformity with the provisions of the WTO agreements. Following the provisions of the WTO agreements and Lithuanian commitments as well as taking into consideration one of the most important WTO *transparency principle*, notification function should be performed, i.e., special documents on all trade measures and legal acts are being prepared and submitted for the WTO members. Necessary to underline, that following the resolution No. 1379 adopted by the Lithuanian Government on 8th November 2001, Lithuanian Ministry of Foreign Affairs is responsible for the coordination and supervision of the implementation of all Lithuanian commitments and fulfillment of all WTO requirements as well as for co-ordination while preparing and submitting aforementioned notifications to the WTO.

In this regard it must be also noted, that the whole package of the accession commitments ("bindings" of customs tariffs, support for agricultural sector, commitments in services sector, market access and etc.) assumed by Lithuania during the accession process as well as GATT provisions and WTO Agreements, to which Lithuania adhered becoming the WTO members, are published in the State Gazette "*Valstybės Žinios*" No.46, 2001, edition.

ORGANISATION FOR ECONOMIC CO-OPERATION AND DEVELOPMENT (OECD)

Seeking to encourage greater economic integration in Western Europe the *Organisation for European Economic Co-operation* (OEEC) was founded in 1948. In 1960-61 after the USA and Canada joined the OEEC, this organisation was transformed into the *Organisation for Economic Co-operation and Development (*OECD). The new body was united by its commitment to democratic government and the market economy. OECD's work covers economic and social issues from macroeconomics, finance policy and capital market, trade, education, development policy, science and innovation. OECD also plays a prominent role in fostering good governance in the public service and in corporate activity, thus contributing to the globalisation processes in the whole world.

Currently, 30 states - Australia, Austria, Belgium, Canada, Czech Republic, Denmark, France, Finland, Germany, Great Britain, Greece, Hungary, Ireland, Island, Italy, Japan, Luxembourg, Mexico, Netherlands, New Zealand, Norway, Poland, Portugal, Slovakia, South Korea, Spain, Sweden, Switzerland, Turkey and USA are members of OECD. All the associated EU members from Central and Eastern Europe in one or another way participate in OECD work: Czech Republic, Hungary, Poland and Slovak Republic are already OECD members. Bulgaria, Slovenia and Romania as well as the Baltic countries – Lithuania, Latvia and Estonia - have special co-operation programs.

The Lithuanian Government acknowledging the necessity to reintegrate the country in the global economic and political structures seeks to become full member of the OECD. The co-operation with OECD is highly important due to several basic reasons: OECD role in the development of global economy and highly valuable OECD know-how assistance to Lithuanian State institutions. Aspiring to become the OECD member, Lithuania should secure the support of the OECD member states; the participation of Lithuanian institutions in different OECD bodies could have also a positive impetus for a full membership in the organisation.

Since 1996 the Government of Lithuania has been pursuing the policy of establishing closer co-operative relations with OECD. In October 1996, Lithuania, Latvia and Estonia issued a Joint Declaration with the aim to get special OECD Programme and to indicate desire to become in future full members of OECD. In response to the Joint Declaration OECD Centre for Co-operation with Non-Members (CCNM) has prepared a Baltic Regional Programme (BRP), that was finally approved in March 1998. While confirming the BRP some OECD Members had different positions over the programme, because it created a competition for the similar OECD programmes for Russia, the Latin America and Asia countries. Only due to the strong support of Scandinavian countries (Sweden, Denmark, Finland, Norway and Island) and Poland OECD Council has approved the Baltic Regional Programme and its implementation started already in 1998. BRP constituting the main tool for OECD's co-operation with Lithuania, Estonia and Latvia, encompasses the activities in such areas as regional co-operation, foreign investment strategies, finance, tax administration, competition policy, social security, employment, science and education, agricultural policy, etc. The fundamental objective of BRP is to promote long-term sustainable economic growth as a basis for the development of democratic society. BRP creates a stable political dialogue between Lithuania and OECD, while seeking these fundamental objectives:

1) to assist in the completion of the transition to market economies;
2) to promote stable integration of Lithuania's national economy into a global economy;
3) using the best practices of OECD, to seek long-term sustainable economic growth and political stability.

Seeking to implement BRP effectively, a special Working Group in the Implementation of the BRP was established in Lithuania in the beginning of 1999 (in 2001 the group has been renewed).

Lithuania highly values OECD initiative under BRP framework to prepare a regional economic assessment study of the three Baltic countries, which was already published under the title "*The Baltic States – a Regional Economic Assessment*". The English version of the study was presented on 8 November 1999, in Paris, in a joint session of the Baltic States and OECD officials. That was a first time in OECD history, when a comparative economic analysis of several countries was prepared and published. Study was translated into the Lithuanian language, published and officially presented on 28 April 2000 in Vilnius, where representatives of the state institutions, NGOs, diplomatic corps, international organisations took part by giving comments on the study.

With the aim to assist the Baltic States' institutions and agencies to formulate the relevant policy in the sphere of small and medium size enterprise development and to encourage the use of international practice in this sector, the Baltic FEED (Forum for entrepreneurship and enterprise development) has been initiated with the aim to give the opportunity for the Baltic States to get acquainted with practice of the OECD countries in the development and facilitation SME friendly legal environment. The identification of the priorities of the enterprise development within FEED and the use of international practice enable the representatives of Lithuanian state and private institutions to find appropriate decisions while solving problems in the SME sector. It is also important, that the Baltic FEED became effectively functioning body that is able to monitor the SME's development and guidelines implementation process. This may lead to the identification of other emerging fields and new issues of concern.

Close Lithuanian and OECD ties could also be proved by the arrangement of regular joint events, in which different Lithuanian institutions take active part. Among these events, there might be mentioned the seminar on diary industry development, organised 4-5 November 2001 in Vilnius by Lithuanian Agricultural ministry and OECD, as well seminar on the openness of the regime in trade in services, held in Tallinn 13-14 December 2001. The latter seminar, held under BRP, was first of such kind and it focused it's attention to the situation of the services sector in the Baltic States, as well as to the international commitments, assumed by the Baltic States in this respect.

Currently OECD is finalising the preparation of the study *Lithuanian Social and Labour Market Review*. This study would greatly contribute to the acquaintance of international research and business community with the social and labour environment realities of Lithuania. It also expected that the Review would provide certain set of recommendations which, in its own turn, may later result in the production of further guidelines to reflect emerging social policy changes, its close interaction with the on-going reforms in Lithuanian insurance and pension sectors.

The Baltic Regional Programme has been highly placed at the latest BRP evaluation meeting that took place in June 2001 in Riga. During this meeting Lithuania presented its paper on the implementation of the BRP Medium term objectives, among other things the BRP activities in the sphere of small and medium size enterprise development, social and labour policies, financial markets and FEED activities were discussed. Additionally, Lithuania, that was the first Baltic state to be granted an observer status in the OECD Competition Committee, presented experience of its work in this OECD body. During the evaluation meeting considerable attention was given also to the future development of the Programme and namely to the membership of the Baltic States in the OECD organisation. Representatives of some OECD member states expressed their notion that the joining of the Baltic States the EU should lead to their eventual membership in the OECD organisation.

The commitment of the Government of Lithuania to become full-fledge OECD member has been reaffirmed during the meeting of Mr. Brazauskas, Lithuanian Prime Minister with Mr. Johnston, OECD Secretary General in Riga in September, 2001. In this meeting the perspective of joining the OECD organisation has been endorsed, also the significance of OECD in bringing closer Lithuania to global world processes has been emphasised. It is foreseen that the BRP would end in the year 2003. Lithuania's interest would be that after the year 2003 this programme would be prolonged or a new form of Lithuanian - OECD dialog, maybe a separate Lithuanian - OECD programme, established.

Lithuania's membership in certain OECD committees and bodies would be highly valuable seeking to established a more close co-operation between Lithuania and OECD and, more importantly, to successfully implement BRP. Following these objectives the official requests of Lithuanian Government were given to the OECD Council in January 1999. Lithuania officially asked for an observer's status in:

Committee on Competition Law and Policy (observer status granted in November 2000);
CIIME - Committee on International Investment and Multinational Enterprises (partial status granted in June 1999);
Trade Committee;
Committee on Fiscal Affairs (application handed in by Lithuania in November 2001).

Lithuania was already granted an observer's status in the following OECD committees and working groups:

Since 15 April 1998 to the Negotiations Group regarding Multilateral Agreement on Investment which preparation was being discussed in OECD framework. Since 21 June 1999, after the failure to conclude MAI, this observer status was transformed into observer status to OECD CIIME discussions on the questions of international investments;
Since 10 December 1998 Lithuania has been granted ad hoc observer status to the Group of Governmental Experts on Third Party Liability in the Field of Nuclear Energy, that was created in the Nuclear Energy Agency (NEA - is a semiautonomous body within OECD www.nea.fr).
Since November 2000 Lithuania (up to now the only Baltic state) has been granted an observer status in OECD Committee on Competition Law and Policy.

Until 1998 the activities of Lithuanian State institutions in OECD mainly took a form of a participation in the thematic programmes organised by OECD CCNM. OECD has given a particular technical and methodological assistance for implementation of Lithuanian tax administration reform. Since the 1992 Lithuanian agricultural policy specialists have started to participate in forums of the non-Members' agricultural experts group. In 1996 Lithuanian Ministry of Public Administration Reforms and Local Authorities started to implement the SIGMA project (state administration reform). After the liquidation of this ministry the implementation of this project has been assigned to the Lithuanian Ministry of Interior Affairs. OECD experts had given a considerable methodological assistance also in other areas, such as environment protection; nuclear energetic; economic, agricultural, FDI statistics, SME etc.

Necessary to mention, that Lithuania also regularly gets OECD publications. For this reason, in 1996 in the premises of Lithuanian Technical Library, in co-operation with Lithuanian Information Institute, the OECD Documentation Centre has been established.

Currently Lithuania is considering the issue of joining the OECD *Convention on Combating Bribery of Foreign Public Officials in International Business Transactions.* At the beginning of 2001 Lithuania has set to make its first steps towards joining OECD Anti-bribery Convention: on February 2001 the official request for acceding to the Convention has been sent to the OECD Secretary General, also the appropriate questionnaire on participation in international trade and investment as well as legal framework regarding combating corruption has been filled and handed over to the OECD officials. The accession to this OECD Convention has been included in the Government's action plan for the period 2000-2004.

Recognising the fact that much of the CIME's work is related to the OECD's investment instruments, in particular to the *Declaration on International Investment and Multinational Enterprises* and related OECD Council decisions, at the beginning of the year 2001, Lithuania has officially expressed its willingness to join this Declaration. Alongside this decision concrete steps have been taken to apply the obligations under the Declaration and its related Decisions and in particular with respect to the establishment of a National Contact Point and other commitments.

As part of the adherence process the examination of the Baltic States FDI policies took place in Paris on 20 June 2001, where Lithuanian delegation presented status-quo of Lithuanian economy, privatisation and structural reforms' processes, particularities of investment and competition policies. As a result of this examination the Secretariat of OECD was recommended to invite Lithuania and Estonia to join the OECD Declaration. The legal procedures of joining the Declaration should be completed in the nearest future. Adherence to the Declaration would provide Lithuania with a comprehensive framework for co-operation with OECD in the medium term. An inseparable part of this would be also the establishment of monitoring procedures, against which Lithuania could be assessed in future.

The extension of the Lithuanian - OEC dialog gains exceptional importance in light of the on-going OECD discussion on the acceptance of new members. Evaluating the criteria OECD has put to the countries, aspiring OECD membership, it could be stated that the membership of the Baltic States in OECD from the political as well as from the economical point of view is not contradicting to the requirements raised. In this respect it should be emphasised that all the EU countries as well as certain applicant countries are already members of the OECD. Active co-operation of Lithuanian Government with OECD and interception of best practices used in the OECD countries would secure the fluent process of Lithuania's transition to market economy, sustainable development and stability as well as it could contribute to the overall integration to the world economy and becoming the true member of the OECD.

COUNCIL OF THE BALTIC SEA STATES

WORKING GROUP ON ECONOMIC CO-OPERATION (WGEC)

In March 1992 the Danish and German foreign ministers invited the foreign ministers of Estonia, Finland, Latvia, Lithuania, Norway, Poland, Russia and Sweden and along with a member of the European Commission, to meet in Copenhagen in order to strengthen existing co-operation between the Baltic Sea states. The ministers found that the recent dramatic changes in Europe heralded a new era in European relations where the confrontation and division of the past have been replaced by partnership and co-operation. Therefore, the Council of the Baltic Sea States

(CBSS) was founded on 6 March 1992. Although, in the beginning CBSS functioned more like a regional political forum, while later when regional co-operation in the CBSS became more intensive, 3 working groups – *Working Group for Assistance to Democratic Institutions and Human Rights* (WGDI), *Working Group for Nuclear Safety* (WGNS) and *Working Group on Economic Co-operation* (WGEC) – were founded in the framework of CBSS.

WGEC is a permanently functioning working group aimed to analyse issues related with the economic co-operation in the region. WGEC has the following priorities of its activities:

- Regional economic co-operation, especially in the fields of investment promotion and small and medium enterprises;
- Transport and energy infrastructure projects development in the region (Baltic Ring, Via Baltica);
- Sub-regional co-operation and more active involvement in the regional co-operation of Russian Federation:
- The implementation of the projects in the environmental and regional development areas.

Having an objective to make WGEC activities more concrete, it has started a more close co-operation with the *Baltic Business Advisory Council* (BBAC). BBAC members representing regional business structures are taking part in every WGEC session and giving their insights to CBSS member-countries on the undergoing economic processes in the region. The representatives of BBAC in WGEC sessions cumulatively represent also the *Baltic Chambers of Commerce Association* (BCCA). BBAC actively participates in the preparation of meetings of CBSS Industry and Trade Ministers. This organisation was granted a *special participant* status in all CBSS activities.
The meetings of Ministers of Trade and Industry of CBSS countries are treated as stimulation for CBSS countries to take active means seeking to stirring up the regional economic co-operation. One of the most significant of the meetings was held in Vilnius 9-10 July 1998. The questions of reduction of barriers to trade, financing of SME's and improvement of their capabilities to compete in the international environment were considered in the meeting. A special action plan named *Vilnius Recommendations* was adopted during the meeting with which the Ministers committed to reduce barriers to trade and investment in the region having the aim of creating better conditions for trade in the Baltic region.

The latest conference of CBSS Ministers of Trade and Industry was held in Bergen on 7-8 February 2000. At this meeting the so-called *Bergen Action Plan* was adopted. The main attention in this Plan is focused on the development of border crossing procedures and simplification of custom formalities, fight against corruption, small and medium enterprise development, protection of the intellectual property rights. The head of Lithuanian delegation Minister of National Economy V. Milaknis in his presentation also outlined the necessity to increase the economic co-operation and to go on reducing the existing administrative barriers in the region. Next meeting of CBSS Ministers of Trade and Industry is scheduled to take place in Moscow on 20 March 2002 and it would focus on the evaluation of the implementation of *Bergen Action Plan*.

The period of July 1998 – July 1999, when Lithuania held the Presidency of CBSS was a very significant for the country. At the same period Lithuania also chaired WGEC as well. During its Presidency Lithuania followed the previously outlined CBSS objectives and aimed the practical implementation of earlier foreseen programmes. Lithuanian Presidency was based on two following guidelines: (1) to seek a greater efficiency in all CBSS activity areas; to give a concrete context to the formulated priorities; via the regional co-operation to create a concrete "value added" to Lithuania's integration into European structures; (2) as far as the regional and sub-regional economic co-operation is one of the most important parts' of Lithuania's integration process into European structure, therefore, Lithuania's objective was to start playing a more active role in CBSS WGEC and, consequently, to take part in the promotion of regional economic co-operation. Opening of the permanent CBSS Secretariat in Stockholm was also one of the most notable events of Lithuania's Presidency. In this manner, Lithuania created the precedent of 'chairing country' and 'working relations of Secretariat', with this creating a possibility to permanently supervise the implementation of the programmes.

Lithuanian participation in the CBSS WGEC activity and initiated projects implementation is very important factor of Baltic Sea states co-operation. Lithuania actively participated in the WGEC work on the preparation of input into the EU *Northern Dimension Action Plan*. Lithuania made input of concrete projects with the main aim of regional development and further co-operation with Kaliningrad oblast.

On March 13 of 2001 the official CBSS web-site (www.balticmarket.org) initiated by WGEC and directed to small and medium business, was officially launched. The main aim of the web-site – to create favourable small and medium business environment. The web-site contains information on Baltic Sea states including also and information on Lithuanian business and investment opportunities.

Lithuania actively supports and participates in the WGEC ad hoc Working Group on Protection of Intellectual Property Rights. On 17 May 2001 the meeting of the ad hoc Working Group in Vilnius, where decision on implementation of two projects on protection of intellectual property rights – 1) the opening of the web-site on intellectual property rights protection and related questions and joining it to the web-site www.balticmarket.org, 2) elaboration of the information campaign project, having the aim to inform the public on the infringement of intellectual right and prevent the usage of pirated goods - was taken.

Lithuania also highly appreciates currently increasing CBSS WGEC and OECD co-operation via implementing respective programmes in such areas as combating with a corruption and bribery in the Baltic Sea region.

Recently, under the Presidency of Russia, on Lithuanian initiative the issues of transport infrastructure development in the region have been included into the programme of WGEC. These questions have been included into the WGEC in connection with the implementation of regional projects such as VIA BALTICA, VIA HANSEATICA and RAIL BALTICA. The strategic aim of Lithuania, as well as of other regional countries, to integrate themselves politically and economically into Europe, predetermines the necessity to unite the existing regional transportation systems with the European networks. In this respect it is of utmost importance for the region to implement the transport corridor projects approved at the *Conference of pan-European Transportation Ministers'* in Crete in 1994 and in Helsinki in 1997. The most important for Lithuania are the above mentioned VIA BALTICA, VIA HANSEATICA and RAIL BALTICA projects, since their implementation could contribute to the more rapid integration of Lithuania and the whole region to the European transportation structures and enhance the opportunities goods and passengers transit. Exceptional role in this regard is played by *Northern Dimension Action Plan*, which implementation is supervised also and by the CBSS. While caring out the projects adopted within the *Northern Dimension*, Lithuania is also assigned to supervise the transportation issues. Additionally it should be noted that Lithuania has presented the CBSS WGEC with the document (prepared by the Ministry of Foreign Affairs) on the Impact of Transport Infrastructure on the Regional Economic Development and Suggestions on the Regional Co-operation in solving transport problems within the CBSS WGEC.

Understanding the importance of economic co-operation in regional intergovernmental relations, Lithuania very favourably values CBSS WGEC objectives. Therefore, Lithuania is strongly committed to actively participate in the activities of this working group and in the future.

FOREIGN TRADE POLICY

Lithuania's foreign trade policy is based on the liberal economic principles. At the present time the formation of the independent foreign trade policy is completed in essence. The main attention in the field of foreign trade policy is focused on:

1) the maintenance of the liberal trade regime,
2) the integration process into the European and World economical structures.

Lithuania has concluded negotiations on its membership to the WTO on 2 October 2000. During the session of WTO General Council held on 8 December 2000 the results of negotiations have been confirmed. After the ratification procedure of negotiation documents by the Lithuanian Parliament is completed, Lithuania will get a full WTO membership status.

De facto, the provisions of the WTO agreements are already applied. Lithuania does not maintain any export or import quantitative restrictions or any other restrictions, which have the same effect. Maintenance of sanitary and phitosanitary measures and technical barriers are in compliance with WTO requirements. A great attention is focused on the protection of the intellectual property.

Negotiating its membership to the European Union, Lithuania has preliminary concluded negotiations on Chapter No 26 "External Relations" on 20 November 2000. This chapter mainly covers the EU obligations to the international organisations as well as obligations under bilateral and multilateral agreements with third countries. Lithuania has committed to undertake all EU foreign trade policy obligations towards third countries and international organisations in accordance with acquis communautaire of Chapter No 26 "External Relations".

The Economic Department of MFA together with the experts from the Ministry of Trade and Industry of Finland have prepared the analysis of possible changes of trade regimes after Lithuania's accession to the EU ("Analysis and evaluation of impact of the changes in trade regime after Lithuania's accession to the European Union). This analysis is available on the webpage of MFA http://www.urm.lt/es-derybos/pasekmes.doc (Lithuanian only).

Free Trade Agreements make great influence on the trade policy's liberalisation. Lithuanian trade turnover with FTA countries is about 70 % of the total foreign trade turnover. Lithuania has signed *Free Trade Agreements* with European Union, European Free Trade Association (EFTA), Latvia, Estonia, Poland, Czech Republic, Slovakia, Slovenia, Turkey, Ukraine and Hungary. Lithuania has conclude the negotiations on Free Trade Agreement with Bulgaria and Romania.

Lithuania applies the *Most Favourable Nation* status (on the base of mutual agreements on economic and trade co- operation or granted unilaterally) to Australia, Belarus, Bulgaria, Georgia, India, Japan, USA, Canada, Kazakhstan, China, Cyprus, Korea, Cuba, Moldova, Romania, Russia, Uzbekistan and Vietnam. Lithuania's trade turnover with MFN countries is about 25 % of the total foreign trade turnover. The Most Favourable Nation status will be applied automatically to all WTO member states after Lithuania's accession to this organisation.

All the negotiations and implementation of the agreements concerning the field of trade and economic relations are supervised by the Economic department of the Ministry of Foreign Affairs of Lithuania concerned with other institutions.

IMPLEMENTATION OF EUROPE AGREEMENT

The **Europe Agreement** forms the legal basis for relations between Lithuania and the EU. Its aim is to provide a framework for political dialogue, promote the expansion of trade and economic relations between the parties, provide a basis for Community technical and financial assistance, and an appropriate framework to support Lithuania's gradual integration into the EU. The institutional framework of the Agreement provides the necessary mechanism for implementation and management of all areas of relations: Sub-committees examine questions at a technical level; the Association Committee, at senior official level, provides for in-depth discussion of and finds solutions to issues arising under the Agreement; the Association Council, at Ministerial level, examines the overall status of relations and provides the opportunity to review Lithuania's progress in preparing for accession.

The First Meeting of the EU-Lithuania Association Council was held in Brussels on 23 February 1998. The rules of procedure of the Association Council and Association Committee and nine Sub-committees under the framework of the Europe Agreement were approved. The First Association Committee was held in Brussels on 25 June 1998. The following Sub-committees were held in 1998:

On 24-25 March - the Sub-committee on Transport and Telecommunications in Vilnius;

On 12 May - the Sub-committee on Trade, Industry and Consumer Protection in Brussels;

On 26 May - the Sub-committee on Co-operation in Customs Matters, Statistics, Drugs and Prevention of Illegal Activities in Brussels;

On 17-18 September - the Sub-committee on Environment, Energy and Regional Development in Brussels;

On 21 September - - the Sub-committee on Economic Issues in Vilnius;

On 6 October - the Sub-committee on Human Resources, Research, Technological Development and Social Policy in Brussels;

On 8 October – the Sub-committee on Financial Services and Establishment, Capital Movements was held in Vilnius;

On 25 November - the Sub-committee on Agriculture and Fisheries was held in Brussels;

On 1-2 December - the Sub-committee on Approximation of Legislation, Competition and Opening up of Community Programmes in Vilnius.

Every month's first Tuesday (as of 3 May) Co-ordination meetings of representatives of the EU Integration and International Relations Divisions of different ministries and departments were organised at the Ministry of Foreign Affairs.

The Second Meeting of the EU-Lithuania Association Council was held on 23 February 1999. The Second Association Committee was held on 18 June 1999. The following Sub-committees were also held in 1999:

On 3 May - the Sub-committee on Trade, Industry and Consumer Protection in Vilnius; On 25 June – the Sub-committee on Transport and Telecommunications in Brussels;

On 12 July – the Sub-committee on Approximation of Legislation, Competition and Opening up of Community Programmes in Brussels;

On 28 July – the Sub-committee on Economic Issues in Brussels;

On 29 July – the Sub-committee on Financial Services and Establishment, Capital Movements will be held in Brussels;

On 15 September – the Sub-committee on Co-operation in Customs Matters, Statistics, Drugs and Prevention of Illegal Activities in Vilnius;

On 8 October – the Sub-committee on Innovation (and Social Policy) in Vilnius;

On 26 November - the Sub-committee on Agriculture and Fisheries will be held in Vilnius.

On 14 December – the Sub-committee on Environment, Energy and Regional Development in Vilnius.

The Third Meeting of the EU-Lithuania Association Council was held on 15 February 2000.

Experience in the monitoring of the Europe Agreement has been accumulated during the three-year process of implementation of the Free Trade Agreement, which was incorporated into the Europe Agreement.

As stated in the European Commission's Opinion, the Free Trade Agreement is fully functioning according to the agreed timetable without posing any major problems over its implementation. After the Agreement has come into force, changes were made in a number of its Annexes and Protocols. On 1 April 1997 a new Protocol allowing for pan-European cumulation of rules of origin entered into force. Since the beginning of 1998 a new Protocol has approved trade liberalisation in trade in textile products.

Other main issues being discussed in the framework of the Agreement are: the political dialogue; approximation of legislation; free movement of goods, services, capital and labour; co-operation in different fields of economics; opening up of Community programmes; certification and standardisation issues; and Third Pillar co-operation in justice and home affairs.

LITHUANIA - EU TRADE

The European Union is the main Lithuania's trade partner. During year 1999, Lithuanian exports to EU amounted to LTL 6.02 billion and imports LTL 8.99 billion. The trade turnover with EU for the year 1999 was 50 per cent of the total trade turnover, and imports and exports amounted respectively 50 and 46 per cent of their total figures (imports according to the country of origin). Since free trade agreement came into force in 1995, the share of EU in Lithuania's trade has constantly increased.

However, the trade turnover with EU did not grow proportionally over the period. The growth of imports was significantly larger than the growth of exports. Only starting with 1998 increase in exports exceeded increase in imports: exports compared with the same figure of 1997 increased by 12.2% whereas imports increased by only 10.7 . In 1999, this trend was even more significant: imports compared with the figure of 1998 decreased by 17.3 , and exports increased by 6.8 . In spite the trade balance in 1999 improved, it remained negative and amounted to LTL3.59 billion.

In 1999, Germany remained the main Lithuania's trade partner. Lithuanian exports to Germany were 16% of the total exports, and imports were 16.5% of the total imports. The other largest trade partners among EU countries were Denmark (6.2% of the total exports and 3.9% of the total imports), UK (5.1% of exports an 4.2% of imports), Italy (4.2% of exports and 4.1% imports), France (4.7% of exports and 3.6% of imports), Sweden (4.2% of exports and 3.4% of imports) and Netherlands (3.5% of exports and 2.3% of imports)

In 1999, the main groups of goods exported to EU by Lithuania were textile, chemicals, machinery and equipment, and wood. These groups together constituted 69% of the total Lithuanian exports to EU.

The leading groups of goods imported from EU were machinery and equipment, textile and its products, transport equipment and products of the chemical industry. In 1999, these groups amounted to 61% of the total imports from EU.

In January-April, 2000 exports to EU constituted 45% of the total Lithuanian exports and compared to the same period in 1999 increased by 11%. In 2000 during the same period Lithuanian imports from EU were 43.7% of the total imports. Compared to the same period last year imports increased by 3.2%.

FOREIGN DIRECT INVESTMENT

Total foreign direct investment to Lithuania at Jan 1, 2000 was LTL8252.12 mln. (USD2063.03). Over the last three years share of EU in FDI in Lithuania constantly increased and this year amounted to 63.14%. The greatest share of investment among EU countries was from Sweden (27.71%), Finland (16.74%) and Denmark (15.37%). Among the countries mentioned above last year the largest increase of investment was from Denmark (87.2%).

FOREIGN DIRECT INVESTMENT FROM EU TO LITHUANIA (MLN. USD)

	1 Jan 1997				1 Jan 1998			
EU Countries	MLN. LTL	MLN. USD	Country/ TOTAL%	Country/ EU%	MLN. LTL	MLN. USD	Country/ TOTAL%	Country/ EU%
Austria	59,08	14,77	2,11	3,62	95,08	23,77	2,28	3,99
Belgium	9,52	2,38	0,34	0,58	12,32	3,08	0,29	0,52
Denmark	156,52	39,13	5,59	9,6	259,68	64,92	6,24	10,91
Finland	130,72	32,68	4,67	8,02	180,76	45,19	4,34	7,6
France	36,12	9,03	1,29	2,22	60,24	15,06	1,45	2,53
Germany	363,68	90,92	12,98	22,31	467,72	116,93	11,24	19,65
Greece	1,08	0,27	0,04	0,07	0,76	0,19	0,02	0,03

Ireland	119,6	29,9	4,26	7,34	202,6	50,65	4,87	8,51
Italy	12,12	3,03	0,43	0,74	56,88	14,22	1,37	2,39
Luxembourg	121,44	30,36	4,34	7,45	161,6	40,4	3,88	6,79
Netherlands	33,12	8,28	1,18	2,03	41,56	10,39	1	1,75
Portugal	0,64	0,16	0,02	0,04	0,8	0,2	0,02	0,03
Spain	1,68	0,42	0,06	0,1	5,88	1,47	0,14	0,25
Sweden	335,96	83,99	11,99	20,61	507,08	126,77	12,18	21,31
United Kingdom	248,88	62,22	8,88	15,27	326,8	81,7	7,85	13,73
Total from EU	1629,96	407,49	58,19	100	2379,8	594,95	57,17	100
TOTAL	2801,24	700,31	100		4162,48	1040,62	100	

1 Jan 1999				1 Jan 2000			
MLN. LTL	MLN. USD	Country/ TOTAL%	Country/ EU%	MLN. LTL	MLN. USD	Country/ TOTAL%	Country/ EU%
84,72	21,18	1,3	2,13	58,35	14,59	0,71	1,12
29,88	7,47	0,46	0,75	34,20	8,55	0,41	0,66
427,8	106,95	6,58	10,75	801,00	200,25	9,71	15,37
693,76	173,44	10,67	17,43	872,14	218,03	10,57	16,74
85,76	21,44	1,32	2,15	96,75	24,19	1,17	1,86
530,32	132,58	8,16	13,32	632,05	158,01	7,66	12,13
1,12	0,28	0,02	0,03	3,16	0,79	0,04	0,06
182,08	45,52	2,8	4,57	231,29	57,82	2,80	4,44
67,88	16,97	1,04	1,71	26,62	6,65	0,32	0,51
302,04	75,51	4,64	7,59	295,28	73,82	3,58	5,67
36,32	9,08	0,56	0,91	116,75	29,19	1,41	2,24
0,52	0,13	0,01	0,01	8,18	2,05	0,10	0,16
1,88	0,47	0,03	0,05	1,74	0,43	0,02	0,03
1096,4	274,1	16,86	27,54	1443,89	360,97	17,50	27,71
440,2	110,05	6,77	11,06	589,32	147,33	7,14	11,31

3980,68	995,17	61,23	100	5210,72	1302,68	63,14	100,00
6501,2	1625,3	100		8252,12	2063,03	100,00	

Source: Department of Statistics of Lithuania

INTEGRATION WITH NATO PROGRAM

MEMBERSHIP ACTION PLAN

To allow applicant countries to better prepare for assuming the responsibilities of membership and to assist the applicants in preparations for eventual accession, NATO has provided a solid mechanism - the Membership Action Plan (MAP). Lithuania expects that the MAP, together with an enhanced PfP programme, will constitute a very practical and membership-tailored element of NATO's "open door" policy. There is an unwavering determination to proceed along this path and make the MAP a real success for Lithuania, for the Alliance, and for our common goal of European security.

GOVERNMENTAL CO-ORDINATION COMMISSION FOR INTEGRATION OF LITHUANIA INTO THE NORTH ATLANTIC TREATY ORGANISATION

On April 29, 1999 Lithuania established a Co-ordination Commission for the Integration into NATO and approved the regulations on its activities. It is meant to enhance Lithuania's administrative capacity and institutionalise internal co-ordination among the government ministries to improve the preparations for the accession negotiations with NATO. The Commission was tasked to prepare a National NATO Integration Programme (NNIP).

In the Commission, headed by the ministers of foreign affairs and national defence, 13 governmental institutions are represented at a vice-ministerial level. It has held two meetings and established six working groups: on Political and Economic, Defence/Military, Resources, Security, and Legal and Public Awareness issues.

The Commission is tasked to report regularly to the Lithuanian Government about Lithuania's implementation of the preparation plans for NATO membership and to make suggestions relating to the implementation of the MAP. The Commission provides the Government with a report on activities and recommendations twice a year, and, when requested, additional projects of decisions to further prepare for NATO membership.

LITHUANIAN NATIONAL NATO INTEGRATION PROGRAMME 2000/2001

Lithuania commits itself to active participation in the Membership Action Plan (MAP) process in its endeavour to assume the obligations of NATO membership. Participation in the MAP process assists Lithuania in its practical preparation for NATO membership and in mobilising national financial and human resources essential for integration into the Alliance.

NATO's "Progress Report" on the implementation of Lithuania's Annual National Programme (ANP) provides a constructive and objective evaluation of progress made by Lithuania. In drawing up the ANP for 2000-2001, the Government of Lithuania has taken into consideration the comments and proposals presented in NATO's "Progress Report."

The Lithuanian NNIP for 2000/2001 was prepared by the Lithuanian Government's Co-ordinating Commission for the Integration into NATO, and on 11 October 2000 was

approved by the Government of Lithuania. The Programme defines objectives and sets forth targets for Lithuania's membership preparations.
On October 31, 2000 Ambassador G.Čekuolis, Director of Multilateral Relations Department, MFA presented the Lithuanian NNIP for 2000/2001 at NATO Senior Political Committee (Reinforced) in Brussels.

TRANSPARENCY AND CO-ORDINATION AMONG THE ASPIRANT COUNTRIES

Having developed intensive political and practical co-operation in preparing fro NATO membership, Lithuania and other NATO candidates contribute to the one of the fundamental tasks envisaged in Alliance's Strategic Concept, to the partnership task, by promoting wide-ranging cooperation and dialogue among the NATO candidates and with the NATO.

Lithuania clearly realises that successful preparation and implementation of the MAP requires transparency between aspirant countries. Therefore, a trilateral consultation with Latvia and Estonia on the MAP were held and an exchange of programmes occurred in August 2000. Political consultations with NATO member states – Czech Republic, Denmark, Poland, the United Kingdom and the United States also took place in the year 2000.

In line with the ongoing processes, the Governments of Lithuania and Slovenia, hosted an international conference **"NATO's Role in the Changing Security Environment in Europe"** in Vilnius on 18-19 May 2000. The conference was organised at the ministerial level. All of the NATO aspirant countries participated at the conference. Nine candidate states issued the "Vilnius statement" that:

underlines NATO candidate's solidarity and ability to work together for the creation of a Europe whole and free in alliance with Europe and North America.
stresses commitment to practical and political efforts to further improve the specific qualifications of nine candidate countries, including implementation of the Membership Action Plan;
calls upon the member states of NATO to invite candidate democracies to begin accession negotiations at the next NATO Summit in 2002.

SUMMARY OF LITHUANIAN NNIP

The Programme addresses Political and Economic, Military and Defence, Resources, Security and Legal issues of Lithuania's integration into the Alliance and defines areas of consultation with NATO.

POLITICAL AND ECONOMIC ISSUES

Lithuania's ANP substantiates its readiness to assume the obligations and responsibilities laid down in the Washington Treaty and the relevant provisions of the "Study on NATO Enlargement." Lithuania shares fully and supports the approach of the Alliance to security in the 21st century, as outlined in the Alliance's Strategic Concept, and seeks to contribute in practical ways to the Alliance's aspiration to preserve peace and reinforce Euro-Atlantic security and stability. Together with the other states aspiring for membership in NATO, in May 2000, Lithuania signed in Vilnius "

The Vilnius Statement" confirming its commitment to the creation of a Europe whole and free and its determination to take practical and political efforts to further improve the specific qualifications, including implementation of the Membership Action Plan, as well as calling on the member states of NATO to invite new members at the next NATO Summit in 2002. The meeting in Vilnius was the beginning of the new-cooperation. In our view, the process in development should not be misinterpreted – this is the process of political and more and more strengthening practical co-operation among NATO candidate countries on their way towards membership and should not be identified with so called "Big bang" theory. We understand, that the Alliance will continue NATO enlargement process by inviting candidate countries, each being considered on the individual basis.

The integration into the European Union (on 15 February 2000, Lithuania commenced accession negotiations) and maintaining of good neighbourly relations with its neighbours as well as the other states of the Baltic Sea region remain to be other top priorities for Lithuania. Lithuania will further develop economic, commercial and cultural relations with the Kaliningrad region of the Russian Federation.
The economic indicators of the first half of 2000 show the recovery of Lithuania's national economy. In the first half of 2000, GDP increased by 2 per cent and exports grew by 26.1 per cent, compared with a respective period of 1999.

DEFENCE/MILITARY ISSUES

Lithuanian defence policy sets two major objectives for the development of national defence in peacetime: to prepare the country for defence and to prepare itself to meet its international commitments to collective defence and support to peacekeeping operations. Lithuania has already developed its Military Strategy, which was approved by State Defence Council on 2 October 2000 and promulgated by the order of the Minister of National defence on 4 October 2000.
With a help of the MAP mechanism Lithuania strengthens its participation in the PfP programme, including PARP. Lithuania commits itself to implementing a package of 66 Partnership Goals (PGs), a part of which is closely related to the DCI. Lithuania's participation in IPP as well as co-operation with other countries under the bilateral format has become a key instrument in the implementation PARP Partnership Goals.
Referring to the Long-Range Security Enhancement Programmes the main priorities in the Annual National Programme are expected to remain unchanged for the forthcoming years:

Enhancement of military education and training;
Quality of life improvement;
Introduction of C3 system;
Development of infrastructure;
Development of logistics system;
Air defence;
Armament and equipment procurement.

RESOURCE ISSUES

Lithuania recognises the necessity of appropriating sufficient human and budget resources to implement both its national self-defence requirements and upon accession, all Alliance commitments, roles and responsibilities. Lithuania's commitment to develop its defence capabilities is demonstrated by the law of Seimas On Financing the System of National Defence" which established defence spending of 1,70-1,75of GDP for the year 2000 and 1,95-2,00 for the year 2001.

To rationalise the management of resources and programming process, the Ministry of National Defence of Lithuania continues to develop the Planning, Programming and Budgeting System, which encompasses all stages of planning. The National Defence System Development Plan includes nine programmes, each of which is based on available resources. Lithuania remains committed to gradually increase defence spending up to 2% of GDP. In modernising its Armed

Forces Lithuania is guided by a realistic approach as to what can be achieved in terms of force structure and capabilities.

SECURITY ISSUES

The work on the establishment of a legal basis essential for assuring effective functioning of the protection of the classified information was completed in 2000. The clearance of personnel, assurance of physical security and procedures for administration of classified documents applied in Lithuania comply with the basic minimum requirements of NATO Security Policy. In 2001 special attention will be paid to the issues of security of communications and information systems security (INFOSEC).

LEGAL ISSUES

Lithuania expects, upon accession to NATO, to make its legal system compatible with basic NATO legal regulations. Our aim in legal sphere is to make sure that there are no potential legal impediments to fulfil Lithuania's obligations stemming from membership. In accordance with the terms outlined in the MAP, Lithuania carries on a review of its domestic legislation and agreements, which regulate the defence/military field and govern wide-ranging cooperation with NATO and its members.

ECONOMY AND ECONOMIC DEVELOPMENT

Currency	Litas (LTL)
Fiscal year	1 January — 31 December
Trade organisations	EU, WTO and OSCE
	Statistics
GDP	$60.38 billion
GDP growth	5,9%
GDP per capita	$19.724
GDP by sector	agriculture (4.37%), industry (21.46%), services (74.18%) (2008)
Inflation (CPI)	3.4% (July
Population below poverty line	4% (2003)
Labour force	1.65 million
Labour force by occupation	services (72.49%), industry (19.58%), agriculture (7.94%)
Unemployment	9.75 %
Average gross salary	2121 LTL / 858 $, monthly
Average net salary	1650 LTL / 668 $, monthly
Main industries	ICT, Biotech, Metal Processing, Machinery and Electric Equipment, Plastics, Furniture, Wood processing & Paper Industry, Textile & Clothing, Food, Real Estate & Construction, Transport & Logistics, Lasers
Ease of Doing Business Rank	27th
	External
Exports	€11.8 billion (2009), €15.6 billion (2010), €20.2 billion (2011)
Export goods	mineral products (21.5%), machinery and mechanical appliances, electrical equipment (10.6%), products of the chemical or allied industries (9.1%)
Main export partners	EU (60.9%), Russia (15.6%), Germany (9.8%), Latvia (9.3%), Poland (7.7%)
Imports	€13.1 billion (2009), €17.6 billion (2010), €22.6 billion (2011)
Import goods	mineral products (29.3%), machinery and mechanical appliances, electrical equipment (13.1%), products of the chemical or allied industries (12.3%) (2009)
Main import partners	EU (56.5%), Russia (32.6%), Germany (10.5%), Poland (8.8%) and Latvia (6.3%)
FDI stock	Eur 10,762 billion
Gross external debt	Eur 7.134 billion (26,6 % of GDP)
	Public finances
Revenues	Eur 9.815 billion
Expenses	Eur 11.502 billion
Economic aid	EU structural assistance: 2.286 Eur billion (est.), assistance from Switzerland: 9.09 Eur Mln.
Credit rating	Standard & Poor's: BBB (Domestic) BBB (Foreign) A (T&C Assessment) Outlook: Stable Moody's:

	Baa1 Outlook: Stable Fitch: BBB Outlook: Positive
Foreign reserves	US$7.851 billion

Lithuania is a member of the European Union and the biggest economy among three Baltic states. GDP per capita reached USD 17,800 in 2008 and was higher than all of its neighbors – Latvia, Poland, Russia and Belarus.

GDP per capita in Lithuania is 70% above the world's average of US$10,500. Lithuania has a favorable legislative basis for business as the country is ranked the 3rd in the region of Eastern Europe and Central Asia and the 26th in the world by the Ease of Doing Business Index prepared by the World Bank Group. Lithuania is ranked the 30th out of 179 countries in the Index of Economic Freedom, measured by The Heritage Foundation. According to the Human Development Report 2011, Lithuania belongs to the group of very high human development countries.

Having moved away from central planning system in the late 1980s, in 1990, Lithuania was the first to break away from the Soviet Union and become an independent capitalist economy. Lithuania soon implemented liberal reforms and became one of the fastest growing countries in the world last decade, as GDP growth rate was positive 9 years in a row till 2009. It enjoyed high growth rates after entering the European Union along with other Baltic states, leading to the notion of a Baltic Tiger. Current excellent telecommunication infrastructure and well-educated, multilingual workforce give the possibility to provide high quality business services and produce manufacturing products worldwide.

In 2005 the GDP grew by 7.5% and the inflation rate was 3%. GDP growth reached its height in 2007, increasing by 8.9%. Lithuania was the last among the Baltic states to be hit by the economic crisis because its GDP growth rate in 2008 was still positive. In the third quarter of 2009, compared to the previous quarter, GDP grew again by 6.9% after 5 quarters with negative numbers. Rebound in Lithuania's economy in the third quarter was the fastest in the EU. In the last quarter of 2009 Lithuanian economy rose moderately by 0.1%, however the Finance Ministry of Lithuania forecasts that Lithuania's economy will keep growing by 1.6% in 2010 and by 3.2% in 2011. In 2011 real growth was higher than expected at first and reached 5.9%

In 2003, before joining the European Union, Lithuania had the highest economic growth rate amongst all candidate and member countries, reaching 8.8% in the third quarter.

In 2004 – 7.4%; 2005 – 7.8%; 2006 – 7.8%; 2007 – 8.9%, 2008 Q1 – 7.0% growth in GDP reflects the impressive economic development and as a result is often termed as a Baltic Tiger. However, 2009 marked a dramatic decline in GDP at -14.74% attributed to overheating of the economy. In 2010, the rate was 1.33%.

As of June 2012, the unemployment rate is 10.2%.

Lithuania has a flat tax rate rather than a progressive scheme. In 2007, personal income tax was reduced to 24% and a reduction to 21% was made in January 2009. Lithuanian income levels are lower than in the older EU Member States. According to Eurostat data, Lithuanian PPS GDP per capita stood at 61 per cent of the EU average in 2008.

Swedbank Headquarters in Vilnius The country boasts a well-developed modern infrastructure of railways, airports and four-lane highways.

Structurally, there is a gradual but consistent shift towards a knowledge-based economy with special emphasis on biotechnology (industrial and diagnostic). The major biotechnology companies and laser manufacturers (Ekspla, Šviesos Konversija) of the Baltics are concentrated in Lithuania. Also mechatronics and information technology (IT) are seen as prospective knowledge-based economy directions.

In 2009, Barclays established Technology Centre Lithuania – one of four strategic engineering centres supporting the Barclays Retail Banking businesses across the globe. In 2011, Western Union officially opened their new European Regional Operating Centre in Vilnius. The stated position of the Lithuanian government is that the focus of Lithuanian economy is high added-value products and services.

Among other international companies operating in Lithuania are: PricewaterhouseCoopers, Ernst & Young, Societe Generale, UniCredit, Thermo Fisher Scientific, Phillip Morris, Kraft Foods, Mars, Marks & Spencer, GlaxoSmithKline, United Colors of Benetton, Deichmann, Statoil, Neste Oil, Lukoil, Tele2, Hesburger and Modern Times Group. TeliaSonera, ICA and Carslberg respectively own local telecommunications company Omnitel, retailer Rimi and beer breweries (Švyturys, Kalnapilis and Utenos Alus).

Lithuanian banking sector is dominated by the Scandinavian banks: Swedbank, SEB, Nordea, Danske Bank, DNB ASA.

Among the biggest Lithuanian companies are: Maxima Group, ORLEN Lietuva, Achema, Lifosa, Apranga.

Corporate tax rate in Lithuania is 15% and 5% for small businesses. The government offers special incentives for investments into the high-technology sectors and high value-added products.

Most of the trade Lithuania conducts is within the European Union.

The litas, the national currency, has been pegged to the euro since 2 February 2002 at the rate of EUR 1.00 = LTL 3.4528, and Lithuania is expecting to switch to the euro on 1 January 2014

The history of Lithuania can be divided into 7 major periods. All the periods have some interesting and important facts that had an impact on the economic situation of the country in those times.

Ancient times – Baltic tribes (until the 13th century)
Grand Duchy of Lithuania (13th century -1569)
Polish-Lithuanian Commonwealth (1569–1795)
Pressure of the Russian Empire (1795–1914)
Independent Lithuania during the interwar period (1918–1940)
Lithuanian Soviet Socialist Republic (1944–1990)
Republic of Lithuania (since 1990)

HISTORY UP TO THE 20TH CENTURY

The first Lithuanians were a branch of an ancient ethnic group known as the Balts. The tribes maintained close trade contacts with the Roman Empire. Amber was the main good provided to the Roman Empire from Baltic Sea coast, by a long route called the Amber Road.

Consolidation of the Lithuanian lands began in the late 12th century. Mindaugas, the first Lithuanian ruler, was crowned as Catholic King of Lithuania in 1253. The expansion of the Grand Duchy of Lithuania reached its height in the middle of the 14th century under the Grand Duke Gediminas, who created a strong central government which later spread from the Black Sea to the Baltic Sea. The duchy was open to everyone. Grand Duke Gediminas issued letters to the Hanseatic league, offering free access to his domains to men of every order and profession from nobles and knights to tillers of the soil. Economic immigrants had a positive impact, improving the level of handicrafts.

In 1569, the Polish–Lithuanian Commonwealth was formed by the union of the Kingdom of Poland and the Grand Duchy of Lithuania. The economy of the Commonwealth was dominated by feudal agriculture based on the exploitation of the agricultural workforce (serfs). Poland-Lithuania played a significant role in the supply of 16th century Western Europe by exporting three sorts of goods, notably grain (rye), cattle (oxen) and fur. These three articles amounted to nearly 90% of the country's exports to western markets by overland and maritime trade.

The Commonwealth was famous for Europe's first and the world's second modern codified national constitution, the so-called Constitution of May 3, declared on the 3rd of May, 1791, after the 1788 ratification of the United States Constitution. Economic and commercial reforms, previously shunned as unimportant by the Szlachta, were introduced, and the development of industries was encouraged.

Following the partitions of the Polish-Lithuanian Commonwealth in 1772, 1793 and 1795, the Russian Empire controlled the majority of Lithuania. One of the most important reforms during the pressure of the Russian Empire that affected economic relations was the Emancipation Reform of 1861 in Russia. The reform amounted to the liquidation of serf dependence previously suffered by peasants and boosted the development of capitalism.

LITHUANIA IN THE 20TH CENTURY

On February 16, 1918, the Council of Lithuania passed a resolution for the re-establishment of the Independent State of Lithuania. Soon, many economic reforms for sustainable economic growth were implemented. A national currency, called the Lithuanian litas, was introduced in 1922. It proved to become one of the most stable currencies in Europe during the inter-war period. During the time of its independence, 1918–1940, Lithuania made substantial progress. For example, Lithuania was the second in the world in exporting flax; Lithuanian farm products such as meat, dairy products, many kinds of grain, potatoes, etc. were of superior quality in the world market.

Having taken advantage of favorable international developments, and driven by its foreign policy aims directed against Lithuanian statehood, the Union of Soviet Socialist Republics (USSR) occupied Lithuania in 1940.

Land and the most important objects for the economy were nationalized, and most of the farms collectivized. Later, many inefficient factories and industry companies, highly dependent on other regions of USSR, were established in Lithuania. Despite that, in 1990, GDP per capita of the Lithuanian Soviet Socialist Republic was USD 8,591, which was above the average for the rest of the Soviet Union of USD 6,871 but lagging behind developed western countries.

The Soviet era brought Lithuania intensive industrialization and economic integration into the USSR, although the level of technology and state concern for environmental, health, and labor issues lagged far behind Western standards. Urbanization increased from 39% in 1959 to 68% in 1989. From 1949–1952 the Soviets abolished private ownership in agriculture, establishing collective and state farms. Production declined and did not reach pre-war levels until the early 1960s. The intensification of agricultural production through intense chemical use and mechanization eventually doubled production but created additional ecological problems. This changed after independence, when farm production dropped due to difficulties in restructuring the agricultural sector.

THE MYTH OF LITHUANIA'S ECONOMIC COLLAPSE

According to official statistics, towards the end of central planning economic output plunged in all Soviet-type countries during the transition from central planning to a market economy. The total registered declines in GDP range from 13 to 77% in Eastern Europe. However, both Soviet period and early transition period statistics were deeply flawed and do not represent the real situation and processes in Eastern Europe and Lithuania.

During the transitional period former USSR republics, including Lithuania, were characterized by these aspects: overproduction reporting; reluctance to pay taxes by people and enterprises; the reduction of value detraction; overestimation of investment ratios; and politically determined trade among the Soviet countries.

Taking into account the shadow economy, value detraction from products and services, doubtful investments and indirect trade subsidies, Lithuania was not faced with such a huge contraction in GDP as was usually thought and represented in official statistics. On the contrary, Lithuania made structural reforms for future growth and welfare.

DEVELOPMENT SINCE THE 1990S

Reforms since the mid-1990s have given Lithuania an open and rapidly growing economy. Open to global trade and investment, Lithuania now enjoys high degrees of business, fiscal and financial freedom. Regulation is relatively transparent and efficient. Foreign capital and domestic capital are subject to the same rules as Lithuania is a member of the EU and the WTO. The financial sector is advanced, regionally integrated, and subject to few intrusive regulations.

One of the most important reforms since Lithuania regained its independence was the privatization of state owned assets. The first stage of privatization was being implemented in 1991–1995. Citizens were given investment vouchers worth LTL 10.5 billion (USD 2.63 billion) in nominal value, which let them participate in assets selling. By October 1995, they were used as follows: 65% for acquisition of shares; 19% for residential dwellings; 5% for agricultural properties; and 7% remained unused. More than 5700 enterprises with LTL 7 billion (USD 1.75 billion) worth of state capital in book value were sold using four initial privatization methods: share offerings; auctions; best business plans competitions; and hard currency sales.

The second privatization step began in 1995 by approving a new law that ensured greater diversity of privatization methods and that enabled participation in the selling process without vouchers. During the period 1996–1998, 526 entities were sold for more than LTL 2.3 billion (USD 0.58 billion). Before the reforms, the public sector totally dominated the economy, where as the current share of the private sector in GDP increased to over 80%.

The implementation of the monetary reform was one of the key success factors for the stability of the economy. Lithuania has chosen a currency board system formed and controlled by the Bank of Lithuania that is independent from any government institution. On 25 June 1993, the Lithuanian litas was introduced as a free convertible currency, but on 1 April 1994 it was pegged to the United States dollar at a rate of 4 to 1. The mechanism of the currency board system enabled Lithuania to stabilize inflation rates to single digits. The litas soon became a reliable currency as the litas is fully backed by foreign currency. The stable currency rate helped to establish foreign economic relations, therefore leading to a constant growth of foreign trade.

By 1998, the economy had survived the early years of uncertainty and several setbacks, including a banking crisis, and seemed poised for solid growth. However, the collapse of the Russian ruble in August 1998 shocked the economy into negative growth and forced the reorientation of trade from Russia towards the West.

Lithuania was invited to the Helsinki EU summit in December 1999 to begin EU accession talks in early 2000.

After the Russian monetary crisis, the focus of Lithuania's export markets shifted from East to West. In 1997, exports to the Soviet Union's successor entity (the Commonwealth of Independent States) made up 45% of total Lithuanian exports. This share of exports dropped to 21% of the total in 2006, while exports to EU members increased to 63% of the total.

Exports to the United States made up 4.3% of all Lithuania's exports in 2006, and imports from the United States comprised 2% of total imports. Foreign direct investment (FDI) in 2005 was 2.6 billion litas, which represented an increase of only 4.6% compared to the same period in the previous year.

Since February 2, 2002 the litas has been pegged to the euro at a rate of 3.4528 to 1. The rate is not expected to change until Lithuania becomes a member of the Eurozone. Lithuania was very close to introducing the euro in 2007, but unfortunately the inflation level was somewhat above the Maastricht requirements. The current tough economic situation precludes compliance with the Maastricht criteria on budget balance, so Lithuania cannot expect to have the euro before 2013–2015.

The Vilnius Stock Exchange (VSE), now renamed the NASDAQ OMX Vilnius, started its activity in 1993 and was the first stock exchange in the Baltic states. In 2003, the VSE was acquired by OMX. Since February 27, 2008 the Vilnius Stock Exchange has been a member of NASDAQ OMX Group, which is the world's largest exchange company across six continents, with over 3800 listed companies. The market cap of Vilnius Stock Exchange was LTL 11.7 billion (EUR 3.4 billion) on November 27, 2009 and was twice as large as the ones of Riga and Tallinn Stock Exchanges.

During the last decade (1998–2008) the structure of Lithuania's economy has changed significantly. The biggest changes were recorded in the agricultural sector as the share of total employment decreased from 19.2% in 1998 to just 7.9% in 2008. The service sector plays an increasingly important role in the economy of Lithuania. The share of GDP in financial intermediation and real estate sectors was 17% in 2008 compared to 11% in 1998. The share of total employment in the financial sector in 2008 has doubled compared with 1998

Structural reform has proceeded rapidly in the privatization of small enterprises and in agriculture. Over 70,000 private farms have been established. However, due to the lack of financial resources and an inefficient credit system, many of the new farmers are operating at subsistence levels. Urban and rural property is being returned to its original owners, but legal mechanisms for title registration, sale and mortgaging of real property are not yet fully developed. About 86% of all enterprises and about 83% of state property included in the initial privatization program have been privatized. Some 5,714 (86%) out of 6,644 eligible companies were privatized during the first stage. In 1999, privatized state-owned capital equaled $850 million or approximately 30% of all the state-owned property . The remaining state-owned property is valued at almost 9.9 billion Litas, or nearly $2.5 billion. In March 1998, the Lithuanian government established the State Property Fund to manage and privatize the remaining state assets which include the energy sector and more of the telecom and transportation sectors.

Currently, privatization of the State property is carried out using the following methods:

1. Public share subscription (large and medium scale enterprises);
2. Auctions (small enterprises or divisions thereof);
3. Tenders or auctions for convertible currency;
4. Direct negotiations;
5. Lease with the option to purchase; and
6. A combination of different methods.

Privatization also includes tenders evaluated for the best business plan, i.e. tenders, which take into account both the financial offer and an overall plan for the development of a company. Open tenders were generally used to privatize large industrial enterprises for hard currency.

Lithuania has historically been an exporter of agricultural products, primarily such as processed meat, dairy products and fish. As part of the Soviet Union, Lithuania exported about 80% of its agricultural production to the other Soviet Republics. Today, owing to the diminished purchase power of the eastern markets and the inadequate restructuring of the agricultural sector, the trade balance to the east is negative.

Major infrastructure projects that are currently being implemented or still pending include the privatization and upgrading of the Mazeikiai oil refinery; safety upgrades of the Ignalina nuclear power plant; construction of the Via Baltica highway connecting the Baltic countries to the rest of Europe; expansion and modernization of Klaipeda sea-port facilities, and construction of the electric power transmission line to the West.

Lithuania's current road network is good especially along the main routes. Likewise, the rail links to Russia are strong, though train tracks and grade crossings need upgrading in order to handle higher speeds and heavier loads. The port of Klaipeda is well equipped but in need of modern management techniques. Vilnius International Airport has been brought up to western standards and is preparing to offer expanded services. Lithuania has two additional international airports- Kaunas and Palanga - and one commercial airport in Siauliai.

TOP TEN FOREIGN INVESTORS IN LITHUANIA

Investor Country Lithuanian Co Sector Value

Amber Swe/Fin Lietuvos telecom 510
Consortium Telekomas

Williams USA Mazeikiu Nafta petroleum 150

International

Telia/Sonera Swe/Fin Omnitel telecom 66

Philip Morris USA Philip Morris tobacco 60
Lietuva products

SEB Swe Vilniaus Bankas banking 57

Tele Denmark DK/Lux Bite GSM telecom 50
Millicom East

Carlsberg DK Svyturys brewery 45

Den Norske Nor Lietuva Statoil petroleum 38
Stats Oljes.

Danisco Sugar DK Lithuanian Sugar sugar prod. 34

Coca-Cola Co. USA Coca-Cola soft drinks 31.5
Bottlers

Lithuania in the 21st century

Real GDP Growth in Lithuania, 1996–2008

Economic sentiment indicator and its components

Balance of Payments in Lithuania, Quarterly Data

The economy of Lithuania was one of the fastest growing in the world last decade (1998–2008) as GDP growth rate was positive 9 years in a row. Since the year 2000 GDP has almost doubled with a growth rate of 77%.

One of the most important factors for substantial economic expansion was the accession to the WTO in 2001 and the EU in 2004, which enabled free movement of the labour force, capital and trade between the Member States. On the other hand, rapid economic expansion has caused some imbalances in inflation and balance of payments. The current account deficit to GDP ratio in 2006–2008 was in double digits and reached its peak at threatening 18.8% in the first quarter of 2008. This was mostly influenced by rapid loan portfolio growth as Scandinavian banks provided cheap credits in Lithuania. The loans directly related to acquisition and development of real estate constituted around half of outstanding bank loans to the private sector. Consumption was affected by credit expansion as well. This led to high inflation of goods and services, as well as trade deficit.

The global credit crunch which started in 2008 affected the real estate and retail sectors. The construction sector shrank by 46.8% during the first 3 quarters of 2009 and the slump in retail trade was almost 30%. GDP plunged by 15.7% in the first nine months of 2009.

Lithuania was the last among the Baltic states to be hit by the economic crisis because its GDP growth rate in 2008 was still positive. In the third quarter of 2009, compared to the previous quarter, GDP again grew by 6.1% after five quarters with negative numbers. The rebound in Lithuania's economy in the third quarter was the fastest in the EU.

A heavy shock to consumers helped to balance the current account in 2009. Net external assets of the Bank of Lithuania are at a record height of EUR 5.46 billion. Inflation in Lithuania is no longer a problem. Economic sentiment and confidence of all business activities have rebounded from a record low at the beginning of the year 2009 and suggest further improvements in the economy.

Sectors related to domestic consumption and real estate are still suffering from the economic crisis. However, exporters have started making profits even with lower levels of revenue. The catalysts of growing profit margins are lower raw material prices and staff expense.

TAX SYSTEM

Lithuania has a favorable tax system. There are four main types of taxes: personal income tax (15% + 6% health insurance contribution); value added tax (21%); corporate profit tax (15%); and social security tax on employers (31% + employee's contribution of 3%).5% corporate tax for small business was introduced on 1 January 2010. Additional taxes are tax on dividends (0-15% - dividends paid or received are not taxed when an investor controls at least 10% of voting shares in the enterprise for the period of at least 12 months), real estate tax (0.3–1.0%) and a land tax of 1.5% on businesses.

The overall tax burden in Lithuania is one of the smallest among all EU countries.

Lithuania attracts foreign investors not only because of small tax burden but also because of a skilled workforce, a well-developed infrastructure and a bigger domestic market than the other two Baltic states combined. Cumulative foreign direct investment (FDI) at the beginning of the year 2009 was LTL 31.6 billion (EUR 9.2 billion).

The manufacturing sector constituted 28% of total FDI, real estate and business activity sector received 20% of total FDI, and financial intermediation a little bit less – 19%. 4/5 of FDI came from the EU countries. Top countries-investors are Sweden (17% of total FDI), Germany (10%) and Denmark (9%).

Lithuania has an ambitious plan to become a Northern European innovation centre by 2020. To reach this goal, it is putting its efforts into attracting FDI to added-value sectors, especially IT services, software development, and consulting services, as well as finance or logistics. Well-known international companies, such as Microsoft, IBM, Transcom, Barclays, Siemens, SEB, TeliaSonera, Paroc, Philip Morris and others, have already established a presence in Lithuania.

Lithuania has prepared an attractive environment for business start-ups in two free economic zones (FEZ) in Kaunas and Klaipėda. FEZs offer not only developed infrastructure for investments and service support but also tax incentives: a FEZ is free from the corporate tax for the first six years, as well as free from tax on dividends and real estate tax.There are nine industrial sites in Lithuania, which can also provide additional advantages by having a well-developed infrastructure, offering consultancy service and some tax incentives.

The transport infrastructure inherited from the Soviet period is adequate and has been generally well maintained since independence. Its single port in Klaipėda is ice-free and supplies ferry services to German, Swedish, and Danish ports. There are a few commercial airports; scheduled international services use the facilities at Vilnius, Kaunas, and Klaipėda. The road system is well developed, including the Via Baltica highway passing through Kaunas.

Border facilities at checkpoints with Poland were significantly improved with the help of EU funds, but long waits had been a frequent phenomenon until 21 December 2007 when the Schengen Agreement came in force in both countries. Telecommunications have improved greatly since independence as a result of heavy investment. There are currently three large companies providing mobile phone services. .

WORKFORCE

Unemployment Rate in Lithuania decreased to 12.30 percent in the third quarter of 2012 from 13.30 percent in the second quarter of 2012. Unemployment Rate in Lithuania is reported by the Statistics Lithuania. Historically, from 1998 until 2012, Lithuania Unemployment Rate averaged 11.7 Percent reaching an all time high of 18.3 Percent in June of 2010 and a record low of 3.9 Percent in September of 2007. In Lithuania, the unemployment rate measures the number of people actively looking for a job as a percentage of the labour force. This page includes a chart with historical data for Lithuania Unemployment Rate.

The number of the population aged 15 years and over is 2.85 million, and 1.52 million of them were employed in 2008. The population with higher education was 0.54 million, or more than 35% of employed people. This ratio demonstrates that workforce in Lithuania is one of the best-educated in Central and Eastern Europe (CEE) and is twice the EU-15 average. About

90% of Lithuanians speak at least one foreign language; every second person speaks two foreign languages and every third person speaks English

Lithuania takes the first position in the EU by the number of students in the country. Compared to the EU's average of 15%, only 7% of 18–24 year-old people in Lithuania are not occupied with studies, the lowest percentage in the EU, announced the European Commission in the end of 2009. School-leavers can choose from 22 universities or 28 colleges for further studies, so 74% of pupils graduated from an upper secondary school continue studies in schools of higher education. Every year more than 30 thousand students graduate from universities or colleges, so the population with higher education is gradually increasing. The most popular higher education programs are business and administration, education science, law, and social sciences.

During the last decade (1998–2008) salaries have more than doubled in Lithuania. Despite this, labour costs in Lithuania are among the lowest in the EU. Average monthly net salary in the third quarter of 2009 was LTL 1665 (EUR 482) and decreased by 6% compared to the same quarter in 2008.The sharpest annual decrease in hourly labour costs in the EU of -10.9% was observed in Lithuania in the third quarter of 2009.

The unemployment rate in Lithuania is very volatile. Since the year 2001, the unemployment rate has decreased from almost 20% to less than 4% in 2007. This could be explained by two main reasons. Firstly, during the time of rapid economic expansion, numerous work places were established. This caused a decrease in the unemployment rate and a rise in staff expenses. Secondly, emigration has also reduced unemployment problems since accession to the EU. However, the current economic crisis has lowered the need for workers, so the unemployment rate increased to 13.8% and then stabilized in the third quarter of 2009.

SECTORS OF ECONOMY

Structure of gross value added by kind of economic activity

Economic activity	2008
Manufacturing	17.9%
Wholesale and retail trade; repair of goods	16.6%
Real estate, renting and business activities	13.1%
Transport, storage and communication	12.1%
Construction	10.0%
Public administration and defense; compulsory social security	6.7%
Education	4.9%
Agriculture, hunting and forestry	4.3%
Financial intermediation	3.5%
Health and social work	3.3%
Electricity, gas and water supply	3.1%
Other community, social and personal service activities	2.5%
Hotels and restaurants	1.3%
Mining and quarrying	0.4%
Activities of households	0.1%
Fishing	0.1%

High value added production is increasing in Lithuania. Several companies produce pharmaceutical substances, components for molecular diagnostics and other sophisticated biotech products. 80% of the production is exported to more than 70 countries. Lithuanian pharmaceutical companies are expanding to foreign markets by acquiring companies in Slovakia and Poland.

Lithuania has over 50% of the world's market for high-energy picosecond lasers, and is a leader in global production of ultra-fast parametric light generators.Lithuanian laser companies were among the first ones in the world to transfer fundamental research into manufacture. Lithuania's laser producers export laser technologies and devices to nearly 100 countries, including EU members, the USA, Japan, Israel, and Switzerland, mostly for universities and corporate laboratories for scientific research purposes.

Recent global broadband Internet studies show that Lithuania has the fastest Internet in the world, as well as is one of the leading countries in terms of Internet service quality. The broadband speed analysis tool that allows anyone to test their Internet connection Speedtest.net places Lithuania as No. 1 on the list of the world's top countries by upload speed. Lithuania is also on the list of the world's top countries of download speed. Lithuania has one of the highest mobile telephone penetration rates, as well. With a subscription rate of 149 per 100 population, Lithuania is ranked the 8th in the world.

An excellent telecommunication infrastructure and a well-educated, multilingual workforce enable Lithuania to provide high quality business services worldwide. Business services vary from financial to accounting and reporting services. The share of value added in this sector reaches 13%.

SERVICE SECTOR

The service sector accounts for the largest share of GDP. One of the most important sub-sectors is information and communication technologies. 37 thousand employees work for more than 2000 ICT companies. ICT received 9.5% of total FDI. 11 out of 20 biggest IT companies from Baltic countries are based in Lithuania. Lithuania exported 31% of its IT services in the first quarter of 2009.

Development of shared services and outsourcing of business processes (BPO) is one of the most promising fields in Lithuania. The research company Datamonitor forecasts a 60% personnel growth by 2009. International companies successfully outsourcing business operations in Lithuania are Barclays Bank PLC, CITCO Group, MIRROR, PricewaterhouseCoopers, Anthill, Ernst&Young and etc.

MANUFACTURING

Manufacturing constitutes the biggest part of gross value added in Lithuania. More than 57 thousand people were employed in food processing in 2008. The food processing sector constitutes 11% of total exports.Dairy products, especially cheese, are well known in neighbouring countries. Another important manufacturing activity is chemical products. 80% of production is exported so chemical products constitute 12.5% of total exports.

Furniture production activity employs more than 50 thousand people. This sector has grown in double-digit numbers over the last three years. The biggest companies in this field work in cooperation with IKEA and provide high quality products at competitive prices. IKEA also owns one of the biggest wood processing companies in Lithuania.

Companies in the automotive and engineering sector are relatively small but offer flexible services for small and non-standard orders at competitive prices. The sector employs about

3% of the working population and receives 5.6% of FDI. Vilnius Gediminas Technical University, the biggest technical university in Baltic countries, prepares experts for the sector.

FINANCIAL SECTOR

Lending and saving data

The financial sector concentrates mostly on the domestic market. There are nine commercial banks holding a license from the Bank of Lithuania and eight foreign bank branches. Most of the banks belong to international corporations, mainly Scandinavian. The financial sector has demonstrated incredible growth in the last decade (1998–2008). Bank assets were only LTL 11.2 billion (USD 2.8 billion) or 25.5% from GDP at the beginning of the year 2000. Half of the bank assets consisted of loan portfolio.

By the beginning of the year 2009, bank assets grew to LTL 89.7 billion (EUR 26 billion) or 80.8% to GDP, the loan portfolio reached LTL 71.4 billion (EUR 20.7 billion). The loan to GDP ratio was 64%. The growth of deposits was not as fast as that of loans. At the end of 2008, the loan portfolio was almost twice as big as that of deposits. It demonstrated high dependence on external financing. Contraction in the loan portfolio has been recorded over the past year, so the loans to deposits ratio are slowly getting back to healthy levels.

UTILITIES SECTOR

Heating energy data

The utilities sector accounts for more than 3% of gross value added in Lithuania. Electricity production exceeded 12 billion kWh in 2007, and consumption exceeded 9.6 billion kWh . Electricity production surplus is exported.

Lithuania had a working nuclear power plant in Visaginas, which had a 72% share in electricity generation. However, the government undertook a commitment to decommission the nuclear power plant by the end of 2009, and the plant was shut on 31 December 2009. The supply of heating energy has been modernized during the last decade (1998–2008). Technological loss in the heat energy system has decreased significantly from 26.2% in the year 2000 to 16.7% in 2008. The amount of air pollution was reduced by one third. The share of renewable energy resources in the total fuel balance for heat production increased to almost 20%.

TOURISM

The tourism sector is becoming increasingly important for the economy of Lithuania. It constituted almost 3% of GDP in 2008. Having an untouched ecological countryside with rich natural resources (22 000 rivers and rivulets, and about 3000 lakes), a well-developed rural tourism network, a unique coastal area of almost 100 km and four UNESCO World Heritage sites, Lithuania receives more than 2.2 million foreign tourists a year. The biggest tourist flows arrive from neighbouring countries: Poland; Russia; Latvia; and Belarus. Other important countries for Lithuania's tourism are Germany, the United Kingdom, Finland and Italy.

AGRICULTURE

Despite a decreased share in GDP, the agricultural sector is still important for Lithuania as it employs almost 8% of the work force and supplies materials for the food processing sector. 44.8% of the land is arable. Total crop area was 1.8 million hectares in 2008. Cereals, wheat and triticale are the most popular production of farms. The number of livestock and poultry has decreased twofold compared to the 1990s. The number of cattle in Lithuania at the beginning of the year 2009 was 770 thousand, the number of dairy cows was 395 thousand, and the number of poultry was 9.1 million. Lithuanians have changed their habits of foodstuff consumption somewhat. During the period 1992–2008, consumption of vegetables increased by 30% to 86 kg per capita, and consumption of meat and its products increased by 23% during the same period to 81 kg per capita. On the other hand, consumption of milk and dairy products has decreased to 268 kg per capita by 21%, and the consumption of bread and grain products decreased to 114 kg per capita by 19% as well.

REGIONAL SITUATION

Lithuania is divided into 10 counties. There are five cities with a population over 100 thousand and twelve cities of over 30 thousand people. The gross regional product is concentrated in the three largest counties – Vilnius, Kaunas and Klaipėda. These three counties account for 70% of the gross domestic product while having just 59% of the population. Service centers and industry are concentrated there. In five counties (those of Alytus, Marijampole, Panevėžys, Šiauliai and Tauragė), GDP per capita is still below 80% of the national average.

In order to achieve balanced regional distribution of GDP, nine public industrial parks (Akmene Industrial Park, Alytus Industrial Park, Kedainiai Industrial Park, Marijampole Industrial Park, Pagegiai Industrial Park, Panevzys Industrial Park, Radviliskis Industrial Park, Ramygala Industrial Park and Šiauliai Industrial Park) and three private industrial parks (Tauragė Private Industrial Park, Sitkunai Private Industrial Park, Ramučiai Private Logistic and Industrial Park) were established to provide some tax incentives and prepared physical infrastructure.

While the growth in the 1990s was largely constrained to the cities of Vilnius and Klaipėda, in the 2000s the situation changed. Babilonas real estate development, the largest in the Baltic States by land area, was conceived in the fifth-largest city Panevėžys in 2004. In years 2006 - 2008 the large-scale development also reached cities of Kaunas and Šiauliai and some smaller towns.

INFRASTRUCTURE

The transport, storage and communication sector has increased its importance to the economy of Lithuania. In 2008, it accounted for 12.1% of GDP compared to 9.1% in 1996. Lithuania became a well-developed transport corridor between the East and the West. Having a high-quality and dense road network, Lithuania has achieved significant growth in the amount of goods carried both by road and by rail transport. The volume of goods transported by road transport has increased fivefold since 1996. The total length of roadways is more than 80 thousand km, and 90% of them are paved. The government is demonstrating high attention to the quality of road infrastructure by increasing their funding. The funding of roads exceeded LTL 1.75 billion (EUR 0.5 billion) in 2008.

Railways

Railway transport in Lithuania provides long-distance passenger and cargo services. Railways carry approximately 50 million tons of cargo and 7 million passengers a year. Direct rail routes link Lithuania with Russia, Belarus, Latvia, Poland, and Germany. Also, the main transit route between Russia and Russia's Kaliningrad Region passes through Lithuania. JSC Lithuanian Railways transports about 44% of the freight carried through the territory of Lithuania. This is a very high indicator compared to other countries of the European Union, where freight transportation by rail amounts to only 10% of the total.

SEA PORT

The northern-most and one of the few ice-free seaports on the eastern shore of the Baltic Sea is located in the western part of Lithuania. The Port of Klaipėda is a regional transport hub connecting the sea, land and railway routes from east and west. Compared to neighbouring Eastern Baltic seaports, the Port of Klaipėda has the widest shipping line network with other seaports. The Port of Klaipėda handles roughly 7,000 ships and 30 million tons of cargo every year, and accepts large-tonnage vessels: dry-cargo vessels up to 70,000 DWT, tankers up to 100,000 DWT and cruise ships up to 270 meters of length. The ice-free seaport of Klaipėda is able to receive Panamax-type vessels. One of the fastest growing segments of sea transport is passenger traffic. Passenger traffic has increased fourfold since 2002.

WAREHOUSING

There are more than 600,000 m2 of modern logistics and warehousing facilities in Lithuania.The biggest supply of new, modern warehousing facilities is in the capital city Vilnius (after the completion of several new projects in the third quarter of 2009, the supply of modern warehousing premises has increased by nearly 12% in Vilnius and currently reaches 334,400 m2 of the rentable area). Kaunas is in the second place (around 200,000 m2), and Klaipėda in the third (122,500 m2). Since the beginning of the year 2009, prices for warehousing premises have dropped by 20–25% in Vilnius, Kaunas and Klaipėda, and the current level of rents has reached the level of 2003. The costs for renting new warehouses in Vilnius, Kaunas and Klaipėda are similar and reach 2.6 to 4.9 LTL/m2 (0.75 to 1.42 EUR/m2), while the rents of old warehouses are 1.2 to 2.3 LTL/m2 (0.35 to 0.67 EUR/m2).

INTERNATIONAL TRADE

International trade for such a small country as Lithuania is crucial. The ratio of foreign trade to GDP has always been at least 100%, and for the last several years exceeded it.

The EU is the biggest trade partner of Lithuania with a 58% of total imports and 64% of total exports during the first ten months of the year 2009. The Commonwealth of Independent States is the second economic union that Lithuania trades the most with, with a share of imports of 34% and a share of exports of 23% during the same period. The vast majority of commodities, including oil, gas and metals have to be imported, mainly from Russia. For this reason, Russia is the biggest import partner of Lithuania.

The import of mineral products has a significant share of 30%, as Lithuania has an oil refinery company owned by Polish concern PKN ORLEN, ORLEN Lietuva, with a refining capacity of 9 million tons a year. The revenues of the company were more than LTL 17 billion (EUR 4.9 billion) in 2008. Orlen Lietuva received 78% of its sales or LTL 13.7 billion (EUR 4 billion) from foreign markets in comparison with total export of Lithuania of LTL 55.5 billion (EUR 16.1 billion) in 2008.

Some sectors are directed mainly at export markets. Transport and logistics export 2/3 of their products and/or services; the biotechnology industry exports 80%; plastics export 52%; laser technologies export 86%; metal processing, machinery and electric equipment export 64%; furniture and wood processing export 55%; textile and clothing export 76%; and the food industry exports 36%.

The total value of natural resources in Lithuania reaches LTL 58 billion (EUR 16.8 billion) or 50% of Lithuania's GDP in 2008. The most valuable natural resource in Lithuania is subterranean water, which constitutes more than a half of the total value of natural resources.

Foreign trade partners, January–December 2011

Country	Import	Country	Export
EU	55.9%	EU	61.4%
Russia	32.8%	Russia	16.6%
Germany	9.7%	Latvia	10.2%
Poland	9.1%	Germany	9.3%
Latvia	6.6%	Poland	6.9%
Netherlands	4.9%	Estonia	6.6%
Sweden	3.3%	Netherlands	6.1%
Italy	3.2%	Belarus	5.2%
Belgium	3.1%	United Kingdom	4.1%
Estonia	2.8%	France	4.1%
Belarus	2.5%	Sweden	3.6%

Foreign trade by product type, January–October 2009

Combined Nomenclature	Export	Combined Nomenclature	Import
Mineral products	21.6%	Mineral products	29.7%
Machinery and mechanical appliances; electrical equipment	9.8%	Machinery and mechanical appliances; electrical equipment	12.6%
Products of the chemical industries	9.3%	Products of the chemical industries	12.4%
Prepared foodstuffs; beverages and tobacco	7.1%	Vehicles and transport equipment	6.4%
Plastics; rubber and articles thereof	6.9%	Prepared foodstuffs; beverages and tobacco	5.9%
Textiles and textile articles	6.7%	Textiles and textile articles	5.2%
Vehicles and transport equipment	6.6%	Base metals and articles of base metal	5.0%
Miscellaneous manufactured articles	6.4%	Plastics; rubber and articles thereof	4.6%
Vegetable products	6.3%	Vegetable products	4.3%
Live animals; animal products	5.7%	Live animals; animal products	3.6%

TRAVEL TO LITHUANIA

US STATE DEPARTMENT SUGGESTIONS

COUNTRY DESCRIPTION: Lithuania is a country undergoing profound political and economic change. Tourist facilities are improving. Many goods and services are now available in the major cities, but may not be fully comparable to Western standards. The capital is Vilnius.

ENTRY REQUIREMENTS: A valid passport is required to enter Lithuania. U.S. citizens do not need Lithuanian visas for most stays of 90 days or less. U.S. citizens may contact the Lithuanian Embassy at 2622 16TH Street N.W., Washington, D.C. 20009, tel. (202) 234-5860 for current information on visa requirements. Travelers who plan to enter Russia, even to transit, need a Russian visa.

MEDICAL FACILITIES: Medical care in Lithuania is slowly improving. Elderly travelers and those with existing health problems may be at risk because medical facilities do not always meet Western standards. However, most medical supplies are now widely available, including disposable needles, anesthetics, antibiotics and other pharmaceuticals. Western-quality dental care can be obtained in major cities. The Lithuanian Government does not require HIV testing for U.S. citizens. Serious medical problems requiring hospitalization and/or medical evacuation to the United States can cost thousands of dollars or more. Doctors and hospitals often expect immediate cash payment for health services.

MEDICAL INSURANCE: U.S. medical insurance is not always valid outside the United States. U.S. Medicare and Medicaid programs do not provide payment for medical services outside the United States. Uninsured travelers who require medical care overseas may face extreme difficulties. Please check with your own insurance company to confirm whether your policy applies overseas, including provision for medical evacuation. Please ascertain whether payment will be made to the overseas hospital or doctor or whether you will be reimbursed later for expenses that you incur. Some insurance policies also include coverage for psychiatric treatment and for disposition of remains in the event of death. Useful information on medical emergencies abroad, including overseas insurance programs, is provided in the Department of State's Bureau of Consular Affairs brochure, *Medical Information for Americans Traveling Abroad*, available via the Bureau of Consular Affairs home page or autofax: (202) 647-3000.

OTHER HEALTH INFORMATION: Information on vaccinations and other health precautions may be obtained from the Centers for Disease Control and Prevention's hotline for international travelers at 1-877-FYI-TRIP (1-877-394-8747); fax 1-888-CDC-FAXX (1-888-232-3299), or via their Internet site at http://www.cdc.gov.

CRIME INFORMATION: The crime rate is relatively low compared to other major European capitals. But street crime does occur. Travelers should exercise the same precautions with regard to their personal safety and belongings that they would practice in any major city in the United States. Muggings and purse snatchings generally take place at night when the victims are walking alone along dimly lit streets. Auto theft is common. Robberies have occurred on trains, in train stations and in hotel rooms. Police forces suffer from lack of manpower, resources and equipment. Local police are not likely to speak English, so it may be difficult to obtain police assistance.

The loss or theft of a U.S. passport should be reported immediately to the local police and the nearest U.S. embassy or consulate. U.S. citizens can refer to the Department of State's pamphlet, *A Safe Trip Abroad*, for hints on a more trouble-free trip. The brochure is available from the Superintendent of Documents, U.S. Government Printing Office, Washington, D.C. 20402, via the Internet at http://www.access.gpo.gov/su_docs, or http://travel.state.gov.

AVIATION SAFETY OVERSIGHT: As there is no direct commercial service at present between the United States and Lithuania, nor economic authority to operate such service, the U.S. Federal Aviation Administration (FAA) has not assessed Lithuania's Civil Aviation Authority for compliance with international aviation safety standards for oversight of Lithuania's air carrier operations.

For further information, travelers may contact the Department of Transportation within the United States at tel. 1-800-322-7873, or visit the FAA Internet web site at http://www.faa.gov/avr/iasa/. The U.S. Department of Defense (DOD) separately assesses some foreign air carriers for suitability as official providers of air services. For information regarding the DOD policy on specific carriers, travelers may contact the DOD at tel. (618) 229-4801.

CUSTOMS REGULATIONS: Lithuanian customs authorities may enforce strict regulations concerning temporary importation into or export from Lithuania of items. It is advisable to contact the Embassy of Lithuania in Washington or one of Lithuania's consulates in the United States for specific information regarding customs requirements.

TRAFFIC SAFETY AND ROAD CONDITIONS: While in a foreign country, U.S. citizens may encounter road conditions that differ significantly from those in the United States. The information below concerning Lithuania is provided for general reference only, and may not be totally accurate in a particular location or circumstance.
Safety of Public Transportation: Good
Urban Road Conditions/Maintenance: Fair
Rural Road Conditions/Maintenance: Fair
Availability of Roadside Assistance: Good

Roads in Lithuania range from two to six-lane highways connecting major cities, to small dirt roads traversing the countryside. Street lanes are not always clearly marked, and lighting is often poor. Drivers always must be alert to visible and hidden dangers on the roads, especially slow-moving horse carts or trucks traveling at night without taillights or reflectors. Dark-clothed pedestrians walking along unlit roads or darting across dimly lit streets or highways pose a risk to unsuspecting drivers. Winter driving can be especially hazardous because roads are not always plowed. Driving with caution is urged at all times.

For specific information concerning Lithuanian driver's permits, vehicle inspection, road tax and mandatory insurance, please contact the Lithuanian National Tourist Organization via the Internet at http://www.tourism.lt/.

DRUG PENALTIES: U.S. citizens are subject to the laws of the country in which they are traveling. Penalties for possession, use, or trafficking in illegal drugs in Lithuania are strict, and convicted offenders can expect jail sentences and heavy fines.

SPECIAL CIRCUMSTANCES: Lithuania is still primarily a cash economy, though an increasing number of hotels, restaurants and other businesses now accept major credit cards.

CHILDREN'S ISSUES: For information on international adoption of children, international parental child abduction, and international child support enforcement issues, please refer to our Internet site at http://travel.state.gov/children's_issues.html or telephone (202) 736-7000.

REGISTRATION/EMBASSY AND CONSULATE LOCATION: Americans are encouraged to register at the Consular Section of the U.S. Embassy where updated information on travel and security within Lithuania is available. The U.S. Embassy in Vilnius is located at Akmenu 6; tel. (370)(2) 223-031.

BUSINESS TRAVEL

U.S citizens are allowed visa-free entry for a period of 90 days.

Phone, cellular phone, fax and e-mail communications are excellent, though the connectivity can be limited in rural areas.

Major hotels, quality restaurants, and some stores accept credit cards, but it is still mainly a cash economy. MasterCard and Visa are the most widely accepted credit cards; Diners Club and American Express are also accepted at a number of hotels and some restaurants and service stations. Budget accommodations, fast-food restaurants, smaller retail establishments and outdoor markets operate on a cash-only basis. A few commercial banks cash traveler's checks or provide cash advances against credit cards but the service charges are high. Lithuanian currency, the Litas, may be bought and sold at numerous currency exchange offices. In rural areas travelers should be prepared to pay cash for most of their expenses.

Lithuania is easily reached by air from Western Europe and, with connecting flights, from the United States. Travel by car is generally the fastest and most convenient mode of transportation within Lithuania and other two Baltic States.

There are today numerous restaurants in the major cities with first class cuisine and service. Supply and diversity of imported food, household supplies, common medications and personal items are excellent. Unleaded gas is available in every gasoline station in the country.

The availability of modern housing is still quite limited though improving. Often, apartments have to be renovated to meet the Western standards. Despite recent improvements, hot water may not always be available through municipal district heating systems; major apartment renovations should include installation of hot water heaters.

Street crime is relatively high in Lithuania. Travelers should take the same precautions, as they would visiting unfamiliar urban centers in the U.S. Although drinking water is chlorinated, it is not considered entirely safe because the filtering system does not remove viruses. Boiling drinking water is recommended. Imported spring water is available at many stores. Food contamination is not a serious problem.

SUPPLEMENTS

LITHUANIA MINISTRY OF FOREIGN AFFAIRS CONTACTS

TELEPHONE DIRECTORY

Address	J.Tumo-Vaizganto 2, LT-2600 Vilnius, Lithuania
Fax	+370 5 2313090
E-mail **Personal emails**	urm@urm.lt name.surname@urm.lt

Information (all days, 24 hours)	**2362444**
Consular information (all days, 24 hours)	**2362400**

MINISTERS OFFICE

Pareigos **Position**	**Vardas, Pavardė** **Name**	**Kabineto Nr.** **Room**	**Darbo tel.** **Office**
Ministras Minister	Antanas Valionis	264	2362401
Ministro patarėja Ministry adviser	Asta Dikčiuvienė	252	2362402
Ministro patarėja Ministry adviser	Violeta Gaižauskaitė	304	2362424
Ministro patarėjas Ministry adviser	Vytautas Plečkaitis	359	2362496
Ministro patarėjas Ministry adviser	Petras Šimeliūnas	251	2362404
Atašė Attaché	Rūta Repečkaitė	264	2362417
Atašė Attaché	Viktorija Urbonavičiūtė	251	2362403
Vyresnioji specialistė Senior Officer	Jurga Tamošaitytė	264	2362401

VICE-MINISTER

Pareigos **Position**	**Vardas, Pavardė** **Name**	**Kabineto Nr.** **Room**	**Darbo tel.** **Office**
Viceministras Vice-Minister	Justas Paleckis	362	2362420

Specialistė Officer	Diana Kancleryté	361	2362420

MFA STATE SECRETARY

Pareigos **Position**	**Vardas, Pavardė** **Name**	**Kabineto Nr.** **Room**	**Darbo tel.** **Office**
Ministerijos valstybės sekretorius MFA State Secretary	Evaldas Ignatavičius	255	2362425
Atašė Attaché	Marijus Dunda	253	2362423
Vyriausioji specialistė Chief Officer	Ernesta Deltuvaitė	254	2362425

MFA UNDERSECRETARIES

Pareigos **Position**	**Vardas, Pavardė** **Name**	**Kabineto Nr.** **Room**	**Darbo tel.** **Office**
Ministerijos sekretorius Undersecretary	Giedrius Čekuolis	363	2362412
Vyresnioji specialistė	Jurgita Murauskienė	361	2362412
Ministerijos sekretorius Undersecretary	Rytis Martikonis	357	2362418
Vyriausioji specialistė Chief Officer	Gitana Bagdonienė	356	2362418
Ministerijos sekretorius Undersecretary	Neris Germanas	353	2362407
Specialistė Officer	Valerija Žeimytė	352	2362407
Pareigos Position	Vardas, Pavardė Name	Kabineto Nr. Room	Darbo tel. Office
Ministerijos sekretorius Undersecretary	Darius Jurgelevičius	366	2362415
Antroji sekretorė Second Secretary	Laimutė Taraškaitė	367	2362415

GENERAL INSPECTORATE

Pareigos Position	Vardas, Pavardė Name	Kabineto Nr. Room	Darbo tel. Office
Skyriaus patarėjas	Jonas Mackevičius	306	2362422

Adviser			

INTERNAL AUDIT DIVISION

Pareigos Position	Vardas, Pavardė Name	Kabineto Nr. Room	Darbo tel. Office
Skyriaus vedėjas Head	Jurgis Akromas	355	2362421
Vyriausioji specialistė Chief Officer	Daiva Cemnolonskienė	356	2362487

MINISTERIAL COUNSELLOR UNIT

Pareigos Position	Vardas, Pavardė Name	Kabineto Nr. Room	Darbo tel. Office
Ambasadorius ypatingiems pavedimams Ambassador at Large	Egidijus Meilūnas	304	2362548
Ambasadorius ypatingiems pavedimams regioninio bendradarbiavimo klausimais Ambassador at Large	Edvardas Borisovas	354	2362577
Ambasadorius ypatingiems pavedimams Ambassador at Large	Ginutis Voveris	305	2362546
Ambasadorius ypatingiems pavedimams Ambassador at Large	Stasys Sakalauskas	253	2362476
Ambasadorius ypatingiems pavedimams garbės konsulų darbo klausimais Ambassador at Large	Kornelija Jurgaitienė	351	2362408
Ambasadorius ypatingiems pavedimams-Europos integracijos studijų centro vadovas Ambassador at Large	Romualdas Kalonaitis	419	2362571
Patarėja žydų bendruomenės klausimais Counsellor	Hilda Griškevičienė	360	2362448
Patarėjas Counsellor	Rimantas Morkvėnas	253	2362620

REGIONAL COOPERATION UNIT

Pareigos Position	Vardas, Pavardė Name	Kabineto Nr. Room	Darbo tel. Office
Antroji sekretorė Second Secretary	Laura Dilytė-Butkienė	354	236257

STATE BORDER GROUP

Pareigos Position	Vardas, Pavardė Name	Kabineto Nr. Room	Darbo tel. Office
Ambasadorius ypatingiems pavedimams Ambassador at Large	Edvardas Gružas	311	2362428
Atašė Attaché	Jurga Vegytė	306	2362429

SECURITY DIVISION

Pareigos Position	Vardas, Pavardė Name	Kabineto Nr. Room	Darbo tel. Office
Skyriaus vedėjas Head	Marius Juška	501	2362430
Vyriausioji specialistė Chief Officer	Rita Razmaitė	501	2362431
Vyriausioji specialistė Chief officer	Snaiguolė Valantinienė	325	2362667
Vyresnioji specialistė Senior Officer	Rūta Lumbienė	326	2362663

PERSONNEL DEPARTMENT

Pareigos Position	Vardas, Pavardė Name	Kabineto Nr. Room	Darbo tel. Office
Departamento direktorius Director	Romanas Podagėlis	215	2362434

PERSONNEL DIVISION

Pareigos Position	Vardas, Pavardė Name	Kabineto Nr. Room	Darbo tel. Office
Skyriaus vedėja Head	Rūta Genienė	216	2362436
Pirmoji sekretorė First Secretary	Irena Strumilienė	212	2362437
Antroji sekretorė Second Secretary	Dalė Mickienė	212	2362437
Vyriausioji specialistė Chief Officer	Rasa Musteikienė	212	2362438

Vyresnioji specialistė Senior Officer	Laimutė Stepancienė	214	362442

TRAINING AND DEVELOPMENT DIVISION

Pareigos Position	Vardas, Pavardė Name	Kabineto Nr. Room	Darbo tel. Office
Skyriaus vedėja Head	Irena Ūsaitė	213	2362440
Atašė Attaché	Giedrė Stagniūnaitė	214	2362441
Vyresnioji specialistė Senior Officer	Jolita Lančinskienė	214	2362426

PERSONNEL DIVISION

Pareigos **Position**	**Vardas, Pavardė** **Name**	**Kabineto Nr.** **Room**	**Darbo tel.** **Office**
Skyriaus vedėja Head	Rūta Genienė	216	2362436
Pirmoji sekretorė First Secretary	Irena Strumilienė	212	2362437
Antroji sekretorė Second Secretary	Dalė Mickienė	212	2362437
Vyriausioji specialistė Chief Officer	Rasa Musteikienė	212	2362438
Vyresnioji specialistė Senior Officer	Laimutė Stepancienė	214	362442

INFORMATION AND CULTURE DEPARTMENT

Pareigos **Position**	**Vardas, Pavardė** **Name**	**Kabineto Nr.** **Room**	**Darbo tel.** **Office**
Pirmoji sekretorė First Secretary	Indrė Dagilienė	353	2362445

INFORMATION DIVISION

Pareigos **Position**	**Vardas, Pavardė** **Name**	**Kabineto Nr.** **Room**	**Darbo tel.** **Office**
Skyriaus vedėjas Head	Tadas Jankauskas	110	2362646
Antroji sekretorė	Gita Blinstrubaitė	102	2362449

Second Secretary			
Trečiasis sekretorius Third Secretary	Antanas Kundrotas	101	2362444
Atašė Attaché	Liutauras Kungys	101	2362452
Vyresnioji specialistė Senior Officer	Jonė Šėmaitė-Deksnienė	102	2362447

PRESS DIVISION

Pareigos Position	Vardas, Pavardė Name	Kabineto Nr. Room	Darbo tel. Office
L.e.p. direktorius Acting Director	Daiva Rimašauskaitė	227	2362453
Skyriaus patarėja Counsellor	Dalia Sukackienė	354	2362455
Antrasis sekretorius Second Secretary	Gytis Marcinkevičius	354	2362454
Trečiasis sekretorius Third Secretary	Darius Budrys	354	2362454
Atašė Attaché	Mindaugas Lašas		2362451

PUBLIC RELATIONS DIVISION

Pareigos Position	Vardas, Pavardė Name	Kabineto Nr. Room	Darbo tel. Office
Skyriaus vedėja Head	Aušra Semaškienė	173	2362456
Pirmoji sekretorė First Secretary	Renata Darulienė	174	2362457
Atašė Attaché	Augusta Lėkaitė	178	2362459

STATE AND DIPLOMATIC PROTOCOL DEPARTMENT

Pareigos Position	Vardas, Pavardė Name	Kabineto Nr. Room	Darbo tel. Office
Departamento direktorius Director	Giedrius Puodžiūnas	256	2362461
Direktoriaus pavaduotoja Acting Deputy Director	Rita Kazragienė	260	2362466

Departamento patarėjas Counsellor	Marijus Nemanis	257	2362583
Atašė Attaché	Aušra Gečaitė	258	2362461

President Protocol Division

Pareigos Position	Vardas, Pavardė Name	Kabineto Nr. Room	Darbo tel. Office
Skyriaus vedėjas Deputy Director	Mindaugas Rukštelė		2664005
Antrasis sekretorius Second Secretary	Damyras Asanavičius	354	2664012

Prime Minister Protocol Division

Pareigos Position	Vardas, Pavardė Name	Kabineto Nr. Room	Darbo tel. Office
Skyriaus vedėja Head	Lina Rukštelienė	340	2663867
Skyriaus patarėja Adviser	Lilija Žinienė	327	2663864
Vyriausioji specialistė Chief Officer	Lineta Maskaliūnaitė	329	2663866

Visits Division

Pareigos Position	Vardas, Pavardė Name	Kabineto Nr. Room	Darbo tel. Office
Skyriaus vedėjas Head	Saulius Labutis	257	2362463
Pirmoji sekretorė First Secretary	Dalia Ambrazevičiūtė	257	2362464

Diplomatic Corps Division

Pareigos Position	Vardas, Pavardė Name	Kabineto Nr. Room	Darbo tel. Office
Skyriaus vedėjas Head	Albertas Dambrauskas	259	2362469
Skyriaus patarėja Adviser	Natalija Bacevičienė	258	2362467
Skyriaus patarėja Adviser	Virginija Klevečkienė	259	2362465

Antroji sekretorė Second Secretary	Danguolė Vinciūnienė	258	2362470

Foreign Policy Planning Division

Pareigos Position	Vardas, Pavardė Name	Kabineto Nr. Room	Darbo tel. Office
Skyriaus vedėja Head	Raimonda Murmokaitė	152	236247
Pirmasis sekretorius First Secretary	Gintautas Šiulys	162	2362477

1ST DEPARTAMENT OF BILATERAL RELATIONS

Pareigos Position	Vardas, Pavardė Name	Kabineto Nr. Room	Darbo tel. Office
Departamento patarėja	Audra Čiapienė	459	2362490
Departamento patarėjas	Algimantas Misevičius	457	2362582

West European Division

Pareigos Position	Vardas, Pavardė Name	Kabineto Nr. Room	Darbo tel. Office
Skyriaus vedėjas Head	Algirdas Paleckis	456	2362482
Skyriaus patarėja Adviser	Aušrinė Venckevičienė	465	2362483
Skyriaus patarėjas Adviser	Artūras Gailiūnas	462	2362484
Antroji sekretorė Second Secretary	Violeta Popovaitė	464	2362483
Trečiasis sekretorius Third Secretary	Nerijus Aleksiejūnas	462	2362484
Trečioji sekretorė Third Secretary	Jurgita Dapkutė	464	2362488

North European Division

Pareigos Position	Vardas, Pavardė Name	Kabineto Nr. Room	Darbo tel. Office
Skyriaus vedėjas Head	Dainius Kamaitis	461	2362489

Skyriaus patarėja Adviser	Lyra Puišytė	459	2362480
Pirmoji sekretorė First Secretary	Irena Skullerud	458	236249
Pirmasis sekretorius First Secretary	Gintaras Pečiukonis	458	2362493
Trečioji sekretorė Third Secretary	Jurgita Usonytė	458	2362491

Central European Division

Pareigos **Position**	**Vardas, Pavardė** **Name**	**Kabineto Nr.** **Room**	**Darbo tel.** **Office**
L.e.p. direktorius Acting Director	Izolda Bričkovskienė	153	2362497
Skyriaus patarėja Counsellor	Audronė Markevičienė	158	2362499
Pirmasis sekretorius First Secretary	Darius Vitkauskas	158	2362499
Pirmasis sekretorius First Secretary	Eduardas Petkevičius	154	2362498
Atašė Attaché	Gediminas Kliukas	154	2362569

2ND DEPARTMENT OF BILATERAL RELATIONS

Pareigos Position	Vardas, Pavardė Name	Kabineto Nr. Room	Darbo tel. Office
Departamento direktorius Director	Ričardas Degutis		2362503

Division of Americas

Pareigos **Position**	**Vardas, Pavardė** **Name**	**Kabineto Nr.** **Room**	**Darbo tel.** **Office**
L.e.p. vedėjas Acting Head	Saulius Jaskelevičius	160	2362557
Antroji sekretorė Second Secretary	Lina Gubrevičiūtė	160	2362506
Trečiasis sekretorius Third Secretary	Kęstutis Vaškelevičius	162	2362475
Atašė	Justas Vaišnoras	161	2362505

Attaché			
Atašė Attaché	Kristina Pakonytė	161	2362558

East European and Central Asia Division

Pareigos Position	Vardas, Pavardė Name	Kabineto Nr. Room	Darbo tel. Office
Skyriaus vedėjas Head	Arvydas Daunoravičius	169	2362507
Pirmasis sekretorius First Secretary	Laurynas Jonušauskas	172	2362473
Pirmasis sekretorius First Secretary	Jonas Mažeika	172	2362508
Antrasis sekretorius Second Secretary	Giedrius Galkauskas	171	2362501
Atašė Attaché	Remigijus Juozaitis	171	2362472

Asian, African,and Pasific Division

Pareigos Position	Vardas, Pavardė Name	Kabineto Nr. Room	Darbo tel. Office
Skyriaus vedėjas Head	Violeta Motulaitė	155	2362509
Pirmasis sekretorius First Secretary	Mindaugas Kačerauskis	157	2362495
Pirmoji sekretorė First Secretary	Valentina Klimišinaitė	156	2362512
Trečiasis sekretorius Third Secretary	Mindaugas Žičkus	157	2362600
Atašė Attaché	Eglė Norvaišienė	156	2362510

DEPARTMENT OF MULTILATERAL RELATIONS

UN and Council of Europe Division

Pareigos Position	Vardas, Pavardė Name	Kabineto Nr. Room	Darbo tel. Office
Skyriaus vedėja Head	Dalia Kraulytė	172	2362524

Pirmoji sekretorė First Secretary	Sandra Paunksnienė	164A	2362526
Antroji sekretorė Second Secretary	Rasa Ostrauskaitė	164	2362566
Antroji sekretorė Second Secretary	Božena Petrauskienė	164	2362526
Atašė Attaché	Valdas Šakalys	172	2362528

SECURITY POLICY DEPARTMENT

Pareigos Position	Vardas, Pavardė Name	Kabineto Nr. Room	Darbo tel. Office
Departamento direktorius Director	Rytis Paulauskas	168	2362516

NATO INTEGRATION DIVISION

Pareigos Position	Vardas, Pavardė Name	Kabineto Nr. Room	Darbo tel. Office
Skyriaus vedėjas Head	Jonas Grinevičius	170	2362619
Skyriaus patarėja Adviser	Loreta Zakarevičienė	169	2362520
Skyriaus patarėjas Adviser	Giedrius Mickūnas	165	2362618
Skyriaus patarėjas Adviser	Andrius Krivas	169	2362527
Pirmasis sekretorius First Secretary	Arūnas Trakimavičius	165	2362517
Antroji sekretorė Second Secretary	Žana Tarasevič	165	2362518
Atašė Attaché	Eglė Morkūnaitė	165	2362518

THREAT ANALYSIS, CRISIS MANAGEMENT AND INTERNATIONAL OPERATIONS DIVISION

Pareigos Position	Vardas, Pavardė Name	Kabineto Nr. Room	Darbo tel. Office
Skyriaus vedėjas Head	Gediminas Varvuolis	169	2362427

ARMS CONTROL, NON-PROLIFERATION AND DISARMAMENT DIVISION

Pareigos Position	Vardas, Pavardė Name	Kabineto Nr. Room	Darbo tel. Office
Skyriaus vedėjas Head	Robertas Rosinas	167	2362521
Pirmoji sekretorė First Secretary	Rosita Šorytė	167	2362522
Atašė Attaché	Donatas Vainalavičius	166	2362579

LAW AND INTERNATIONAL TREATIES DEPARTMENT

Pareigos Position	Vardas, Pavardė Name	Kabineto Nr. Room	Darbo tel. Office
Departamento direktoriaus pavaduotojas Deputy Director	Ričardas Pikutis	318	2362533
Departamento patarėjas Counsellor	Saulius Valainis	316	2362534
Specialistė Officer	Gitana Masaitytė	319	2362530

INTERNATIONAL TREATIES DIVISION

Pareigos Position	Vardas, Pavardė Name	Kabineto Nr. Room	Darbo tel. Office
Skyriaus vedėjas Head	Ridas Petkus	321	2362543
Pirmasis sekretorius-poskyrio vedėjas First Secretary - Head of Subdivision	Tomas Bliznikas	310	2362534
Pirmasis sekretorius First Secretary	Rytis Satkauskas	312	2362544
Trečiasis sekretorius Third Secretary	Audrius Paksas	308	2362545
Atašė Attaché	Natalija Točickienė		2362535

LAW DIVISION

Pareigos Position	Vardas, Pavardė Name	Kabineto Nr. Room	Darbo tel. Office
Skyriaus vedėja Head	Jurgita Virbickaitė	322	2362542
Skyriaus patarėjas	Darius Staniulis		2362409

Adviser			
Trečioji sekretorė Third Secretary	Jurgita Satkūnienė	321	2362550
Atašė Attaché	Laima Mašalaitė	313	2362537
Trečiasis sekretorius Third Secretary	Michail Cvelich	315	2362500
Atašė Attaché	Neringa Juodkaitė	313	2362538

International Treaties Register Division

Pareigos Position	Vardas, Pavardė Name	Kabineto Nr. Room	Darbo tel. Office
Skyriaus vedėjas Head	Julius Rakitskis	307	2362539
Antroji sekretorė Second Secretary	Liana Vazbienė	307	2362540

EUROPEAN INTEGRATION DEPARTMENT

Pareigos Position	Vardas, Pavardė Name	Kabineto Nr. Room	Darbo tel. Office
Departamento direktorius Director	Žygimantas Pavilionis	421	2362570
Departamento direktoriaus pavaduotojas Deputy Director	Gintautas Vasiulis		2362564
Specialistė Officer	Irma Jagminaitė	419	2362570

Political Cooperation Division

Pareigos Position	Vardas, Pavardė Name	Kabineto Nr. Room	Darbo tel. Office
Skyriaus vedėjas Head	Egidijus Navikas	413	2362555
Skyriaus patarėjas Adviser	Ramūnas Misiulis	422	2362563
Pirmasis sekretorius First Secretary	Jurgis Vilčinskas	423	2362531
Trečiasis sekretorius Third Secretary	Julius Pranevičius	401	2362568

Economic Cooperation Division

Pareigos Position	Vardas, Pavardė Name	Kabineto Nr. Room	Darbo tel. Office
Skyriaus vedėjas Head	Sigitas Mitkus	425	2362560
Pirmasis sekretorius First Secretary	Dainoras Žiukas	401	2362565
Skyriaus patarėja Adviser	Janė Petuchienė	402	2362576
Pirmoji sekretorė First Secretary	Sigrida Mulevičienė	401	2362561
Antroji sekretorė Second Secretary	Rasa Žemaitytė	402	2362562
Vyriausioji specialistė Chief Officer	Vita Naujokaitytė	401	2362561

Common Foreign and Security Policy Division

Pareigos Position	Vardas, Pavardė Name	Kabineto Nr. Room	Darbo tel. Office
Skyriaus vedėjas Head	Tomas Gulbinas	164	2362513
Skyriaus patarėjas Adviser	Tomas Irnius	423	2362554
Atašė Attaché	Inga Maskelytė	420	2362573

Economics Department

Pareigos Position	Vardas, Pavardė Name	Kabineto Nr. Room	Darbo tel. Office
Departamento direktorius Director	Romas Švedas	452	2362585
Departamento patarėja Counsellor	Dalia Kadišienė	414	2362560
Specialistė Officer	Inga Lasevičiūtė	453	2362593

Foreign Trade Policy Division

Pareigos Position	Vardas, Pavardė Name	Kabineto Nr. Room	Darbo tel. Office
Skyriaus vedėjas Head	Albinas Zananavičius	470	2362587

Skyriaus patarėjas Adviser	Regimantas Jablonskas	451	2362590
Pirmoji sekretorė First Secretary	Renata Rinkauskienė	451	2362592
Pirmoji sekretorė First Secretary	Irena Urbutytė	470	2362588
Antroji sekretorė Second Secretary	Lina Viltrakienė	473	2362589
Antrasis sekretorius Second Secretary	Donatas Tamulaitis	470	2362591
Trečioji sekretorė Third Secretary	Dalia Kreivienė	470	2362589

INTERNATIONAL ECONOMIC ORGANISATIONS DIVISION

Pareigos Position	Vardas, Pavardė Name	Kabineto Nr. Room	Darbo tel. Office
Skyriaus vedėja Head	Gitana Grigaitytė	469	2362594
Skyriaus patarėjas Adviser	Vaidotas Karvelis	455	2362595
Pirmoji sekretorė First Secretary	Dangirutė Vest	452	2362596
Antroji sekretorė Second Secretary	Jurgita Bilvaisienė	455	2362598
Trečiasis sekretorius Third Secretary	Tomas Valiukas	469	2362603
Trečiasis sekretorius Third secretary	Simonas Šatūnas	468	2362597
Trečioji sekretorė Third secretary	Diana Čistovaitė	452	2362596

ECONOMIC ANALYSIS AND EXPORT DEVELOPMENT DIVISION

Pareigos Position	**Vardas, Pavardė Name**	**Kabineto Nr. Room**	**Darbo tel. Office**
Skyriaus vedėjas Head	Lina Antanavičienė	468	2362601
Skyriaus patarėja Adviser	Sigita Kavaliūnaitė	466	2362668
Skyriaus patarėja Adviser	Irena Vedrickaitė	466	2362604

Pirmoji sekretorė First Secretary	Lina Žukauskaitė	467	2362575
Trečioji sekretorė Third Secretary	Skirmantė Aliukonienė	467	2362605
Trečiasis sekretorius Third Secretary	Donatas Kušlys	467	2362602
Atašė Attaché	Donatas Butkus	469	2362603

DEVELOPMENT ASSISTANCE DIVISION

Pareigos Position	**Vardas, Pavardė Name**	**Kabineto Nr. Room**	**Darbo tel. Office**
Skyriaus vedėjas Head	Gediminas Levickas	364	2362572
Trečioji sekretorė Third Secretary	Virginija Umbrasienė	365	2362581
Atašė Attaché	Liliana Jaroslavska	365	2362584

CONSULAR DEPARTMENT

Pareigos Position	**Vardas, Pavardė Name**	**Kabineto Nr. Room**	**Darbo tel. Office**
Departamento direktorius Director	Gediminas Šiaudvytis	218	2362607
Departamento direktoriaus pavaduotojas Deputy Director	Petras Anusas	219	2362608

CONSULAR ASSISTANCE DIVISION

Pareigos Position	**Vardas, Pavardė Name**	**Kabineto Nr. Room**	**Darbo tel. Office**
Skyriaus vedėja Head	Irena Valainytė	224	2362611
Pirmoji sekretorė First Secretary	Vilija Jatkonienė	203	2362610
Pirmasis sekretorius First Secretary	Arvydas Miknevičius	206	2362612
Antrasis sekretorius Second Secretary	Sigitas Cirtautas	105	2362613
Antrasis sekretorius	Regimantas Gecevičius	206	2362612

Second Secretary			
Antrasis sekretorius Second Secretary	Arūnas Kaminskas	212	2362624
Atašė Attaché	Laura Tilūnaitė	327	2362567
Atašė Attaché	Aidas Sunelaitis	212	2362614
Atašė Attaché	Audrius Bendinskas	203	2362547
Vyriausioji specialistė Chief Officer	Saulė Šarpytė	203	2362616

Visas Division

Pareigos **Position**	**Vardas, Pavardė** **Name**	**Kabineto Nr.** **Room**	**Darbo tel.** **Office**
Skyriaus vedėjas Head	Rimgaudas Lošys	207	2362622
Pirmasis sekretorius First Secretary	Alvydas Vaitkūnas	223	2362617
Pirmoji sekretorė First Secretary	Andra Kašubienė	105	2362623
Antrasis sekretorius Second Secretary	Dainius Šriubša	202	2362626
Trečiasis sekretorius Third Secretary	Ugnius Labutis	220	2362621
Atašė Attaché	Kristina Babičienė	205	2362633
Atašė Attaché	Asta Slavinskaitė	221	2362625
Atašė Attaché	Rimas Kungys	223	2362617

Consular Information and Analysis Division

Pareigos **Position**	**Vardas, Pavardė** **Name**	**Kabineto Nr.** **Room**	**Darbo tel.** **Office**
Skyriaus vedėjas Head	Gvidas Kerušauskas	222	2362627
Pirmasis sekretorius First Secretary	Jonas Kindurys	205	2362599
Atašė	Darius Nevulis	327	2362567

Attaché			
Atašė Attaché	Gabrielė Klimaitė	204	2362400
Atašė Attaché	Evelina Kuzmickaitė	205	2362629
Vyresnioji specialistė Senior Officer	Aldona Volodkienė	204	2362400
Vyresnioji specialistė Senior Officer - Secretary	Vida Čižienė	218	2362607

CONSULAR TREATIES DIVISION

Pareigos **Position**	**Vardas, Pavardė** **Name**	**Kabineto Nr.** **Room**	**Darbo tel.** **Office**
Skyriaus vedėjas Head	Saulius Kašuba	201	2362632
Pirmasis sekretorius First Secretary	Vytautas Velička	202	2362615
Atašė Attaché	Giedrius Granickas	220	2362628
Atašė Attaché	Dalija Ignatavičiūtė	105	2362613

FINANCE DEPARTMENT

Pareigos **Position**	**Vardas, Pavardė** **Name**	**Kabineto Nr.** **Room**	**Darbo tel.** **Office**
Departamento direktorė Director	Jolanta Tubaitė	406	2362635

BUDGET AND FINANCE MANAGEMENT DIVISION

Pareigos **Position**	**Vardas, Pavardė** **Name**	**Kabineto Nr.** **Room**	**Darbo tel.** **Office**
Skyriaus vedėjas Head	Vilius Stulpinas	407	2362647
Vyriausioji specialistė Chief Officer	Kristina Jančienė	409	2362638
Vyriausioji specialistė Chief Officer	Audronė Vabinskienė	410	2362639
Vyresnysis specialistas Senior Officer	Geraldas Daublys	410	2362640
Vyresnioji specialistė	Ilona Mikštienė	407	2362637

Senior Officer			

ACCAUNTANCY DIVISION

Pareigos Position	**Vardas, Pavardė Name**	**Kabineto Nr. Room**	**Darbo tel. Office**
Skyriaus vedėja Head	Žibutė Čiurlionienė	409	2362642
Vyriausioji specialistė Chief Officer	Inga Adinec	412	2362643
Vyriausioji specialistė Chief Officer	Sigita Vaitkevičiūtė	412	2362643
Vyresnioji specialistė Senior Officer	Janina Cilcienė	411	2362641
Vyresnioji specialistė Senior Officer	Jolanta Kareckienė	411	2362644
Vyresnioji specialistė Senior Officer	Asta Fergizienė	408	2362634
Vyresnioji specialistė Senior Officer	Auksė Lukošienė	405	2362645

INFORMATION TECHNOLOGIES DEPARTMENT

Pareigos Position	Vardas, Pavardė Name	Kabineto Nr. Room	Darbo tel. Office
Departamento direktorius Director	Vytautas Pinkus	208	2362651

INFORMATION SYSTEMS DESIGN DIVISION

Pareigos Position	**Vardas, Pavardė Name**	**Kabineto Nr. Room**	**Darbo tel. Office**
Skyriaus vedėjas Head	Viktoras Dagilis	418	2362673
Vyriausioji specialistė Chief Officer	Laima Kairytė	415	2362676
Vyriausiasis specialistas Chief Officer	Jonas Umbrasas	413	2362657
Vyriausiasis specialistas Chief Officer	Marius Kaziliūnas	415	2362658

COMPUTERS SYSTEMS DIVISION

Pareigos **Position**	**Vardas, Pavardė** **Name**	**Kabineto Nr.** **Room**	**Darbo tel.** **Office**
Skyriaus vedėjas Head	Jurgis Černiauskas	414	2362670
Vyriausiasis specialistas Chief Officer	Marius Šveckus	416	2362672
Vyriausiasis specialistas Chief Officer	Vidmantas Šveiteris	413	2362671
Vyresnysis specialistas Senior Officer	Edvinas Kerza	413	2362541
Vyresnysis specialistas Senior Officer	Artūras Janušis	416	2362656
Vyresnysis specialistas Senior Officer	Irmantas Grucė	416	2362674
Vyresnysis specialistas Senior Officer	Miroslavas Lašinskas	416	2362675

COMMUNICATIONS SYSTEMS DIVISION

Pareigos Position	Vardas, Pavardė Name	Kabineto Nr. Room	Darbo tel. Office
L.e.p. vedėjas Acting Head	Petras Pietaris	413	2362677
Specialistas Officer	Virgilijus Mikalkevičius	127	2362678

ADMINISTRATIVE DEPARTMENT

Pareigos **Position**	**Vardas, Pavardė** **Name**	**Kabineto Nr.** **Room**	**Darbo tel.** **Office**
Departamento direktorius Director	Remigijus Motuzas	210	2362630
Trečioji sekretorė Third Secretary	Kristina Nepaitė	130	2362683

EMBASSIES DIVISION

Pareigos **Position**	**Vardas, Pavardė** **Name**	**Kabineto Nr.** **Room**	**Darbo tel.** **Office**
Skyriaus vedėjas Head	Saulius Butkus	129	2362652
Skyriaus patarėjas	Romualdas Šemeškevičius	130	2362649

Adviser			

DIPLOMATIC MAIL DIVISION

Pareigos **Position**	**Vardas, Pavardė** **Name**	**Kabineto Nr.** **Room**	**Darbo tel.** **Office**
Skyriaus vedėjas Head	Saulius Genys	327	2362654
Vyriausiasis specialistas Chief Officer	Raimundas Marcinkevičius	125	2362655

CLERICAL DIVISION

Pareigos **Position**	**Vardas, Pavardė** **Name**	**Kabineto Nr.** **Room**	**Darbo tel.** **Office**
Skyriaus vedėja Head	Žana Kotova	112	2362660
Vyriausioji specialistė Chief Officer	Veronika Malerova	126	2362662
Vyriausioji specialistė Chief Officer	Rūta Staniulienė	114	2362665
Vyriausioji specialistė Chief Officer	Diana Gabrilevičienė	113	2362661
Vyriausioji specialistė Chief Officer	Svajonė Martutaitienė	113	2362661
Vyresnioji specialistė Senior Officer	Jolanda Radvilavičienė	126	2362662
Specialistė Officer	Jurgita Kalesnykienė	114	2362661
Specialistė Officer	Inga Marcinkevičienė	112	2362661
Specialistė Officer	Nerija Porutienė	113	2362665

CONSTRUCTION DIVISION

Pareigos **Position**	**Vardas, Pavardė** **Name**	**Kabineto Nr.** **Room**	**Darbo tel.** **Office**
Skyriaus vedėjas Head	Antanas Butrimas		2362680
Vyriausiasis specialistas Chief Officer	Vytautas Paukštė	128	2362681
Vyriausiasis specialistas	Kęstutis Genevičius		2362682

Chief Officer			

LIBRARY

Pareigos Position	Vardas, Pavardė Name	Kabineto Nr. Room	Darbo tel. Office
Vyriausioji specialistė Chief Officer	Patricija Vitkauskienė	103	2362685
Vyresnioji specialistė Senior Officer	Liongina Stanienė	103	2362685

MAINTENANCE DIVISION

Pareigos Position	Vardas, Pavardė Name	Kabineto Nr. Room	Darbo tel. Office
Skyriaus vedėjas Head	Bronius Stankevičius	108	2362688
Vyriausiasis specialistas Chief Officer	Romualdas Mickus	108	2362693
Vyriausiasis specialistas Chief Officer	Tadas Svenčkauskas	108	2362687
Vyriausiasis specialistas Chief Officer	Kęstutis Navikas	108	2362686
Vyresnioji specialistė Senior Officer	Leokadija Orševska	108	2362691
Specialistas Officer	Algimantas Cesiulis	055	2362692
Sandėlininkas Suplies Manager	Jonas Kunigėlis	058	2362689
Darbininkas Technical personnel	Konstantinas Ustinovičius	056	2362690
Vairuotojas Driver	Viktor Tomaševič	055	2362692
Vairuotojas Driver	Laimutis Nargelas	055	2362692
Vairuotojas Driver	Vytautas Černiauskas	055	2362692
Vairuotojas Driver	Valerijanas Orševskis	055	2362692
Vairuotojas Driver	Vytautas Rudokas	055	2362692
Mechanikas	Montanas Smagurauskas	108	2362693

Mechanic			

EMBASSIES

EMBASSY OF THE REPUBLIC OF LITHUANIA TO THE REPUBLIC OF ARGENTINA, TO THE REPUBLIC OF COLOMBIA, TO THE ORIENTAL REPUBLIC OF URUGUAY AND TO THE BOLIVARIAN REPUBLIC OF VENEZUELA

Gelly 3530
Capital Fedral
Buenos Aires
Argentina
Tel.: (54) 11 48016007
Fax.: (54) 11 4805 8238
E-mail: amb.ar@urm.lt

LR AMBASADA AUSTRIJOS RESPUBLIKOJE, SLOVĖNIJOS RESPUBLIKAI, SLOVAKIJOS RESPUBLIKAI IR KROATIJOS RESPUBLIKAI

EMBASSY TO THE REPUBLIC OF AUSTRIA, TO THE REPUBLIC OF SLOVENIA, TO THE REPUBLIC OF SLOVAKIA AND TO THE REPUBLIC OF CROATIA

Löwengasse 47/4
1030 Vienna
AUSTRIA
Tel.: (43 1) 718 5467, (43) 664 451 00 73
Fax.: (43 1) 718 5469

E-mail: amb.at@urm.lt

LR AMBASADA BALTARUSIJOS RESPUBLIKOJE

EMBASSY TO THE REPUBLIC OF BELARUS

ul. Zacharova 68
220088 Minsk
BELARUS
Tel.: (375 17) 2852 448, (375 17) 2852 449
Fax.: (375 17) 2853 337
E-mail: amb.by@urm.lt
WWW: http://by.urm.lt/

LR AMBASADA BELGIJOS KARALYSTĖJE IR LIUKSEMBURGO DIDŽIAJAI HERCOGYSTEI

EMBASSY OF THE REPUBLIC OF LITHUANIA TO THE KINGDOM OF BELGIUM AND TO THE GRAND DUCHY OF LUXEMBOURG

Rue Maurice Lietart 48
1150 Bruxelles
BELGIUM
Tel.: (32 2) 772 27 50
Fax.: (32 2) 772 17 01
E-mail: amb.be@urm.lt

LR AMBASADA ČEKIJOS RESPUBLIKOJE IR VENGRIJOS RESPUBLIKAI

EMBASSY TO THE CZECH REPUBLIC AND TO THE REPUBLIC OF HUNGARY

Pod Klikovkou 1916/2
15000 Praha 5, Smichov
CZECH REPUBLIC

Tel.: (42 02) 572 101 22 , (42 02) 572 101 23
Fax.: (42 02) 572 101 24
E-mail: amb.cz@urm.lt

LR AMBASADA DANIJOS KARALYSTĖJE IR ISLANDIJOS RESPUBLIKAI
EMBASSY TO THE KINGDOM OF DENMARK AND TO THE REPUBLIC OF ICELAND
Bernstorffsvej 214
DK-2920 Charlottelund
Copenhagen
DENMARK
Tel.: (45 39) 636 207
Fax.: (45 39) 636 532
E-mail: amb.dk@urm.lt
WWW: http://dk.urm.lt

LR AMBASADA EGIPTO ARABŲ RESPUBLIKOJE
EMBASSY OF THE REPUBLIC OF LITHUANIA TO THE ARAB REPUBLIC OF EGYPT
47 Ahmed Heshmat Street
Zamalek
Cairo
Arab Republic of Egypt
Tel.: (20) 2 736 4329
Tel/Fax: (20) 2 736 4326
E-mail: amb.eg@urm.lt

LR AMBASADA JUNGTINĖJE DIDŽIOSIOS BRITANIJOS IR ŠIAURĖS AIRIJOS KARALYSTĖJE IR AIRIJOS RESPUBLIKAI
EMBASSY TO THE UNITED KINGDOM OF GREAT BRITAIN AND NORTHERN IRELAND AND TO THE REPUBLIC OF IRELAND
84 Gloucester Place
London W1U 6AU
UNITED KINGDOM
Tel.: (44 20) 7486 64 01, (44 20) 7486 64 02
Fax.: (44 20) 7486 64 03
E-mail: amb.uk@urm.lt
WWW: http://www.users.globalnet.co.uk/~lralon/

LR AMBASADA ESTIJOS RESPUBLIKOJE
EMBASSY TO THE REPUBLIC OF ESTONIA
Uus tn. 15
Tallinn EE 0100,
ESTONIA
Tel.: (372) 631 40 30, (372) 631 40 53
Fax.: (372) 641 20 13
E-mail: amb.ee@urm.lt

LR AMBASADA GRAIKIJOS RESPUBLIKOJE, BULGARIJOS RESPUBLIKAI, RUMUNIJAI IR ALBANIJOS RESPUBLIKAI
EMBASSY TO THE HELLENIC REPUBLIC, TO THE REPUBLIC OF BULGARIA, TO ROMANIA AND TO THE REPUBLIC OF ALBANIA
49, Vasilissis Sofias Ave.
GR - 106 76 Athens
GREECE

Tel.: (30) 210 72 94 356, (30) 210 72 94 357
Fax.: (30) 210 72 94 347
E-mail: amb.gr@urm.lt

LR AMBASADA ISPANIJOS KARALYSTĖJE, ANDOROS KUNIGAIKŠTYSTEI, BRAZILIJOS FEDERACINEI RESPUBLIKAI IR MAROKO KARALYSTEI

EMBASSY TO THE KINGDOM OF SPAIN, TO THE PRINCIPALITY OF ANDORRA, TO THE FEDERATIVE REPUBLIC OF BRAZIL AND TO THE KINGDOM OF MOROCCO

C.Fortuny 19
28010 Madrid
SPAIN
Tel.: (34 91) 702 21 16, (34 91) 310 20 75 (konsuliniai kl.)
Fax.: (34 91) 310 40 18
E-mail: amb.es@urm.lt
WWW: http://www.emblituania.es

LR AMBASADA ITALIJOS RESPUBLIKOJE, MALTOS RESPUBLIKAI, ŠVEICARIJOS KONFEDERACIJAI IR JUGOSLAVIJOS FEDERACINEI RESPUBLIKAI

EMBASSY TO THE ITALIAN REPUBLIC, TO THE REPUBLIC OF MALTA, TO THE SWISS CONFEDERATION AND TO THE FEDERAL REPUBLIC OF YUGOSLAVIA

Viale di Villa Grazioli 9
00198 Rome
ITALY
Tel.: (39 06) 855 90 52, (39 06) 854 04 82
Fax.: (39 06) 855 90 53
E-mail: amb.it@urm.lt

LR AMBASADA IZRAELIO VALSTYBĖJE, PIETŲ AFRIKOS RESPUBLIKAI IR KIPRO RESPUBLIKAI

EMBASSY TO THE STATE OF ISRAEL, TO THE REPUBLIC OF SOUTH AFRICA AND TO THE REPUBLIC OF CYPRUS

Top Tower 14th floor
Dizengoff 50,
Suite 1404
Tel Aviv 64332
ISRAEL
Tel.: (972 3) 528 85 14
Fax.: (972 3) 525 72 65
E-mail: amb.il@urm.lt

LR AMBASADA JAPONIJOJE IR FILIPINŲ RESPUBLIKAI

EMBASSY TO JAPAN AND TO THE REPUBLIC OF THE PHILIPPINES

401 Pure City Roppongi
7-11-12 Roppongi, Minato
-ku
Tokyo 106-0032
JAPAN
Tel.: (81 3) 5414 3433
Fax.: (81 3) 5414 3434
E-mail: amb.jp@urm.lt
WWW: http://www2.gol.com/users/lithemb/

LR AMBASADA JAV IR JUNGTINĖMS MEKSIKOS VALSTIJOMS

EMBASSY TO THE UNITED STATES OF AMERICA AND TO THE UNITED MEXICAN STATES

2622 16th Str.,
N.W.,
Washington,
D.C., 20009
USA
Tel.: (1 202) 234 5860
Fax.: (1 202) 328 0466
E-mail: amb.us@urm.lt
WWW: http://www.ltembassyus.org

LR AMBASADA KANADOJE

EMBASSY TO CANADA

130 Albert Str., Suite 204,
Ottawa, Ontario K1P 5G4
CANADA
Tel.: (1 613) 567 54 58
Fax.: (1 613) 567 53 15
E-mail: amb.ca@urm.lt
WWW: http://www.lithuanianembassy.ca/

LR AMBASADA KAZACHSTANO RESPUBLIKOJE

EMBASSY TO THE REPUBLIC OF KAZAKHSTAN

Gornij Gigant
Iskenderovo 15
480099 Almaty
KAZAKHSTAN
Tel.: (7 3272) 934 606 (kanceliarija), (7 3272) 532 505 (konsulinis sk.)
Fax.: (7 3272) 935 153
E-mail: amb.kz@urm.lt

LR AMBASADA KINIJOS LIAUDIES RESPUBLIKOJE, KORĖJOS RESPUBLIKAI IR MONGOLIJAI

EMBASSY TO THE PEOPLE'S REPUBLIC OF CHINA, TO THE REPUBLIC OF KOREA AND TO MONGOLIA

#B-30 King's Garden Villa
18 Xiaoyun Road,
Chaoyang District
100016 Beijing
PEOPLE'S REPUBLIC OF
CHINA
Tel.: (86 10) 845 185 20
Fax.: (86 10) 845 144 42
E-mail: amb.cn@urm.lt

LR AMBASADA LATVIJOS RESPUBLIKOJE

EMBASSY TO THE REPUBLIC OF LATVIA

Rupniecibas iela 24
LV-1010 Riga
LATVIA
Tel.: (371 7) 321 519, (371 7) 320 948, (371 7) 320 919
Fax.: (371 7) 321 589

E-mail: amb.lv@urm.lt
WWW: http://lv.urm.lt

LR AMBASADA LENKIJOS RESPUBLIKOJE
EMBASSY TO THE REPUBLIC OF POLAND

Al. Jana Chrystiana Szucha 5
00-580 Warszawa
POLAND
Tel.: (48 22) 625 33 68
Fax.: (48 22) 625 34 40
E-mail: amb.pl@urm.lt
WWW: HTTP://www.poland.ambasada.lt.

LR AMBASADA NORVEGIJOS KARALYSTĖJE
EMBASSY TO THE KINGDOM OF NORWAY

Gimle Terrasse 6
0244 Oslo
NORWAY
Tel.: (47) 225 581 50, (47) 225 514 71
Fax.: (47) 225 567 30
E-mail: amb.no@urm.lt
WWW: http://no.urm.lt

LR AMBASADA NYDERLANDŲ KARALYSTĖJE
EMBASSY TO THE KINGDOM OF THE NETHERLANDS

Koninginnegracht 78
2514 AH The Hague
THE NETHERLANDS
Tel.: (31 70) 385 5418
Fax.: (31 70) 385 3940
E-mail: amb.nl@urm.lt
WWW: http://nl.urm.lt

LR AMBASADA PORTUGALIJOS RESPUBLIKOJE
EMBASSY TO THE PORTUGUESE REPUBLIC

Av. 5 de Outubro, 81 - 1
Esq.
Apartado 14160
1064-002 Lisboa Codex
PORTUGAL
Tel.: (351 21) 799 01 10
Fax.: (351 21) 799 63 63
E-mail: amb.pt@urm.lt

LR AMBASADA PRANCŪZIJOS RESPUBLIKOJE IR TUNISO RESPUBLIKAI
EMBASSY TO THE FRENCH REPUBLIC AND TO THE REPUBLIC OF TUNISIA

22, bd de Courcelles
75017 Paris
FRANCE
Tel.: (33) 1 40 54 50 50
Fax.: (33) 1 40 54 50 75
E-mail: amb.lituanie@magic.fr
WWW: http://www.amb-lituanie-paris.fr

LR AMBASADA RUSIJOS FEDERACIJOJE IR ARMĖNIJOS RESPUBLIKAI
EMBASSY TO THE RUSSIAN FEDERATION AND TO THE REPUBLIC OF ARMENIA

Borisoglebskij per. 10
121069 Moscow
RUSSIA
Tel.: (7 095) 785 86 05, (7 095) 785 86 25 (konsulinis sk.)
Fax.: (7 095) 785 86 00, (7 095) 785 86 49 (konsulinis sk.)
E-mail: amb.ru@urm.lt
WWW: http://ru.urm.lt

LR AMBASADA SUOMIJOS RESPUBLIKOJE
EMBASSY TO THE REPUBLIC OF FINLAND

Rauhankatu 13 A
00170 Helsinki
FINLAND
Tel.: (358 9) 608 210, (358 9) 278 10 05
Fax.: (358 9) 608 220
E-mail: amb.fi@urm.lt
WWW: http://fi.urm.lt/

LR AMBASADA ŠVEDIJOS KARALYSTĖJE
EMBASSY TO THE KINGDOM OF SWEDEN

Grevgatan 5, BV
114 53 Stockholm
SWEDEN
Tel.: (46 8) 667 54 55; (46 8) 103 018
Fax.: (46 8) 667 54 56
Konsulinis skyrius: (46 8) 103 565
E-mail: amb.se@urm.lt, litemb@telia.com
WWW: http://se.urm.lt/

LR AMBASADA PRIE ŠVENTO SOSTO IR MALTOS ORDINUI
EMBASSY TO THE HOLY SEE AND TO THE MALTESE ORDER

Via G.G.Porro, 4
00197 Roma
ITALY
Tel.: (39) 06 807 8259
Fax.: (39) 06 807 8291
E-mail: amb.va@urm.lt
WWW: http://va.urm.lt

LR AMBASADA TURKIJOS REPUBLIKOJE, AZERBAIDŽANO RESPUBLIKAI IR UZBEKISTANO RESPUBLIKAI
EMBASSY TO THE REPUBLIC OF TURKEY, TO THE REPUBLIC OF AZERBAIJAN AND TO THE REPUBLIC OF UZBEKISTAN

Mahatma Gandi Cad. No. 17/8-9
06700 G.O.P.
Ankara
TURKEY
Tel.: (90 312) 447 07 66
Fax.: (90 312) 447 06 63
E-mail: amb.tr@urm.lt

LR AMBASADA VOKIETIJOS FEDERACINĖJE RESPUBLIKOJE

EMBASSY TO THE FEDERAL REPUBLIC OF GERMANY

Botschaft der Republik Litauen
Charitestr. 9
10117 Berlin
GERMANY
Tel.: 4930-890 681 0
Fax.: 4930-890 681 15
E-mail: info@botschaft-litauen.de
WWW: http://de.urm.lt

LR AMBASADOS VOKIETIJOJE BONOS SKYRIUS

EMBASSY TO THE FEDERAL REPUBLIC OF GERMANY (BONN OFFICE)

Konstantinstrasse 25 A
53179 Bonn-Bad Godesberg
GERMANY
Tel.: (49 228) 9149112, (49 228) 9149113
Fax.: (49 228) 9149115
E-mail: amb.bona.de@urm.lt

LR AMBASADA UKRAINOJE, MOLDOVOS RESPUBLIKAI IR GRUZIJOS RESPUBLIKAI

EMBASSY TO UKRAINE, TO THE REPUBLIC OF MOLDOVA AND TO THE REPUBLIC OF GEORGIA

21 Buslivska str.
010901 Kyiv
UKRAINE
Tel.: (380 44) 254 09 20
Fax.: (380 44) 254 09 28
E-mail: amb.ua@urm.lt

LR MISIJA PRIE EUROPOS BENDRIJŲ

MISSION TO THE EUROPEAN COMMUNITIES

Rue Belliard 6
1040 Brussels
BELGIUM
Tel.: (32 2) 771 01 40
Fax.: (32 2) 771 45 97
E-mail: office@lt-mission-eu.be
WWW: http://users.skynet.be/lt-mission-eu/

LR NUOLATINĖ ATSTOVYBĖ PRIE ET

PERMANENT REPRESENTATION AT THE COUNCIL OF EUROPE

42, Rue Schweighaeuser
67000 Strasbourg
FRANCE
Tel.: (33) 390 411750
Tel/Fax: (33) 390 411759
E-mail: atstovybe.et@urm.lt

LR NUOLATINĖ MISIJA JT

PERMANENT MISSION TO THE UNITED NATIONS

420 Fifth Avenue, Third Floor
New York, NY 10018
USA
Tel.: (1 212) 354 7820
Fax.: (1 212) 354 7833
E-mail: misija.jt@urm.lt
WWW: http://www.undp.org/missions/lithuania/lithuania.html

LR NUOLATINĖ MISIJA JUNGTINIŲ TAUTŲ SKYRIUJE ŽENEVOJE
PERMANENT MISSION TO THE UNITED NATIONS IN GENEVA

18, Avenue du Bouchet
1209 Geneva
SWITZERLAND
Tel.: (41 22) 734 51 01
Fax.: (41 22) 734 50 70
E-mail: misija.zeneva.jt@urm.lt

LR MISIJA PRIE NATO
MISSION OF THE REPUBLIC OF LITHUANIA TO THE NORTH ATLANTIC TREATY ORGANIZATION

Boulevard Leopold III
NATO HQ
1110 Brussels
BELGIUM
Tel.: (32 2) 707 28 49
Fax.: (32 2) 707 28 50
E-mail: misija.nato@urm.lt
WWW: http://www.nato.int/pfp/lt/

LR NUOLATINĖ ATSTOVYBĖ PRIE TARPTAUTINIŲ ORGANIZACIJŲ VIENOJE
PERMANENT REPRESENTATION AT THE INTERNATIONAL ORGANIZATIONS IN VIENNA

Löwengasse 47/8
1030 Vienna
AUSTRIA
Tel.: (43 1) 710 9780
Fax.: (43 1) 710 9759
E-mail: atstovybe.esbo@urm.lt

NUOLATINĖ ATSTOVYBĖ UNESCO
PERMANENT REPRESENTATION AT THE UNESCO

1, Rue Miollis
Piece No. 1.10
75015 Paris
FRANCE
Tel.: (33 1) 456 833 20
Fax.: (33 1) 456 736 89
E-mail: atstovybe.unesco@urm.lt

LR GENERALINIS KONSULATAS ČIKAGOJE (JAV)
CONSULATE GENERAL IN CHICAGO (USA)

211 E. Ontario, Suite 1500
Chicago, IL 60611
USA

Tel.: (1 312) 397 0382
Fax.: (1 312) 397 0385
E-mail: kons.cikaga@urm.lt

LR GENERALINIS KONSULATAS NIUJORKE (JAV)
CONSULATE GENERAL IN NEW YORK (USA)

420 Fifth Avenue, 3 Floor
New York, N.Y., 10018
USA
Tel.: (1 212) 354 78 40, (1 212) 354 78 49
Fax.: (1 212) 354 79 11
E-mail: kons.niujorkas@urm.lt

LR GENERALINIS KONSULATAS SANKT-PETERBURGE (RUSIJOS FEDERACIJA)
CONSULATE GENERAL IN ST. PETERSBURG (RUSSIAN FEDERATION)

Gorokhovaya ul., 4
190000 St.Petersburg
RUSSIA
Tel.: (7 812) 314 58 57
Fax.: (7 812) 315 89 91
E-mail: st.peterburgas@mail.linkey.ru

LR GENERALINIS KONSULATAS GARDINE
CONSULATE GENERAL IN GRODNO (REPUBLIC OF BELARUS)

ul. Gorkogo 104,
Grodno
BELARUS
Tel.: (375 15) 2780 130; (375 15) 2780 176
Fax.: (375 15) 2780 130

LR GENERALINIS KONSULATAS VARŠUVOJE(LENKIJOS RESPUBLIKA)
CONSULATE GENERAL IN WARSAW (REPUBLIC OF POLAND)

ul. Zakroczymska 13,
00-225 Warszawa
POLAND
Tel.: (48 22) 635 97 94
Fax.: (48 22) 635 60 54
Konsulinis skyrius: 815007 LITEM PL
E-mail: kons.varsuva@urm.lt

LR KONSULATAS DAUGPILYJE (LATVIJOS RESPUBLIKA)
CONSULATE IN DAUGAVPILS (REPUBLIC OF LATVIA)

Teatra iela 8
LV-5401 Daugavpils
LATVIA
Tel/Fax: (371 54) 228 04
E-mail: kons.daugpilis@urm.lt

LR GENERALINIS KONSULATAS KALININGRADE (RUSIJOS FEDERACIJA)
CONSULATE GENERAL IN KALININGRAD (RUSSIAN FEDERATION)

Proletarskaja 133
Kaliningrad
RUSSIA

Tel.: (7 0112) 55 71 70, (7 0112) 55 14 44 (vizų išdavimo sk.)
Fax.: (7 0112) 55 68 38
E-mail: kons.kaliningradas@urm.lt

LR KONSULATAS SEINUOSE(LENKIJOS RESPUBLIKA)
CONSULATE IN SEJNY (REPUBLIC OF POLAND)

ul. 22 LIPCA 9,
16-500 Sejny
POLAND
Tel/Fax: (48 87) 5162 273
E-mail: kons.seinai@urm.lt

SELECTED BUSINESS CONTACTS

GOVERNMENT MINISTRIES

Government of the Republic of Lithuania
Gedimino pr. 11, 2600 Vilnius
Tel.: (370 2) 629 038; Fax: (370 2) 227 452
www.lrvk.lt
E-mail: kanceliarija@lrvk.lt

Ministry of Agriculture
Gedimino pr. 19, 2600 Vilnius
Tel.: (370 2) 391 032; Fax: (370 2) 224 440
www.zum.lt
E-mail: zum@zum.lt

Ministry of Environment
Jaksto 4/9, 2600 Vilnius
Tel.: (370 2) 616 148; Fax: (370 2) 220 847
www.gamta.lt
E-mail: info@aplinkuma.lt

Ministry of Culture
Basanaviciaus 5, 2683 Vilnius
Tel.: (370 2) 610 458; Fax: (370 2) 220 886
www.muza.lt
E-mail: culture@muza.lt

Ministry of National Defence
Totoriu 25/3, 2001 Vilnius
Tel.: (370 2) 735 745; Fax: (370 2) 226 082
www.kam.lt
E-mail: vis@kam.kam.lt

Ministry of Education and Science
Volano 2/7, 2600 Vilnius
Tel.: (370 2) 622 483; Fax: (370 2) 612 077
www.smm.lt
E-mail: smmin@smm.lt

Ministry of Finance
J. Tumo-Vaizganto 8a/2, 2600 Vilnius
Tel.: (370 2) 390 005; Fax: (370 2) 791 481

www.finmin.lt
E-mail: finmin@finmin.lt

Ministry of Foreign Affairs
J. Tumo-Vaizganto 2, 2600 Vilnius
Tel.: (370 2) 362 444; Fax: (370 2) 313 090
www.urm.lt
E-mail: urm@urm.lt

Minister of Health Care
Vilniaus 33, 2001 Vilnius
Tel.: (370 2) 661 400; Fax: (370 2) 661 402
www.sam.lt
E-mail: ministerija@sam.lt

Ministry of Interior
Sventaragio 2, 2600 Vilnius
Tel.: (370 2) 717 130; Fax: (370 2) 718 551
http://www.vrm.lt
E-mail: spaudavrs@vrm.lt

Ministry of Justice
Gedimino pr. 30/1, 2600 Vilnius
Tel.: (370 2) 226 615; Fax: (370 2) 625 940
www.min.tm.lt
E-mail: tminfo@tic.lt

Ministry of Economy
Gedimino pr. 38/2, 2600 Vilnius
Tel.: (370 2) 629 412; Fax: (370 2) 623 974
www.ekm.lt
E-mail: kanc@po.ekm.lt

Ministry of Social Security and Labour
Vivulskio 11, 2693 Vilnius
Tel.: (370 2) 603 773; Fax: (370 2) 603 813
www.socmin.lt
E-mail: post@socmin.lt

Ministry of Transport
Gedimino pr. 17, 2679 Vilnius
Tel.: (370 2) 393 911 ; Fax: (370 2) 224 335
www.transp.lt
E-mail: info@transp.lt

OTHER GOVERNMENTAL INSTITUTIONS

European Committee under the Government of Lithuania
Gedimino pr. 56, 2685 Vilnius
Tel.: (370 2) 661 700; Fax: (370 2) 612 178
www.euro.lt
E- mail: mail@www.euro.lt

Lithuanian State Property Fund
Vilniaus 16, 2600 Vilnius
Tel.: (370 2) 684 999; Fax: (370 2) 684 997
www.vtf.lt
E-mail: info@vtf.lt

Department of Statistics
Gedimino pr. 29, 2746 Vilnius
Tel.: (370 2) 364 822; Fax: (370 2) 364 845
www.std.lt
E-mail: statistika@mail.std.lt

State Patent Bureau
Kalvariju 3, 2600 Vilnius
Tel.: (370 2) 780 250; Fax: (370 2) 750 723
www.is.lt/vpb/engl/index.htm
E-mail: spb@vpb.lt

Tourism Department
Vilniaus 4/35, 2600 Vilnius
Tel.: (370 2) 622 610; Fax: (370 2) 226 819
www.tourism.lt
E-mail: info@tourism.lt

Bank of Lithuania
Gedimino pr. 6, 2001 Vilnius
Tel.: (370 2) 680 001; Fax: (370 2) 221 501
www.lbank.lt
E-mail: lb_spauda@lbank.lt

Customs Department
Jaksto 1/25, 2600 Vilnius
Tel.: (370 2) 226 415; Fax: (370 2) 224 948
www.cust.lt
E-mail: tara@cust.lt

Central Mortage Office
Tilto 17/4, 2001 Vilnius
Tel.: (370 2) 313 490; Fax: (370 2) 313 491
http://www.lhr.lt
E-mail: info@lhr.lt

MUNICIPALITIES

Vilnius Municipality
Gedimino pr. 9, 2600 Vilnius
Tel.: (370 2) 226 977; Fax: (370 2) 629 064
www.vilnius.sav.lt
E-mail: savivaldybe@vilnius.lt

Kaunas Municipality
Laisves al. 96, 3000 Kaunas
Tel.: (370 7) 425 088; Fax: (370 7) 220 443
http://www.kaunas.lt
E-mail: savivaldybe@kaunas.sav.lt

Klaipeda Municipality
Liepu 11, 5800 Klaipeda
Tel.: (370 6) 396 001; Fax: (370 6) 213 343
http://www.klaipeda.lt
E-mail: bendras@klaipeda.lt

Siauliai Municipality
Vasario 16-osios 62, 5400 Siauliai

Tel.: (370 1) 596 302; Fax: (370 1) 524 116
http://www.siauliai.sav.lt
E-mail: meras@siauliai.sav.lt

Panevezys Municipality
Laisves 20, 5300 Panevezys
Tel.: (370 5) 501 250; Fax: (370 5) 501 351
http://www.panevezys.sav.lt
E-mail: admins@panevezys.sav.lt

Utena Municipality
Utenio 4a, 4910 Utena
Tel.: (370 39) 61 611; Fax: (370 39) 61 615
http://www.utena.lt
E-mail: infosav@utena.sav.lt

FOREIGN BUSINESS ASSOCIATIONS

American Chamber of Commerce
Lukiskiu 5-204, 2600 Vilnius
Tel.: (370 2) 611 181; Fax: (370 2) 226 128
www.acc.lt
E-mail: acc@post.omnitel.net

Austrian Trade Association
Kastonu 6/3-133, 2600 Vilnius
Tel./Fax: (370 2) 616 732
E-mail: a80645@post.omnitel.net

Belgian Trade and Economic Representative
Kalinausko 2 B, 2009 Vilnius
Tel.: (370 2) 313 595; Fax: (370 2) 313 596
E-mail: vlev.vilnius@post.omnitel.net

British Chamber of Commerce
Fabijoniskiu 2, 2001 Vilnius
Tel./Fax: (370 2) 301 731
E-mail: british.chamber@takas.lt

Canada-Lithuania Business Association
Gedimino pr. 64, 2001 Vilnius
Tel.: (370 2) 220 853; Fax: (370 2) 220 884
E-mail: canambv@aiva.lt

Chinese Trade Mission
Blindziu 34, 2004 Vilnius
Tel.: (370 2) 722 375; Fax: (370 2) 722 161
www.chinesecomoffice.lt

Finish Trade Office
Dominikonu 5, 2001 Vilnius
Tel.: (370 2) 223 221; Fax: (370 2) 224 288
E-mail: vilna@finpro.fi

French-Lithuanian Chamber of Commerce
Seimyniskiu 21, 2051 Vilnius
Tel.: (370 85) 77 012; Fax: (370 2) 613 087
www.cci-fr.lt

French Trade Mission
Didzioji 1, 2001 Vilnius
Tel.: (370 2) 223 786; Fax: (370 2) 223 898
E-mail: ambra-fr-vilnius@post.omnitel.net

German Business Mission
Kudirkos 6, 2009 Vilnius
Tel.: (370 2) 231 122; Fax: (370 2) 231 013
E-mail: info-ahklit@post.omnitel.net

Holland House
Didzioji 13-13, 2001 Vilnius
Tel.: (370 2) 224 085; Fax: (370 2) 224 084
E-mail: hollandhouse@eunet.lt

Italian Foreign Trade Institute
Universiteto 4, 2600 Vilnius
Tel.: (370 2) 223 744; Fax: (370 2) 223 449
http://www.ice.it
E-mail: icevilnius@takas.lt

Norwegian Trade Council
Didzioji 25-20, 2004 Vilnius
Tel.: (370 2) 624 020; Fax: (370 2) 223 186
E-mail: vilnius@ntc.no

Polish Commercial Advisory Bureau
Kastonu 2/14, 2001 Vilnius
Tel.: (370 2) 617 960; Fax: (370 2) 224 084
E-mail: brh@takas.lt

Swedish Trade Council
Vokieciu 26, 2600 Vilnius
Tel.: (370 2) 226 155; Fax: (370 2) 226 697
E-mail: litauen@swedishtrade.se

BUSINESS ORGANISATIONS

Lithuanian Entrepreneurs' and Employers' Confederation
Rotundo 5, 2600 Vilnius
Tel.: (370 2) 629 729; Fax: (370 2) 220 448
195.182.80.20/lvdk
E-mail: lvdk@post.omnitel.net

Confederation of Lithuanian Industrialists
Vienuolio 8, 2000 Vilnius
Tel.: (370 2) 225 217; Fax: (370 2) 225 209
www.lpk.lt
E-mail: info@lpk.lt

Association of Lithuanian Chambers of Commerce, Industry and Crafts
J. Tumo-Vaizganto 9/1-63a, 2600 Vilnius
Tel.: (370 2) 612 102; Fax: (370 2) 612 112
www.chambers.lt
E-mail: info@chambers.lt

Vilnius Chamber of Commerce, Industry and Crafts
Algirdo 31, 2600 Vilnius
Tel.: (370 2) 235 550; Fax: (370 2) 235 542

www.cci.lt
E-mail: vilnius@cci.lt

Kaunas Chamber of Commerce, Industry and Crafts
Donelaicio 8, 3000 Kaunas
Tel.: (370 7) 229 212; Fax: (370 2) 208 330
www.chamber.lt
E-mail: chamber@chamber.lt

Siauliai Chamber of Commerce, Industry and Crafts
Vilniaus 88, 5400 Siauliai
Tel.: (370 1) 525 504; Fax: (370 1) 523 903
www.rumai.lt
E-mail: siauliai_cci@siauliai.omnitel.net

Klaipeda Chamber of Commerce, Industry and Crafts
Danes 17, 5800 Klaipeda
Tel.: (370 6) 410 625; Fax: (370 6) 410 626
E-mail: klaipeda@chambers.lt

Panevezys Chamber of Commerce, Industry and Crafts
Respublikos 34, 5319 Panevezys
Tel.: (370 5) 463 687; Fax: (370 5) 462 227
www.ccic.lt
E-mail: panevezys@chambers.lt

National Regional Development Agency
Kalvariju 3-327, 2005 Vilnius
Tel./Fax: (370 2) 731 254
www.nrda.lt
E-mail: nrda@nrda.lt

Association of Information Technology, Telecommunications and Office Equipment Companies - "Infobalt"
Vokieciu 28/17-6, 2001 Vilnius
Tel.: (370 2) 622 623; Fax: (370 2) 622 629
www.infobalt.lt
E-mail: office@infobalt.lt

Lithuanian Agricultural Technics Association
Kalvariju 62-30, 2005 Vilnius
Tel.: (370 2) 734 411; Fax: (370 2) 734 411

Lithuanian Breweries Association
Aludariu 1/2, 2600 Vilnius
Tel.: (370 2) 222 495; Fax: (370 2) 628 916
E-mail: alusasoc@takas.lt

Lithuanian Builders Association
Vytauto 14, 2004 Vilnius
Tel.: (370 2) 734 676; Fax: (370 2) 225 901
E-mail: lsa@post.omnitel.net

National Association of Business Administrators
Gedimino pr. 38/2, 2600 Vilnius
Tel.: (370 2) 617 174; Fax: (370 2) 616 674
E-mail: nvaasoc@iti.lt

Association of Lithuanian Chemical Industry Enterprises
Vienuolio 8, 2600 Vilnius
Tel./Fax: (370 2) 224 175
www.tdd.lt/lchpia
E-mail: lchpia@tdd.lt

Lithuanian Association of Directors of Colleges
Didlaukio 45, Vilnius
Tel.: (370 2) 764 871; Fax: (370 2) 769 496
E-mail: vaem@is.lt

Association of Communication Construction Enterprises
Draugystes 15A, 3003 Kaunas
Tel./Fax: (370 7) 231 735
www.krst.lt
E-mail: krs@takas.lt

Association of Construction Industry
Sevcenkos 19, 2009 Vilnius
Tel.: (370 2) 233 479; Fax: (370 2) 635 641
E-mail: scancem@post.omnitel.net

Lithuanian Consumer Cooperative Societies Union
Gedimino pr. 28, 2600 Vilnius
Tel.: (370 2) 623 797; Fax: (370 2) 226 663
www.lvks.lt
E-mail: litkoop@mail.lt

National Association of Customs Brokers
Kalvariju 133, 2600 Vilnius
Tel.: (370 2) 315 816; Fax: (370 2) 315 818
www.draginta.lt
E-mail: asista@aiva.lt

Lithuanian Dairy Association "Pieno Centras"
Vykinto 7, 2004 Vilnius
Tel.: (370 2) 715 552; Fax: (370 2) 715 553
E-mail: pienocentras@post.omnitel.net

Engineering Ecology Association
Dominikonu 4, 2001 Vilnius
Tel./Fax: (370 2) 223 879
E-mail: rimasbudrys@takas.lt

Association "Lithuanian Food Industry"
Vienuolio 8, 2600 Vilnius
Tel.: (370 2) 627 022; Fax: (370 2) 224 447

Association of Lithuanian Foundries
Kalantos 49, 3718 Kaunas
Tel.: (370 7) 454 469; Fax: (370 7) 451 612
E-mail: ketus@takas.lt

Lithuanian National Freight Forwarders Association "LINEKA"
Verkiu 44-306, 2600 Vilnius
Tel.: (370 2) 779 036; Fax: (370 2) 779 036
www.lineka.lt
E-mail: lineka@post.5ci.lt

Associations of Lithuanian Glassmakers
Dzuku 2, 2600 Vilnius
Tel.: (370 2) 330 419; Fax: (370 2) 654 009
E-mail: lsa@takas.lt

Lithuanian Grain Processors Association
Kauno 1A, 2600 Vilnius
Tel.: (370 2) 335 615; Fax: (370 2) 236 175
E-mail: stanislavas@takas.lt

Association of Lithuanian International Airports
Rodunes kelias 10 A, 2038 Vilnius
Tel.: (370 2) 336 342; Fax: (370 2) 262 135
www.vilnius-airport.lt/asociacija.html
E-mail: vilnius-airport@post.omnitel.net

Association of Investment Companies
Juozapaviciaus 6/2, 2686 Vilnius
Tel.: (370 2) 425 571; Fax: (370 2) 725 685
E-mail: invalda@aiva.lt

Association of Leather Producers and Consumers of Lithuania
Tilzes 225, 5400 Siauliai
Tel.: (370 1) 431 861; Fax: (370 1) 426 562
E-mail: office@siauliu-stumbras.lt

Association of Lift Enterprises
Taikos pr. 110, 3031 Kaunas
Tel.: (370 7) 333 054; Fax: (370 7) 313 823
E-mail: kaunoliftai@ijo.lt

Association of Light Industry Enterprises of Lithuania
Saltoniskiu 29, 2677 Vilnius
Tel.: (370 2) 751 877; Fax: (370 2) 721 127
www.lpia.lt
E-mail: llpia@post.5ci.lt

Lithuanian National Road Carriers Association "LINAVA"
Basanaviciaus 45, 2009 Vilnius
Tel.: (370 2) 237 585; Fax: (370 2) 232 242
www.linava.lt
E-mail: office@linava.lt

Association of Machines and Appliances Industry Enterprises
Vienuolio 8, 2600 Vilnius
Tel./Fax: (370 2) 312 520
E-mail: beker@auste.elnet.lt

Lithuanian Meat Makers Association
Savickio 4, 2001 Vilnius
Tel./Fax: (370 2) 222 009
E-mail: g.radzevicius@post.omnitel.net

Association of Lithuanian Companies for Melioration
Juozapaviciaus 9, 2686 Vilnius
Tel.: (370 2) 723 213; Fax: (370 2) 728 124
E-mail: lmia@takas.lt

Association of Enterprises "Lithuanian Peat"
Kestucio 54, 3000 Kaunas
Tel.: (370 7) 227 721; Fax: (370 7) 201 243

Association of Enterprises of Pharmaceutical Industry
Vytauto pr. 3, 3000 Kaunas
Tel.: (370 7) 226 725; Fax: (370 7) 223 696
E-mail: sanitas@post.sonex.com

Association of the Polytechnic Schools Principals of the Republic of Lithuania
Pamenkalnio 11, 2600 Vilnius
Tel./Fax: (370 2) 625 764
v1pm.w3.lt
E-mail: v1pm@centras.lt

Enterprises Association "Praktika"
Vilniaus 137 A, 2400 Siauliai
Tel.: (370 1) 434 653; Fax: (370 1) 438 881
http://www.praktika.lt
E-mail: praktika@siauliai.omnitel.net

Association of Retail Trade Enterprises
Vienuolio 8, 2600 Vilnius
Tel./Fax: (370 2) 312 522
E-mail: zizysg@takas.lt

Shipowners Association
Janonio 24, 5813 Klaipeda
Tel.: (370 6) 393 120; Fax: (370 6) 393 121
E-mail: lsa@hq.lisco.lt

Lithuanian Association of Stevedoring Companies
Nemuno 2, 5802 Klaipeda
Tel.: (370 6) 395 570; Fax: (370 6) 395 572
E-mail: a.kuzmarskis@bega.lt

Association of Lithuanian Sugar Enterprises "CUKRUS"
Savickio 4, 2001 Vilnius
Tel./Fax: (370 2) 628 422
E-mail: asocukrus@takas.lt

Association "Lithuanian Timber"
Savanoriu 178, 2600 Vilnius
Tel.: (370 2) 237 325; Fax: (370 2) 237 326
http://www.tdd.lt/lm
E-mail: l.m@tdd.lt

Lithuanian Association of the Trade Intermediators
Verkiu 7, 20 korp., 2042 Vilnius
Tel./Fax: (370 2) 727 728

FOREIGN CONSULTING COMPANIES

Andersen
Subaciaus 7, 2600 Vilnius
Tel.: (370 2) 313 063; Fax: (370 2) 620 743
www.andersen.com
E-mail: Lithuania@lt.andersen.com

PricewaterhouseCoopers
Sevcenkos 21, 2009 Vilnius
Tel.: (370 2) 392 300; Fax: (370 2) 392 301
www.pwc.lt
E-mail: vlnius@lt.pwcglobal.com

Aon Consulting
Vilniaus 39, 2600 Vilnius
Tel.: (370 2) 626 640; (370 2) 220 870
www.aon.lt
E-mail: centeuro@hrs.omnitel.net

Deloitte&Touche
Jaksto 13, 2600 Vilnius
Tel.: (370 2) 250 425; Fax: (370 2) 226 844
www.deloitte.com
E-mail: lietuva@deloitteCE.com

KPMG Lietuva
Vytauto 12, 2001 Vilnius
Tel.: (370 2) 687 500; Fax: (370 2) 687 599
http://www.kpmg.com
E-mail: vilnius@kpmg.lt

Ernst&Young
Labdariu 5, 2600 Vilnius
Tel.: (370 2) 616 610; Fax: (370 2) 227 128
www.ey.com
E-mail: eyi@eyi.lt

Scandinavian Accounting and Consulting
Kestucio 79-7, 3000 Kaunas
Tel.: (370 7) 204 928; Fax: (370 7) 320 811

De Facto
Sv. Ignoto 5, 2600 Vilnius
Tel.: (370 2) 227 040; Fax: (370 2) 685 377
E-mail: defacto@takas.lt

Kredoline (Dun and Bradstreet)
Svitrigailos 7-406, 2009 Vilnius
Tel.: (370 2) 310 024; Fax: (370 2) 233 128
www.5ci.lt/kredoline
E-mail: kredoline@post.5ci.lt

LITHUANIAN CONSULTANTS

Abisala & Partners
Gostauto 40, 2001 Vilnius
Tel.: (370 2) 362 755; Fax: (370 2) 362 754

Mickeviciaus 29-4, 3000 Kaunas
Tel.: (370 7) 204 520; Fax: (370 7) 320 606
www.abisala.com
E-mail: abisala@abisala.com

Economic Research Centre
Vrublevskio 4, 2600 Vilnius

Tel.: (370 2) 619 919; Fax: (370 2) 615 712
www.erc.lt
E-mail: info@erc.lt

Lithuanian Free Market Institute
Birutes 56, 2004 Vilnius
Tel.: (370 2) 722 584; Fax: (370 2) 721 279
www.lrinka.lt
E-mail: lfmi@lrinka.lt

Economic Consultancy and Research
Smolensko 6, 2600 Vilnius
Tel.: (370 2) 333 990; Fax: (370 2) 235 006
www.ekt.lt
E-mail: ekt@ekt.lt

New Marketing Systems
Zirmunu 68, 2600 Vilnius
Tel.: (370 2) 700 570; Fax: (370 2) 700560
www.nms.lt
E-mail: info@nms.lt

Intellectual Resource Systems
Kestucio 19/18, 2001 Vilnius
Tel.: (370 2) 750 688; Fax: (370 2) 750 438
www.irs.lt
E-mail: info@irs.lt

Vilnius Consulting Group
Vokieciu 26, 2001 Vilnius
Tel.: (370 2) 661 100; Fax: (370 2) 611 671
www.vkg.lt
E-mail: vkg@vkg.lt

Mercuri International
Lukiskiu 5-519, 2600 Vilnius
Tel.: (370 2) 617 574; Fax: (370 2) 224 829
www.mercuri.lt
E-mail: vilnius@mercuri.lt

Alliance for Integrated Development
Raugyklos 15, 2001 Vilnius
Tel.: (370 2) 332 829; Fax: (370 2) 627 134
www.aid.lt
E-mail: office@bemi-bfic.com

EKO RIVI
Gedimino pr. 10/1, 2001 Vilnius
Tel.: (370 2) 224 153; Fax: (370 2) 626 538
www.ekorivi.freeservers.com
E-mail: ekorivi@post.omnitel.net

Banking Consultations
Gedimino pr. 26, 2600 Vilnius
Tel.: (370 2) 616 274; Fax: (370 2) 628 756

SIC Market Research (Gallup)
Raugyklos 15, 2001 Vilnius

Tel.: (370 2) 310 121; Fax: (370 2) 627 134
www.sic.lt
E-mail: sic@sic.lt

People Management
Vytenio 9/25, 2600 Vilnius
Tel.: (370 2) 683 444; Fax: (370 2) 683 442
www.peoplemanagement.fi
E-mail: atranka@peoplemanagement.lt

LAW FIRMS

Lideika, Petrauskas, Valiunas & Partners
Labdariu 5, 2001 Vilnius
Tel.: (370 2) 681 888; Fax: (370 2) 225 591
www.lpvp.lt
E-mail: lpvp@lpvp.lt

Bishop and Robertson Chalmers
Vytauto 8/7, 2004 Vilnius
Tel.: (370 2) 614 875; Fax: (370 2) 624 147
www.icclaw.com
E-mail: office@bishops.lt

McDermott, Will and Emery
Smetonos 6-6, 2000 Vilnius
Tel.: (370 2) 791 000; Fax: (370 2) 227 955
www.mwe.lt
E-mail: office@mwe.lt

Foresta, Business Law Group
Kudirkos 22, 2001 Vilnius
Tel.: (370 2) 224 564; Fax: (370 2) 233 749
www.foresta.lt
E-mail: lawfirm@foresta.lt

AAA Legal Services & Real Estate Development
Rudininku 18/2, 2001 Vilnius
Tel.: (370 2) 613 232; Fax: (370 2) 220 422
www.aaa.lt
E-mail: info@aaa.lt

S. Katauskas Law Firm
Jaksto 11-4, 2001 Vilnius
Tel./Fax: (370 2) 616 052
E-mail: s.katauskas@post.inet.lt

Glimstedt Law Firm
Gostauto 12 A, 2001 Vilnius
Tel.: (370 2) 683 700; Fax: (370 2) 225 649
www.glimstedt.lt
E-mail: glimstedt@glimstedt.lt

Sorainen Law Office
Gedimino pr. 3A-2, 2600 Vilnius
Tel.: (370 2) 685 040; Fax: (370 2) 610 667
www.sorainen.lt
E-mail: sorainen@sorainen.lt

Rodl and Partners
Totoriu 21/6-10, 2001 Vilnius
Tel.: (370 2) 223 590; Fax: (370 2) 791 514
www.rodl.de
E-mail: info@roedl.lt

Baublys & Partners Law Firm
Gostauto 40, 2001 Vilnius
Tel.: (370 2) 362 708; Fax: (370 2) 362 709
www.baublys.lt
E-mail: lawfirm@baublys.lt

Jurevicius, Balciunas an Partners
Pamenkalnio 23/5-6, 1st floor, 2001 Vilnius
Tel.: (370 2) 685 533; Fax: (370 2) 685 534
www.jbp.lt
E-mail: advocate@jbp.lt

INSURANCE COMPANIES

Lietuvos Draudimas
Basanaviciaus 12, 2737 Vilnius
Tel.: (370 2) 686 300; Fax: (370 2) 314 138
www.ldr.lt
E-mail: info@ldr.lt

Drauda
Gelezinio Vilko 6A, 2001 Vilnius
Tel.: (370 2) 683 001; Fax: (370 2) 683 005
www.drauda.lt
E-mail: info@drauda.lt

Lithuanian Export and Import Insurance
Vilniaus 23, 2600 Vilnius
Tel.: (370 2) 791 727; Fax: (370 2) 791 754
www.leidas.lt
E-mail: info@leidas.lt

Lindra
Jasinskio 16, 2005 Vilnius
Tel.: (370 2) 611 905; Fax: (370 2) 610 937
www.lindra.lt
E-mail: info@lindra.lt

Preventa
Kudirkos 7; 2009 Vilnius
Tel.: (370 2) 225 552; Fax: (370 2) 263 183
www.preventa.lt
E-mail: info@preventa.lt

Finalas Insurance Brokers
Algirdo 2/22-15, 2001 Vilnius
Tel.: (370 2) 227 301; Fax: (370 2) 227 491
www.finalas.lt
E-mail: mail@finalas.lt

STOCK BROKERS

Baltijos vertybiniai popieriai
Gedimino pr. 60, 2001 Vilnius
Tel.: (370 2) 313 833; Fax: (370 2) 313 840
www.bvp.lt
E-mail: bvp@nse.lt

VB Vilfima
Jogailos 9/1, 2600 Vilnius
Tel.: (370 2) 681 400; Fax: (370 2) 681 499
www.vilfima.lt
E-mail: mail@vilfima.lt

Suprema
Gostauto 40, 2600 Vilnius
Tel.: (370 2) 362 770; Fax: (370 2) 362 771
www.suprema.lt
E-mail: suprema@suprema.lt

VB Investiciju valdymas (Investment Management)
Jogailos 9/1, 2600 Vilnius
Tel.: (370 2) 681 579; Fax: (370 2) 681 575
www.vbiv.lt
E-mail: info@vbiv.lt

Alpha Baltic
Ukmerges 41-507, 2001 Vilnius
Tel.: (370 2) 724 774; Fax: (370 2) 725 254
E-mail: alpha@nse.lt

Finasta
Ukmerges 41-510, 2600 Vilnius
Tel.: (370 2) 723 463; Fax: (370 2) 723 491
www.finasta.lt
E-mail: info@finasta.lt

PUBLIC RELATIONS

Komunikacija ir konsultantai
Pamenkalnio 5-9, 2600 Vilnius
Tel.: (370 2) 313 003; Fax: (370 2) 312 908
www.koko.lt
E-mail: koko@koko.lt

Network Gulliver
Aguonu 10, 2001 Vilnius
Tel.: (370 2) 312 382; Fax: (370 2) 312 383
E-mail: gulliver@post.omnitel.net

Jonkus ir partneriai
Klaipedos 1/16, 2001 Vilnius
Tel.: (370 2) 312 634; Fax: (370 2) 612 328
www.jonkus.lt
E-mail: info@jonkus.lt

Hill & Knowlton
Pilies 25A, 2600 Vilnius
Tel.: (370 2) 685 135; Fax: (370 2) 685 133

www.hillandknowlton.lt
E-mail: info@hill.lt

GCI Lithuania
Ukmerges 12, 2005 Vilnius
Tel.: (370 2) 754 686; Fax: (370 2) 755 030
E-mail: gci@havera.lt

ADVERTISING

Media House
Pylimo 38/1, 2600 Vilnius
Tel.: (370 2) 222 075; Fax: (370 2) 222 108
www.media-house.com
E-mail: vytas@media-house.com

Lukrecijos grupe
Sevcenkos 19, 2600 Vilnius
Tel.: (370 2) 334 599; Fax: (370 2) 263 037
www.lukrecija.lt
E-mail: lukrecija@lukrecija.lt

Adell Saatchi & Saatchi
Ligonines 4, 2600 Vilnius
Tel.: (370 2) 791 640; Fax: (370 2) 628 412
E-mail: kristina@saatchi.lt

Leo Burnett Dvyniu Ratas
Donelaicio 3A, 2009 Vilnius
Tel.: (370 2) 262 587; Fax: (370 2) 263 335
www.leoburnett.com
E-mail: office@leoburnett.lt

DDB (Brand Sellers)
Dominikonu 5, 2600 Vilnius
Tel.: (370 2) 312 190; Fax: (370 2) 312 191
www.ddb.com
E-mail: ddb@bsddb.com

McCann Ericson
Ausros Vartu 17-1, 2001 Vilnius
Tel.: (370 2) 224 509; Fax: (370 2) 223 816
www.mccann.com
E-mail: astos.dizainas@taide.lt

Age Advertising
Zemaites 21, 2001 Vilnius
Tel.: (370 2) 310 630; Fax: (370 2) 310 600
E-mail: office@age.lt

Havera (Grey Worldwide)
Ukmerges 12, 2000 Vilnius
Tel.: (370 2) 754 686; Fax: (370 2) 728 663
E-mail: info@havera.lt

MEDICAL CARE

Baltic-American Medical and Surgical Clinic
Antakalnio 124, 2001 Vilnius
Tel.: (370 2) 342 020; Fax: (370 2) 767 942

Cor Sanum (Cardiology)
Pamenkalnio 25-2, 2601 Vilnius
Tel.: (370 2) 220 329

Medical Diagnostic Center
Grybo 32, 2001 Vilnius
Tel.: (370 2) 709 120

Kardivita (Cardiology)
Kolektyvo 13, 2600 Vilnius
Tel.: (370 2) 700 669

Denticija (Dentists)
Grybo 32, 2001 Vilnius
Tel.: (370 2) 709 125

Heart Surgery Center
Laisves 64A, 2010 Vilnius
Tel.: (370 2) 390 500

AIRLINE CONTACT INFORMATION

Lithuanian Airlines
Gustaicio 4, 2038 Vilnius
Tel.: (370 2) 306 017; Fax: (370 2) 266 828
www.lal.lt
E-mail: info@lal.lt

Air Lithuania
Svitrigailos 26/40-18, 2600 Vilnius
Tel.: (370 2) 231 322; Fax: (370 2) 231 566
www.airlithuania.lt
E-mail: hdoffice@airlithuania.lt

Aeroflot
Pylimo 8/2, 2600 Vilnius
Tel./Fax: (370 2) 224 189
www.aeroflot.ru

Austrian Airlines
Basanaviciaus 11/1, 2001 Vilnius
Tel.: (370 2) 313 137; Fax: (370 2) 313 136
www.aua.com
E-mail: egle.ragauskaite@aua.com

Estonian Airlines
Rodunios kelias 2, 2600 Vilnius
Tel.: (370 2) 739 022; Fax: (370 2) 739 016
www.estonian-air.ee
E-mail: vilnius@estonian-air.ee

Finnair
Rodunios kelias 2, 2600 Vilnius
Tel.: (370 2) 619 393; Fax: (370 2) 232 247
www.finnair.com

LOT
Rodunios kelias 2, 2600 Vilnius
Tel./Fax: (370 2) 739 020
www.lot.com
E-mail: lotvno@lot.com

Lufthansa
Rodunios kelias 2, 2600 Vilnius
Tel.: (370 2) 262 222; Fax: (370 2) 230 889
www.lufthansa.com
E-mail: ticketing@litcargus.lt

SAS
Rodunios kelias 2, 2600 Vilnius
Tel.: (370 2) 395 500; Fax: (370 2) 395 501
www.scandinavian.net

Czech Airlines
Valanciaus 4/9, 2600 Vilnius
Tel.: (370 2) 251 503; Fax: (370 2) 251 511
www.czechairlines.com
E-mail: csavilnius@czechairlines.lt

INTERNET PROVIDERS

Aiva Sistema
Aguonu 10, 2600 Vilnius
Tel.: (370 2) 227 654; Fax: (370 2) 227 905
www.aiva.lt
E-mail: sales@office.aiva.lt

Delfi
Juozapaviciaus 6/2, 2001 Vilnius
Tel.: (370 2) 732 656; Fax: (370 2) 732 657
www.delfi.lt
E-mail: info@delfi.lt

Elnet
Vytenio 53-2, 2600 Vilnius
Tel.: (370 2) 250 471; Fax: (370 2) 263 948
www.elnet.lt
E-mail: info@elnet.lt

Eunetas
Jogailos 8-16, 2600 Vilnius
Tel./Fax: (370 2) 791 213
www.eunet.lt
E-mail: info@eunet.lt

Informacijos tiltas
Smolensko 6, 2600 Vilnius
Tel.: (370 2) 231 944; Fax: (370 2) 333 457
www.iti.lt
E-mail: office@iti.lt

Infostruktura
Pilies 23/15, 2001 Vilnius
Tel.: (370 2) 791 321; Fax: (370 2) 791 331

www.is.lt
E-mail: info@is.lt

Omnitel
Vytenio 18, 2600 Vilnius
Tel.: (370 2) 747 474; Fax: (370 2) 231 313
www.omnitel.lt
E-mail: info@omnitel.lt

Penki kontinentai
Stulginskio 5, 2600 Vilnius
Tel.: (370 2) 239 279; Fax: (370 2) 239 280
www.5ci.lt
E-mail: info@5ci.lt

Ralinga
Pylimo 20, 2600 Vilnius
Tel.: (370 2) 611 966; Fax: (370 2) 661 188
www.ralinga.lt
E-mail: info@ralinga.lt

Takas (Lithuanian Telecom)
Savanoriu pr. 28, 2600 Vilnius
Tel.: (370 2) 367 611; Fax: (370 2) 226 665
www.takas.lt
E-mail: info@telecom.lt

MOBILE PHONE PROVIDERS

Bite GSM
Zemaites 15, 2600 Vilnius
Tel.: (370 2) 232 323; Fax: (370 2) 231 010
www.bite.lt
E-mail: info@bite.lt

Omnitel
Vytenio 18, 2600 Vilnius
Tel.: (370 2) 747 474; Fax: (370 2) 231 313
www.omnitel.lt
E-mail: info@omnitel.lt

Tele2
Sporto 7A, 2051 Vilnius
Tel.: (370 2) 366 300; Fax: (370 2) 366 301
www.tele2.lt
E-mail: tele2@tele2.lt

Comliet
Savanoriu pr. 28, 2600 Vilnius
Tel.: (370 2) 367 403; Fax: (370 2) 231 139
www.comliet.lt

TRADE FAIRS AND EXHIBITIONS

AUGUST 29 - SEPTEMBER 2
BABY LAND
Children's clothing, footwear, toys, games, school articles, baby care

SEPTEMBER 11 - 14
BALTIC TEXTILE AND LEATHER
Textiles, clothing, footwear, textile industries and raw material

SEPTEMBER 25 - 28
BALTMEDICA
Medical equipment, pharmacy, dentistry and optics

OCTOBER 9 - 12
SECURITY
Security and safety systems

OCTOBER 24 - 27
INFOBALT
Information technologies, computers, telecommunications and office systems

NOVEMBER 8-11
HOUSEHOLD
Domestic appliances, kitchen and housewares

NOVEMBER 22 - 24
BALTGASTRO
Shop, hotel and restaurant equipment, groceries

DECEMBER 13 - 16
WINTER BOUQUET
Competition of florists, Christmas fair

LITHUANIA'S REPRESENTATION IN THE UNITED STATES

Embassy of Lithuania
Ambassador Mr. Stasys Sakalauskas
2622 Sixteenth St., NW
Washington DC 20009
Tel: (202) 234-5860
Fax: (202) 328-0466
E-mail: admin@ltembassyus.org
Internet site: www.ltembassyus.org

Consulate General of Lithuania
Mr. Rimantas Morkvenas
Consul General
420 Fifth Ave.
New York, NY 10018
Tel: (212) 354-7849
(212) 354-7840
Fax: (212) 354-7911
E-mail: lrgkn@msn.com

Consulate General of Lithuania
Mr. Giedrius Apuokas,
Consul General
211 East Ontario Street
Suite 1500
Chicago, IL 60611
Tel: (312) 397-0382
Fax: (312) 397-0385

E-mail: admin@ltconchi.org

Honorary Consulate General
Mr. Vytautas Cekanauskas,
Honorary Consul General
3236 N. Sawtooth Ct.
Westlake Village, CA 91362
Tel: (805) 496-5324
Fax: (805) 496-7435
cglalith@gte.net

Honorary Consulate
Mr. W. Richard Bingham,
Honorary Consul
One Maritime Plaza, Suite 2525
San Francisco, CA 94111
Tel: (415) 788-7354
Fax: (415) 788-5302

Honorary Consulate General
Ms. Ingrida Gertruda Bublys,
Honorary Consul
18021 Marcella Rd., Suite 101
Cleveland, OH 44119
Tel: (216) 486-8692
Fax: (216) 486-8612
ibcommo@aol.com

Honorary Consulate
Mr. Stanley Balzekas, Honorary Consul
230 Royal Palm Way
Suite 204
Palm Beach, FL 33480
Tel: 561-832-2232

Honorary Consulate
Mr. Al Karnavicius, Honorary Consul
1101 First Avenue South
St. Petersburg, FL 33705
Tel.: (727) 895-4811
Fax: (727) 822-2252
Email: LTconsulFL@bayprintonline.com

Lithuanian Mission to the UN
Ambassador Oskaras Jusys
Tel: (212) 354-7820
Fax: (212) 354-7833
litun@undp.org

Lithuanian-American Community, Inc.
Public Affairs Office
Ms.Audrone Pakstiene,
Director

11250 Roger Bacon Drive
#17 C
Reston, VA 22090
Tel: (703) 397-0950
Fax: (703) 397-0951
www.JAVLB.org

U.S. AND LITHUANIAN CONTACTS

OFFICE OF THE GOVERNMENT OF THE REPUBLIC OF LITHUANIA

Algirdas Šemeta	Government Secretary	626595	a.semeta@lrvk.lt
Irena Butrimienė	Deputy Government Secretary, Director of the Department of Public and Municipal Economy	626509	i.butrimiene@lrvk.lt
Vygantas Švoba	Government Press Service	625651	kasp@lrvk.lt

ADVISORS ON SPECIFIC MATTERS

Deividas Matulionis	Advisor on Foreign Relations	615334	d.matulionis@lrvk.lt
Algimantas Slivinskas	Advisor on Economy	626605	a.slivinskas@lrvk.lt
Aloyzas Duksa	Advisor on Property Management and Use	628771	kppr@lrvk.lt
Vaclovas Medišauskas	Advisor on Treasury	227792	medis@lrvk.lt
Stasys Čipkus	Advisor on Finance	625908	s.cipkus@lrvk.lt
Jonas Olšauskas	Advisor on Trade	621702	j.olsauskas@lrvk.lt
Arvydas Basiulis	Advisor on Rural Matters	625746	a.basiulis@lrvk.lt
Irena Pilypienė	Advisor on Environmental Protection	627956	i.pilypiene@lrvk.lt
Gintautas Asadauskas	Advisor on Transportation	627186	g.asadauskas@lrvk.lt
Stanislovas Trilikauskis	Advisor on Labour and Social Affairs	627450	s.trilikauskis@lrvk.lt
Petras Plumpa	Advisor on Religions	620607	p.plumpa@lrvk.lt
Gintautas Vilkelis	Advisor on National Security	627959	g.vilkelis@lrvk.lt
Egidijus Šileikis	Advisor on Public Administration	622698	e.sileikis@lrvk.lt

HEADS OF DIVISIONS OF THE OFFICE OF THE GOVERNMENT

Ramutė Ruškytė	Director of the Department of Law and Law Enforcement	227764	r.ruskyte@lrvk.lt
Juozas Linartas	Reception Office	626982	
Olegas Romančikas	Deputy Government Secretary - Director of Administration Department	621697	o.romancikas@lrvk.lt
Gediminas Samulionis	Head of Editorial Division of Government Documents of Administration Department	626486	g.samulionis@lrvk.lt

Birutė Skinkienė	Personnel Division	623912	b.skinkiene@lrvk.lt
Viktorija Tichonova	Translation Division	615592	v.tichonova@lrvk.lt
Edmundas Kazakevičius	Information Technologies Division	629817	edka@lrvk.lt
Zita Riškuvienė	Finance Division	628158	z.riskuviene@lrvk.lt
Jonas Šniaukšta	Maintenance Division	629856, fax.220470	j.sniauksta@lrvk.lt
Marius Nemanis	Protocol of the Office of the Prime Minister Diplomatic Protocol of the Ministry of Foreign Affairs	628523, fax.227783	m.nemanis@lrvk.lt

REPRESENTATIVE OFFICES OF THE INTERNATIONAL AND FOREIGN INSTITUTIONS BASED ON THE PREMISES OF THE GOVERNMENT OFFICE

Mark Alan Horton	International Monetary Fund Representative in Lithuania	620893, fax 290248
Lynn Willenbring	Advisor of the USA Treasury Department	627729, fax 226289

Lithuanian Embassy: 2622 16th Street N.W. Washington D.C. 20009; ph: 202-2345860; fax: 202-3280466. Homepage: http://www.ltembassy.org

Lithuanian Development Agency: Sv Jono str. 3, 2001 Vilnius, Lithuania; ph: 370-2 627438; fax: 370-2 220160. Homepage: http://www.lda.lt

Customs Department: A. Jaksto str. 1/25, LT-2600 Vilnius, Lithuania; ph: 370-2 226415; fax: 370-2 224948. Homepage: http://www.cust.lt

State Competition and Consumer Protection office: Vienuolio str. 8, LT-2600 Vilnius, Lithuania; ph: 370-2 226492; fax: 370-2 226412. Homepage: http://www.konkuren.lt

Lithuanian Standardization Board: Kosciuskos str. 30 LT-2600 Vilnius, Lithuania; ph: 370-2 226252; fax: (370-2) 226252. Homepage: http://www.lsd.lt

National Stock Excange of Lithuania: Ukmerges str. 41, LT- 2662 Vilnius, Lithuania; ph: 370-2 723611; fax: 370-2 724894. Homepage: http://www.nse.lt

State Veterinary Service: Siesiku str. 19, LT- 2010 Vilnius, Lithuania; ph: 370-2 404361; fax: 370-2 404362. Homepage: http://www.vet.lt

State Patent Bureau: Algirdo str. 31, LT-2025 Vilnius, Lithuania; ph: 370-2 233349; fax: (370-2) 233357. Homepage: http://www.is.lt/vpb/liet/vpbhome.HTML

State Tax Inspection under the Ministry of Finance: Sermuksniu str. 6, LT-2695 Vilnius, Lithuania; ph: 370-2 620060; fax: 370-2 621924. Homepage: http://www.vmi.lt

State Property Fund: Vilniaus str. 16, LT-2600 Vilnius, Lithuania; ph: 370-2 684 902; fax: 370-2 684901. Homepage: http://www.vtf.lt

Commercial Court of the Republic of Lithuania: Gedimino pr. 39/1, LT-2640 Vilnius, Lithuania; ph: 370-2 622843; fax: 370-2 619927

Association of Lithuanian Entrepreneurs: A. Jaksto str. 9, LT-2600 Vilnius, Lithuania: ph: 370-2 614963; fax: 370-2 220448

Association of Lithuanian Chambers of Commerce and Industry: V. Kudirkos str. 18, LT-2600 Vilnius, Lithuania; ph: 370-2 222630; fax: 370-2 222621

American Chamber of Commerce: Room 204, Lukiskiu str.5, 2600 Vilnius, Lithuania; ph: 370-2 611181; fax: 370-2 226128; email: acc@post.omnitel.net Homepage: http://www.acc.lt

The Bank of Lithuania: Gedimino pr. 6, LT-2001 Vilnius, Lithuania; ph: 370-2 224008; fax: 370-2 628124. Homepage: http://www.lbank.lt

Major Commercial Banks

Vilniaus Bankas: Gedimino pr. 12, LT-2600 Vilnius, Lithuania; ph: 370-2 610723; fax: 370-2 626557. Homepage: http://www.vb.lt

Hermis Bank: Jogailos str. 9/1, LT-2001 Vilnius, Lithuania; ph: 370-2 226165; fax: 370-2 224477. Homepage: http://www.hermis.lt

Snoras Bank: Tilzes str. 170, LT-5400 Siauliai, Lithuania; ph: 370-1 426338; fax: 370-1 426592 Homepage: http://www.snoras.com

U.S. Department of Commerce Contacts
Karen Pilmanis, Principal Commercial Officer
Tuula Javanainen, Commercial Specialist
American Embassy,
Dag Hammarskjolds Vag 31
11589 Stockholm, Sweden
ph: 46-8 7835346; fax: 46-8 6609181

Jonas Vasilevicius, Commercial assistant
US Embassy
Pranciskonu 3/6
2001 Vilnius, Lithuania
ph. 370 2 223 031; fax: 370 2 222 779

Export-Import Bank of the U.S.: International Business Development, 811 Vermont Ave, N.W., Washington, D.C. 20571,
tel: (202) 565-3913; fax: (202) 566-7524

Overseas Private Investment Corporation (OPIC): Central/Eastern Europe and Central Asia, Investment Development, 1100 New York Avenue, N.W., Washington D.C. 20527, tel: (202) 336-8617, fax: (202) 408-5145

U.S. Trade and Development Agency: Central, Eastern & Southern Europe, Room 309 SA-16, Washington D.C. 20523-1602, tel: (702) 875-4357, fax: (703) 875-4009

PROGRAM OF THE GOVERNMENT OF THE REPUBLIC OF LITHUANIA

1. PERSONAL SAFETY AND LEGAL SYSTEM

The primary function of the state, among many others, is to guarantee the inalienable rights and freedoms of the individual, and the security of personal property, including home and business security. The successful exercise of this function is heavily dependent on the adequate development of its forms resting on the reinforcement of the principles of the constitutional state, i.e. supremacy of the law, inviolability of individual rights and personal freedoms, separation of powers, mutual responsibility of citizens and the state and, last but not least, democracy. The development of the role of conventional forms in exercising the functions of the state, establishment of the adequate relationship between the legal system and legislation thereby facilitating greater accessibility and transparency in legal documents as well as their compatibility and proper application constitute essential prerequisites that assist the safeguarding of personal safety and the coherent development of the legal system.

Legislation on the Safeguarding of Human Rights

The redundant and petty provisions of legal regulations shall be ruled out wherever possible and the freedom of contract for legal entities shall remain intact.

Legislation shall not be passed in a desultory and hasty manner. The development and deliberation of any legislative act shall rest on its major principles and goals.

The preliminary and independent expertise of basic draft legislation shall be guaranteed.

The impact of every new legislative act submitted for parliament approval shall be assessed in real terms as well as in relation to the legal system, and shall be will be made freely and publicly available.

The major objective is the consolidation of legislation, codification of separate branches of law and preservation of the subject matter stability of codified laws.

Legislation in force shall be systematically arranged into the uniform code of laws of the Republic of Lithuania.

The development and adoption of legislative acts shall be made public, special expert groups shall be set up to draw up and codify consolidated legislation.

The date of entry into force of legally binding laws for private business entities shall be established with the view to providing all possibilities for private entities to get ready to comply with laws.

The imperative regulations shall be established by law only. Subordinate legislation shall regulate the implementation procedure only.

Legislation shall be harmonised with the *acquis communautaire* of the European Union; the requirements and recommendations of the United Nations Organisation and the Council of Europe shall be observed with respect to the needs of the people of Lithuania.

Proposed legislation will aim at transposing basic provisions of the European Convention for the Protection of Human Rights and Fundamental Freedoms and its Protocols.

Protection of Human Rights and Interests. Law Implementation

The powers of public institutions and officials shall be clearly defined.

The aim is to establish a system that shall assist in efficiently examining the legality, validity and purposefulness of the application of repressive measures of the state.

The state authority and public servants shall be deprived of any opportunity to make wilful (i.e. not provided or stipulated by legislation) decisions dealing with the granting or cancellation of privileges, incentives, and exceptions or cancellation of the latter.

Public institutions and civil servants shall be held personally responsible for the violations of law caused by their actions.

The "one-stop shop" principle shall apply: a person shall be able to settle his/her matters in one institution. Documents will be sent by an institution itself within the strict time limit. Moreover, possibilities will be provided to settle matters by post or electronic mail.

An efficient compensation procedure for the compensation for moral and material damage shall be introduced.

No restrictions or privileges on grounds of gender, race, nationality, faith, language, origin, social status, beliefs, convictions or views shall apply.

Petitions shall be investigated comprehensively and to the heart of the matter.

Public institutions shall be prohibited from making decisions based on documents which were not publicly announced or classified for internal use only.

The reform of the bailiff's office system shall be further pursued thereby ensuring efficient execution of court decisions.

Conditions provoking corruption and bribery shall be eliminated: functions failing to qualify as suitable for public authorities shall be either eliminated or transferred into non-governmental sector.

The upgrading of professional skills shall be promoted with a clear orientation towards contemporary law doctrine and integration into the European Union and protection of human rights.

Legal information technologies assisting in greater accessibility to legislative acts and relevant drafts as well as to the application of legislative acts.

Protection of Human Rights and Interests. Legal Protection

The Government plans to establish an efficient dispute settlement system which would guarantee proper application of legal acts.

Social and legal mechanisms minimising possible grounds for dispute.

Alternative dispute settlement systems will be promoted encouraging arbitration, mediation, and legal activities.

Self-regulation of judges, lawyers and notaries will be advocated on the basis of their professional codes.

A coherent and effective fight against corruption, smuggling, shadow economy, drugs and organised crime shall be introduced in the law enforcement system: each institution will have clear-cut functions, powers and authority. The activities of these institutions will be co-ordinated.

Police shall respond, with no exceptions, to all violations of law.

Crime at school, especially against schoolchildren and drug crimes shall be severely persecuted.

A number of "office" officials shall be reduced in law enforcement institutions.

Structural reforms of law enforcement institutions shall continue, overlapping functions will be eliminated in different institutions.

Public initiative ("safe neighbourhood" and likewise initiatives) shall be promoted which would increase security of people and their property.

Crime victims shall be compensated for moral and material damage as compensation will be considered a major goal of crime detection.

Necessary material procurement shall be provided for law enforcement institutions to guarantee public security. Financing of the police structures should depend on their work rather than on the crime rate and a number of offenders.

Better conditions shall be created for private security firms to guarantee personal safety and property security.

Functions of the security police shall be transferred to private hands.

Functions of public order shall be decentralised and will be partly transferred to municipalities.

Effective protection of intellectual property shall be introduced.

The law enforcement system shall be restructured to make punishment for crime unavoidable, and to avoid protracted crime investigation procedures.

The system of punishments and penalties shall undergo partial changes, i.e. the system of adequate punishments for violations of the law shall apply. Repressive punishment will be rarer in use as the Government will seek the reformation and social integration of those who have served out their sentence. The 'economical punishment' principle shall be pursued: a minimum punishment shall would be enough to influence a convict and to encourage him/her to change his/her conduct.

Deprivation of freedom shall apply less often. Instead, public works, financial and other penalties that will help eliminate overcrowding in prisons and save the taxpayers' money shall apply more often.

More humane conditions shall be ensured in confinement institutions and detention centres as required by international standards. Humiliation of human dignity shall not be tolerated.

A system of penalties for administrative offences shall be changed; unreasonably high sanctions shall be lifted.

An early prevention system for juvenile delinquents shall be further developed.

Programmes for the employment of minors and drug prevention programmes shall be developed.

Maximum pretrial detention time shall be clearly set.

2. PUBLIC ADMINISTRATION

The Government admits that recent legislation adopted by the previous Seimas in the field of public administration was mostly targeted to address just a number of issues related to the internal problems of the public service. The Government refusing to accept these current trends in public administration and seeking to improve it in principle, to reduce the influence exerted by central authorities, being confident of still unused more efficient, less costly and more transparent working capacities of municipalities, being interested in ensuring that all level public institutions and officials work for the benefit of people and the community, sets the following goals and targets:

To prepare amendments to the Constitution of the Republic of Lithuania:

to establish that mayors and municipal councils are elected by secret ballot on the basis of universal, equal, and direct suffrage for the term of 4 years. Municipal elections shall be organised halfway through the Seimas' term in office;

to legalise five administrative territorial units of the second level in compliance with the requirements of regional policy of the European Union;

to approve legal provisions regulating ownership rights on land for legal entities (irrespectively of its use) on the territories defined under the relevant conditions and terms of the constitutional law.

To restructure the Government:

to develop a relevant project for government restructuring which would define separation of functions and goals, and to develop new Draft of Government Law.

during the transitional period to retain thirteen ministries, but later reduce a number till twelve with a possibility for further reduction of ministries.

To concentrate functions of ministries on the development of administration policy and strategy, to separate enforcement and control functions:

to perform audits of the functions of every ministry and of the institutions under their responsibilities;

to establish strategic goals of each ministry and to assign functions thereto

to systemise and co-ordinate institutions under the responsibility of the ministries;

to outline in detail the functions of all public and municipal institutions, to remove overlapping functions, to maximally specify their capacities and limit their powers. Public institutions are not policy-makers, but rather tools of implementing a specific policy, therefore they are obliged to professionally organise the work, be able to flexibly and rapidly restructure themselves in implementing new goals set by the Seimas;

to establish an effective law enforcement mechanism ensuring that any public or municipal institution complies with the legislation enforced;

to give up practice when content of the law is changed in the process of the adoption of secondary legislation. Before any norm (rule) is introduced it is essential to ascertain whether it is in compliance with the strategy approved and to assess its costs for the state and its future effects on an entity falling under its regulation.

To rationally use tax payers' revenues and public financial resources.

To implement the reform of counties and to expand the rights of municipalities:

to dismiss administrations of ten counties, and establish five representative administrative territorial units instead;

to assign to the regional representative institutions the functions qualified as the second level self-governance functions which municipalities fail to perform;

to transfer land and land management matters to municipalities;

to transfer all institutions accountable to county administrations to the municipalities of those towns or regions on which territories they are located;

to gradually phase out the centralised redistribution of budgetary funds. To provide municipalities with the possibility to form their budgets from local taxes and levies. To establish that both natural and legal entities pay taxes in two shares: a fixed amount to the state and to the municipality;

to establish the ceilings allowing a municipality itself to establish amounts of municipal taxes by legislation;

to prepare and submit to the Seimas a draft of the law on the management of municipal securities;

in the process of resetting the administrative boundaries of municipalities to pay due respect to the public opinion and to establish procedures for the compensation of possible losses;

to transfer to municipalities the property which is not essential for public needs and which is not to be given back to former owners.

To restructure the system of civil service:

before establishing a new administrative institution or before authorising the already existing institution to perform a new function, to assess its purposefulness and implementation costs for the state as well as for its future regulation object;

to establish an efficient system of motivation (promotions and penalties) for civil servants;

after the establishment of a new or reorganisation of the existing institution the general number of public servants of a ministry or other institution should not increase;

To define the responsibility of civil service and public administration:

to establish that rights are inseparable from responsibilities: administrative bodies of any level shall be responsible for whatever they have the right to administer;

to demand that the responsibilities of public institutions of any level be generally understood, and their activities be targeted and yield results, and also be based on strategic planning;

to establish an order that public and municipal institutions adopt the rules of their activities themselves and announce them publicly, and also provide information comprehensible to people about activities of the institutions and who controls them;

to demand that civil servants (state and municipal institutions) pleasantly provide services to people, and upon making a wrong decision to apologise them and immediately rectify the mistake. Moreover, any state or municipal institution shall be obliged to publicly announce the procedure of complaints which could be lodged against their public servants;

to establish the procedure whereby moral and material damages incurred by people due to public servants' activities be covered by state or municipal institutions which should exact adequate amounts from the civil servants personally responsible for the damage.

To develop the state register system which would be suitable for the operational and efficient public work.

To decentralise territorial state administration:

to analyse the need of transferring institutions (agencies, departments, inspectorates, and likewise) to the regional centres to which they relate by their activities;

to develop and implement the strategy of transferring institutions (in case their transfer is useful) to regional centres.

To involve the public in the major decision-making process. The Government undertakes the commitment, before adopting resolutions of greatest relevance to the people, to assess the public opinion, to co-ordinate different interests of stakeholders and, by reducing the number of legal acts to be adopted, to focus its attention on their quality, enactment possibilities and control.

3. ECONOMY

The authorities and businesses shall base their relations on mutual trust and co-operation. Public institutions of different levels shall base their relations with the business community on dialogue rather than confrontation.

Budgetary and Financial policy

In the realm of budgetary and financial policy it is essential to ensure that:

in the forthcoming year the budgetary deficit of the state not exceed 2-3 per cent and shall have an annual downturn tendency until it is fully balanced;

the responsibility of budgetary allocations lie with the Seimas alone, moreover, the use of approved budgetary funds fall under strict regulation and scrutiny;

the consolidated budget be built up while the state budget be considered concurrently with all extra-budgetary funds (as long as they exist);

only those measures which are provided by a specific law to achieve a specific goal be financed from the state budget, rather than the fields "traditionally" supported by the state;

the resources of the state budget be allocated with respect to the efficiency of the budget allocated by the assignations manager within the previous year;

amount of taxes and their redistribution through the budget be reduced;

the budget planning be approximate without including revenues planned from penalties and forfeits for tax administrative institutions and not be indicated in the budget;

public investment be gradually limited except for those public investments which are essential for the achievement of goals set or which are needed to co-finance the assistance provided by international organisations;

the state address the issue of liabilities to private economic entities;

public structural borrowing be limited to only such cases when it is reasonable and necessary by way of defining specific fields or conditions;

members of the credit market should not be discriminated and equal borrowing conditions be created for everyone;

in changing the anchor currency from the US dollar to EURO the co-operation with the Bank of Lithuania be maintained retaining the currency board arrangement as an essential precondition for sustaining economic growth and preventing official interference in people's finance.

Tax Policy

The Government shall draft amendments to the existing legislation, seek that legal acts set forth clear-cut, precise and unequivocal tax calculation rules and a flat-rate tax tariff, and plans to:

gradually reduce the personal income tax to 24 per cent;

increase the tax exempt minimum of the personal income tax up to 320 Litas;

replace the corporation tax with dividend taxation;

complete the unification of the tax administration of the State Social Insurance Fund and the state budget to simplify the tax administration and reduce the expenditure thereof;

create conditions for the functioning of private pension funds thereby smoothly moving over towards private cumulative insurance;

create preconditions for independent work on obtaining a single-use patent;

impose the excise duty on goods (including luxury items) whenever found relevant to Lithuania's integration into international organisations;

change the road tax imposition procedure by discontinuing its calculation on the basis of the capital turnover of companies;

change the valuation procedure of customs goods and gradually reduce customs duties;

in applying the VAT differentiation set a 5 per cent VAT for construction works and the construction of residential houses and a 9 per cent VAT for central heating;

gradually phase out tax incentives and exemptions;

by encouraging residents to save money and foster investment culture, to annul the capital gains tax (CGT) as the total administrative costs exceed the income it generates;

delegate no functions to municipalities until adequate financing has been given;

introduce a general assets and income tax return.

Tax Administration

In the area of tax administration it is essential to:

pass a uniform law on the fundamentals of the tax system specifying all the taxes, their subjects and entities, mutual responsibility of tax payers and tax collectors, dispute settlement procedure; The law would set the maximum ceiling on taxes and all compulsory contributions and levies to extra-budgetary funds;

introduce new taxes and amendments to tax laws (excluding reduction of taxes) only from the beginning of the next fiscal year after the publication in the *Valstybės Žinios* not later than 3 months before the introduction thereof.

introduce a regular tax collection audit and set the maximum time limits thereof;

hold the State Tax Inspectorate financially responsible for illegal tax collection or suspension of operation;

separate tax evasion from accounting mistakes and impose different sanctions for these actions.

Liberalisation of Business Environment

For the liberalisation of business environment we shall:

immediately draft and implement proposals on the liberalisation of business environment;

make no public investments into private business;

restructure the remaining natural monopolies and strategic entities and carry out their full or partial privatisation; introduce the efficient management of the above entities and seek their competitiveness and higher quality services;

ensure the transparency of privatisation process of the state property, guarantee equal market conditions for all investors, i.e. offer a public share of stock in joint stock companies for sale through the securities exchange, widely use the capital market infrastructure and impose no additional restrictions and preconditions for investors;

create a favourable business climate for the establishment and activities of new and existing institutional investors, i.e. liberalise investment conditions for commercial banks, insurance companies, investment pension funds in accordance with the European Union legal framework and practice;

introduce no retrospective legislation regulating business and business environment;

specify the authority and responsibility of supervisory institutions and their public servants as well as the responsibility for illegal actions; and also establish that an official of a supervisory institution should prove an error on the part of a businessman rather than otherwise; establish the compensation mechanism for material damages caused by officials of supervisory institutions due to their illegal actions;

make an impartial assessment of both domestic and foreign investments;

encourage the restructuring of enterprises under bankruptcy procedure;

legalise gambling casinos with a view to developing tourism and entertainment industry.

Liberalisation of Labour Relations

For the liberalisation of labour relations we shall implement the following provisions:

an approved typical form of an employment contract shall be recommended but not compulsory;

all restrictions to conclude any type of civil contracts between natural persons as well as between natural and legal persons shall be lifted;

restrictions on temporary employment contracts shall be gradually phased out;

equal rights of employers and trade unions shall be enforced;

quotas, permits, licences, prohibitions, and other restrictions for European Union citizens to work in Lithuania shall be no longer applicable;

statutory requirements for an employer to inform Sodra on the employment of a person on the same day and dismissal from employment within three working days will be no longer applicable;

mandatory working time track records shall be no longer kept;

a requirement that employees need to have employment identification documents shall be waived;

legislation regulating labour relations will be co-ordinated with the European Social Charter;

compensation for public servants and other employees as provided by the legislation in effect will be reduced in amount;

4. DEVELOPMENT OF INFORMATION SOCIETY

The development of information society becomes an essential part of the establishment of economic, public and state infrastructure. The development of information society is an urgent task of the Lithuanian national strategy.

In implementing this task the government plans:

to put allocations for the development of information society under the separate budget item regarding the above allocations as investments into the country's future;

to seek that all school graduates schoolchildren finishing the school should be computer literate;

to implement the computer literacy programme among civil servants;

to encourage the development of communications, data transfer and Internet infrastructure by promoting competition in the telecommunications sector;

to reduce the monopoly of service providers, to seek that all information technologies and communications should be accessible to all people of Lithuania;

to provide the conditions for e-business and digital economy and to establish relevant legal framework;

to implement the e-government programme in seeking to better service the population, improve the performance of the public administration and cut down on public expenditure;

to introduce a digital signature, to ensure the general electronic identification of a person and data protection;

to make the impact on the decision-making process in the social sector through the development of information society (e.g. integration of the disabled persons into public life);

to develop annual action plans according to the Long-term National Information Society Development Strategy approved by parliament (Seimas).

5. ENVIRONMENT AND URBAN DEVELOPMENT

The environmental protection system shall be guided by the principle of "clean development" by way of passing from administrative regulation to economic regulation, implementing mutually balanced programmes of urban and forestry development as well as programmes for the protection of environment and cultural heritage, and also reviewing and co-ordinating laws and other legislation regulating the process. Consequently, we shall:

in the area of environmental protection:

pass from administrative regulation to economic regulation of environmental protection - implement and enforce economic regulation measures (according to the "polluter-pays" principle);

draft new and improve the existing laws and other legislation on the exploitation of natural resources as well as regulation of economic activities and environmental protection with a view to creating conditions for the balanced development of the country's territory as well as rational exploitation of natural resources;

develop waste (*esp.* hazardous) management programmes;

improve the monitoring of environmental pollution, assessment of environmental impact and its control system, promote the use of environmentally friendly energy sources, reduce the level of hazardous waste by introducing more advanced technologies;

develop forestry, expand the forest land by growing forests in areas not suitable for agricultural activity, exploit it in a more economical and efficient way, develop its recreational functions, and promote tourism as well as other activities;

reduce water, air, soil, and physical contamination, prevent the decline of unique countryside in protected territories;

in the area of urban development and construction:

amend the existing legislation with a view to simplifying construction designing and licensing procedures to avoid unnecessary interference of public servants into these matters;

introduce essential changes to the functions of public institutions, municipalities, and counties with regard to construction processes, i.e. transfer all the rights and responsibilities to municipalities;

promote implementation and development of latest construction methods and technologies;

on the basis of approved programmes develop general and engineering infrastructure of towns and settlements;

use financial means of banks and financial resources to ensure the renovation and modernisation of educational and pre-school as well as other public institutions and residential houses with a view to saving public funds and energy resources;

in the area of housing policy:

start implementing housing programmes - resolve issues related to the provision of long-term credits for construction, attract investments in the housing development by taking advantage of the tax system;

promote the development of social housing in municipalities, provide public support to socially vulnerable persons and young families;

encourage economic entities and private residents to renovate and modernise their houses or apartments with a view to saving funds and energy resources;

in the area of cultural heritage protection:

draft regulations of the cultural heritage protection policy and the strategy for their implementation in accordance with the requirements of the public and the present day to ensure clear distribution of functions and responsibilities;

set priorities of the cultural heritage protection and their implementation principles, and also ensure that the public is informed about the requirements and purpose of the cultural heritage protection. All restrictions shall be clear and made known in advance;

create and impose the compensation system for owners of cultural heritage and investors as well as the system of their promotion, improve the existing and draft new legislation and methodologies with a view to creating a unified management and regulation system of heritage safety.

6. TRANSPORT

In view of the geographical location of Lithuania, it is planned to maximise the use of national capacities in the transit services market and simplify transit procedures. To this end, promotion of private initiatives should become the focus of our attention; no less important is to attract investments for the establishment of combined transport and logistics centres, develop international relations and international agreements, and improve the process of the passenger and freightage transport under the terms of international conventions.

In the medium term while pursuing the national transport policy, the Government shall:

Road Transport

Develop the network of motorways and national roads.

Remove restrictions for the development of the network of commercial units and facilities adjacent to the motorways and other roads of national importance.

Remove bureaucratic obstacles detrimental to the business of road carriers. Apply the simpler customs clearance, border, sanitary and other transport export, import and transit procedures - the procedures must be speedy, cheap and ensure the safe delivery of cargo.

Reform the institutional management of public transport by creating equal business opportunities for private and municipal carriers.

Put the mandatory car insurance into operation.

Water Transport

Modernise the Klaipėda State Seaport infrastructure - build new quays or reconstruct those already in use, deepen the harbour water area to a depth of 14 metres and reorganise the harbour landing-stage infrastructure.

Improve the Klaipėda Seaport interoperability with other types of transport and modernise the infrastructure of service roads and railways.

Continue the development of the shipping network with other foreign ports.

Apply a flexible tariff system of harbour dues, lading, warehousing and transportation on the territory of Lithuania.

Introduce a free seaport status in the Klaipėda State Seaport.

Railway Transport

Make improvements to the main railway lines of Lithuania until they meet the terms of the European Agreement on Main International Railway Lines.

Ensure equal operating conditions for private and public railway carriers.

Air Transport

Draft the privatisation model of national airlines that will guarantee the long-term development and privatisation transparency of the company.

Modernise the landing monitoring system and introduce flight safety facilities in the international airports.

Implement the Multilateral Agreement on the Establishment of the European Common Aviation Area, i.e. accede to the liberalised global airspace.

7. EDUCATION AND SCIENCE

Education Reform Priorities

The key objective of the education reform is a young man's preparation for life. This objective might be achieved by meeting the following priorities:

Education of an open-minded Lithuanian citizen;

Education of the new information society;

Development of a private education sector;

Improvement of education management.

General Education

To rationalise a general education school network - to make an evaluation of both regional and public needs as well as capacities based on social, cultural and economic grounds.

To create equal opportunities for rural and urban pupils to acquire proper education in pursing rational school specialisation, school renovation and school transportation programmes.

To ensure the attendance of all school-age children instructed by the qualified teaching staff.

To use education-related funds in an efficient way, to improve education services and to create real conditions to provide education services for citizens according to their capacities and needs.

To finance schools according to the "money follow the child" principle and guarantee equal opportunities for private and public education institutions.

To ensure the self-government of pupils and their involvement in addressing school community issues.

Additional Education

To develop additional education activities, especially the informal education of children and young people as the top priority in the prevention and socialisation sector. To promote and support democracy and civil education programmes.

To implement the "money follow the child" principle in the additional training area as well.

To promote the activities of non-governmental organisations (NGOs) and provide support to the initiatives of young people.

Pre-school Education

To establish a teacher training, psychological and social services system that will guarantee the proper education of the children of pre-school age.

To implement comprehensive pre-school education and guarantee an equal opportunities for a successful adaptation of children at primary school.

Vocational Technical Training

To direct vocational training towards the dynamically changing labour market.

To create equal operating opportunities for public and private institutions in the vocational training sector.

Adult Education

Continuous learning and training must be available to all society members.

Retraining programmes must be directed to address the emerging social problems.

Teaching Staff Qualification Improvement and Testing

Qualification improvement is one of the key education reform factors contributing to the renewal of the teaching staff.

The state passes decisions to develop qualification improvement programmes vital for the implementation of public education policy provisions.

To place the teaching staff qualification improvement into private hands (partially) and adopt the independent assessment method to guarantee the quality of the above system.

To develop the training system of education institution managers.

To reform the teaching staff testing system by linking it with the funding system of education institutions and develop plans for the re-qualification of the teaching staff on a systematic basis.

Science and Studies

To carry out the high school studies programme audit according to specialities through unification.

To ensure the necessary knowledge standard of every relevant speciality.

The amount of funds earmarked for science and studies must total 1.5 per cent of GDP, and to transfer a part of funds to the studies crediting fund.

To seek that the salary of the high school staff would not be below the average salary in the public service sector.

To develop the long-term programmes dealing with public science and research investments.

To reform the scientific research sector funding and seek to provide funding for specific purposes and through tenders.

To set out innovative policy guidelines and strategy according to the EU recommendations.

To develop a national innovative process development programme along systematic approach and science-business integration lines.

8. CULTURE

Recognising that culture is one of key guarantees of the establishment and existence of a democratic state, we consider the preservation and fostering of the identity of traditional cultural values and the assurance of most favourable creative conditions of modern cultural phenomena to be a long-term political goal of the Lithuanian national cultural policy. On the basis of the principles of democracy, open culture and the creative self-expression of every citizen we will pay special attention to the identification and purposeful implementation of the priorities of the national culture policy, i.e.:

the consolidation of the authority of professional art in the global cultural development process, support and distribution of the works of prominent Lithuanian artists contributing to the positive image of our state in the world;

the diversification of assistance to young creative minds and assessment as well as presentation of works produced owing to this support;

the promotion of a native language and literature as well as the publishing and dissemination of valuable cultural periodicals and publications, literature, Lithuanian linguistics, history, ethnology, art criticism, art books and great world literature in Lithuania and abroad; the development of information society;

the management and protection of national heritage, funding of the activities of the cultural heritage institutions and implementation of significant projects in the above field, introduction of new technologies, presentation of the national heritage and promotion of cultural tourism.

With the implementation of above priorities the Government shall:

conduct a systematic audit of national culture institutions (including public institutions founded by the state) and their relevant functions as well as subsidies they received;

promote the creative activities of NGOs and young people;

decentralise and liberalise the management of Lithuanian culture;

foster the development and funding of culture and art programmes by the rational use of the resources of culture institutions, national ones in particular. To contribute to the research of new purposeful culture funding resources and forms and capital investments in cultural establishments;

seek the strengthening of legal grounds for the financing and propagation of culture and the author's status and copyright protection; improvement of culture support and charity legislation;

encourage private and collective creative initiatives, co-operation of national and public culture institutions in the regions and exchange with foreign cultural institutions in the regions;

proceed with the implementation of the integrated modernisation programme of libraries;

seek to make efficient use of the intellectual and financial support of European institutions and co-ordinate art-related regulations by integrating Lithuanian culture into the general European culture; take active part in the EU cultural programmes and organisations;

maintain support to the cultural expression of national minorities in Lithuania;

being fully confident that physical training, sport, tourism and adequate recreation facilities should be made available to every Lithuanian citizen, encourage local governments and private business to develop and implement new initiatives in the above sector;

create favourable conditions for professional sportsmen with the best track record in sports to spread the fame of Lithuania throughout the world as the creation of the above conditions proves to be one of the best investments of effort into the formation of the Lithuanian image.

9. RURAL POLICY

Being well aware of a very complicated and still deteriorating agrarian and rural situation and seeking a fundamental solution to the economic problems of rural regions, the Government is fully committed to:

develop a new national long-term strategy for rural and agricultural development and improve current legislation (draft new relevant legislation if need be) instrumental in the implementation of the strategy;

improve agriculture-related legislation and adopt new legislation if need be once it facilitates preparations for the integration into the Common Agricultural Policy (CAP) of the EU;

complete land restitution and speed up the land reform;

discontinue the division of land lots on the basis of its use;

grant land ownership rights to legal entities;

create conditions for the operation of land and credit markets;

separate social assistance to rural population from industrial support and provide it under social programmes;

seek that 10 percent of the state budget would be earmarked for primary agricultural industry, development of processing industry and rural regions;

assure gradual transition from agricultural industry subsidies to direct payments;

establish agricultural quotas for the coming year (wherever these quotas apply) by 1 June of the current year;

draft legislation on timely payments for sales of agricultural and food products;

implement the ecological farming development programme in a more efficient way;

introduce a farmer compensation mechanism for expenditure on diesel oil;

make an in-depth analysis of compensation for excise taxes on diesel and develop proposals addressing the relevant issue;

improve the protection of the internal market from poor quality, illegally imported agricultural and food products;

strengthen the protection of consumer rights;

pursue the policy of economic sanctions in dumping cases;

protect and take care of land and soil productivity, operate, renovate and modernize land reclamation facilities;

develop and implement the policy of foreign trade in agricultural products;

make adequate preparations for the use of EU structural funds and intake as much EU funds as possible lest the allocated funds might remain unused;

make use of EU funds under the consistent development strategy (the so-called National Regional Development Plan).

10. LABOUR AND SOCIAL CARE

The primary goal of the government labour and social policy is to create conditions for every person to work, regulate his life in his own way, look to the future with a sense of responsibility and freedom, and offer special assistance to those who are unable to provide for themselves for reasons beyond their control.

In the social insurance and pension sector, determined to achieve the set goal the Government shall:

immediately launch a social insurance pension reform and gradually move over towards a more flexible multi-tier pension system by introducing a mandatory retirement saving scheme and creating an additional private social insurance system and preventing the reduction of the amount of current social insurance contributions during the reform;

strive to combine the State Social Insurance Fund with the national budget;

proceed with the social insurance reform on the basis of privatisation receipts and the national budget, starting with the introductory stage of the reform;

cut the budget deficit of the State Social Insurance Fund;

reorganise the granting of non-insurance pensions;

proceed with the gradual increase of retirement age, also providing an opportunity for earlier retirement;

ensure the stable level of the purchasing capacity of pension; for this purpose and depending on the country's financial condition, arrange the adequate indexing of pensions to the Consumer Price Index established as a measure for a fixed market basket of consumer goods and services.

In the social assistance sector the Government shall:

enhance the efficiency of social assistance system now under development and assure assistance to persons in need of help.

combine social assistance with personal income and property by the introduction of a general income tax and assets return system;

discontinue the system of benefits and compensation payments via grants to service providers and move over towards the system of direct payments;

develop a family assistance system that will guarantee independence and stability of it as a social institution and ensure the generation transition laying special emphasis on young families;

enact the UN Convention on the Rights of the Child protecting the social guarantees and economic rights of the child as a citizen;

decentralize social services provisions transferring more functions to local authorities;

improve efficiency in using a private sector by developing the social services of the community and creating conditions for private initiatives;

give priority to assistance and care at home rather than to senior care facilities (rest homes, nursing homes, etc.);

develop and enact a social integration programme for disabled persons;

develop and enact a new disability assessment procedure;

develop and launch an efficiently operating housing credits programme with young families being given priority;

In the labour sector the Government shall:

decrease the level of unemployment, create more favourable conditions for job growth and promote solidarity between employers and employees;

direct a professional training system to meet market needs;

develop and put into operation a tender-run re-qualification system;

increase efficiency in using a public works option; in certain cases make payments for public works in preference to unemployment benefits;

11. HEALTH CARE

The Government stands ready to take decisions leading to the transformation of the present health system into an accessible, safe and efficient system stimulating medical persons to be more involved in the care of a patient and make the most efficient use of resources available and encouraging people to take care of their health.

For this purpose the Government shall:

assure instant medical aid accessible to everyone, create a preventive health care system based on real health insurance and the patient's right to choose a doctor on his/her own discretion and any public or private health care institution he/she likes;

promote a voluntary health care insurance scheme and the establishment and operation of health funds in enterprises closely linked to economic levers and a social insurance system;

in addition to health insurance funds, legitimate an option for patients to make additional payments for services provided once the value of services exceeds mandatory health insurance payments;

move over towards the financing of health care for services provided;

unify the operating conditions private and public health institutions (contracts with patients' funds, VAT rules, etc.)

specify and differentiate tariffs for medical services on grounds of the complexity of services in a more accurate way;

improve the self-regulation of health care institutions;

improve health system management by including management experts and relevant public administration institutions operating in the health system;

optimise a network of health institutions;

improve primary health care; support and promote the development of primary health care institutions in rural areas and strengthen the general practitioner's institution;

assure the rights of municipalities in planning and organising population health care; develop regional health care networks more efficiently in economic terms for better assistance in emergencies;

deal with the improvement of health care quality on a regular basis, i.e. install information systems operating under the terms of quality indicators; assure the impartial control of public health care accessibility, safety and efficiency;

privatise and commercialise state controlled pharmacies, sanatoriums and other inefficiently governed establishments;

utilise the allocations for health care pursuant to the principles of democracy and openness;

improve a drug compensation policy;

advocate the principles of healthy life, implement public education programmes based on global medical practices dealing with health issues and develop health information services.

12. NATIONAL SECURITY AND DEFENCE

The internal and external security of the state forms two inherent parts of national security. The national security policy of the Government must assure the smooth functioning of a national security system and proper readiness of defence institutions to counter aggression, to protect the independence, territorial integrity and constitutional order of the State of Lithuania, and to assure the relevant place of Lithuania in European and transatlantic security institutions.

In developing the national security and defence system, the Government shall:

thoroughly strengthen democracy, protection of human rights and fundamental freedoms, promote the speedier economic development and other initiatives of people and public groups. The national security will be strengthened through different public management sectors (economy, social security, health, security of citizens and their property, other) enhancing national security;

draft or specify a public administration, fight against crime and anti-corruption, power stability, ecological safety and other programmes enhancing national security in the short term; assure the implementation thereof;

reduce the spread of alcoholism, suicides, drug abuse, AIDS and other mass diseases; draft and implement preventive programmes to address the above issues in a more active way;

analyse emerging threats to the internal security and take preventive measures thereof;

further develop the democratically controlled Armed Forces of the Republic of Lithuania in accordance with the long-term army development plan adjusted by the Government and ensure its efficient operation;

seek to make the professional army equipped with modern arms and equipment and interoperable with NATO armed forces as the defence foundation of Lithuania in the future;

train the armed forces and the national defence system to operate under the terms and conditions of NATO; seek Lithuania's accession to NATO at the 2002 NATO Summit;

proceed with the improvement of the defence system legislative framework and other relevant legislation;

make an analysis and evaluation of external threats and design preventive measures on a regular basis.

In meeting the above goals the Government shall:

increase the income and employment of population, proceed with the health and pension reforms, other measures ensuring the security of the state and its citizens;

develop the armed forces, other national security institutions and infrastructure so as to make them ready to protect the state and citizens from possible external threats and aggression;

seek the successful completion of the reorganisation of national defence institutions; assure the military and technical capacities of the armed forces to operate jointly with the NATO forces; give priority to the improvement of the privates and officers training and instruction;

take part in the Partnership Planning and Revision Process (PARP), Partnership for Peace programme and the Euro-Atlantic Partnership Council (EAPC); update Lithuania's NATO membership preparations programme in the military and defensive area; implement the programme of activities outlined in the Membership Action Plan (MAP) designed to assist aspiring countries in their for future NATO membership;

ensure the implementation and funding of the defence programmes drafted or in progress in accordance with the long-term national defence development programmes and international commitments by the rational utilisation and planning of defence allocations (will seek to increase defence spending to 2 per cent of GDP);

put forward a proposal of a gradual transition to the professional army without increasing the number of conscripts; ensure the implementation of the alternative military service; develop mobilisation reserves both for the additional capacities of the armed forces following the declaration of mobilisation and for actions on the territorial defence principles; improve the National Defence Volunteer Forces (NDVF) and reorganise the internal troops;

develop bilateral international and regional military co-operation; assure that the armed forces would participate in the internal peacekeeping operations under the leadership of the UN, OECD and NATO pursuant to Lithuanian international commitments;

ensure the protection of land and sea borders of the state; develop an integrated civil-military airspace and sea surveillance and control systems;

make every effort to use the scientific, technological and industrial capabilities of Lithuania for the security reinforcement needs of Lithuania and to this end utilise a part of budget allocations for national defence.

13. FOREIGN POLICY

The foreign policy of Lithuania shall be open, transparent, active, continuous and based on clear-cut principles.

The major foreign policy objectives are the following:

accession to the European Union under the most favourable conditions for Lithuania as possible;
further close co-operation with NATO and membership aspirations therein;
good relations with neighbourly states;
preservation of existing markets and vigorous search for new ones.

EU AND NATO MEMBERSHIP

The EU and NATO membership aspirations are considered of equal value.

The Government will not spare effort to get Lithuania ready to accede to the EU by 2004. Lithuanian people will be gradually introduced to the EU financial assistance mechanism and instructed on its use.

It is planned to continue active involvement in the common and foreign policy of the European Union; we will seek to contribute to the implementation of the ongoing security and defence policy of the European Union. Lithuania will seek to contribute to the processes keeping the NATO role intact in the creation process of a new security architecture in Europe.

The Government will make much effort to get Lithuania ready for NATO membership and will seek to become a full-fledged member in 2002.

The Government will seek the mature and active involvement of Lithuania in the international organisations, especially in the United Nations, the European Security and Co-operation in

Europe, the World Trade Organisation and others; it also plans to join the Organisation for Economic Co-operation and Development (OECD).

Relationship with Neighbourly Countries

Lithuania will continue co-operation with Poland as its strategic partner on the way towards the EU and NATO.

The Baltic States and the Baltic Sea Region remain a foreign policy priority.

As far as Russia is concerned, the Government will pursue its policy based on good neighbourly relations, aiming at creating better conditions for Lithuanian businesses and financial institutions to look for partners in the Russian and CIS markets. Lithuania will make effort to enter into closer economic relations with Kaliningrad. Also, Lithuania will take an active part in the implementation of the initiatives of EU and the United States focusing on the involvement of Kaliningrad in the European process.

The Government intends to preserve pragmatic and mutually beneficial economic relations with Belarus, also contributing to the democratic tendencies in this country.

Economic Interests

The Government will be involved in the search for newly emerging and promising global markets. The development of diplomatic representatives will proceed along with the economic priorities of the country.

The Government will not spare efforts to make the widest possible use of the advantages rising from the accession to the WTO in the establishment of more favourable trade regimes with different countries in the world.

Implementation of Foreign Policy

The training and support of the diplomatic service merits our particular attention.

The Government will promote the widest possible relations of Lithuanian people with foreign NGOs and individuals depending on the field of their interests.

The Government intends to encourage the contributions of Lithuanians resident in other countries of the world to the key goals of the Lithuanian foreign policy, primarily to NATO and EU membership.

GLOSSARY

Cheka (Vserossiyskaya chrezvychaynaya komissiya po bor'be s kontrrevolyutsiyey i sabotazhem--VChK)

All-Russian Extraordinary Commission for Combating Counterrevolution and Sabotage. The political police created by the Bolsheviks in 1917, the Cheka (also known as the Vecheka) was supposed to be dissolved when the new regime, under Vladimir I. Lenin, had defeated its enemies and secured power. But the Cheka continued until 1922, becoming the leading instrument of terror and oppression in the Soviet Union, as well as the predecessor of other secret police organizations. Members of successor security organizations continued to be referred to as "Chekisty" in the late 1980s.

Commonwealth of Independent States (CIS)

A loosely structured alliance of most of the former republics of the Soviet Union that facilitates consultation and cooperation in economic and security matters of common concern. Members in 1995 were Armenia, Azerbaijan, Belarus, Georgia, Ka-zakhstan, Kyrgyzstan, Moldova, Russia, Tajikistan, Turkmenistan, Ukraine, and Uzbekistan.

Communist International (Comintern)

An international organization of communist parties founded by Russian Communist Party (Bolshevik) leader Vladimir I. Lenin in 1919. Initially, it attempted to control the international socialist movement and to foment world revolution; later, it also became an instrument of Soviet foreign policy. The Comintern was dissolved by Soviet leader Joseph V. Stalin in 1943 as a conciliatory measure toward his Western allies.

Conference on Security and Cooperation in Europe (CSCE)

Established in 1972, the group in 1995 consisted of fifty-three nations--including all the European countries--and sponsored joint sessions and consultations on political issues vital to European security. The Charter of Paris (1990) changed the CSCE from an ad hoc forum to an organization having permanent institutions. In 1992 new CSCE roles in conflict prevention and management were defined, potentially making the CSCE the center of a Europe-based collective security system. In the early 1990s, however, applications of these instruments to conflicts in Yugoslavia and the Caucasus were largely ineffective. In January 1995, the organization was renamed the Organization for Security and Cooperation in Europe (OSCE).

Congress of People's Deputies

Established in December 1988 in the Soviet Union by constitutional amendment, the Congress of People's Deputies was the highest organ (upper tier) of legislative and executive authority in the Soviet Union. As such, it elected the Supreme Soviet of the Soviet Union. The Congress of People's Deputies that was elected in March through May 1989 consisted of 2,250 deputies. The Congress of People's Deputies ceased to exist at the demise of the Soviet Union.

Council of Europe

Founded in 1949, the Council of Europe is an organization overseeing intergovernmental cooperation in designated areas such as environmental planning, finance, sports, crime, migration, and legal matters. In 1995 the council had thirty-five members.

European Community (EC)

A grouping of primarily economic organizations of West European countries, including the European Economic Community (EEC), the European Atomic Energy Community (Euratom or EAEC), and the European Coal and Steel Community (ECSC). The name changed to European Union (*q.v.*) in November 1993. Members in 1993 were Belgium, Britain, Denmark, France, Germany, Greece, Ireland, Italy, Luxembourg, the Netherlands, Portugal, and Spain.

European currency unit (ECU)

Established in 1979 as a composite of the monetary systems of European Community (*q.v.*) member nations, the ECU functions in the European Monetary System and serves as the unit for exchange-rate establishment, credit and intervention operations, and settlements between monetary authorities of member nations.

European Union (EU)

Successor organization to the European Community (*q.v.*). The EU was officially established by ratification of the Maastricht Treaty of November 1993. The aim of the EU is to promote the economic integration of Europe, leading to a single monetary system and closer cooperation in matters of justice and foreign and security policies. In 1995 members consisted of Austria, Belgium, Britain, Denmark, Finland, France, Germany, Greece, Ireland, Italy, Luxembourg, the Netherlands, Portugal, Spain, and Sweden.

glasnost

Russian term for public discussion of issues; accessibility of information so that the public can become familiar with it and discuss it. *Glasnost* is the name given to Soviet leader Mikhail S. Gorbachev's policy in the Soviet Union in the mid- to late 1980s of using the media to make information available on certain controversial issues to provoke public discussion, challenge government and party bureaucrats, and mobilize greater support for the policy of *perestroika* (*q.v.*).

gross domestic product (GDP)

A measure of the total value of goods and services produced by the domestic economy during a given period, usually one year. GDP is obtained by adding the value contributed by each sector of the economy in the form of profits, compensation to employees, and depreciation (consumption of capital). Only domestic production is included, not income arising from investments and possessions owned abroad, hence the use of the word "domestic" to distinguish GDP from the gross national product (*q.v.*). Real GDP is the value of GDP when inflation has been taken into account.

gross national product (GNP)

The gross domestic product (*q.v.*) plus the net income or loss stemming from transactions with foreign countries. GNP is the broadest measurement of the output of goods and services by an economy. It can be calculated at market prices, which include direct taxes and subsidies. Because indirect taxes and subsidies are only transfer payments, GNP is often calculated at factor cost, removing indirect taxes and subsidies.

International Monetary Fund (IMF)

Established along with the World Bank (*q.v.*) in 1945, the IMF has regulatory surveillance and financial functions that apply to its more than 150 member countries and is responsible for stabilizing international exchange rates and payments. Its main function is to provide loans to its members (including industrialized and developing countries) when they experience balance of payments difficulties. These loans often have conditions that require substantial internal economic adjustments by the recipients, most of which are developing countries. Estonia, Latvia, and Lithuania joined the IMF and the World Bank in 1992.

Karaites

Members of a religious group practicing Karaism, a Jewish doctrine originating in Baghdad in the eighth century A.D. that rejects rabbinism and talmudism and bases its tenets on Scripture alone.

kroon (EKR)

Estonia's prewar currency (1928-40), reintroduced in June 1992 after Estonia became the first former Soviet republic to leave the Russian ruble zone. The kroon was officially pegged to the deutsche mark (DM) within 3 percent of EKR8 = DM1. In March 1996, the exchange rate was EKR11.83 = US$1.

lats (LVL)

Latvia's unit of currency prior to the Soviet annexation in 1940. Reintroduced in March 1993, the lats became the sole legal tender in Latvia in October 1993. In March 1996, the exchange rate was LVL0.55 = US$1.

Latvian ruble

Interim unit of currency introduced in Latvia in May 1992 and circulated in parallel to and valued at par with the Russian ruble, a vestige of Soviet rule, until July 1992. Sole legal tender until March 1993. Replaced by the lats (*q.v.*).

litas (pl., litai)

Lithuania's unit of currency prior to the Soviet annexation in 1940. Reintroduced in June 1993, the litas became the sole legal tender in Lithuania in August 1993. In March 1996, the exchange rate was 4.0 litai = US$1.

nomenklatura

The communist party's system of appointing key personnel in the government and other important organizations, based on lists of critical positions and people in political favor. The term also refers to the individuals included on these lists.

Nordic Council
Founded in 1952, the Nordic Council promotes political, economic, cultural, and environmental cooperation in the Nordic region. Members in 1995 were Denmark, Finland, Iceland, Norway, and Sweden.

Old Believers
A sect of the Russian Orthodox Church that rejects the reforms of liturgical books and practices carried out by the head of the church, Patriarch Nikon, in the mid-seventeenth century.

perestroika
Literally, restructuring. The term refers to Mikhail S. Gorbachev's campaign in the Soviet Union in the mid- to late 1980s to revitalize the economy, communist party, and society by adjusting political, social, and economic mechanisms.

value-added tax (VAT)
A tax levied on the value-added income of a business. The VAT is defined as the difference between the total sales revenue and the costs of intermediate inputs, such as raw materials, used in the production process.

World Bank
Name used to designate a group of four affiliated international institutions that provide advice on long-term finance and policy issues to developing countries: the International Bank for Reconstruction and Development (IBRD), the International Development Association (IDA), the International Finance Corporation (IFC), and the Multilateral Investment Guarantee Agency (MIGA). The IBRD, established in 1945, has the primary purpose of providing loans to developing countries for productive projects. The IDA, a legally separate loan fund administered by the staff of the IBRD, was set up in 1960 to furnish credits to the poorest developing countries on much easier terms than those of conventional IBRD loans. The IFC, founded in 1956, supplements the activities of the IBRD through loans and assistance designed specifically to encourage the growth of productive private enterprises in less developed countries. The president and certain senior officers of the IBRD hold the same positions in the IFC. The MIGA, which began operating in June 1988, insures private foreign investment in developing countries against such noncommercial risks as expropriation, civil strife, and inconvertibility. The four institutions are owned by the governments of the countries that subscribe their capital. To participate in the World Bank group, member states must first belong to the International Monetary Fund (*q.v.*).

BASIC TITLES ON LITHUANIA

Title	ISBN
Lithuania A "Spy" Guide - Strategic Information and Developments	1433030144
Lithuania A Spy" Guide"	1438729464
Lithuania Air Force Handbook	1433030152
Lithuania Army Weapon Systems Handbook	1433061783
Lithuania Army Weapon Systems Handbook	1433061783
Lithuania Army Weapon Systems Handbook - NATO Weapons	1433061783
Lithuania Army, National Security and Defense Policy Handbook	1433030160
Lithuania Banking & Financial Market Handbook	1433030179
Lithuania Business and Industrial Directory	1438729472
Lithuania Business and Industrial Directory	1433030187
Lithuania Business and Investment Opportunities Yearbook	1433030195
Lithuania Business and Investment Opportunities Yearbook	1438729480
Lithuania Business and Investment Opportunities Yearbook Volume 1	1438777205

Title	ISBN
Strategic Information and Opportunities	
Lithuania Business and Investment Opportunities Yearbook Volume 2 Leading Export-Import, Business, Investment Opportunities and Projects	1577519361
Lithuania Business Intelligence Report - Practical Information, Opportunities, Contacts	1433030209
Lithuania Business Intelligence Report - Practical Information, Opportunities, Contacts	1438729499
Lithuania Business Law Handbook - Strategic Information and Basic Laws	1438729502
Lithuania Business Law Handbook - Strategic Information and Basic Laws	1433030217
Lithuania Business Law Handbook - Strategic Information and Basic Laws	1438770332
Lithuania Business Law Handbook - Strategic Information and Basic Laws	1438770332
Lithuania Business Law Handbook Volume 2 Investment and Trade Laws Volume 2 Investment and Trade Laws	1577518063
Lithuania Clothing & Textile Industry Handbook	1438729510
Lithuania Clothing & Textile Industry Handbook	1433030225
Lithuania Company Laws and Regulations Handbook	1433070200
Lithuania Constitution and Citizenship Laws Handbook - Strategic Information and Basic Laws	1438779348
Lithuania Country Study Guide - Strategic Information and Developments	1438729529
Lithuania Country Study Guide - Strategic Information and Developments	1433030233
Lithuania Country Study Guide - Strategic Information and Developments Volume 1 Strategic Information and Developments	1438774877
Lithuania Customs, Trade Regulations and Procedures Handbook	1433030241
Lithuania Diplomatic Handbook - Strategic Information and Developments	143303025X
Lithuania Diplomatic Handbook - Strategic Information and Developments	1438729537
Lithuania Ecology & Nature Protection Handbook	1433030268
Lithuania Ecology & Nature Protection Handbook	1438729545
Lithuania Ecology & Nature Protection Laws and Regulation Handbook	1433074249
Lithuania Economic & Development Strategy Handbook	1438729553
Lithuania Economic & Development Strategy Handbook	1433030276
Lithuania Education System and Policy Handbook	1433066912
Lithuania Energy Policy, Laws and Regulation Handbook	1433072009
Lithuania Export-Import and Business Directory	1438729561
Lithuania Export-Import and Business Directory	1433030284
Lithuania Export-Import Trade and Business Directory	143872957X
Lithuania Export-Import Trade and Business Directory	1433030292
Lithuania Foreign Policy and Government Guide	1433030306
Lithuania Government and Business Contacts Handbook	1433030314
Lithuania Government and Business Contacts Handbook	1438729588
Lithuania Immigration Laws and Regulations Handbook - Strategic Information and Basic Laws	1438782950
Lithuania Industrial and Business Directory	1438729596
Lithuania Industrial and Business Directory	1433030322
Lithuania Insolvency (Bankruptcy) Laws and Regulations Handbook - Strategic Information and Basic Laws	9781433085451

Title	ISBN
Lithuania Internet and E-Commerce Investment and Business Guide - Strategic and Practical Information: Regulations and Opportunities	143872960X
Lithuania Internet and E-Commerce Investment and Business Guide - Strategic and Practical Information: Regulations and Opportunities	1433030330
Lithuania Investment and Business Guide - Strategic and Practical Information	1433030349
Lithuania Investment and Business Guide - Strategic and Practical Information	1438768052
Lithuania Investment and Business Guide - Strategic and Practical Information	1438768052
Lithuania Investment and Business Guide - Strategic and Practical Information	1438729618
Lithuania Investment and Business Guide Volume 2 Business, Investment Opportunities and Incentives	157751856X
Lithuania Investment and Trade Laws and Regulations Handbook	1433076217
Lithuania Justice System and National Police Handbook	1433030357
Lithuania Justice System and National Police Handbook	1438729626
Lithuania Labor Laws and Regulations Handbook - Strategic Information and Basic Laws	1438781156
Lithuania Land Ownership and Agriculture Laws Handbook	1438759452
Lithuania Medical & Pharmaceutical Industry Handbook	1438729634
Lithuania Medical & Pharmaceutical Industry Handbook	1433030365
Lithuania Mineral & Mining Sector Investment and Business Guide - Strategic and Practical Information	1438729642
Lithuania Mineral & Mining Sector Investment and Business Guide - Strategic and Practical Information	1433030373
Lithuania Mining Laws and Regulations Handbook	1433077779
Lithuania Privatization Programs and Regulations Handbook	1438729650
Lithuania Privatization Programs and Regulations Handbook	1433030381
Lithuania Recent Economic and Political Developments Yearbook	1433063409
Lithuania Recent Economic and Political Developments Yearbook	1433063409
Lithuania Recent Economic and Political Developments Yearbook	1433063409
Lithuania Research & Development Policy Handbook	1433063247
Lithuania Research & Development Policy Handbook	1433063247
Lithuania Research & Development Policy Handbook	1433063247
Lithuania Starting Business (Incorporating) in....Guide	1433066920
Lithuania Tax Guide	1438729669
Lithuania Tax Guide	143303039X
Lithuania Taxation Laws and Regulations Handbook	1433080281
Lithuania Telecom Laws and Regulations Handbook	1433082101
Lithuania Telecommunication Industry Business Opportunities Handbook	1433030403
Lithuania Telecommunication Industry Business Opportunities Handbook	1438729677
Lithuania Transportation Policy and Regulations Handbook	1433066939
Lithuania: How to Invest, Start and Run Profitable Business in Lithuania Guide - Practical Information, Opportunities, Contacts	9781433083853

WORLD COUNTRY STUDY GUIDE LIBRARY

Strategic political, geographic, economic, business information, contacts and important developments

Price: $149 each

Afghanistan Country Study Guide
Aland Country Study Guide
Albania Country Study Guide
Algeria Country Study Guide
Andorra Country Study Guide
Angola Country Study Guide
Anguilla Country Study Guide
Antigua and Barbuda Country Study Guide
Antilles (Netherlands) Country Study Guide
Argentina Country Study Guide
Armenia Country Study Guide
Aruba Country Study Guide
Australia Country Study Guide
Austria Country Study Guide
Azerbaijan Country Study Guide
Bahamas Country Study Guide
Bahrain Country Study Guide
Bangladesh Country Study Guide
Barbados Country Study Guide
Belarus Country Study Guide
Belgium Country Study Guide
Belize Country Study Guide
Benin Country Study Guide
Bermuda Country Study Guide
Bhutan Country Study Guide
Bolivia Country Study Guide
Bosnia and Herzegovina Country Study Guide
Botswana Country Study Guide
Brazil Country Study Guide
Brunei Country Study Guide
Bulgaria Country Study Guide
Burkina Faso Country Study Guide
Burundi Country Study Guide
Cambodia Country Study Guide
Cameroon Country Study Guide
Canada Country Study Guide

Cape Verde Country Study Guide
Cayman Islands Country Study Guide
Central African Republic Country Study Guide
Chad Country Study Guide
Chile Country Study Guide
China Country Study Guide
Colombia Country Study Guide
Comoros Country Study Guide
Congo Country Study Guide
Congo, Democratic Republic Country Study Guide
Cook Islands Country Study Guide
Costa Rica Country Study Guide
Cote d'Ivoire Country Study Guide
Croatia Country Study Guide
Cuba Country Study Guide
Cyprus Country Study Guide
Czech Republic Country Study Guide
Denmark Country Study Guide
Djibouti Country Study Guide
Dominica Country Study Guide
Dominican Republic Country Study Guide
Ecuador Country Study Guide
Egypt Country Study Guide
El Salvador Country Study Guide
Equatorial Guinea Country Study Guide
Eritrea Country Study Guide
Estonia Country Study Guide
Ethiopia Country Study Guide
Falkland Islands Country Study Guide
Faroes Islands Country Study Guide
Fiji Country Study Guide
Finland Country Study Guide
France Country Study Guide
Gabon Country Study Guide
Gambia Country Study Guide
Georgia Country Study Guide
Germany Country Study Guide
Ghana Country Study Guide
Gibraltar Country Study Guide
Greece Country Study Guide
Greenland Country Study Guide
Grenada Country Study Guide
Guam Country Study Guide
Guatemala Country Study Guide
Guernsey Country Study Guide
Guinea Country Study Guide
Guinea-Bissau Country Study Guide
Guyana Country Study Guide
Haiti Country Study Guide
Honduras Country Study Guide
Hungary Country Study Guide

Iceland Country Study Guide
India Country Study Guide
Indonesia Country Study Guide
Iran Country Study Guide
Iraq Country Study Guide
Ireland Country Study Guide
Israel Country Study Guide
Italy Country Study Guide
Jamaica Country Study Guide
Japan Country Study Guide
Jersey Country Study Guide
Jordan Country Study Guide
Kazakhstan Country Study Guide
Kenya Country Study Guide
Kiribati Country Study Guide
Korea, North Country Study Guide
Korea, South Country Study Guide
Kosovo Country Study Guide
Kurdistan Country Study Guide
Kuwait Country Study Guide
Kyrgyzstan Country Study Guide
Laos Country Study Guide
Latvia Country Study Guide
Lebanon Country Study Guide
Lesotho Country Study Guide
Liberia Country Study Guide
Libya Country Study Guide
Liechtenstein Country Study Guide
Lithuania Country Study Guide
Luxembourg Country Study Guide
Macao Country Study Guide
Macedonia,Country Study Guide
Madagascar Country Study Guide
MadeiraCountry Study Guide
Malawi Country Study Guide
Malaysia Country Study Guide
Maldives Country Study Guide
Mali Country Study Guide
Malta Country Study Guide
Man Country Study Guide
Marshall Islands Country Study Guide
Mauritania Country Study Guide
Mauritius Country Study Guide
Mayotte Country Study Guide
Mexico Country Study Guide
Micronesia Country Study Guide
Moldova Country Study Guide
Monaco Country Study Guide
Mongolia Country Study Guide
Monserrat Country Study Guide
Morocco Country Study Guide

Mozambique Country Study Guide
Myanmar Country Study Guide
Namibia Country Study Guide
Nauru Country Study Guide
Nepal Country Study Guide
Netherlands Country Study Guide
New Caledonia Country Study Guide
New Zealand Country Study Guide
Nicaragua Country Study Guide
Niger Country Study Guide
Nigeria Country Study Guide
Niue Country Study Guide
Northern Mariana Islands Country Study Guide
Norway Country Study Guide
Oman Country Study Guide
Pakistan Country Study Guide
Palau Country Study Guide
Palestine (West Bank & Gaza) Country Study Guide
Panama Country Study Guide
Papua New Guinea Country Study Guide
Paraguay Country Study Guide
Peru Country Study Guide
Philippines Country Study Guide
Pitcairn Islands Country Study Guide
Poland Country Study Guide
Polynesia French Country Study Guide
Portugal Country Study Guide
Qatar Country Study Guide
Romania Country Study Guide
Russia Country Study Guide
Rwanda Country Study Guide
Saint Kitts and Nevis Country Study Guide
Saint Lucia Country Study Guide
Saint Vincent and The Grenadines Country Study Guide
Samoa (American) A Country Study Guide
Samoa (Western) Country Study Guide
San Marino Country Study Guide
Sao Tome and Principe Country Study Guide
Saudi Arabia Country Study Guide
Scotland Country Study Guide
Senegal Country Study Guide
Serbia Country Study Guide
Seychelles Country Study Guide
Sierra Leone Country Study Guide
Singapore Country Study Guide
Slovakia Country Study Guide
Slovenia Country Study Guide
Solomon Islands Country Study Guide
Somalia Country Study Guide
South Africa Country Study Guide
Spain Country Study Guide

Sri Lanka Country Study Guide
St. Helena Country Study Guide
St. Pierre & Miquelon Country Study Guide
Sudan Country Study Guide
Sudan South Country Study Guide
Suriname Country Study Guide
Swaziland Country Study Guide
Sweden Country Study Guide
Switzerland Country Study Guide
Syria Country Study Guide
Taiwan Country Study Guide
Tajikistan Country Study Guide
Tanzania Country Study Guide
Thailand Country Study Guide
Togo Country Study Guide
Tonga Country Study Guide
Trinidad and Tobago Country Study Guide
Tunisia Country Study Guide
Turkey Country Study Guide
Turkmenistan Country Study Guide
Turks & Caicos Country Study Guide
Tuvalu Country Study Guide
Uganda Country Study Guide
Ukraine Country Study Guide
United Arab Emirates Country Study Guide
United Kingdom Country Study Guide
United States Country Study Guide
Uruguay Country Study Guide
Uzbekistan Country Study Guide
Vanuatu Country Study Guide
Vatican City Country Study Guide
Venezuela Country Study Guide
Vietnam Country Study Guide
Virgin Islands, British Country Study Guide
Wake Atoll Country Study Guide
Wallis & Futuna Country Study Guide
Western Sahara Country Study Guide
Yemen Country Study Guide
Zambia Country Study Guide
Zimbabwe Country Study Guide

www.ingramcontent.com/pod-product-compliance
Lightning Source LLC
LaVergne TN
LVHW080036210926
848481LV00011B/3203